HR Reporting with SAP®

 PRESS

SAP PRESS is a joint initiative of SAP and Galileo Press. The know-how offered by SAP specialists combined with the expertise of the publishing house Galileo Press offers the reader expert books in the field. SAP PRESS features first-hand information and expert advice, and provides useful skills for professional decision-making.

SAP PRESS offers a variety of books on technical and business related topics for the SAP user. For further information, please visit our website: *www.sap-press.com*.

Christian Krämer, Sven Ringling, and Song Yang
Mastering HR Management with SAP
2006, 630 pp., ISBN 978-1-59229-050-7

Christos Kotsakis and Jeremy Masters
SAP ERP HCM Performance Management
2007, 302 pp., ISBN 978-1-59229-124-4

Christian Krämer, Christian Lübke, and Sven Ringling
HR Personnel Planning and Development Using SAP
2004, 552 pp., ISBN 978-1-59229-024-8

Valentin Nicolescu, Katharina Klappert, and Helmut Krcmar
SAP NetWeaver Portal
2007, 400 pp., ISBN 978-1-59229-145-8

Norbert Egger, Jean-Marie Fiechter, Sebastian Kramer, Ralf-Patrick Sawicki, Peter Straub, and Stephan Weber
SAP Business Intelligence
2007, 656 pp., ISBN 978-1-59229-082-6

Hans-Jürgen Figaj, Richard Hassmann, and Anja Junold

HR Reporting with SAP®

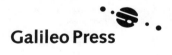

Galileo Press

Bonn • Boston

ISBN 978-1-59229-172-4

1st edition 2007

Editor Meg Dunkerley
Translation Lemoine International, Inc., Salt Lake City, UT
Copy Editor Ruth Saavedra
Cover Design Silke Braun
Layout Design Vera Brauner
Production Iris Warkus
Typesetting Typographie & Computer, Krefeld
Printed and bound in Germany

Contents at a Glance

Contents at a Glance

Contents

13   Personnel Development 311

14   Benefits 325

16 Personnel Cost Planning 361

PART IV Retrieving Reports

17 Area Menu 371

18 Human Resources Information System 377

19 Manager's Desktop (MDT) 383

20 SAP NetWeaver Portal 395

Appendix 413

Acknowledgments

This book is the product of a team effort. Our thanks are due to several people without whom the project would not have been possible, especially at this level of quality. Particularly deserving of mention are our colleagues in the AdManus consulting network (*http://www. admanus.de/int/index.php*), who supported us in word and deed, especially Martin Esch, who contributed to the Authorizations topic in Section 2.4, and Jörg Edinger, who gave us the benefit of his project experience with SAP NetWeaver BI.

We would also like to thank the staff of our partner, PIKON International Consulting Group, for their advice and support in setting up the system examples in SAP NetWeaver BI.

Thanks are also due to the staff of SAP PRESS for their positive, constructive, and friendly collaboration, which made the publication of this book possible. We must mention in particular Eva Tripp, who supported us with the concept of this book, and Frank Paschen, who encouraged the progress of the book with patience and determination.

Hans-Jürgen Figaj, Richard Hassmann, and Anja Junold

What is the goal of this book? Who will benefit from reading it? How is the book structured, and how can readers get the optimum benefit from it? This introductory chapter answers these questions.

Introduction

The reporting requirements in human resources (HR) are many and varied, and in many cases, the solutions are, too. This book will show you how you can use the powerful reporting tools of the SAP® system to fulfill your HR reporting requirements in a targeted and effective way. It contains detailed descriptions of all the relevant tools and the options for making reports accessible to users.

Goal of this book

Our goal is to give you a clear idea of how the reporting tools are used in practice. In doing so, we devote more space to certain tools that offer particularly flexible options in terms of structuring and designing reports. These are SAP Query, Ad-hoc Query, and SAP NetWeaver® BI, and they are extremely powerful when used in the optimal way.

In the chapter on SAP NetWeaver BI, we concentrate on HR Reporting, explain the tools available for creating and retrieving queries in Excel and on the Web, and outline the HR-specific aspects of using SAP NetWeaver BI. In terms of technical topics, we refer you to the further reading material contained in the appendix.

SAP NetWeaver BI

The topic of customer reports is a very wide one, so we restrict ourselves in this book to providing guidelines and tips on developing customer reports. You will also become familiar with the benefits of having your own logical database. Because the programming tools and options are, again, numerous, we refer you in the appendix to a more detailed book on the topic of programming in the HR area.

Customer reports

We also use several screenshots from Release SAP ERP 6.0 (SAP ERP 2005 was recently renamed SAP ERP 6.0) to help you visualize how the tools are used in practice. The screenshots are also intended to

SAP ERP 6.0

introduce you to some tools that you may not yet be using and will provide insight into the system even to readers who as yet have little or no practical experience with the SAP system.

In practice, a lot of time is often spent on compiling and formatting data and figures. This book is intended to help you reduce the amount of time wasted on formatting data and thus increase the time you have for analyzing report data and planning targeted activities.

Target Audience of this Book

The following groups of readers will find valuable information in this book:

▸ This book will give **decision-makers in HR and IT departments** an overview of the reporting options available in SAP and the strengths and weaknesses of the tools. These readers will be able to use this information to create a strategy within their own companies.

▸ Many sections of the book will enable **key users and regular users** to become familiar with how to use the SAP system in practice. In particular, the functions and flexibility of SAP Query, Ad-hoc Query, and SAP NetWeaver BI will be of interest to these users. They will also find useful the overview of the reports contained in the standard SAP system.

▸ **Project leaders and team members** will learn how important it is to include the issue of reporting in HR projects right from the beginning, in other words, to take reporting requirements into account as early as the process design stage. These requirements comprise the definition of key figures, the creation and retrieval of reports, and data security.

▸ **Programmers of customer reports in the SAP ERP Human Capital Management (SAP ERP HCM) field** will learn about and get tips on alternatives to ABAP-only reports, such as InfoSets with added customer-specific fields and custom-built logical databases.

▸ **Students and other interested parties** who would like to become familiar with the topic of HR reporting will also get insight into the practice of reporting with SAP ERP HCM from this book.

▶ This book will also be of use to **any readers who have previously used other software packages** and would like to learn about the possibilities of SAP software in the area of reporting.

Structure of the Book

Following from this introductory chapter, we describe in Part 1 of the book some important fundamentals of HR reporting in SAP. **Chapter 1** introduces a *Process-Oriented Reporting Concept*. This includes the definition of key figures, the creation and retrieval of reports, and data security. In **Chapter 2**, we describe the *Basics of Reporting in SAP ERP HCM*. This chapter covers data structures, logical databases, report classes, authorization checks, and the basis on which reports are run.

Part I – Fundamentals

Part II looks in detail at the tools you can use to create reports. These tools are as follows:

Part II – Reporting Tools

▶ **Chapter 3: Standard SAP Report**
The standard SAP report is the longest-established reporting tool. Before SAP changed its strategy and moved most new reporting requirements to SAP NetWeaver BI, all basic reporting requirements were fulfilled by the standard SAP report. The first module to which the new strategy applied was Personnel Cost Planning, which was developed from scratch for Release R/3 4.7 Enterprise. The new direction was clear in this module: There would be only a few reports in the R/3 system from now on, and additional reporting options would be contained in SAP NetWeaver BI.

The standard SAP report was designed for only a small number of reporting options at most and is thus quite inflexible. Even though frequent attempts were made to provide more structuring options in the standard report — such as the flexible employee list — every report can still be used for only a very limited number of analyses.

▶ **Chapter 4: Queries**
SAP Query and Ad Hoc Query are tools that enable programmers and nonprogrammers alike to compile reports using their own selection of fields from different infotypes. From this point on,

the query replaced several customer developments, and some standard SAP reports were also created using the query tools.

► **Chapter 5: HR Reporting with SAP NetWeaver BI**
The flexible analysis options of SAP NetWeaver BI brought a new dimension to reporting. Queries that are based on multidimensional InfoCubes make flexible navigation possible in queries, something that was not possible with earlier tools. The standard content for HR that comes with SAP NetWeaver BI is comprehensive and can be used directly in reports. The time required to roll out this tool is therefore significantly reduced.

► **Chapter 6: Customer Report**
The individualized customer report remains the answer to all unresolved requirements. Such reports can deliver almost everything the customer requires. The central question is that of how much time and effort to put into creating these reports.

Part III – Reporting in HCM Modules

After a short *Introduction to Part III* of the book in **Chapter 7**, we look at selected standard reports and the standard BI content of the individual HCM modules:

► Personnel Administration (Chapter 8)

► Organizational Management (Chapter 9)

► Recruitment (Chapter 10)

► Payroll (Chapter 11)

► Personnel Time Management (Chapter 12)

► Personnel Development (Chapter 13)

► Benefits (Chapter 14)

► Training and Event Management (Chapter 15)

► Personnel Cost Planning (Chapter 16)

These chapters provide useful examples of standard reports and queries in SAP NetWeaver BI. Combined with the illustrations and descriptions, these chapters will give you a good idea of the possibilities offered by the standard SAP system.

Part IV – Retrieving Reports

Part IV contains an overview of the interfaces available for retrieving reports. In this part, we look at the following options:

► **Chapter 17: Area Menu**
The area menu allows you to combine standard SAP reports and

customer reports in user-defined tree structures. This makes it much easier for the user to search for specific reports. The structures can also be created in a role-based way.

▶ **Chapter 18: Human Resource Information System (HIS)**
The HIS enables you to link structures in organizational management and event management with reports in all HCM modules. Simply selecting a substructure and then starting one of the available reports is enough to automatically start the report with the selected objects; it is not necessary to fill out a selection screen.

▶ **Chapter 19: Manager's Desktop (MDT)**
The Manager's Desktop is tailored to the requirements of managers with line management responsibilities. You use it to provide reports that managers can use directly in their areas of responsibility.

▶ **Chapter 20: SAP NetWeaver Portal**
The SAP NetWeaver Portal enables users to access the SAP system via a Web browser. Because there is no need to install the SAP GUI, it is much easier to roll out the portal for decentralized use. Its close integration with SAP ERP 6.0 and SAP NetWeaver BI make the portal an almost indispensable component, including in the reporting area.

Working with this Book

You can read the chapters in any order you like. At several points throughout the book, we provide references to other sections of the book that explain a topic in greater detail. If you have questions about specific topics, you can use the index to go directly to that topic in the book.

Of course, some topics will be of particular interest to you, whereas you will already be familiar with others, and you should feel free to skip any chapters that are less relevant to you. However, we do recommend that you read **Chapter 1**, *Process-Oriented Reporting Concept*.

Terminology

HR or HCM

The term *HR* (Human Resources) is still a common one, although SAP's software product in this area is now called SAP ERP Human Capital Management (HCM). We use both terms in this book: HCM when we are referring to the SAP product and its processes and HR when we are referring to human resources processes in general.

Special icons To make it easier for you to work with this book, we use icons to highlight certain sections. These icons have the following meanings:

[!] **Attention**
We use this icon to warn you about frequent errors or problems that you may encounter in your work.

[+] **Tip**
We use this icon to highlight tips that may make your work easier and to help you find additional information on the current topic.

[Ex] **Example**
We use examples to explain and give more information on the current topic. Many of the examples in this book are based on our own consulting experience.

PART I
Fundamentals

In the first part of this book, you will become familiar with a process-oriented reporting concept and the basics of reporting in SAP ERP HCM.

If you want to set up a human resources (HR) reporting system for the first time, or reorganize your existing one, HR processes will play a major role in this undertaking. They are the basis for defining key figures and for generating reports. This chapter presents an efficient procedure for creating a reporting concept.

1 Process-Oriented Reporting Concept

To create a new reporting concept, you first have to define your requirements. There is no shortage of procedures for doing this. One approach would be to ask the users what reports they need for their daily work. However, this step would not be enough on its own, because the role of the modern HR department is no longer a purely administrative one. HR is in a state of change; it is becoming a business partner, and what is more, a value-added partner of company management that actively supports the goals of the enterprise. Therefore, HR strategy has to be based on the company strategy, and HR controlling, for its part, has to be based on the HR strategy. It has to deliver figures that optimally support the company strategy.

How can you identify the key figures that you need for a professional, consulting-style HR concept? How do you avert the risk of overlooking important key figures? How do you create a comprehensive reporting concept right from the start? Clearly, the reporting concept should be set up in such a way that new key figures can be integrated easily. An HR strategy is not meant to be cast in stone; however, the more fully you define the requirements at the beginning of the concept creation process, the more closely the reporting concept can be oriented to the HR strategy. Also, the more key figures that are known at the beginning, the more efficiently they can be coordinated, calculated, and processed.

Defining the requirements

Thus, in this chapter, we present to you a procedure that you can use to determine key figures from your company's HR processes in an efficient and target-oriented way (see Section 1.1). We then deal with how to define reports (see Section 1.2). What figures are contained in what reports? How many reports or report variants should there be? In Section 1.3, we explain how to select the most suitable tool for creating your reports. Last, in Section 1.4, we look at the issues you need to be aware of when making reports available to different user groups.

1.1 Determining Key Figures

HR services tree

First, you need a good overview of all the relevant services your HR department provides. Your process documentation can serve as the basis of this overview of services. Another tried-and-trusted starting point is the reference service catalog that is increasingly used and extended on an ongoing basis by the authors (for further information see *http://www.iprocon.de/referencemodel*).

This model is currently composed of approximately 800 services that are typically provided by HR departments, subdivided into the main HR processes (see Figure 1.1). If you decide to use the reference service catalog, you first have to adapt it to your company's specific situation by deleting any services that are not relevant, adding ones that are missing, and adjusting the terminology to fit your company's standards.

Also, because not all services are equally important for determining key figures, or even necessary at all, you first have to evaluate the services. To do this, you should define characteristics such as the following:

▶ Strategic purpose from company viewpoint (yes/no)
▶ Stakeholders
▶ Number of cases per year

This enables you to prioritize what is important and whose interests are to be represented. The various interest groups will have a position of lesser or greater power, depending on the company's position in the market (for example, job applicants are in a strong position if the company is experiencing growth and a lack of qualified staff). Setting priorities in this way also clarifies how important the role of HR controlling is when changes occur in the market.

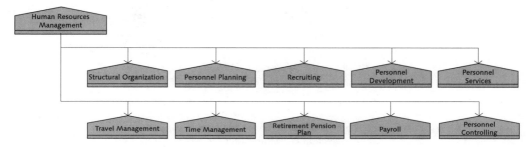

Figure 1.1 Upper Level of "HR Services Tree" by iProCon GmbH

After evaluating the services and defining the characteristics, you will be in a position to decide what services you want to use. You then need to look in detail at these services. It may be necessary at this stage to model the process — if it is very extensive, for example.

The key figures can now be determined either directly from the service or from the process steps.

> Growth is one of your company's stated goals. To achieve this, you need **[Ex]**
> new employees. Because the job market for qualified staff does not offer
> your industry a great selection, your company's Controlling department is
> required to provide figures on the selection procedure. The most useful
> information is how many applications are received per month and how
> many of these applicants are actually suitable. Based on this information,
> a decision can be made about whether the current job advertisement pro-
> cedure is suitable for your company's purposes or whether it needs to be
> adapted. Figure 1.2 shows an evaluation of the Organization of Selection
> Procedures service, a part of the associated process, and the key figures
> derived from this service.
>
> Proceed in this way for all the services you have prioritized.

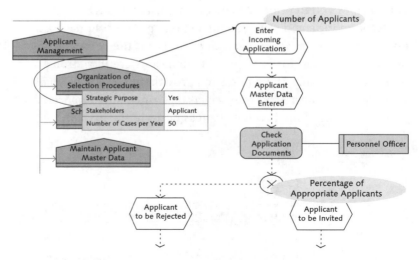

Figure 1.2 Determining Key Figures from the Organization of Selection Procedures Process

1.2 Defining Reports

Checking the data basis

Once you have defined the required key figures, you have to check whether the data used to calculate the key figures exist in the SAP system, in other words, whether the information has been entered into SAP Enterprise Resourse Planning Human Capital Management (ERP HCM) and, if so, in what form it is stored there.

For information on the various data structures in SAP ERP HCM and their characteristics, see Chapter 2, *Basics of Reporting in SAP ERP HCM*. If the system does not contain all the data you need, you may have to make organizational changes to the way data is recorded and stored so that you can access the required data basis in the future.

Recommendations on defining reports

Note the following points when defining reports:

▸ **Calculation procedure for key figures**
Specify how you calculate the key figures. In practice, the calculation should be performed only once (centrally), if possible, so that all reports use the same figures and can be compared afterwards.

▸ **Avoid redundancies as much as possible**
If different user groups need reports with similar content but different layouts (for example, aggregated data and individual data),

you do not have to program two separate reports. Instead, use layout variants to fulfill the different layout requirements.

▶ **Manageable number of reports**
The more reports you create, the more maintenance work is required. Try to fulfill several requirements with one report and to make parts of the report available as layout variants.

▶ **Comprehensibility**
When naming key figures and report fields, use your company's standard terminology. Also, create documentation for each report and make sure this documentation contains the key figures calculation, as otherwise, the key figures will be interpreted differently.

▶ **Different user groups**
Not every user should be able to run Excel reports or modify the layout of a list. Thus, you need to define in advance which user groups are allowed to run the report and what functions they are allowed to access.

The *HR controlling* subtree in the *HR services tree* reference model already contains a range of standard reports and statutory lists, subdivided by topics such as working time, recruitment, and employee movements. If you use this reference model, you can simply extend the subtree and create various characteristics (such as user, frequency of use, and report name) for every report. This form of documentation can also be used as an orientation aid for new employees.

1.3 Selecting Tools

In Part II, *Reporting Tools*, we describe in detail the tools available in SAP ERP HCM for creating reports:

Part II: Reporting Tools

▶ Standard reports

▶ Queries

▶ SAP NetWeaver Business Intelligence (BI)

▶ Programming customer reports

The decision of which tool you use, and when, depends on the circumstances in each case and especially on whether you need to create only one new report or a whole range of new reports as part of a redesign process.

If only a single report is required, you should first check whether it is already contained in the standard reports. Our report overview in Appendix B should be your first port of call for this purpose; it contains the name and transaction code of all the available reports in every HCM module.

Part III: Reporting in HCM Modules Also, as well as a list of the most important standard reports, Part III of the book provides tips on using these reports and describes their strengths and weaknesses. If you are already using SAP NetWeaver BI, you will also find out in Part III whether the report you require is contained in the standard content of the relevant HCM module.

Queries If it is not, the next question is whether it can be created using the query tool. The answer depends on the complexity of the report. Simple reports based on infotype fields are easy to create with SAP Query or Ad Hoc Query, and can be adapted at any time without the need for programming know-how. This gives the creator of the report much more flexibility and the ability to react more quickly to new requirements, such as additional fields in the report. The Ad Hoc Query is particularly suitable for individual requests for once-off reports. The following are some characteristics of reports that cannot be created using the query tools:

- They compare multiple time periods.
- They track employee movements.
- They report on cross-module data.
- They include complex calculations.
- They have high layout requirements.
- They enable interaction.

Customer reports The only option for fulfilling these kinds of requirements is to program individual customer reports. With customer reports, you can implement anything the customer wants; the only question is what input of time and effort is justified. You have to decide the answer individually in each case.

The danger is that there can be a tendency to respond to almost every new requirement with programming, and the number of programmed reports thus increases infinitely. In this situation, key figures are continuously re-calculated, and the results may not always be identical. The result of this is that the reports can then no longer be used for comparative purposes, and maintenance becomes more and more time-consuming. At this point, if not before, it is worthwhile to redesign your reporting concept to reduce the number of reports and to carry out calculations centrally. Clear programming guidelines (see Section 6.2) also help reduce the amount of maintenance work required.

Before you get started with any complex programming, you should first establish whether the report will be needed in the same form in the future or whether the request is a once-off one. In the latter case, it may make sense to gather the data in a slightly less convenient way (for example, via various queries and standard reports) and to further process it outside the SAP system (for example, with Microsoft® Excel® or Microsoft Access™). If you do this, you will need to carefully document how you created the report to ensure that any subsequent queries can be answered and that the report's comparability with other reports can be evaluated.

For a future-oriented reporting concept, there are alternatives: You could roll out SAP NetWeaver BI, or you could program your own logical database. Chapter 5, *HR Reporting with SAP NetWeaver BI*, and Section 6.3 provide detailed information on both tools, explain their advantages and disadvantages, and provide you with tips on how to decide which tool is best suited to your reporting concept.

Alternatives to customer reports

When defining reports, remember to specify the distribution of roles between the HR Controlling Department, the HR Department, and management. Do not forget to include other report recipients such as employee representative bodies, the Risk Management Department, and the Auditing Department. Also, define a procedure for implementing future reports well in advance.

[!]

1.4 Retrieving Reports for Users

In Part IV of this book, *Retrieving Reports*, we introduce you to the tools you need to retrieve reports. Our tool selection criteria are as follows:

PART IV: Retrieving Reports

▶ **User's SAP know-how**

Is the user familiar with the structure of the data — that is, the infotype concept, including time constraints and history? Is the user a competent user of the SAP ERP HCM system interface?

▶ **Frequency of use**

Will the report be requested only once or regularly?

Table 1.1 shows an overview of the retrieval tools based on the criteria described above.

	Low SAP Know-How	High SAP Know-How
Once-off request	▶ MS Office document ▶ Paper report	▶ Ad Hoc Query with corresponding InfoSet ▶ BI Query of corresponding InfoCube
Regular request	▶ User menu with restricted selection criteria ▶ Manager's Desktop (MDT) ▶ SAP NetWeaver Portal (Web Reporting)	▶ User menu with full selection criteria ▶ SAP NetWeaver BI

Table 1.1 Report Retrieval Options

[Ex] Assuming that you are using the SAP NetWeaver Portal, but not SAP NetWeaver BI, the four scenarios shown above could be distributed as follows:

▶ Once-off request–low SAP know-how

Answers to Ad Hoc Queries are supplied to the board of directors or company management in the form of Office documents or printed reports.

▶ Regular request–low SAP know-how

▷ The company's union can use the portal to access a wide range of standard reports. Some of these reports are legally required, and some have been agreed to within the framework of the reporting concept.

▷ The Risk Management Department also has access via the portal to a number of defined standard reports in the area of HR risk management (turnover, age structure, remaining leave, time accounts, and so on).

> ▹ Area managers and heads of departments use Manager Self-Services in the portal to access a number of standard reports.

- ▶ Once-off request–high SAP know-how

  HR employees can use InfoSets, which provide very wide coverage of each activity area, to run their own Ad Hoc Queries. They can then further process the data in Office.

- ▶ Regular request–high SAP know-how

  Within their area of responsibility, HR employees can access data relating to the employees for whom they are responsible. Standard reports, company-specific reports, and queries are included in the user menu.

The following statements are true on a general level about reporting situations with a high number of users, a very complex reporting concept, and the appropriate budget:

- ▶ Portal solutions such as Web Reporting and Self-Services are to a large extent replacing the user menu and the SAP Easy Access menu.

- ▶ Standard query tools and report programming are in many cases being replaced by SAP NetWeaver BI.

When determining how reports will be retrieved in your reporting concept, you should draw up a detailed access authorization plan. Section 6.8 contains detailed information on the authorization concept in HR reporting.

[!]

In the next chapter, *Basics of Reporting in SAP ERP HCM*, you will first learn which data is available for reporting in SAP ERP HCM and how this data is stored in the system. You will also learn what you need to take into account when setting up access to this data, and what authorizations are required for access.

Before running a report, you first have to examine the data that you intend to use as a basis for the report. Among the things you need to look at are the data's technical structure and content. The latter has to contain information that is relevant to the purpose of the report. We explain these basic topics in this chapter.

2   Basics of Reporting in SAP ERP HCM

SAP ERP HCM contains many different data structures. These data structures can be divided into three areas:

Data structures in SAP ERP HCM

- ▶ Personnel administration master data
- ▶ Payroll and time management results data
- ▶ Personnel planning data

The structures of the data in each of these areas are fundamentally different.

> The structure of applicant management data is identical to that of personnel administration data, so we mention it here only when we want to draw your attention to something in particular.

[+]

Personnel administration master data is the basis of all SAP ERP HCM modules. When an employee's data is entered in the system, the data is stored in what are known as *infotypes*. Once the employee is "created" in this way, the data can then be used in other modules. The payroll and time management areas, for example, use this data and store their results in *data clusters*. The structure of these data clusters consists of several related tables that are different for each application. Personnel planning data consists of a wide variety of objects that are related to each other by means of links. The individual properties of these objects are also stored in *infotypes*. Section 2.1 deals with these data structures in more detail.

Logical database   The fundamental technology provided by SAP for reporting on these structures is the *logical database*. Almost every report is based on the functionalities of a logical database, which retrieves data for reporting purposes from any infotype you want. The logical database presents you with a selection screen for the settings and carries out the standard authorization checks without system downtime. From the user's viewpoint, there is a single, unified interface for dealing with all kinds of reports. Section 2.2 contains information about the logical databases that are available in the HCM system.

Authorization concept   HR data is particularly sensitive, which creates considerable demands of the authorization concept. See Section 2.4 for important information on the authorizations required in the HR reporting area.

Reporting basics   Even the best report cannot compensate for inadequate data quality and missing information. Section 2.5 of this chapter describes the most important things you need to know to create a good basis for your reports.

2.1   Data Structures in SAP ERP HCM

In this section, we introduce the three data structures of the HCM system that we mentioned above: payroll and time management data clusters, the employee master data (personnel administration) infotypes, and the personnel planning infotypes. Because these infotypes have different structures and uses, we will look at them separately.

2.1.1   Personnel Administration Infotypes

Interrelated content is stored in infotypes in SAP ERP HCM. The division of data into infotypes is based mainly on business criteria. This concept enables you to decide freely which infotypes to use and not use. However, certain infotypes, such as IT0002 (Personal Data), are mandatory, as some basic functions would not be possible without them. The decision about which of the different infotypes to use depends on which processes you intend to use. Another option is to use data fields within an infotype. In this case, as before, there are differences: Certain fields are mandatory, whereas others can be used or hidden, as you require.

[Ex]

The Personal Data infotype (see Figure 2.1) contains the personal details of the person in question, divided into the blocks *Name*, *Birth data*, and *Marital status/religion*. This infotype is clearly one of the mandatory ones (without a person's name, for example, most reports would be useless). Examples of optional infotypes are IT0040 (Objects on Loan) and IT0035 (Company Instructions).

Only a few fields in Personal Data are not mandatory, such as the fields under *Marital status/religion*; you use these only if you choose to.

[!]

The example above illustrates the disadvantage of the infotype concept: some data applies to multiple infotypes. For example, data on marital status and religion is also relevant for taxation purposes (in Germany), so the *Number of children* (*No. child.*) and *Religion* fields are also included in the infotype IT0012 (tax data D). Therefore, as you can see, data redundancy exists in the system. There are only a few cross-infotype checks, and you have to program these yourself in user exits.

Thus, multiple options sometimes exist for reporting on data, and in these cases you have to establish which source will deliver data reliably and is easiest to report on. For example, if you require a report on religious affiliation, the infotype IT0012 (tax data D) is the most reliable source, as this data is relevant to payroll and is therefore carefully maintained.

SAP provides you with tools that enable you to quickly develop your own infotypes and to extend existing ones by adding your own fields to them. This has no detrimental effect on the SAP standard, and any changes are retained in updates.

Customer extensions

The main advantage of this function is that any custom development work that you carry out is available in the logical database without the need for further adaptations (see Section 2.2) and can also be used in SAP Query and Ad Hoc Query InfoSets (see Section 4.1).

The infotypes can be time-specific; that is, they are saved with a start date and an end date. This often poses a major challenge in reports, especially when information from several infotypes with different validity periods have to be combined for reporting purposes. If you make a selection over a period of time, there may be multiple records of an infotype in this period, with the result that multiple rows are output in the report.

History capability

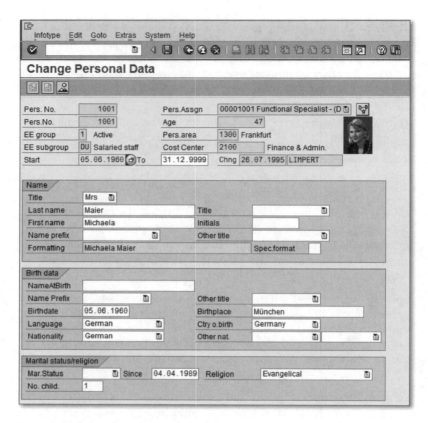

Figure 2.1 Infotype (Personal Data)

[+] The reporting requirements are an important consideration in deciding what infotypes and data fields to use, as a lot of data is maintained for reporting purposes only. This is why analyzing the data basis is always the first step in designing a reporting concept.

2.1.2 Payroll and Time Management Data Clusters

Payroll and time management results are stored in data clusters, which are stored in database table PCL2. Every cluster has its own structure, consisting of multiple tables. Whereas time management is international in nature and always uses cluster B2, there is an individual payroll cluster for each country version, as statutory regulations require specific data in each country.

Figure 2.2 shows the data structure PAYUS_RESULT, which makes reporting on payroll results easier. The structure contains three areas: EVP, the cluster directory; INTER, international payroll result objects; and NAT, national payroll result objects with the US payroll tables. The INTER and NAT areas are based on several tables.

Data structure of payroll result

You can use the sample report RPMUST01 as a template for your own reports. This report is an example of how payroll results are read on the basis of the PAYUS_RESULT structure.

[+]

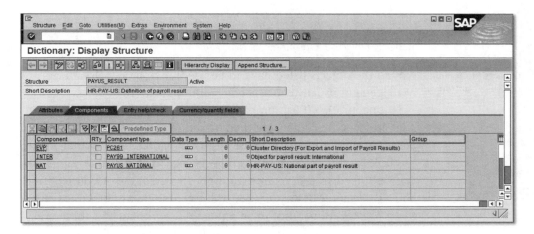

Figure 2.2 Structure of the Payroll Data Cluster

Reporting on payroll and time management results is technically more complex and less convenient than other data types, as you will see in Chapter 4, *Queries*, in particular. There is no logical database that directly retrieves payroll or time management results, so the programmer always has to use function modules to provide the data required for the report.

2.1.3 Personnel Planning Infotypes

The object-based data model for personnel planning consists of objects that are interrelated by links. Each of these objects has properties that are stored in infotypes.

There are many object types in the various personnel planning modules. Table 2.1 lists the object types in the *Organizational Management* module.

Object Type	Text
O	Organizational unit
S	Position
C	Job
T	Task
A	Work center
P	Person
K	Cost center

Table 2.1 Objects in Organizational Management

Objects in Organizational Management

Not all the objects listed have to be used; in practice, Organizational Management usually consists of a hierarchy with the objects O (Organizational unit), S (Position), and C (Job). The external objects P (Person) and K (Cost center) are then linked to these objects. Person and cost center do not originally belong to Organizational Management, but links can be set to external objects such as these. Also, a position can be linked to a personnel number in Personnel Administration, and a cost center in the CO (Controlling) module can be linked either to an organizational unit or to a position. Links such as these create hierarchy trees, and reports can then be run based on these structures.

Links

Links describe a relationship between two objects. They are defined in two directions: A (bottom-up) and B (top-down), and thus, reports can be run in two directions. For example, starting from a manager, the system can find all his subordinates, while starting from an employee, the system can identify his manager.

Staff assignments

The *organizational structure* is the basis of Organizational Management. The organizational units are arranged hierarchically in this structure. One position per employee is assigned to these organizational units in a concept known as *staff assignments* (see Figure 2.3).

Positions are also linked to jobs. Whereas a position corresponds to the employee's exact role, such as *Secretary Plant Manager Plant 1*, a job provides a general description only, such as *Secretary*.

A position can also be vacant; the property **Vacant** specifies that a position is either to be filled or that it will remain vacant (see Figure 2.3).

Staff Assignments (Structure)	Code	ID	Chief
▽ ☐ Human Resources	Hum Res -US	O 50000595	Mr. Mark Taylor
▷ 🙎 Vice President of Human Resources (US)	VPHR	S 50013548	
🙎 Director, HR Initiatives (US)	Dir. HR I-US	S 50000089	
▷ 🙎 Receptionist	Receptionist	S 50013593	
▷ ☐ Compensation and Benefits - (US)	Comp_Ben-US	O 50000603	Mrs Joanne Pawlucky
▽ ☐ Labor Relations - (US)	Lab.Rel. -US	O 50000604	Mrs Ann Takahashi
▽ 🙎 Manager of Labor Relations (US)	Mgr LbRel-US	S 50000205	
👥 Mrs Ann Takahashi	Takahashi	P 00100202	
🙎 Supervisor of Labor staff (US)	Supervisor	S 50013097	
🙎 Legal Advisor	Advisor	S 50006267	
▽ 🙎 Legal Advisor	Advisor	S 50013053	
👥 Mr. Michael Houseman	Houseman	P 00100144	
🙎 Administration Staff (US)	Administratn	S 50006266	
▷ 🙎 Administration Staff (US)	Administratn	S 50013399	
▷ 🙎 Functional Specialist (US)	Func.Spec-US	S 50000206	
▷ 🙎 Functional Specialist (US)	Func.Spec-US	S 50000243	
▷ ☐ Human Resources Administration - (US)	HR Adm. -US	O 50000605	Mr. Tom Peterson
▷ ☐ Development and Training Admin - (US)	Dev/Educ -US	O 50000606	Mr. David Payne
▷ ☐ Payroll Administration - (US)	Payroll -US	O 50000610	Mr. Timmy Tabasco
▷ ☐ Talent Relationship Management(US)	TalRel(US)	O 50012007	Mr. Jack Kincaid
▷ ☐ Workforce Planning	Wrkfrce -US	O 50018722	Mrs Jennifer Morris
▷ ☐ HR Information Systems (US)	HRIS -US	O 50025100	Mrs Patricia Otto

Figure 2.3 Staff Assignments

The evaluation path determines which objects are processed. Processing starts with an initial object and proceeds through all other objects that are connected to the initial object via the links defined in the evaluation path (see Figure 2.4).

Evaluation path

Evaluation Path	0-S-P		Internal persons per organizational unit				
No.	Obj.Type	A/B	Relat'ship	Relationship name	Priority	Rel.obj.type	Skip
10	0	B	003	Incorporates	▴	S	☐
20	S	A	008	Holder	▴	P	☐
30	0	B	002	Is line supervisor of	▴	0	☐

Figure 2.4 Evaluation Path — Customizing

The evaluation path starts with the organizational unit and searches for all positions linked to that unit. It then reads all the persons assigned to a position and proceeds from there with the next subordinate organizational unit.

This data model can be extended flexibly; for example, you can create your own objects, add your own links, and create your own evaluation paths for reporting purposes.

Extensibility

Organizational Management data is relevant at various points throughout the reporting process. This data is reported on directly in reports, such as a list of open or vacant positions. However, it can also be used to select employees if you select an organizational unit as the root object and use all employees assigned to the subordinate positions as the selected set. Managers often use this approach for reporting purposes. Therefore, you should take reporting aspects into account when setting up the Organizational Management structure.

2.2   Logical Databases

In the previous section, you learned about the complex structures of SAP ERP HCM. To save you having to reprogram the complex data-reading process every time in every report, SAP provides ready-to-run program routines in what are known as logical databases.

2.2.1   Properties of a Logical Database

A logical database is an ABAP program. It is the basis of reports and InfoSets of the query tools (see Chapter 4, *Queries*) and provides data for reporting and processing purposes. The logical database contains the following functions:

▶ **Data retrieval**
Data is read from the database and made available in main memory. Internal tables within the program store data from various infotypes, ready for further processing. The logical database is not a real physical database; instead, it provides access to database tables at the runtime of the report.

▶ **Selection screen**
The standard selection screen enables you to restrict the data selection by a variety of criteria. Various fields are available as selection parameters, depending on the structure of the logical database. In many cases, you do not need to define any additional selections in the report.

▶ **Authorization check**
The logical database checks whether the user has the appropriate permissions to view the requested data.

[+]   The authorization concept in HR is subject to particularly high demands. We strongly recommend that you use a logical database when programming customer reports.

The logical databases in the HCM system are as follows: PNP and PNPCE for personnel administration, PAP for recruitment, and PCH for the Organizational Management, Personnel Development, and Event Management modules.

2.2.2   Logical Database PNP

The logical database PNP is used in the Personnel Administration, Time Management, and Payroll modules. The selection screen of this logical database consists of the areas shown in Figure 2.5:

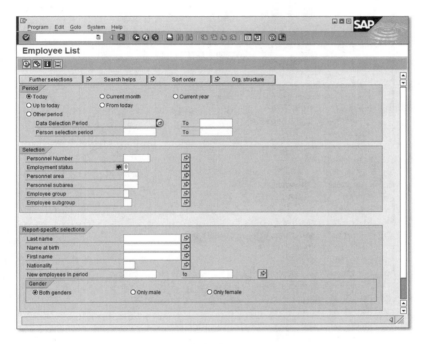

Figure 2.5 Selection Screen of Logical Database PNP

▶ **Application toolbar**

The application toolbar contains more functions for making selections, using search help, setting the sort order, and making selections using the organizational structure.

The **Further selections** button gives you access to additional fields for employee selection. To keep the selections area manageable, not all selection fields are visible by default; use this button to activate them.

The **Search helps** button links the selection and sort order areas in one function. For example, you can use it to select a search help screen for personnel numbers from the list of available search helps (Figure 2.6). You can also define your own search helps.

[Ex] A cost center, for example, can be entered in search help K (Organizational assignment). This has the effect that only employees who are assigned to this cost center are output. At the same time, the sorting process is carried out in accordance with the order of fields in search help K.

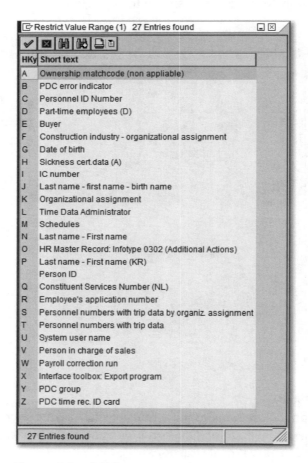

Figure 2.6 Search Helps

The list of employees is processed and output based on personnel numbers in ascending order. You can use the **Sort order** button to select the order of these fields. This functionality is more convenient and therefore preferable to using search helps.

The **Org. structure** button lets you select organizational units and thus restrict the list of employees in accordance with the organizational units you selected.

▶ **Dynamic selection**

The button for dynamic selection is located in the general toolbar. Users of this tool rarely use it to its full capacity. The fields available here can be used to create the selection view that is assigned in the HR report category (see Section 2.3). This selection view can contain data from various infotypes, including customer-specific infotypes. The dynamic selection functionality can be used to add any field you want to the Selection block, which consists of fields of the infotypes 0000 (Actions) and 0001 (Organizational Assignment).

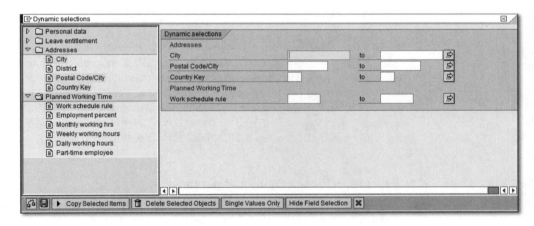

Figure 2.7 Dynamic Selection

▶ **Period**

The options under "Period" differentiate between the data selection period and the person selection period. The person selection period refers to the employee selection that has been carried out (see the example below). The data selection period refers to the data to be reported on and displayed.

[Ex]

We want to select all employees who are active on 12/31/2006. We also want to display the salary development of these employees during the year 2006.

To select the employees, we set 12/31/2006 as the start date and end date of the person selection period. (It is sufficient to enter the start date only. If the end date field is left empty, the end date is automatically set to be the same as the start date.) We also set the "Employment status" as "not equal to" 0. This selects all employees who are active on 12/31/2006.

We then set the period from 01/01/2006 to 12/31/2006 as the data selection period, as we want the report to read data for the whole year in order to represent the historical development. The report then outputs all data records that exist for that year.

► **Selection**
This area restricts the list of employees used for the report. All employees are selected who have matched the time period specified under person selection period for at least one day (also see Section 3.1).

[Ex]

The person selection period starts on 01/01/2006 and ends on 12/31/2006. Enter 1000 as the personnel area. All employees are then selected who were in this personnel area at some point during this period. (In other words, an employee does not have to have been in this personnel area for the entire period; it is sufficient for each employee simply to have been in this personnel area on 01/01/2006, even if he then moved to another personnel area on 01/02/2006, for example.)

► **Report-specific selections and parameters**
This screen area has nothing to do with the logical database; it is specific to the individual report. Here, you can define other selection options and program control parameters.

2.2.3 Logical Database PNPCE

The logical database PNPCE has existed since the SAP R/3 Enterprise release and is a successor of PNP. The selection screen shown in Figure 2.8 has undergone the following improvements:

► Simple and clear representation of data selection period and person selection period

▶ Integration of evaluation period and payroll dates in a single screen, so time periods and key dates can now be selected without the need to switch screens

▶ Inplace display of dynamic selection

▶ Integration of buttons into general toolbar

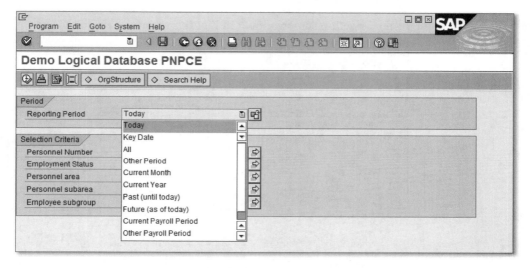

Figure 2.8 Selection Screen of Logical Database PNPCE

The most important new addition is support for concurrent employment. In other words, the person identifier is used as a selection criterion, making it possible to process employees with multiple contracts and, therefore, to process multiple person identifiers. This functionality has to be explicitly activated in the customizing.

Concurrent employment

> For more information on the topic of concurrent employment, see Note 517071 in the SAP Service Marketplace.

[+]

The general improvements to PNPCE can also be used without concurrent employment. SAP recommends that you use them in custom development work. However, most standard SAP reports still use the logical database PNP. SAP is switching over its reports step by step as new developments become necessary.

> See Section 6.3 on the specific weaknesses of this logical database.

[+]

2.2.4 Logical Database PCH

The logical database PCH was designed for the personnel planning data model, in which objects such as organizational units, positions, qualifications, and events are interrelated by links. PCH is used in Organizational Management, Personnel Cost Planning, Event Management, and Personnel Development.

In the selection screen shown in Figure 2.9, one or more objects can be specified as starting points. You can include other objects in the report by specifying an evaluation path.

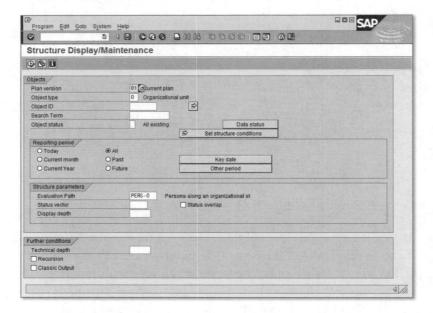

Figure 2.9 Selection Screen of Logical Database PCH

2.2.5 Logical Database PAP

The logical database PAP is used to report on recruitment data. The structure of the data in this database is similar to that of personnel administration data and uses largely the same infotypes, although PAP also uses some infotypes that are required specifically to administrate job applications.

The data is stored in its own area of the database.

Some terms have a different meaning in the "Applicant" context. In appli-   **[+]**
cant administration, the personnel number is called the applicant number,
the employee subgroup is the applicant range, and the employee group is
the applicant group.

Figure 2.10 shows the selection screen of the logical database PAP,
which is similar to the logical database PNP. However, some of the
fields in this screen are specially designed for applicant administration. The receipt of application period and the data selection period
are the available time periods. Also, **Advertisement** and **Unsolicited
application group** are data items that exist only in applicant administration.

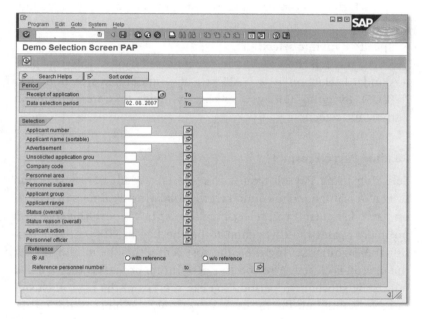

Figure 2.10 Selection Screen of Logical Database PAP

2.3 HR Report Categories

HR report categories enable you to fine-tune the selection screens of   Fine-tuning the
the PNP and PNPCE logical databases. You can make the following   selection screen
settings:

▸ **Key date, payroll period**
You can enter the payroll periods as the time periods. You can also restrict your entry to a key date.

▸ **Data selection period and person selection period**
You can interlink the data selection period and the person selection period. This means only one entry is required, and the periods are then always identical. It depends on the requirements of the report whether the periods remain identical or whether they will have to be entered separately later on.

▸ **Permitted selection options**
This setting enables you to select the selection options you require. In doing so, you specify which ones appear straight away and which ones can be activated using the **Further selections** button.

▸ **Specify dynamic selection**
Select the selection view for dynamic selections. This can be a standard selection view (SAP) or a custom-defined selection view (CUS). By doing this, you specify the fields that are available in dynamic selection.

Reading Payroll results

Selection using Payroll results

Selection using Payroll results is a special variant of the selection screen. It is intended to counteract the following weakness in reports on payroll results. If you select a cost center in a report, this selection normally causes the cost center to be checked in IT0001 (Organizational Assignment). However, the cost center may be modified after the payroll is closed. A retroactive accounting process is then carried out in the subsequent period. You can see this in the payroll cluster in table WPBP, but the infotype shows only the most recent status. Selection using Payroll results uses the field in table WPBP and not the infotype fields. This table is read not from the cluster, but from the tables HRPY_WPBP and HRPY_RGDIR. The content of the tables in the payroll cluster have been available in these transparent tables since release R/3 4.6C to make this selection type possible. This modifies the selection screen only; it does not cause any payroll results to be read. The payroll results have to be read using the usual function modules, as before.

To view the HR report category, open the properties of a report in the ABAP Editor (transaction SE38). Figure 2.11 shows the button you use to access the settings for the HR report category.

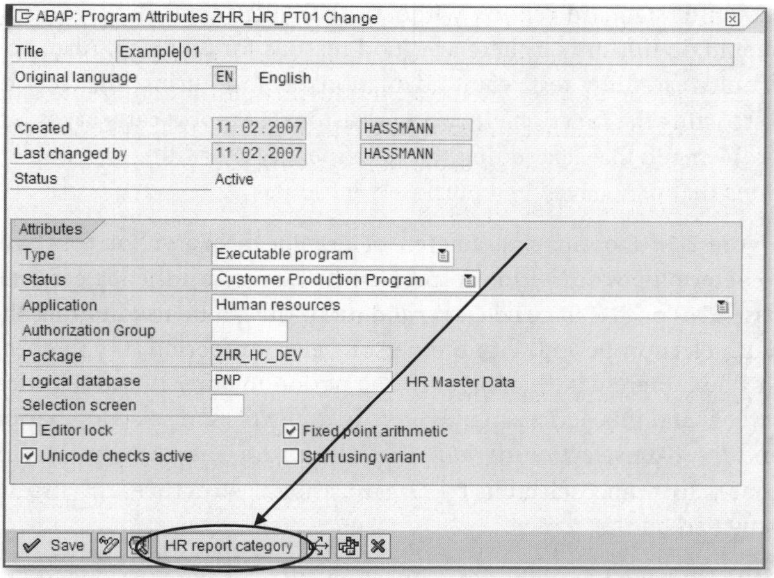

Call HR report category

Figure 2.11 ABAP Program Attributes

Click on the **HR report category** button to open the **Report category assignment** window shown in Figure 2.12. Here, you can select a report category or go to the report categories maintenance screen.

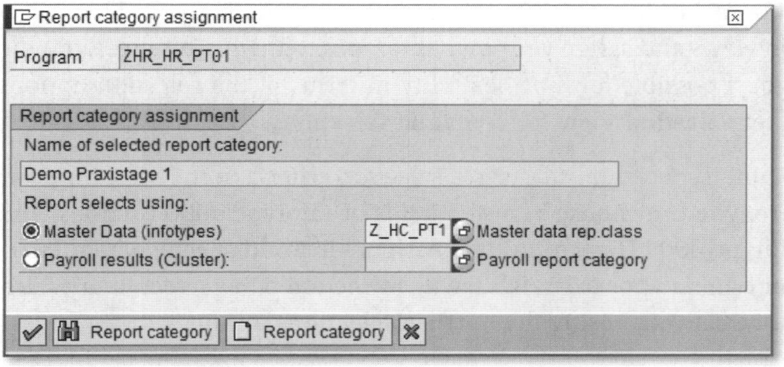

Figure 2.12 Report Category Assignment

You can also adapt the HR report category in the Customizing under the IMG path **Personnel Management · Human Resources Information System · Reporting · Adjusting the Standard Selection Screen · Assign Report Categories**. This enables you to adapt the selection screen of standard reports without modifying them. However, you should do this only if there are good reasons for doing so. Also, you should carefully test your adaptations before using the report. Restricting the functionality using a custom HR report category is less problematic than extending the functionality by adding more selections that may have been purposely left out.

Create a report category

Figure 2.13 shows the parameters of a report category. You first have to determine whether to use the report category for the logical database PNP or PNPCE. The **General data** block can be used to link the data selection period with the person selection period. If you check this box, there will then be only one period to enter in the selection screen, and this period applies equally to the person selection period and the data selection period. The buttons for **Search help** (Matchcode), **Sort,** and selection by **Organizational structure** can also be activated on this screen.

You also have the option to reduce the entry of time periods to key dates or to read the period from the data in the Payroll administration record.

The next step is to assign the **Selection view for dynamic selections**.

Selection view for dynamic selection

Selection views are a little-used but very useful selection option. These can be used to include additional infotype fields that are not contained in the standard selection. You can define your own selection views and assign your own infotypes to them. This gives you the highest possible level of flexibility in terms of the selection options under **Selection View for Dynamic Selections**.

You then specify the allowable selection criteria in the next window. Here, you can choose between fields of infotype 0000 (Actions) and infotype 0001 (Organizational Assignment) and specify which selection criteria appear straight away in the selection screen and which can be activated using the **Further Selections** button.

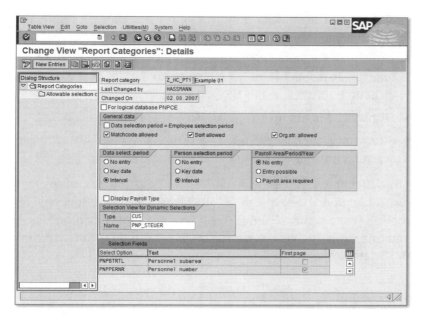

Figure 2.13 Creating a Report Category

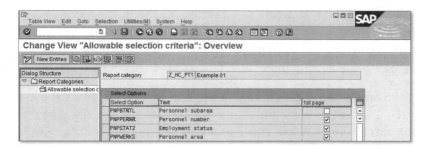

Figure 2.14 Specifying Allowable Selection Criteria

2.4 Authorization Checks in HR Reporting

As a basic rule, the same authorization checks are used in reporting as in the display and maintenance transactions in the HCM system. This applies in particular to the following authorizations:

Usual HR authorizations

▶ Display and maintenance authorizations for object types, infotypes, and subtypes in Organizational Management (authorization object PLOG)

▶ Display and maintenance authorizations for infotypes and subtypes in Applicant Management (P_APPL)

▶ Display and maintenance authorizations for infotypes and subtypes in Personnel Administration (P_ORGIN or P_ORGINCON, or both, P_ORGXX, P_PERNR)

▶ Display and maintenance authorizations for clusters (P_PCLX)

▶ Structural authorizations for Organizational Management and Personnel Administration

The following sections deal with how authorizations other than those mentioned above can be or have to be used specially for reporting in SAP ERP HCM. We also go into some detail on cluster authorizations in these sections, as these authorizations are very important in the reporting context.

2.4.1 Calling Reports

There are two authorization options for calling reports.

Starting Reports Using the SAP Easy Access Menu

To authorize users to start reports using the SAP Easy Access menu, go to the **Menu** tab (see Figure 2.15) and open the role maintenance function (transaction PFCG).

Link variants to reports   The **Transaction** button is used to add transactions directly. **Report** is used to create a transaction for a report if one does not already exist. On this screen, you can also create a transaction that calls a specific variant of the report and link a report to a variant using the transaction maintenance function (transaction SE93).

The Profile Generator creates entries in the authorization object **Transaction Code Check for Transaction Start** (S_TCODE) from the transactions that you maintained in the menu. These entries can be modified via the menu only.

To avoid a situation where every transaction is processed using the role maintenance function, the authorization object S_TCODE can also be transferred manually to the profiles and maintained without having to go through the menu. You can also use the placeholder "*" here — for example, "ZPT" would allow all transactions that start with ZPT.

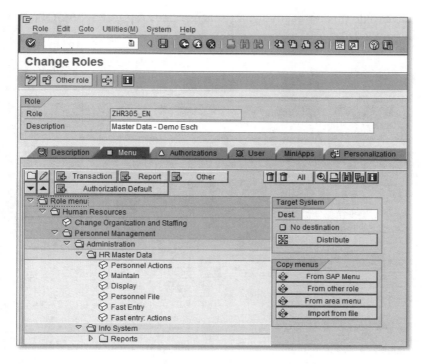

Figure 2.15 Creating an Authorization to Start Reports Using the SAP Menu

Starting Reports Using Transaction SA38

You can start any report by entering its name in transaction SA38 (**System • Services • Reporting**). In doing this, you are initially creating the option on a general level to start reports, rather than assigning an individual authorization for a specific report, so you need to be very careful when assigning authorizations in this way. This is particularly true because there are a few reports in the standard in which no authorization checks are run.

Start reports using SA38

To create authorization protection in this situation, you have to use the authorization object **ABAP: Program Flow Check** (S_PROGRAM) in conjunction with the authorization group. This field is located in the program attributes, which can be maintained by the programmer.

Authorization groups

Because the authorization group is not maintained in several standard SAP programs (or not maintained in the way you require), you have to do this retroactively. Do this using the report RSCSAUTH (*see* Figure 2.16).

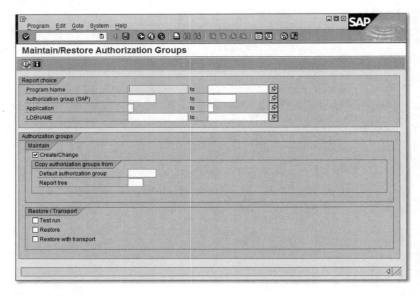

Figure 2.16 Maintaining Authorization Groups in Reports

In the upper part of the screen, use specific criteria to select the standard reports to which you want to assign the authorization groups entered under **Default authorization group**. If you have also created authorization groups in report trees, include these using the **Report tree** option.

The Restore options are needed after upgrades and other new releases of standard programs.

[+] As part of the process of defining your authorization concept, you should decide whether reports will be called using the menu or SA38. If you decide against the SA38 option, you will not need to maintain the authorization groups. Instead, you will have to explicitly assign permission for every report or group of reports.

2.4.2 Simplified Authorization Check for Reports

Authorization object P_ABAP

Because the process of checking read authorizations for master data takes up a lot of computing time, especially in the running of reports, you may want to restrict or deactivate the check for certain reports. Do this using the authorization object **HR: Reporting** (P_ABAP).

P_ABAP does not replace the basic authorization required to start a report. This basic authorization is administrated by the authorization objects mentioned in the previous section. Rather, P_ABAP simplifies and speeds up the process of checking the reported data. If you assign full authorization for this object, a user can view all the HR master data in the reports, even if he does not have authorization for the relevant infotypes and personnel numbers.

P_ABAP has an effect only in reports that use the personnel administration logical database (PNP). **P_ABAP for PNP only**

To maintain authorizations, enter the report name and one of the following two "simplification forms": **Two forms of simplification**

▶ Infotypes and organizational assignment are checked independently of each other. In other words, users can view all infotypes for all personnel numbers to which they have access. This approach speeds up the authorization check.

▶ When the report is run without checks, no checks of HR master data or structural checks are carried out. This approach makes sense for "uncritical" reports, such as a room directory, and for users who already have full read access to HR master data.

> P_ABAP can be used to deactivate the authorization check for all users in the case of a report of employee data that do not have to be protected (such as name, date of birth, and organizational unit). **[Ex]**
>
> For example, this authorization object is assigned specially for reports with a critical runtime to users in the central HR department who have full read access to HR master data.

2.4.3 Cluster Authorizations

The authorization object P_PCLX is used for the following, frequently used clusters: **Frequently used clusters**

▶ Master data

   ▹ TX: infotype texts

   ▹ LA: Master data change documents (LB for applicants)

- Time management
  - PC: single-character abbreviation for the monthly calendar, generated every time a presence or absence is updated
  - B1: interface to positive time management, read and written from RPTIME00
  - B2: central time evaluation cluster
- Payroll
  - RU: payroll results (USA)
  - CU: cluster directory
  - PS: generated payroll schema
  - PT: texts for generated schema

The input help for the **Area ID for Cluster** field in the authorization maintenance function of the cluster authorization object provides a full list of all the clusters in the PCL* tables.

2.4.4 Query

If a user is assigned to a user group (see Section 4.1.4) and has access in the user menu to queries via the SAP Query or Ad Hoc Query transaction, he is already able to run queries. This user has access to queries of the InfoSets that are assigned to his user group. Also, this user can run queries that you add directly to his user menu using the role maintenance function.

Authorization object S_QUERY

However, this user cannot save modifications to the queries. Thus, for more advanced work in the query area, you need the authorization object S_QUERY. With this object, you can grant access to the following activities:

- **Create and modify queries**
  The user can create new queries on the basis of the InfoSets in his user group(s) and save modifications to existing queries. You can reserve permission to modify queries for individual users by means of the user group assignments.

- **Maintain environment (InfoSets, user groups)**
  The user can execute transactions SQ02 (InfoSet maintenance) and SQ03 (user group maintenance) and transports. Ideally, end users should not have this authorization.

To extend InfoSets using ABAP code, the additional authorization object S_DEVELOP is also required with the value AQ* for the object name field and PROG for the object type field.

▶ **Translation (language comparison for SAP Query objects)**
The user can translate the texts or carry out a language comparison.

If a user has authorization to create and modify queries and to maintain InfoSets and user groups, he has access to the queries of all user groups without being explicitly assigned to them.

> If a query accesses tables outside the logical database, the authorization **[+]**
> object S_TABU_DIS is also checked.
>
> Access to the HR data to be reported on is administrated by the usual HR
> authorization objects and the structural or context-sensitive authorization
> check. If a field is included in the InfoSet as an additional field by directly
> reading the database table rather than by means of the logical database,
> no authorization check is carried out.
>
> However, this would enable you to fulfill the following requirement: A
> user wants to report on the internal address of infotype 0032 (internal
> data) but is not authorized to view company car data and thus cannot
> have full authorization for this infotype.

Since Release 4.6C, there is another maintenance tool that serves as an alternative to user group maintenance (SQ03). You can access this tool using transaction SQ10 or by choosing **Environment • Role Administration** in the InfoSet maintenance function (SQ02). Here, you can directly assign the user group to the role. In the next step, assign the InfoSets from the user group. Now every user with this role can run queries of these InfoSets. If a user also has the authorization object S_QUERY with change authorization, he can modify the queries of all other roles. This tool cannot be used to override the change authorization for each user group. This can be done in the user group maintenance function only (see Section 4.1.4).

*Role adminis-
tration*

Another way of restricting access to queries and InfoSets is to use the authorization group that you maintain in the InfoSet. The authorization group is located in the first screen after the InfoSet is created. For an InfoSet that has already been saved, you can open this screen from the menu by choosing **Goto • Global properties**. The authorization group assigned here has to be entered in the role in the S_PRO-

*Authorization
groups*

GRAM authorization object under **ABAP/4 Program Authorization Group** (see Section 2.4.1).

If you are not using authorization groups, this field remains empty in the InfoSet maintenance function. In this case, you do not need the S_PROGRAM authorization object either.

[+] To make it as easy as possible for the user to use SAP Query, we recommend that you prespecify the work area. Do this in the user maintenance function on the **Parameters** tab. The "AQW" and "Blank" entries have the effect that the relevant standard work area is displayed when SAP Query is called.

2.4.5   Manager's Desktop

The authorization object **BC-BMT-OM: Allowable Function Codes for Manager's Desktop** (S_MWB_FCOD) checks each function's authorization for individual users for all the possible functions in the Manager's Desktop (MDT). The input help of the **Function code** field contains a list of the function codes.

2.4.6   Customer Reports

In SAP ERP HCM, authorization checks are carried out in the application system rather than on the database level. Therefore, every authorization check has to be programmed in ABAP/4.

Use logical databases

The most secure and easiest way of checking authorizations in customer reports is therefore to use the relevant logical database, that is, PAP for applicant data, PNP or PNPCE for HR master data, and PCH for data in Organizational Management, Personnel Development, and similar modules. The logical database carries out all the necessary checks. Data that is accessed via the GET command when a user wants to read HR data in the program is thus secure from the authorization point of view.

Use standard function modules

As soon as the need arises in the program to read external data, or in cases where, for example, the logical database cannot be used for performance reasons, the code has to ensure the completeness of the authorization check. Usually, this is done using the *standard function modules* of the SAP system. These function modules usually contain parameters for administrating the authorization check, some of which are divided up into "normal" authorization checks and structural checks. It is advisable to activate these parameters so that the standard function modules run the authorization checks.

The correct functioning of any standard function modules you use has to be checked as part of upgrades. This also applies when your company starts using new authorization objects.

The code should specify that data be read directly from the database only in very exceptional circumstances. In such cases, the whole authorization check has to be carried out individually for each authorization object with the AUTHORITY-CHECK command.

Also, as indicated above, simple read commands to the database enable *program developers* to view all the data in clients in which they create programs. Special read commands can also be used to give programmers access to data in other clients in the same system.

Remember authorizations for programmers

2.4.7 Special Issues

You need to take the following special issues into account.

Access to Aggregated Data

Often a user has to process the statistics of a specific user group but is not allowed access to the source of this data.

Total yes, details no

> An HR controller is not allowed to know the salaries of the board members, but the statistical report he is creating has to include the total salaries of everyone in the company, including the board members.

[Ex]

This is not possible using the standard means, as without the corresponding authorization to the individual data, the report cannot generate the required totals. However, as soon as the required authorization is assigned, the user can view them — in the HR master data display screen, for example.

There are two possible solutions to this problem:

▶ Use authorization object P_ABAP to deactivate the authorization check (see Section 2.4.2). However, with this approach, there is always the danger that the user runs the report for one person only and accesses the confidential information in this way.

▶ Create a customer-specific report especially for this purpose. This report would not carry out any authorization check but would have to ensure that the report could not be run for individual personnel numbers.

Behavior of Reports in the Case of Insufficient Authorizations

If a user runs a report but does not have authorization for the data in question, the report skips all rows that contain "forbidden" data.

[Ex] A report contains the names and powers of attorney of all employees. However, a user who runs the report does not have read access to the power of attorney data for some of the selected employees; in these cases, he has access to the names only. The report does not output the data of the employees in question (not even their names). Instead, it simply displays a warning message at the end of the report: "Personnel number skipped due to insufficient authorization."

2.5   Reporting Basics

Reliable data basis   In previous sections, you saw that successful reporting requires a data basis that contains solid information. The data has to be maintained thoroughly, and the relevant information has to be reliable.

Data required for payroll or time management purposes is usually very carefully maintained. If errors are made or data forgotten in these areas, the employee will notice this immediately, and the required corrections are made. Therefore, this data is a solid basis and is frequently used for reports.

[+] As a rule of thumb, you can assume that data will be insufficiently maintained if it is relevant to only a small number of processes and if the user does not have sufficient knowledge of the content or relevance of the data.

In other areas, such as job vacancies, data may be maintained, but inconsistently. If the information on the vacancy is required in a number of different processes that are not functioning correctly because the data hasn't been maintained sufficiently, data quality will increase if data maintenance is carried out properly. In the example of the vacancy, the process in question could be Personnel Cost Planning, which requires the vacancy information for personnel cost planning, or it could be a process for approving positions for each workflow, for which adequate data maintenance or integration into applicant management are necessary.

Therefore, when new processes are rolled out, you need to check which of the new key figures and information are relevant and how to support full, correct data maintenance through appropriate plausibility checks in the system. For new reports on the basis of existing processes, the data on which the reports are based has to be validated, Field prepopulation and plausibility checks may also be necessary to enable retroactive maintenance and to support data maintenance.

2.5.1 Central Data for Successful Reports

Certain central data in the HCM system needs to be carefully designed and structured, as this data is intensively used both in multiple processes and in reporting.

This central data includes the following:

Infotypes 0000 (Actions) and 0001 (Organizational Assignment)

Data of the infotypes 0000 (Actions) and 0001 (Organization Assignment) are the basis of authorization checks and are used in the selection screens of the logical databases PNP and PNPCE. Therefore, you need to take reporting aspects into consideration when customizing these infotypes. These aspects include the following:

Customizing the enterprise structure and personnel structure

▶ **Actions and action reasons**
Entry and leaving, as well as leaving reasons, are particularly important for creating key figures. You have to design a definition concept for leaving reasons for reporting purposes. The important information here is whether the employee in question is leaving the company for his own reasons, or whether there were internal company reasons.

▶ **Employee group and employee subgroup**
Employee groups and employee subgroups are important for selecting relevant employees. A frequently used approach is to

create an "inactive" employee group, so that these employees can be omitted from reports. Reporting requirements also need to be taken into account when you are designing the employee subgroups. You should try to keep the number of employee groups and subgroups as small as possible, but an extra employee group or subgroup can often make reporting easier.

▶ **Personnel area and personnel subarea**
Personnel areas and personnel subareas can play an important role in reporting — for example, if you want to make divisions or independent parts of the company easy to select for reporting purposes.

Structure of Organizational Management

Structure formation

The structure(s) specified in organizational management are used for reports but are also the basis of employee selection and possibly also of authorization checks for reports. You should take into account the following aspects in relation to these structures:

▶ **Job catalog**
There are various requirements of the job catalog, most of which are closely related to reporting requirements. The challenge is to come up with job definitions that apply throughout the company. One reporting requirement would be a salary comparison between employees with the same job.

▶ **Organizational units**
The need to assign the information of a hierarchy level — such as board area, department, or team — to an organizational unit is a common one, and you need to take it into account when setting up your organizational structure. One option in this regard is to store the extra information in the object abbreviation. An alternative is to create a special infotype in which the hierarchy level is stored. You could also create the structure numerically; for example, the first level could be equivalent to the board area, the second level to the department, and so on. However, none of these three solutions are directly accessible to reporting in the SAP standard, so you have to decide which solution you prefer and how you are going to incorporate it into your reporting concept.

▶ **Staff assignments structure**

The easiest way to select employees in reports for managers is to use the staff assignments. However, if the hierarchy does not reflect the reporting structure, you have to invest extra time and effort, for example, create a special evaluation path or use other information, to correctly assign the areas of responsibility. This is something to keep in mind when creating the organizational structure.

Another challenge is posed by multidimensional structures, in which the business and disciplinary assignments are different from each other.

The fact that you can define your own evaluation paths creates flexibility in reports. It also shows that reporting plays an important role in modeling organizational management structures.

Wage Types in Payroll and Time Types in Time Management

The creation of wage types and time types for reporting can make reporting tasks easier. For example, it is considerably easier to answer a query regarding how many hours an employee was sick with and without continued pay if there are time types and wage types in which these hours can be saved. Sickness statistics can then be created with a simple wage type or time type report. Alternatively, you could calculate these hours on the basis of the work schedule and absences, but this would require much more programming.

Check which key figures can be reported on on the basis of wage types **[+]**
and time types.

2.5.2   Special Features of International Reporting

Many companies also use SAP ERP HCM for their foreign subsidiaries. This situation involves additional challenges.

Unified Definitions of Terms

The data used as a basis for reports has to be comprehensible and usable on an international level. However, in practice, definitions are often based on country-specific conditions, such as the definition of employee groups and subgroups. For example, few countries differentiate between salaried employees and industrial workers. In Germany, this differentiation is based on past pension regulations that no longer apply but is still enshrined in some collective agreements. It is therefore common practice in Germany to reflect this differentiation in various employee subgroups. This situation is difficult for other countries to understand, as they have no legal basis for the differentiation. Therefore, as this example illustrates, it is important in international reporting to use universal definitions. To give another example, the differentiation between *office worker* and *factory worker* could be changed to create a single internationally applicable term.

Because employee subgroups contain several technical SAP Customizing settings that affect payroll and time management, it is difficult to roll out definitions of employee subgroups on a global level. Some countries manage to do so, whereas others use their own employee subgroups to fulfill payroll and time management requirements. For this reason, you should define a concept that allows for multiple equivalent employee subgroups — for example, by creating defined areas containing employee subgroups with the same definition; 10–20 could correspond to an office worker. Alternatively, you could use the first character to identify the employee subgroup and the second character for the country code.

In Germany, the status **Inactive** also often depends on German legal conditions, such as the end of continued pay. The concept of continued pay as it exists in Germany is unknown in other countries. If someone outside Germany is using a report that is based on German social insurance regulations, such as days that qualify for social insurance coverage, that person will have no basis on which to run the report. Therefore, in this case, the person running the report will have to use the first full month in which no remuneration was paid, for example, as the inactive period.

These parameters have to be agreed upon and embedded in a concept.

Data Harmonization

It is easier to implement key figure definitions for international reporting if you design and implement guidelines for doing so before rolling out your SAP system. It is difficult to make retroactive data changes (and almost impossible in some areas) such as definitions of employee subgroups. A possible option here would be to load the data into an SAP NetWeaver BI system and harmonize the data when it is loaded. However, the question is still open as to whether this alone would create comparable data, as certain information may not exist at all, such as separate definitions of *office worker* and *factory worker*, or may be used differently in different systems.

Programming Requirements

Programs created in-house are subject to certain requirements. However, these requirements are often not taken into account from the start.

If the system allows users to log on in different languages, tables in the logon language have to be read. Check whether the reading of tables has been programmed with the required level of flexibility. If the system is Unicode-enabled, the programs also have to adhere to Unicode guidelines (see *service.sap.com/unicode*). Program texts have to be translated, and text symbols have to be used rather than text that is embedded in the code.

You also have to ensure that country-specific settings in the program are read correctly. For example, the country modifier (MOLGA) is often preset to **01** in the code, which makes it impossible for users in other countries to use the program.

The resources required to adapt in-house programs for international use should be incorporated into the roll-out schedule.

2.6 Summary

The data structures in SAP ERP HCM are very complex, as there are various modules with different requirements. In addition, not all modules are used to the same level in practice. Therefore, a basic requirement of reporting is that you analyze the data basis to define the data to be output in reports.

In certain modules, such as Payroll, careful data maintenance is a must, whereas in other modules, data is often only maintained sporadically. To create a solid data basis, which results in complete and useful reports, you need to decide what processes to install that support and manage data maintenance. In some cases, it is sufficient to carry out retroactive maintenance in response to gaps in data maintenance that are highlighted in reports themselves.

Authorizations are particularly important when it comes to reports involving HR data. You should always strive to avoid the worst-case scenario, in which poorly maintained authorizations enable users to view data for which they do not have the required authorization.

PART II
Reporting Tools

Human resources management requires reports and analyses relating to employee data and key figures on an ongoing basis. The SAP system provides a range of tools with various options for this purpose, which are introduced in this second part of the book. Specifically, these tools are standard SAP reports, queries, SAP NetWeaver BI, and customer reports.

The standard report is the most widely used SAP tool in the context of HR. This chapter provides some useful tips on how to use this tool.

3   Standard SAP Report

Standard SAP reports fulfill all the standard reporting requirements. In the payroll area, in particular, the standard SAP report is the ideal tool for creating reports. It is also in this area that the standard report covers the greatest number of requirements because these are predominantly based on legal regulations that apply to all companies. In other modules, such as Organizational Management and Personnel Development, requirements may vary widely in practice, and the standard report covers only the basic reporting requirement.

3.1   Starting a Report

You can start a report in one of the following ways:

▶ In the ABAP Editor (Transaction SE38)

▶ By executing the ABAP program (in Transaction SA38 or by selecting **System · Services · Reporting** from the menu)

▶ From the SAP Easy Access menu

It is preferable to start a report from the SAP Easy Access menu or from the individual menu of a role (see Chapter 16, *Area Menu*, and Section 2.4) for the following two reasons: Reports are easier to use this way, and the assignment of authorizations is simpler and more secure.

Reports can be organized by area in a menu, and it is possible to search for specific reports.

SAP has grouped together the available reports in *information systems*.

SAP information systems

The following information systems are available:

▶ **The component information system**
You can find the information systems of the individual HR components under the following paths:

  ▶ **Human Resources • <component> • Information System • Reports**

  ▶ **Human Resources • Payroll • <continent> • <country> • Information System**

  ▶ **Human Resources • Time Management • <component> • Information System**

▶ **The HR information system**
The HR information system contains all HR-specific reports and reporting tools. It is organized by component and, within each component, according to content-based criteria. You can find it under: **Human Resources • Information System • Reports • <component>**

▶ **The SAP information system**
The reports in the HR information system are also contained in the SAP information system. This is found under both paths specified below:

  ▶ **Information Systems • Human Resources • Reports • <component>**

  ▶ **Information Systems • General Report Selection • Human Resources • <component>**

3.2 Period Selection

Time-dependent data maintenance in SAP ERP HCM is often relatively difficult when it comes to reporting. If key date reports are executed, the result is unique and traceable. With period-based reports, on the other hand, an interpretation of results is frequently required. Duplicated data records occur, employees may appear in unexpected cost centers, or employees who have already left the company may turn up again in the results of the report.

To ensure a reliable result, a distinction must be made between the data selection period and the person selection period.

The selection screen in Figure 3.1 shows both periods, which must be examined separately.

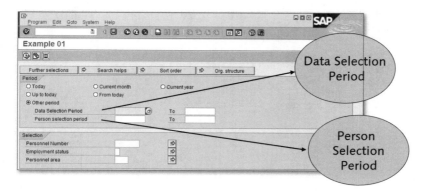

Figure 3.1 Data Selection Period and Person Selection Period

The **data selection period** is used once the relevant employees have been identified. It determines the period for which the employee data is to be processed.

Data selection period

The **person selection period** is based on the restrictions made under **Selection**. Employees who fulfill all criteria entered here during the specified period are included in the set of persons for whom data is to be processed. The criteria do not have to be fulfilled for the entire period. Even if a criterion is fulfilled for a single day within the period, this is sufficient. This explains why an employee who leaves the company in January still appears in the results of a report executed for the entire year.

Person selection period

You need to ensure that the selections you make for both periods suit your specific requirements. For example, to calculate the amount of overtime worked over the course of a year, you must include all employees who were active in the company during the year. You must select a data selection period and a person selection period of January 1 to December 31. Employees who left the company at the end of January have to be included in the report.

[Ex]

If, on the other hand, you want to calculate the number of hours of overtime completed over the last year to determine the bonuses to be paid to employees, anyone who has left the company is no longer of interest for your report. Therefore, the data selection period is still January 1 to December 31, but the person selection period is limited to a single date, that is, December 31. This means only those employees who were still active in the company on December 31 are included in your report.

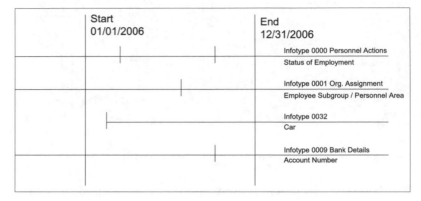

Figure 3.2 Infotype Selection

Another obstacle to overcome in reports is the time constraint. Infotypes may exist:

▶ Without time gaps or overlaps

▶ With time gaps but without overlaps

▶ With both time gaps and overlaps

▶ Only once

An example is shown in Figure 3.2. Duplicate rows will appear in the results of reports with this query.

It is important to understand the effect of this in order to verify and evaluate the results.

3.3   Selection Variables

You can use selection variables to prefill fields dynamically in a report variant. This option saves you from having to always change variants (see Figure 3.3) and is particularly useful for reports that run in the background.

There are two different types of variable: table variables (T) and dynamic date calculation (D).

A table variable fills the content of the selection variable with a value stored in the TVARVC table. If these table variables change in accordance with a certain logic, it is advisable to write a report that runs in the background on a regular basis and updates the variables in the table.

Table variables

Dynamic date calculation uses integrated functions to calculate key dates (for example, the last day of the current month or the previous month) and uses these as default values for date fields on selection screens.

Dynamic date calculation

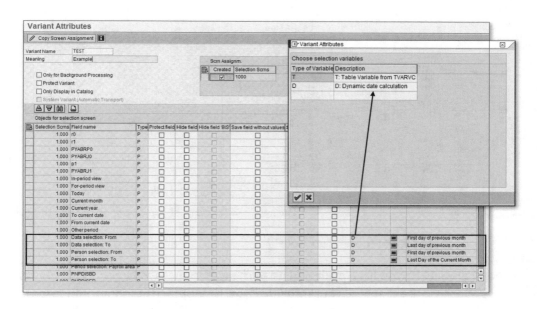

Figure 3.3 Selection Variable

3.4 Using ALV Lists

The flexible display with the *ALV Grid* (ABAP List Viewer) is now used in most standard SAP reports, and we recommend that you also use it in customer reports (see Chapter 6). ALV lists give you a great deal of flexibility when designing reports. You can configure sorting of the results, show or hide fields, and use filtering and totaling functions in order to use reports for various purposes and user groups.

The layout you configure can be reused and saved as the default setting, so that it is used automatically the next time the report is started.

Changing a layout   Press the **Change layout** button to see which fields are available in the column set. Often not all available fields are displayed when you start a report. Therefore, you should check whether the fields you require are included in the column set (see Figure 3.4).

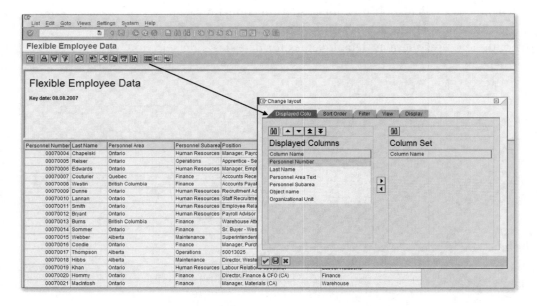

Figure 3.4 Changing a Layout

Saving a layout   If you have made extensive changes to the layout, you can save it as a separate layout, provided you have sufficient authorization to do so. This is shown in Figure 3.5. Note that if you save a layout for a specific user, it cannot be used by any other users. If you do not save the layout for a specific user, it is available to all users.

User-specific layouts must start with a letter, whereas general layouts must start with a forward slash (/). You can also define a layout as the default layout. It will then be used automatically the next time the report is started.

[!]   If you save a general layout as the default layout, it is used as the default layout for all users. You should only do this as system administrator.

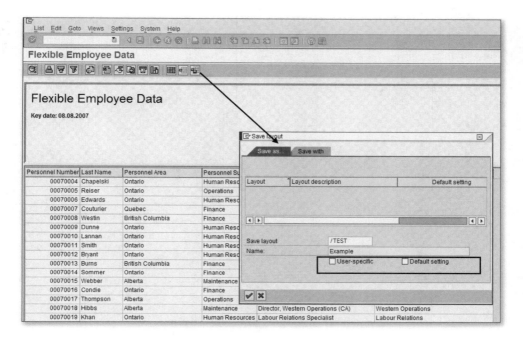

Figure 3.5 Saving a Layout

3.5 Summary

The standard report is the report of choice for meeting legal requirements, for example, in relation to the subsequent activities in payroll. Standard reports fulfill the greatest number of requirements in this area because the same legal requirements apply to all companies. Requirements differ to a greater degree in other modules, such as Personnel Development, and, accordingly, cannot be fulfilled to the same degree by standard reports. In addition, standard reports are losing some ground due to SAP's new strategy of increasingly mapping reporting requirements in SAP NetWeaver BI. Reports in the BI system are considerably more flexible and easier to adapt to suit individual requirements, provided that an InfoCube exists with the necessary key figures and characteristics.

Standard reports have become more flexible thanks to the use of ALV lists, which enable a variable design. However, it is still the case that a suitable standard report must exist for the specific requirement and that this report must come very close to fulfilling this requirement.

This chapter explains how to create reports without any programming expertise. Specifically, we will demonstrate the various functions available with QuickViewer, Ad Hoc Query, and SAP Query. You will also learn which tool can best fulfill which requirements.

4   Queries

Ad Hoc Query and QuickViewer are generally used for short-term requests. Both tools are intuitive and are therefore particularly suitable for beginners. SAP Query is predominantly used to create reports that are executed periodically. QuickViews and ad hoc queries can be processed further with SAP Query. SAP queries can also be converted into ad hoc queries, with some restrictions. You can then use the *set operations* and *report-report interface* functions, which are not available with SAP Query (see Table 4.1).

QuickViewer,
Ad Hoc Query, and
SAP Query

Table 4.1 provides an overview of the three tools in terms of application options, user friendliness, data basis, functions, and list types. The tools and their functions are discussed in detail in Sections 4.2 to 4.4.

	QuickViewer	Ad Hoc Query	SAP Query
Applications	Ad Hoc Reporting	Ad Hoc Reporting	Standard Reporting
User friend-liness	Intuitive	Intuitive	Some instruction would be helpful
Data basis	InfoSet or table, table join, logical database	InfoSet	InfoSet

Table 4.1 A Comparison of QuickViewer, Ad Hoc Query, and SAP Query

	QuickViewer	Ad Hoc Query	SAP Query
Functions	No additional functions	Set operations Report-report interface	Multiline lists Additional local fields Interactive lists
Lists	Basic list	Basic list Statistics Ranked list	Basic list Statistics Ranked list

Table 4.1 A Comparison of QuickViewer, Ad Hoc Query, and SAP Query (cont.)

A query can be processed in all three tools thanks to the shared data basis, that is, InfoSets. The following section explains how to create a unified data basis for the creation of queries.

4.1 InfoSets

InfoSets normally contain fields belonging to various infotypes from a component (such as Personnel Administration or Recruitment). The fields are provided by a logical database. A logical database exists for each component (see Section 2.2, Logical Databases).

Standard InfoSets   SAP provides standard InfoSets in the **global area**. Personnel Administration contains only *one* (international) InfoSet by default. To create a customer-specific InfoSet, you must copy a standard InfoSet, transport it into the client-specific standard area (see Section 4.7), and adapt and extend it there. First, we explain how to create a new InfoSet.

4.1.1 Creating Your Own InfoSets

You can access InfoSet maintenance in one of the following ways:

▸ In the SAP Easy Access menu, select **Human Resources • Information System • Reporting Tools • SAP Query** and then select the menu option **Environment • InfoSets**.

▸ Enter "Transaction SQ02" in the command field and press Enter on your keyboard.

Is the **global area** set as the query area? If so, you must first change the query area. Select the menu option **Environment • Query areas** and switch to the **standard area** (see Figure 4.1).

To work in the global area, cross-client changes must be permitted. We therefore recommend that you work in the client-specific standard area.

[!]

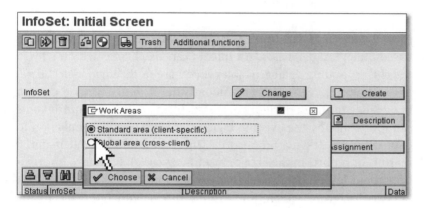

InfoSet: Initial Screen

Trash | Additional functions

InfoSet | | 🖉 Change | 📄 Create

Work Areas

⦿ Standard area (client-specific)
○ Global area (cross-client)

📄 Description

ssignment

✓ Choose | ✖ Cancel

Status InfoSet | Description | Data

Figure 4.1 Changing the Query Area

If you want to access the standard area directly the next time you call up InfoSet or query maintenance, simply enter the parameter AQW with a blank value in your user master. To do this, select the menu option **System • User Profiles • Own Data** and select the **Parameters** tab.

[+]

1. To create a new InfoSet, enter a name for the InfoSet and click on the **Create** button.

2. Maintain a description for the InfoSet in the dialog box that appears. Refer to the discussion of query-specific authorizations in Section 4.1.4 in relation to authorization groups.

3. Select the logical database PNPCE as your data source.

In this example, the following data is available in PNPCE:

[Ex]

▶ All infotypes in Personnel Administration and Time Management

▶ The Payroll results, provided that they are stored in a "Payroll results" infotype

> ▶ The results from Time Management, provided that they are included in Customizing for simulated infotypes
>
> ▶ Long texts for most relevant keys stored in the infotypes that have already been specified
>
> ▶ A comprehensive set of additional fields, for example, from PD info-types, where a reference can be created to an individual personnel number (e.g., a manager)

Using logical databases

In SAP ERP HCM, an InfoSet can be easily defined and generated based on logical databases. An InfoSet can also be created directly in the corresponding database tables if you are not using a logical database. However, we only recommend this if you have a thorough knowledge of the underlying data structures and if the requirements cannot be met by the existing logical database (e.g., a connection to data from the HR master record, Time Management and material master for reports in the area of incentive wages). For more information about logical databases, refer to Section 2.2, *Logical Databases*. Reports based on a table join are explained with reference to the QuickViewer (see Section 4.2). Unlike a query, a QuickView may also be based directly on tables or table joins.

4. Confirm your entries. You can now select the required infotypes.

5. The InfoSet maintenance screen then appears. The system proposes the most frequently used fields and assigns them to the field groups according to infotype (see Figure 4.2).

You can simply delete any automatically proposed fields that are not maintained or are not required for the report. Fields can only be removed later if they have not already been used in a query. However, fields can be added at any stage.

Maintaining meaningful texts

We also strongly recommend that you maintain your own texts. Default texts are proposed, but these are often not self-explanatory or are only meaningful within a certain context. For example, if an InfoSet contains wage type and amount fields from various info-types, it will be impossible to tell from the titles whether the wage type/amount is from infotype 0008, 0014, or 0015. An InfoSet with well-chosen texts can save you a lot of time later. When you double-click on a field, the field label appears on the bottom-right of the screen and can be overwritten (see Figure 4.2).

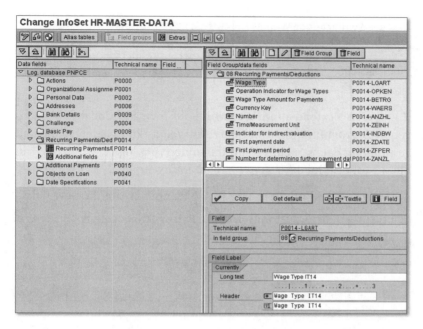

Figure 4.2 InfoSet Maintenance — Selecting a Meaningful Field Label for a Wage Type from Infotype 0014

6. After you create or change an InfoSet, you must generate it.

> When maintaining InfoSets, you must always bear in mind that they will be used in the future as the basis for numerous queries and ad hoc queries. For this reason, it is worth investing a little extra time when creating an InfoSet. It is only possible to make a limited number of changes to an InfoSet for which queries already exist. However, it is normally possible to add new fields.

[«]

4.1.2 Extending InfoSets

InfoSets contain other fields in addition to infotype fields. These additional fields are located in the relevant field groups and are closely connected to the fields in the infotype. Frequently used additional fields include:

▸ Infotype 0001: Personnel number and name of superior

▸ Infotype 0002: Age of employee, day and month of date of birth

▸ Infotype 0008: Annual salary

[!] Proceed with caution with the additional fields provided. It is tempting to use the additional fields for entry and leaving dates from infotype 0000. However, these sometimes return unexpected results, depending on the data selection period. Check the contents of these fields carefully.

You can also extend an InfoSet with your own additional fields. This requires programming experience, as well as knowledge of the corresponding data structures and the underlying logical database. This allows user-defined fields to be read, for example.

Creating an additional field

1. Select the field group in which you want to create the new field.

2. Press the **Extras** button, select the **Extras** tab, and click on the **Create** button (see Figure 4.3).

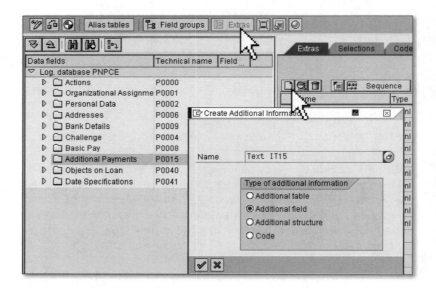

Figure 4.3 Defining an Additional Field

3. Enter a name for the additional field and select the **Additional field** radio button. Press Enter.

4. Maintain a format for the **Additional field**.

5. Make the data declaration on the **Code** tab in the **DATA** code section.

6. For the code to fill the new field, select the **Extras** tab, place the cursor in the field, and click on the **CodingForAddition** button (Figure 4.4).

7. Finally, save and check the code and generate your InfoSet.

Last name	Wage Type	Wage Type	Amount	Curre	Additional Text of IT 15
MacDonald	6M03	Bonus	200.00	CAD	for great achievments

Figure 4.4 Result: Displaying a User-Defined Field in the Output List

You can find sample code for reading text clusters in Appendix C.   **[+]**

4.1.3   Special "Switches"

You can use *switches* to influence the processing logic of an InfoSet. *General switches* affect all Infotypes. They allow you to execute functions that deviate from the standard, including the following:

General switches

▸ Process persons for whom only partial authorization is available because the query excludes all Personnel numbers for which no authorization is available for at least one field (PROC_PERNR_PARTIAL_AUT switch)

▸ Take locked data records into account (PROCESS_LOCKED_RECORDS switch)

Infotype-specific switches refer to a specific infotype (to be specified). These allow you to execute, for example, the following functions:

Infotype-specific switches

▸ Output data records in the logon language only if objects from Personnel Development (for example, events) have been created in several languages (NO_DUPLICATE_LANGU switch)

▸ Ignore the operation indicator (for deduction wage types from infotypes 0008, 0014, 0015, and 0052) (the IGNORE_WAGE_TYPE_OPERA switch)

You can find a complete list of all switches with detailed descriptions in the Implementation Guide (IMG) documentation under **Personnel Management • Human Resources Information System • HR Settings for SAP Query • Create InfoSets for HR**.

It is important that you are aware that these switches may have a direct effect on the processing logic of InfoSets. Therefore, they should only be used meet a few very specific requirements.

Switches are integrated using additional code in the InfoSet. In InfoSet maintenance, click on the **Extras** button and then select the **Code** tab on the right of the screen. For infotype-specific switches, specify the relevant infotype or infotypes in square brackets as shown in the example below. For general switches, Common must be entered in square brackets:

```
*$HR$ [P0008, P0014, P0015]
*$HR$ IGNORE_WAGE_TYPE_OPERA = 'X'
```

[+] These switches are available as of SAP R/3 Enterprise Release 4.7. For earlier releases, refer to SAP Note 305118.

Note that queries must be regenerated after you add or change a switch.

4.1.4   Enabling the Use of InfoSets

Special authorization is required in the queries context to access InfoSets. This must be configured in addition to role maintenance (see Section 2.4.4).

User groups
You can use various user groups to determine which users can access which InfoSets. You can determine whether a user can create and change queries in this InfoSet or can only execute queries. If a user is permitted to change all queries, you can revoke change authorization for queries in this InfoSet from this user. In this case, the relevant checkmark must not be set (see Figure 4.5).

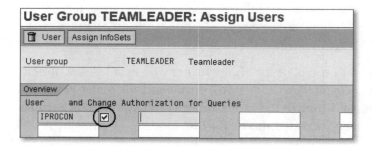

Figure 4.5 Assigning user IPROCON to the Teamleader User Group

You can access user maintenance from the SAP Easy Access menu under **Human Resources · Information System · Reporting Tools · SAP Query · Environment · User groups**. Define a new user group and click on **Create**.

When you have defined a user group and assigned users to this group, you must then assign the InfoSet. To do this, click on the **Assign InfoSets** button. A list of all InfoSets is then displayed. Set a checkmark next to the InfoSets you want to assign to the user group and save your settings.

4.2 QuickViewer

Of the three tools, the QuickViewer is the easiest to use. However, it is not a reporting tool per se. With the QuickViewer, you can quickly and easily create a query in "what you see is what you get" format using drag and drop. However, this generates a QuickView rather than a report. A QuickView can only be seen by the user who created it, but it can be converted into an SAP query, in which case the list will also be available to other users. The QuickViewer is characterized by a simple and intuitive user interface. In contrast to the other query tools, no programming skills are required to use the Quick-Viewer. However, the QuickViewer offers no additional functions, such as those provided with Ad Hoc Query and SAP Query. Furthermore, you can only create basic lists rather than statistics or ranked lists with this tool.

Whereas SAP queries and ad hoc queries are always created on the basis of an InfoSet, QuickViews can also be created directly based on database views, tables, table joins, and logical databases.

You can access the QuickViewer from the SAP Easy Access menu under **Tools · ABAP Workbench · Utilities · QuickViewer** or in SAP Query by clicking on the **QuickViewer** button.

Instructions to help you create a QuickView are provided on the left of the screen in the QuickViewer.

We will now show you how to create a table join. First, give the QuickView a name and click on the **Create** button on the next screen (see Figure 4.6), enter a title and select the **data source**.

Table join

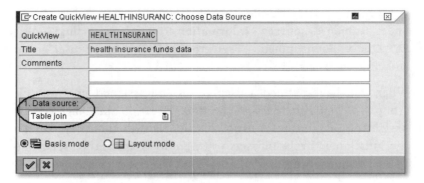

Figure 4.6 Creating a Table Join

On the next screen, insert the relevant tables using the button shown in Figure 4.7. The tables are displayed with all available fields. If you click on the **Join conditions** button, the tool proposes possible join conditions.

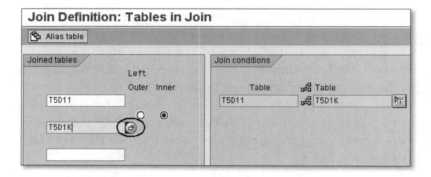

Figure 4.7 Selecting Tables for the Creation of a Table Join

Use the **Back** button to navigate to the QuickViewer. Two work modes are available in the QuickViewer: basis mode and layout mode. You can switch modes at any time using the [Layout mode] and [Basis mode] buttons. In basis mode, you can copy the relevant fields into the output list on the **List fld. select.** (i.e., **List field selection**) tab (see Figure 4.8). In layout mode, select the relevant fields by setting checkmarks in the **List fields** column (see Figure 4.9).

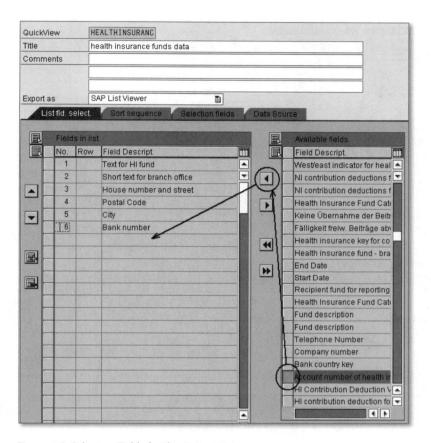

Figure 4.8 Selecting Fields for the Output List

On the other tabs, you can determine the sort sequence by column, create the selection screen using the available fields, and change the data source (in this case the table join). Click on the **Execute** button to display the selection screen and, after making a selection, to output the list.

Layout mode provides various options for adjusting the list layout, for example, by adding headers and footers or by changing the output length of the list field (see Figure 4.9).

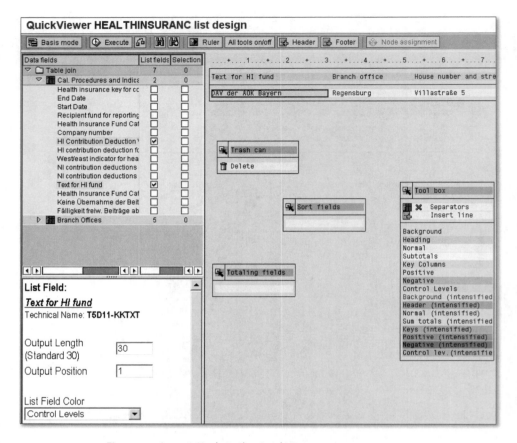

Figure 4.9 Layout Mode in the QuickViewer

Converting a QuickView into an SAP query QuickViews can be converted into SAP queries. An SAP query offers additional editing options and allows you to make the report available to other users (see Section 4.4). Access the SAP Query environment from the SAP Easy Access menu under **Human Resources • Information System • Reporting Tools • SAP Query**. You must be in the standard query area (see Section 4.1.1), and the user group to which you want to add the QuickView must be selected. To change user group if necessary, select the menu option **Edit • Other user group**. Next, select the menu option **Query • Convert QuickView**. Give the query a name and specify the InfoSet (see Figure 4.10). A new InfoSet is then created (in this case, consisting of a table join). The InfoSet is automatically assigned to the selected user group. All users assigned to this user group can now execute the former Quick-View.

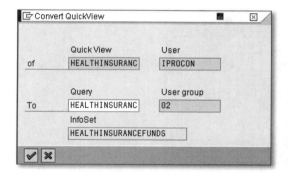

Figure 4.10 Converting a QuickView into an SAP Query

4.3   Ad Hoc Query

Outside of the HR area, Ad Hoc Query is also referred to as *InfoSet Query*. Since it is much easier to use than SAP Query, it has greater application possibilities in business departments, as well as for management and administrative staff.

Ad Hoc Queries are based on the definition of InfoSets and user groups, which we discussed earlier in Section 4.1. Ad hoc queries allow you to use simple (single-line) lists, based on an InfoSet.

You can access Ad Hoc Query from the SAP Easy Access menu under **Human Resources • Personnel Management • Administration • Info System • Reports • Ad Hoc Query**. The menu item **Reports/Reporting Tools** is also contained in other component info systems and in cross-application info systems. You can also access Ad Hoc Query from SAP Query by clicking on the **InfoSet Query** button.

If the user is assigned to a suitable user group, to which several InfoSets are also assigned, the initial screen shown in Figure 4.11 appears.

The Ad Hoc Query appears on the maintenance screen after you select the InfoSet. Figure 4.12 shows the individual screen areas of Ad Hoc Query. The top part of the screen is divided into two areas. The area on the left shows the **field groups/fields** of the available infotypes based on the selected InfoSet. On the right are the **reporting period**, the restriction of the **reporting set**, the **selections**, and the **hit list**.

Maintaining an Ad Hoc Query

Figure 4.11 Selecting an InfoSet for the Teamleader User Group

The hit list displays the number of data records selected. The lower half of the screen contains the **preview of output**.

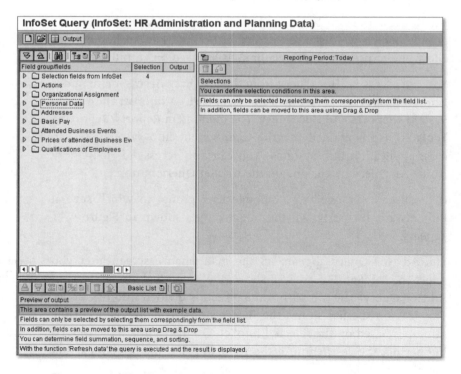

Figure 4.12 Ad Hoc Query Initial Screen

Define the query itself in the top-left section of the screen. As a rule, any field can be used for output and/or selection. For each field, you can also specify whether the key or the long text is to be used (for example, if you were using the **Personnel Subarea** field, **you could decide whether to use 0001** or **Boston**). The name of the employee is stored as a long text together with the Personnel number. Simply right-click to choose between the **value** (key) or **text** (see Figure 4.13).

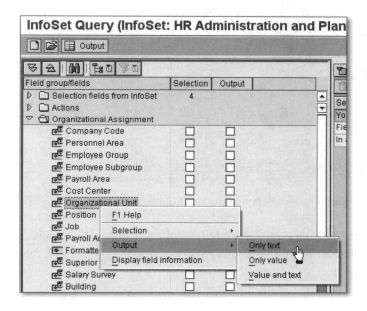

Figure 4.13 Selecting the Output format in the Context Menu

Next, select the relevant fields from the infotypes by setting check-marks in the **Selection** or **Output** column. When you choose the **Selection** option, the corresponding selection field is added to the table on the right of the screen. You can use options and values to enter default values there. Check your selection first using the **Hit list** button.

To display the result of your ad hoc query, click on the **Output** button. The **Output preview** button in the lower part of the screen displays the layout of the list. You can click on a column header to select a column and then move it using the drag-and-drop function.

You can select the menu option **Edit • Settings** (see Figure 4.14) to determine whether the default selection screen of the logical database is to be displayed before the output. You can use this screen to restrict the set of results further, for example, by period (data selection period and person selection period). For more about the significance of period selection, refer to Section 3.2, *Period Selection*.

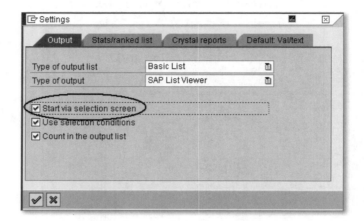

Figure 4.14 Selection Screen Before the Ad Hoc Query is Output

Go back to the selection screen. Make any necessary corrections to your selection and save the query. Saving not only saves the definition of selection and output fields, but also saves the selection that has actually been made (in the same way as when you save a variant for standard reports).

Using the organizational structure to make a selection

Restricting the reporting set using object selection is particularly useful. For example, you can define a basic restriction using the organizational structure. To activate or deactivate object selection, select the menu option **Extras • ... object selection**. Figure 4.15 shows the **Reporting set: not restricted** bar on the right of the screen. Click on this and then select the **Persons along organizational structure** option under **restrict by**. This improves performance if you have a large HR master record. However, the object selection activated only allows for selection by keys, not by text fields. To view the set of results from the restriction, press the **Display** button. From there, you can also access the screen for maintaining an employee's **HR master data**.

Take a look at the other tabs on the screen under **Edit • Settings** and refer   **[+]**
to the [F1] help for explanations where required.

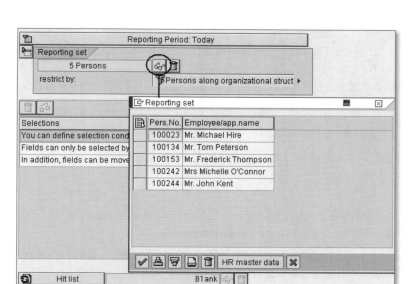

Figure 4.15 Displaying the Resulting Set of the Object Selection, with Optional Access to HR Master Data

4.3.1   Set Operations

The option of linking various selection quantities within an query offers considerable flexibility. It allows you to map intersections, set unions and quantity differences. You can, for example, select all employees who do not have infotype 0017 (Travel Privileges). This is because the system can only ever find data that exists. With set operations, you simply subtract the subset of employees with the relevant infotype from your initial set (for example, all employees or employees within a particular personnel subarea) to get your resulting set.

1. First, activate object selection (under **Extras • ... object selection** in the menu). Then display the **Set operations** tab (select **Extras • Show set operations**).

2. Copy the initial set into the **Hit list** and then click on the **Plus** button on the left to copy it into **Set A** (see Figure 4.16).

3. Make a selection (for example, enter **> 0** in the Employee Grouping for **Travel Expense** field.

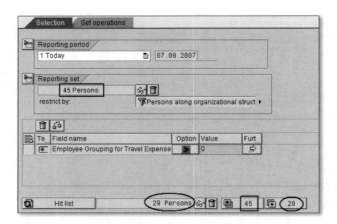

Figure 4.16 Selection for Set Operations

4. Refresh the **Hit list** and then click on the **Plus** button on the right (i.e. **Set B**). Switch to the **Set operations** tab.

5. Select the **Set A minus set B** option and click on **Carry out operation** (see Figure 4.17).

6. At the bottom of the screen, copy this resulting set into the **Hit list** and click on **Copy resulting set**.

7. Switch to the **Selection** tab and click on **Output** to output the personnel numbers without the Travel Privileges infotype.

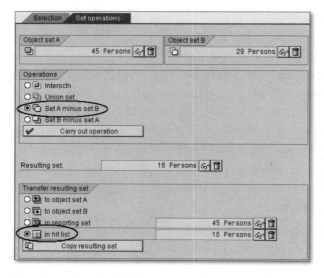

Figure 4.17 Executing Set Operations

When you execute set operations, you must not select the "Use selection conditions" setting on the **Output** tab under **Edit • Settings**. If you do, the results list will be empty.

[!]

The extensive selection options in Ad Hoc Query, in particular for set operations, can be used for other reports also (see Section 4.3.2).

4.3.2 The Report-Report Interface

You can copy the resulting set of your Ad Hoc Query for all reports (both standard reports and those you have developed yourself). This allows you to make more extensive selections than would otherwise be possible with a standard selection screen, for example.

Proceed as follows:

1. Start Ad Hoc Query with a relevant InfoSet. Make the relevant selection and update the hit list.
2. Select the menu option **Goto • Start report**.
3. Enter the name of the report. (Select **Start via selection screen** if you want the selection screen of the report to be displayed before you execute the report.)
4. Press Enter.

The report is then executed for the hit list copied from Ad Hoc Query.

4.3.3 Applications and Limitations of Ad Hoc Query

Ad Hoc Query can be used by a wide range of users only if the InfoSets and user groups are clearly defined according to the specific requirements. Even if, at first glance, the tool seems easy to use, users should be trained or at least have access to high-quality, company-specific documentation. Otherwise, experience shows that errors that occur when selecting data and interpreting the results often lead to confusion and contradictory lists.

> **Note the following points in particular:**
>
> ▶ Meaningful field texts
> Use clear, self-explanatory terms when naming fields (especially for terms such as basic salary, *variable salary*, basic pay, or hourly rate, which are often understood differently by employees in Payroll and by managers. It is important to clearly define exactly what these mean).
>
> ▶ Importance of the selection period
> Be aware, in particular, that many reports only provide useful information when they are executed for a specific key date.
>
> ▶ Evaluation of actions
> Note the difference between infotypes 0000 and 0302.
>
> ▶ Significance of object selection
> Preselection based on the organizational structure enhances performance.

Nevertheless, we strongly recommend the use of Ad Hoc Query within the restrictions imposed by data security considerations and training costs. A central concept must be created for this purpose (i.e. Personnel Controlling). To do this, extensive knowledge of HCM data and functionality is required.

Ad Hoc Query reaches its limits where more comprehensive calculation logic, group levels, special layouts or multiline lists are required. These requirements are partly fulfilled by SAP queries, the creation of which is covered in the next section.

4.4   SAP Query

Access SAP Query from the SAP Easy Access menu under **Human Resources • Information System • Reporting Tools • SAP Query**. After you enter a name for the query and click on the **Create** button, a wizard appears to guide you through the steps involved in creating a query.

1. As a first step, determine the title and the output format (usually **SAP List Viewer**; for a multiline list, select **ABAP List** [see Section 4.4.1]). Click on the **Next screen** button.

2. Select the field groups (infotypes) that contain the required fields.

3. Select the fields you require for selection and/or output.

4. On the next screen, select the fields required for selection.

If the InfoSet is based on a logical database (such as PNPCE), the standard **[«]**
selection screen is also available. Therefore, fields that are already contained in the standard selection screen should not be defined as selection
fields again. Otherwise, they will appear twice on the selection screen.

5. Click on the **Basic list** button and, on the next screen that appears,
   specify the sequence of fields for the output list.

6. On the same screen, click on the **Test** button to display the result
   of the query for a limited selection of data records. To execute the
   query, go back to the initial query maintenance screen and click
   on the **Execute** button (see Figure 4.18).

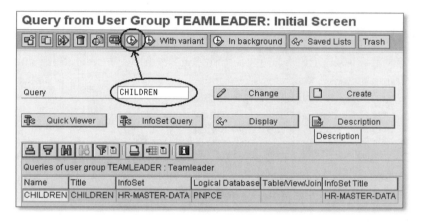

Figure 4.18 Executing a Completed Query

If you click on the **Basic list** button when creating or changing a
query and then click on the **Next screen** button to proceed, you can
make the following layout settings:

▶ **List line output options**
For example, you can choose to highlight the first line (see Figure
4.20).

▶ **Field output options**
For example, you can choose to round numeric field content.

▶ **Basic list header**
As shown in Figure 4.19, you can fill the page header and footer
with dynamic fields. The field help ([F1] key) for the page header

provides additional examples. You can also change the title. Double-click to open the **Column header of a field** dialog box.

Note that the header and footer are only visible in the **ABAP list** output format (which you select as the first step in query maintenance under **Output format** or on the selection screen).

In contrast to standard query maintenance, you can also use the graphical Query Painter (which is equivalent to layout mode in the QuickViewer; see Section 4.2). To switch from normal mode to graphical mode, select the menu option **Settings • Settings**.

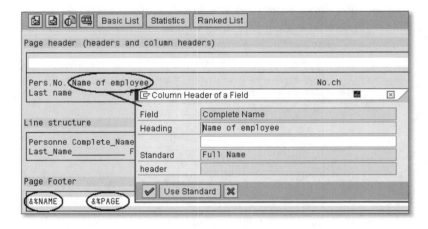

Figure 4.19 Changing Headers and the Dynamic Page Footer

[+] The field help (use the F1 key) in query creation is very helpful for most of the fields, and you should make full use of it from the start.

4.4.1 Multiline Lists

You are probably wondering what is so special about multiline lists. After all, more than one line is normally displayed in your reports anyway. However, *multiline* means the column information is divided over two lines. The result is a structured list (see Figure 4.20).

```
┌──────────────────────────────────────────────────────────────────────┐
│ Children of employee                                                   │
│ ┌───┬───┬───┬───┬───┐ ┌──────────┐                                     │
│ │ 🔲 │ 🔲 │ 🔲 │ Σ │ 🔲 │ │ Selections │                                   │
│ └───┴───┴───┴───┴───┘ └──────────┘                                     │
│                                                                        │
│ Pers.No. name of employee                             No.ch           │
│ Last name              First name       Birth date                     │
│ ─────────────────────────────────────────────────────────────────     │
│ 00000069 Horatio Holder                                  1             │
│ Holder                 Harriet          01.01.1960                     │
│ Holder                 Harold           01.01.1998                     │
│ 00001007 Hanna    Ulrich                                 3             │
│ Ulrich                 Wolfgang         07.11.1952                     │
│ Ulrich                 Michelle         29.05.1982                     │
│ Ulrich                 Ludwig           19.10.1984                     │
│ Ulrich                 Stefan           21.05.1986                     │
│ 00210004 Margret Bush                                    3             │
│ Bush                   Bert             23.12.1952                     │
│ Bush                   Rene             01.04.1986                     │
│ Bush                   Maja             23.08.1978                     │
│ Bush                   Peter            01.05.1974                     │
│ ─────────────────────────────────────────────────────────────────     │
│ Overall total                                            7  *          │
│ ─────────────────────────────────────────────────────────────────     │
│ User: Iprocon                                  Page:       1           │
└──────────────────────────────────────────────────────────────────────┘
```

Figure 4.20 Multiline List: Children of Employee

A multiline list can only be displayed with the ABAP List. In Figure **ABAP list**
4.20, information about the employee appears in the first line, with
the names of the employee's children in the subsequent lines. This
type of division of information may be required if, for example:

▶ You use a column to calculate a total and several records exist for
each personnel number

▶ You want to run a report on general trip data together with document data. Due to the structure of the logical database PTRVP
(travel management), the header information about the trip, such
as personnel number, trip number, total costs and trip country,
must appear in the first line. The second line contains the information about travel documents (document number, travel expense
type and document amount). Without a multiline list, it would be
impossible to calculate the total costs correctly.

> If you want to process the results of the query further in a spreadsheet, **[+]**
> you should only use single-line lists.

In contrast to the procedure described in Section 4.4 for creating a
single-line list, only the **basic list line structure** (see Figure 4.21) and

the **list line output options** (see Figure 4.22) change when you create a multiline list .

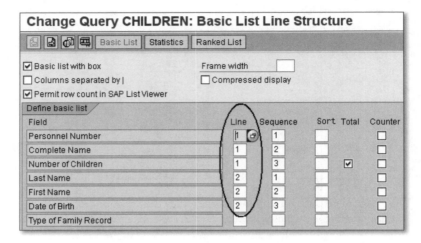

Figure 4.21 Line Structure of a Multiline List

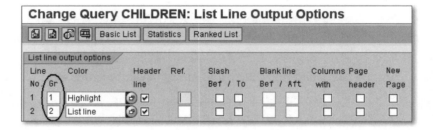

Figure 4.22 Output Options for a Multiline List

[+] Multiline lists can only be created and output with SAP Query. If, for example, you tried to generate a trip report with general trip data and document data in Ad Hoc Query, an error message would appear. When you call up a multiline list created with SAP Query in Ad Hoc Query, the tool automatically deletes the information from the second line.

4.4.2 Additional Local Fields

You can create additional local fields in SAP Query. This requires no programming skills. An additional local field may be derived or calculated from other fields in the query or defined as an input field on the selection screen, for example. Possible additional local fields include:

- Calculation fields
- Date fields
- Time fields
- Conditional numeric fields
- A combination of existing text fields
- A fixed value from the selection screen
- Traffic lights
- Symbols/icons

Let's take a look at an example: Assume that the vacation bonus for all **[Ex]** employees is to be increased by 5%. You can calculate the increased vacation bonus in a new field in the query. To do this, follow the steps below:

1. Create a new query.
2. Select the relevant field groups (the **Recurring Payments/Deductions** group is required in this case).
3. Select the relevant fields (here we require the **Wage Type** from infotype 0015 and the **Wage Type Amounts for Payments**).
4. On the same screen, select the menu option **Edit • Short names • Switch on/off**. Enter any name in the **Short Name** column for the **Wage Type Amounts for Payments** field.
5. Select **Edit • Local field • Create** and maintain the field definition as follows (see Figure 4.23):
   - Specify the names and the column header.
   - Select **Recurring Payments/Deductions** as the field group.
   - Under **Properties**, select **Same attributes as field** and enter the short description you have just defined in the field (for example, BONUSOLD).
   - Under **Calculation Formula**, enter "BONUSOLD * 1.05."

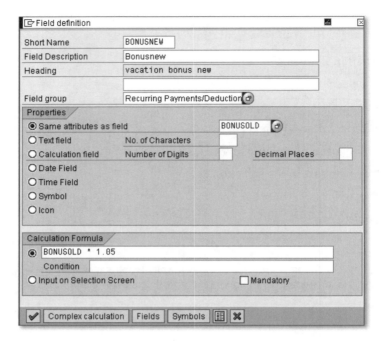

Figure 4.23 Defining a Local Field

6. The new field is created. Follow the remaining steps for query definition outlined in Section 4.4. Make sure to define the wage type as a selection field so you can select the **Vacation bonus** wage type for the output, rather than having all wage types displayed. Incorporate the new field into the output. The result is shown in Figure 4.24.

Increase of vacation bonus

Pers.No.	Last name	Wage Type	Wage Type	Σ Bonus old	Crcy	Σ Bonus new	Crcy
00001006	Awad	M110	Vacation bonus	672.69	EUR	706.32	EUR
00001019	Thomson	M110	Vacation bonus	1,683.68	EUR	1,767.86	EUR
00001038	Loewe	M110	Vacation bonus	647.64	EUR	680.02	EUR
00001043	Twin	M110	Vacation bonus	613.55	EUR	644.23	EUR
00001205	Schwarz	M110	Vacation bonus	725.18	EUR	761.44	EUR
				▪ 4,342.74	**EUR**	▪ 4,559.87	**EUR**

Figure 4.24 BONUSNEW Local Field in a Query

Ampel-Icon Let's assume the vacation bonus can never exceed EUR 1,300. In this case, a red traffic light can be used to indicate that this limit has been exceeded. To implement this, you need to create another local field as described above. This time, enter **Icon** as the property (see Figure 4.23). Press the **Complex Calculation** button to enter the data as shown in Figure 4.25. To view the names of the icons, press the **Icons** button (to the right of the **Symbols** button) (Figure 4.26).

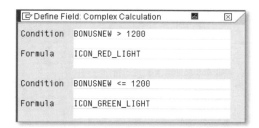

Figure 4.25 Using Traffic Light Color Changes to Indicate Changes to the Vacation Bonus

Increase of vacation bonus								
Pers.No.	Last name	Wage T...	Wage Type	Σ Bonus old	Crcy	Σ Bonus new	Crcy	Bonus too high
00001006	Awad	M110	Vacation bonus	672.69	EUR	706.32	EUR	◯◯◯
00001019	Thomson	M110	Vacation bonus	1,683.68	EUR	1,767.86	EUR	◉◯◯
00001038	Loewe	M110	Vacation bonus	647.64	EUR	680.02	EUR	◯◯◯
00001043	Twin	M110	Vacation bonus	613.55	EUR	644.23	EUR	◯◯◯
00001205	Schwarz	M110	Vacation bonus	725.18	EUR	761.44	EUR	◯◯◯
				■ 4,342.74	EUR	■ 4,559.87	EUR	

Figure 4.26 Additional Local Field with Traffic Light Icon

You can make this query even more flexible by specifying the percentage increase on the selection screen and using this value for the calculation. You must define a calculation field for this purpose. Under **Calculation Formula**, select **Input on Selection Screen** (see Figure 4.23). Then use this calculation field instead of the fixed value in the calculation rule for the BONUSNEW field.

4.4.3 Interactive Lists

SAP Query also allows you to create interactive lists. From the output list, you can, for example:

▶ start another query

▶ start an ABAP report

▶ call a transaction

In SAP query maintenance (Transaction SQ01), select a query (standard or customer specific) and click on **Change**. On the following screen, select the menu option **Goto • Report assignment**. On the **Assign reports** screen, click on the **Insert row** button and then on Other report type . You can then select the report type, as shown in Figure 4.27.

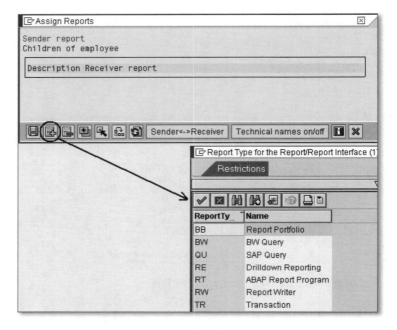

Figure 4.27 Creating an Interactive List

[Ex]   To access master data maintenance for an employee from the output list, for example, select the Transaction report type and enter "Transaction PA30" on the screen that appears. The output list must contain the "Personnel number" field. Double-click on the line to copy the personnel number directly into master data maintenance.

To access one query from another, you must explicitly enter the transfer parameter (for example, the personnel number or personnel subarea) as a selection parameter in the query you want to call. The next query is then called for the selected line.

You can make any number of assignments in SAP Query. If you then double-click on a line, a selection list of possible navigation options is displayed (see Figure 4.28). In each report that you call from here, you can also configure an additional assignment to yet another report. This means the drill-down options are endless. You can, for example, call up personnel subareas from a company view and then, from there, call up organizational units and, ultimately, individual personnel numbers.

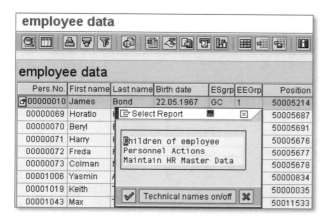

Figure 4.28 Several Interactions in a Query

4.5 Integration of Payroll Results

You can also evaluate payroll results in a query. Before you can access payroll wage types and amounts, they must be available in an infotype. The **Payroll results** infotype is provided for this purpose. After you make the corresponding settings in Customizing, the system can create person-specific infotypes containing the values for specific wage types after each payroll run. These infotypes can be displayed the same way as normal infotypes in Transaction PA20. Like other customer-specific infotypes, you can add these infotypes to an InfoSet and evaluate them in queries and reports.

The relevant Customizing settings are made in the IMG under **Personnel Management • Human Resources Information System • Payroll Results** as follows:

Customizing

1. **Define evaluation wage types**
   These are the wage types you will see later in the newly defined infotype.

2. **Assign "real" wage types**
   This assignment is made from the payroll results for the evaluation wage types. This can be a 1:1 assignment. However, it is also possible to add or subtract several real wage types in an evaluation wage type.

3. **Set up one or more payroll infotypes**
   You do this by assigning evaluation wage types.

4. **Define the update procedure**
   The payroll infotypes can either be filled directly from payroll or by using the RPABRI00 report. To optimize performance for payroll, we generally recommend that you update the infotypes separately using the report. If you use the Payroll Process Manager, you can add this update at the end of the process.

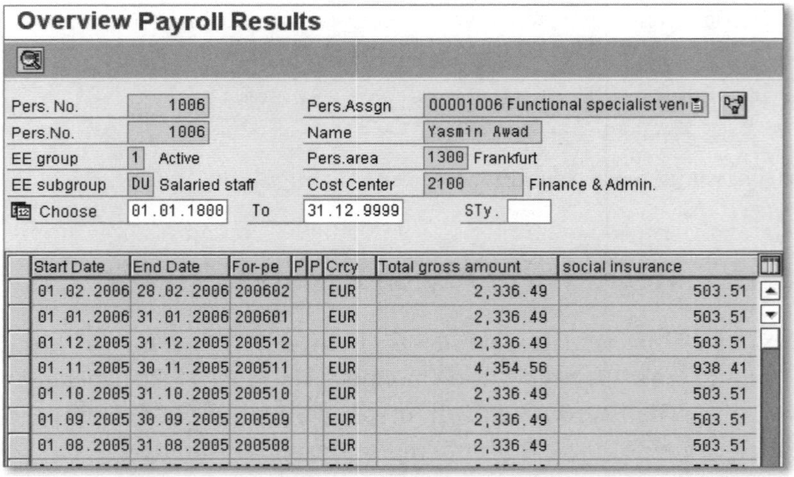

Figure 4.29 Payroll Infotype — List Screen

Figure 4.29 displays the list screen for a payroll infotype. This is a typical example, in which various gross salaries and employee/employer contributions are stored that are often required in reporting. Hourly or daily rates are stored with equal frequency, as is the monetary value of a lifetime working account.

4.6 Integration of Time Evaluation Results

The result clusters for time evaluation are also not directly available for evaluation via the query. In this case, however, SAP uses a different approach to the one used for payroll results. Instead of actually storing the results in an infotype, *simulated infotypes* are used. These are defined in Customizing, and their "content" is calculated when a query is run, without ever being stored in a database table.

Simulated infotypes may contain different results for time evaluation. These are then summarized again, if necessary:

▶ Time types (values from the day table — but not the monthly cumulation) are summarized in reporting time types.

▶ Time wage types are summarized in reporting time types.

▶ Attendance and absence values are summarized in reporting time types.

▶ Attendance and absence quotas are summarized in reporting quota types.

▶ Leave quotas are summarized in reporting quota types.

The daily values of time types are unsuitable for most applications. As a rule, cumulated monthly values are relevant for evaluations. A workaround is required to integrate these with the simulated infotypes. For example, it is possible to store the monthly values in specially defined time types or time wage types as a daily value at the end of the month. To do this, you must include a corresponding calculation rule in the time evaluation schema. Make the relevant Customizing settings in the IMG under: **Time Management · Information System · Settings for Reporting**.

You also have the option of including the time balances in the InfoSet using additional fields. Each time type is a separate field and therefore has its own column in the evaluation. A function module reads the data from the clusters for each employee, year, month, and time type. The additional fields are created in the InfoSet (for example, infotype 0007 [Planned working time]) with reference to PC2B5-ANZHL. YEAR(4) and MONTH(2) must be declared in the **DATA** coding section. The code for each additional field differs only in terms of the time type and the name of the additional field.

Simulated time management infotypes

Sample code in the appendix

You can find sample code for the function module and the additional field in Appendix C.

The result is a list, as shown in Figure 4.30.

Time balances

Pers.No.	Last name	First name	Age	Personnel Area	Organizational Unit	Monthly hours	Planned time	Productive hours	Abscence	Abscence on pub.holiday
00001208	Hintz	Michael	44	Hamburg	Pump pre-assembly (D)	141.55	122.75	121.25	15.50	15.50
00001266	Effenberg	Manfred	34	Hamburg	Pump final assembly (D)	141.55	138.25	149.00	6.25	6.25

Figure 4.30 Various Time Balances for Each Employee

4.7   SAP Query Transport Tool

The SAP Query Transport Tool allows you to exchange and copy queries, InfoSets, and user groups without using the standard transport procedure. You can do this:

▶ between the standard area and global area query areas

▶ between clients

▶ between systems

From the global area to the standard area

If you use a standard InfoSet as a template to create your own InfoSet in the standard area or if you have already created queries based on standard InfoSets in the global area and want to copy these into the standard area, then you need to use the SAP Query transport tool. You can find this tool in InfoSet maintenance (Transaction SQ02). You will see the **Transport** icon 🚚 in the toolbar. When you press this, the RSAQR3TR report is executed (see Figure 4.31).

Under **Transport Action Selection**, select the **Copy Global Area • Standard Area** option. If you simply want to copy the InfoSet, select the standard InfoSet under the **Transport InfoSets** option. If you want to transport queries of this InfoSet, select **Transport InfoSets and Queries**, enter the standard InfoSet, and leave the input field next to **Queries** blank to ensure that all queries of this InfoSet are transported. Execute the report in a **test run** first, check the copy log, and make any necessary changes to the selection.

Cross-client transport

Queries are normally created in the standard area, which means they are only visible within a specific client. However, the transport tool allows you to transport the SAP Query objects from the standard area into other clients or systems.

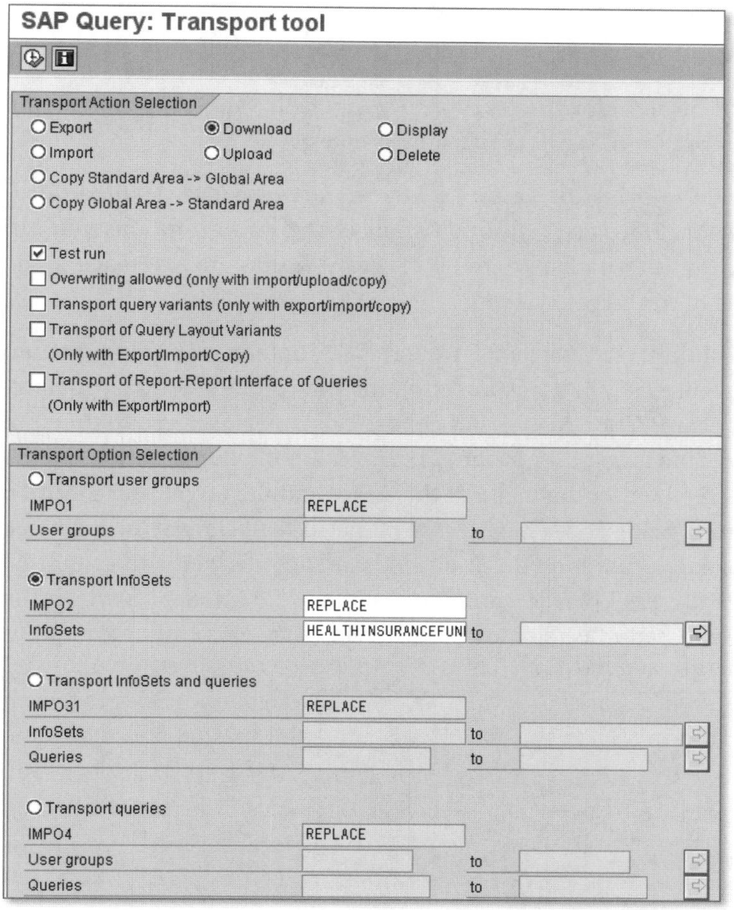

Figure 4.31 Downloading the Health Insurance Funds InfoSet in a Test Run

Select **Download** to download the relevant objects into a local file in the source system. If you do not specify any objects under **Transport Option Selection**, all objects from the selected group are transported. Click on **Execute** and enter the relevant download path on the screen that appears. After you save your entries, the export log displays the list of exported objects. Next, log on to the target system to import the file containing the query objects using the same report. To do this, select the **Upload** option. After a successful import, a log is displayed, showing the imported objects.

[»] When you have imported InfoSets, access these again in Transaction SQ02 and click on **Generate**. If the InfoSet contains additional fields that refer to customer programs or function modules, an error message will appear. These programs must be imported separately.

Instead of downloading and generating a file, you can also use the **Export** option to create a transport request.

The blue information button in the report provides detailed documentation. Here you will find details of the import options you can use as an alternative to the REPLACE option (i.e., replacing the objects in the target system).

Copying a query into a new user group

If you simply want to transfer queries to another user group, you do not need to use the transport tool. Instead, open SAP query maintenance (Transaction SQ01) and choose the **Other user group** function to select the target user group. Then click on the **Copy** button. On the next screen, enter the name of the query and the target user group in the **From** fields and a new query name in the relevant **To** field (see Figure 4.32). The target user group is already defined and cannot be changed. Press Enter to confirm. Note that the InfoSet on which the query is based must already be assigned to the target user group.

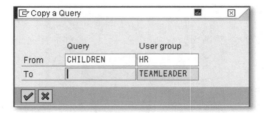

Figure 4.32 Copying the Children Query to the Teamleader User Group

4.8 Critical Success Factors

To conclude this chapter, a list is provided below of the factors that are critical to the successful use of queries:

▶ Work out a concept for how the query is to be used. Who is permitted to maintain InfoSets? Who can create SAP queries and make them available? Who can create reports based on simple

InfoSets? Can these be saved? In which query area are queries maintained?

▶ Never use standard InfoSets without checking them first. These may contain many fields that are not required. In addition, many field names are not self-explanatory. Additional fields often have unexpected content. Therefore, you should take time to invest sufficient effort in adjusting and renaming field names. This also increases user acceptance later.

▶ Before you program a report, check whether a query could also meet your requirements if one or more additional fields were programmed in the InfoSet. This considerably reduces the effort involved in maintenance. Adjustments to the list can be made directly by the business departments.

▶ Make full use of the various functions provided with Ad Hoc Query and SAP Query. These can often fulfill many more requirements than you might imagine.

▶ In particular, the integration of payroll results into queries meets many requirements in the Payroll area. Once you have made the necessary Customizing settings, you can use the data in reports after each payroll run.

Intensive technical enhancements and the provision of a comprehensive Business Content have made SAP NetWeaver BI a powerful tool for analytical reporting. In this chapter, you will be given an overview of the technology and structure of SAP NetWeaver BI and learn about the flexible evaluation options available.

5 HR Reporting with SAP NetWeaver BI

SAP NetWeaver BI is establishing a foothold in the area of HR Reporting. The integration of data from different systems and flexible evaluation and analysis options offer you new insights into your enterprise data. A comprehensive Business Content with predefined evaluation options for all modules of SAP ERP HCM provides a basis whereby the time required to implement the system is greatly reduced.

After SAP BW 3.5, SAP NetWeaver 2004s BI is available as a fully revised release that has been enhanced with many new functions.

If we do not expressly indicate that the descriptions refer to Version 3.x, the details in this chapter describe the current release.

SAP BW and SAP NetWeaver BI

We begin this chapter in Section 5.1 with an introduction to the architecture and structure of SAP NetWeaver BI. This section contains basic terms and describes functions required to help you understand the other contents.

Sections 5.2 to 5.6 are dedicated to the individual reporting tools. You will become familiar with executing a query integrated in Microsoft Excel using the Business Explorer Analyzer, learn how to create queries using the Query Designer, gain insights into the browser-based Web Tools, Web Analyzer and Web Application Designer, and the options of automated reporting available with Information Broadcasting.

In Section 5.7, you will be given an overview of the standard Business Content of SAP NetWeaver BI. Part III of this book contains more detailed examples of the Business Content in the areas of the individual HCM modules.

Since authorizations also always play a particularly important role in the HR environment, you will learn about the special characteristics of authorizations in SAP NetWeaver BI in Section 5.8.

In Section 5.9, you will discover how you can use the structural authorization from SAP ERP HCM in SAP NetWeaver BI.

This chapter concludes with Section 5.10. In this section, we have compiled tips to help you implement SAP NetWeaver BI successfully into the HR environment.

5.1   Architecture of SAP NetWeaver BI

SAP NetWeaver BI is a standalone system environment that is optimized for queries and analyses. The data can be retrieved from different systems.

[+]   Even though the SAP NetWeaver BI Data Warehouse in SAP ERP 6.0 is already integrated into the application, we advise against an integrated operation for performance reasons. You should install SAP NetWeaver BI as a standalone system, in order not to impair the daily operations of SAP ERP HCM.

Three-tier architecture   The SAP NetWeaver BI architecture consists of three layers: the *extraction layer*, which controls the transfer of data into the BI system, the *modeling layer*, where the data structures are defined and the data is stored, and the *reporting and analysis layer*, where the tools for evaluations are provided. Figure 5.1 provides a simplified overview of the SAP NetWeaver BI architecture.

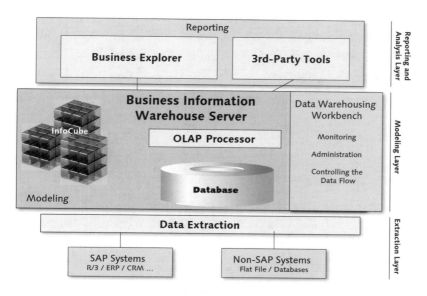

Figure 5.1 Simplified Illustration of the SAP NetWeaver BI Architecture

5.1.1 Extraction Layer

The process of transferring data, also called the ETL process, is composed of the components extraction, transformation, and loading. Relevant data is selected from the source system for the *extraction*. Data can be compressed, harmonized and changed for the *transformation*. The *loading process* then follows. In the following sections, you will see how this process was implemented in SAP NetWeaver BI.

ETL process

The following options for extracting data from an SAP system are available:

Extraction

▶ **Extraction from a database table**
You can use this method to transfer the content of an infotype or other transparent tables into SAP NetWeaver BI.

▶ **Extraction from an InfoSet of the SAP Query**
For the extraction, you can create InfoSets in the SAP Query, the fields of which are transferred.

▶ **Extraction from a function module**
Data is read for each function module and transferred to a defined structure.

▸ **Extraction from domain fixed values**

Allowed values are frequently stored as fixed values in a domain of the data dictionary. These values can be read easily.

Figure 5.2 shows the IMG section for Customizing the data extraction.

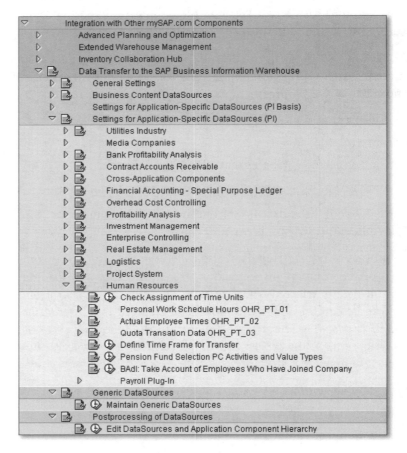

Figure 5.2 Customizing the Data Extraction

[+]   The Business Content extractors are not automatically available in an active status. Before you can use them, you must activate them in Customizing by selecting the path **Integration with Other SAP Components • Data Transfer to the SAP Business Information Warehouse • Business Content DataSources • Transfer Business Content DataSources**.

Some extractors, in the area of time management in particular, provide Customizing options. For example, this means that you can convert attendances and absences or time types into reporting time types for SAP NetWeaver BI, which enables you to compress and rename the extracted data. Do this by selecting the path **Integration with other SAP Components • Data Transfer to the SAP Business Information Warehouse • Settings for Application-Specific Data-Sources (PI) • Human Resources • Personal Work Schedule Hours.**

Customizing extractors

SAP NetWeaver BI also provides methods for retrieving data from different systems using different techniques. Data can be transferred from the following sources:

▶ From structured files, for example, Excel files

▶ From XML files

▶ From connected databases that allow the DBConnect

▶ From third-party systems that can retrieve data using BAPIs

Figure 5.3 shows the data flow from the source system to the Info-Cube (this InfoCube term is explained in Section 5.1.2). The data can be retrieved from one or several systems into an InfoCube for evaluations. If the data for small plants from other countries are not entered in the ERP system, you can load this data into the BI using Excel files to enable you to perform evaluations across the entire company.

Data flow from the source to the InfoCube

The DataSource that transfers a quantity of logically related data into the BI system in a flat structure is assigned to exactly one source system. This DataSource consists of logically related fields in a flat structure. A PSA table is assigned to the DataSource, and the incoming data is stored temporarily in this table.

DataSource

The delivered data is stored temporarily unchanged in the *Persistent Staging Area (PSA)*, which means you can control the delivered data and separate the loading of data from the further processing of data. This increases the speed of the loading process.

PSA

The PSA tables are not deleted automatically after processing, so the data of all loading processes are retained. Consequently, the tables can become very large and must be reorganized regularly. You can define a retention period after which the data is deleted for each job.

[+]

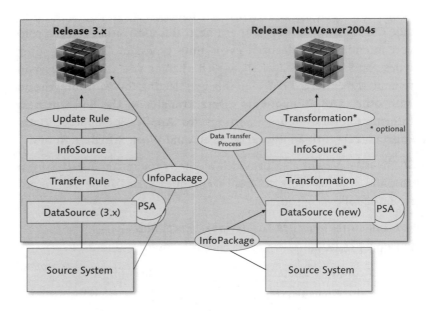

Figure 5.3 Data Flow in SAP BW 3.x and SAP NetWeaver 2004s BI

Transformation The concept of transferring data was revised in Release SAP NetWeaver 2004s. This includes revised DataSources and the new concept of transformation. In accordance with the new concept, the transformation converts the data from the format of the source structure into the format of the target structure and defines the formation of key figures; the transformation consists of at least one transformation rule.

3.x DataSources You can still transfer data on the basis of the 3.x concept. Instead of the transformation, this concept included the transfer and update rule. The delivered data is converted into data compatible for SAP NetWeaver BI according to a transfer rule. You can update master data directly into the InfoObject, whereas an additional step, the update rule, is required for the update process for transaction data into InfoProviders. You must define an update rule for each key figure and the corresponding characteristics. You can use the following types of updates:

- No update
- Adding or calculating minimums or maximums
- Overwriting (for DataStore objects and InfoObjects only)

In the end, the updating of the data is stored in one or more Info-Cubes.

5.1.2 Modeling Layer

The modeling objects include InfoProviders and InfoObjects, which **InfoProviders** form the smallest data unit of SAP NetWeaver BI (this will be discussed further at a later stage). *InfoProviders* form the basis for evaluations in SAP NetWeaver BI. Each query is based on exactly one Info-Provider. These InfoProviders can be physically available and filled with data, like the InfoCube, or they can represent a logical view that refers to data from other physical objects such as the MultiCube, for example. Figure 5.4 displays the **Plan/Actual Comparison of Personnel Costs** MultiCube, which is based on two InfoCubes, **Personnel Cost Plans** (with the personnel cost planning data) and **Auditing Information on Postings Relevant to Cost Accounting**, which contains the CO-relevant data of the posting document for the payroll results.

Figure 5.4 A MultiCube and the InfoCubes It Contains

The *InfoCube* describes a self-contained dataset that forms the basis **InfoCube** of the reporting in SAP NetWeaver BI. The InfoCube is a set of tables that are arranged in a star schema (see Figure 5.5). A fact table in the middle is surrounded by several dimensions. The fact table contains the key figures of the InfoCube, for example, **Number of Employees**. In terms of SAP NetWeaver BI, key figures are any values or quantities.

The dimension tables contain one or more characteristics, as shown in Figure 5.6. The **Employee Status** master data table is assigned to the **Employee** dimension table.

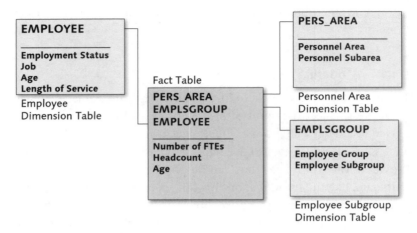

Figure 5.5 Star Schema of an InfoCube

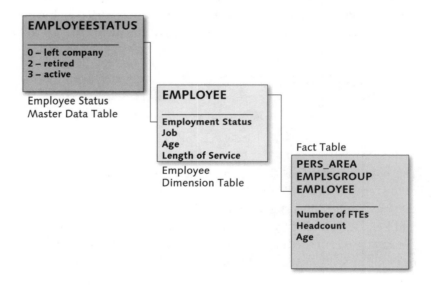

Figure 5.6 Master Data and Dimensions of an InfoCube

You will be able to recognize these properties by the **Headcount and Personnel Actions** InfoCube (see Figure 5.7). The **Personnel Area** dimension is composed of the **Personnel Area** and **Personnel Subarea** characteristics. The key figures include the **Number of Employees**, for example, or **Headcount FTE**, which contains the number of FTEs (full time equivalent).

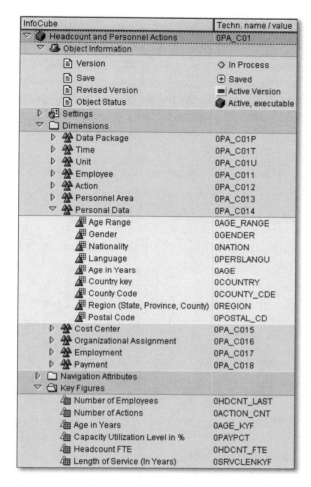

InfoCube	Techn. name / value
▽ 🎲 Headcount and Personnel Actions	0PA_C01
▽ 📚 Object Information	
📄 Version	◇ In Process
📄 Save	⊕ Saved
📄 Revised Version	═ Active Version
📄 Object Status	🎲 Active, executable
▷ 🗄 Settings	
▽ 📁 Dimensions	
▷ 🔼 Data Package	0PA_C01P
▷ 🔼 Time	0PA_C01T
▷ 🔼 Unit	0PA_C01U
▷ 🔼 Employee	0PA_C011
▷ 🔼 Action	0PA_C012
▷ 🔼 Personnel Area	0PA_C013
▽ 🔼 Personal Data	0PA_C014
📇 Age Range	0AGE_RANGE
📇 Gender	0GENDER
📇 Nationality	0NATION
📇 Language	0PERSLANGU
📇 Age in Years	0AGE
📇 Country key	0COUNTRY
📇 County Code	0COUNTY_CDE
📇 Region (State, Province, County)	0REGION
📇 Postal Code	0POSTAL_CD
▷ 🔼 Cost Center	0PA_C015
▷ 🔼 Organizational Assignment	0PA_C016
▷ 🔼 Employment	0PA_C017
▷ 🔼 Payment	0PA_C018
▷ 📁 Navigation Attributes	
▽ 📑 Key Figures	
📊 Number of Employees	0HDCNT_LAST
📊 Number of Actions	0ACTION_CNT
📊 Age in Years	0AGE_KYF
📊 Capacity Utilization Level in %	0PAYPCT
📊 Headcount FTE	0HDCNT_FTE
📊 Length of Service (In Years)	0SRVCLENKYF

Figure 5.7 Headcount and Personnel Actions InfoCube

The InfoCube consists of a number of InfoObjects that correspond exactly to a data field. The term stands comprehensively for characteristics as well as key figures. InfoObjects contain general properties such as **Field Type** and **Field Size** and a range of additional information such as reporting parameters and the use of master data. In the case of key figures, the aggregation type is defined in the InfoObject. All InfoProviders use the InfoObjects, which are the smallest data unit of SAP NetWeaver BI.

InfoObjects

InfoObjects are divided into:

▶ **Characteristics**
You can store master data, texts, and hierarchies in characteristics. They contain classification keys such as personnel area or employee subgroup, for example. You can store a multilingual name in the text (for example, personnel area or employee subgroup).

▶ **Key figures**
Key figures deliver values such as quantities and amounts that you can evaluate in queries. They also contain properties that are relevant for loading data and controlling evaluations. This is how amounts are expressed in currencies and can be calculated into other currencies (for example, number of employees or number of FTEs).

▶ **Time characteristics**
Time characteristics contain data such as month, year, or periods (for example, payroll period, year, or month).

▶ **Units**
Units describe the properties of key figures. The currency is specified for amounts, and the unit of measurement is specified for quantities.

▶ **Technical characteristics**
Technical characteristics only have organizational significance within SAP NetWeaver BI. One such example is the request number that is created when you load data into the data package. This helps you to retrieve the request (for example, the request number).

Data Warehousing Workbench

The central tool of the modeling layer is the Data Warehousing Workbench (see Figure 5.8), which you can call from transaction RSA1. You can use this tool to:

▶ Perform the modeling of the InfoProviders and InfoObjects

▶ Activate the standard content

▶ Set up and manage the transfer of data

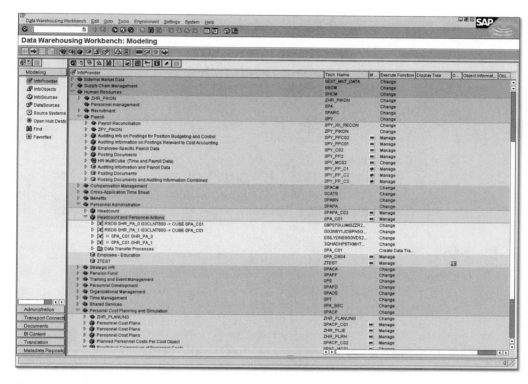

Figure 5.8 Data Warehousing Workbench

5.1.3 Reporting and Analysis Layer

The Business Explorer Suite provides tools that enable you to perform flexible evaluations and analyses of the data saved in SAP NetWeaver BI (see Figure 5.9).

The query is the basis of all evaluations, and you create it using the BEx Query Designer (see Section 5.3). Based on an InfoProvider, a combination of characteristics and key figures is defined for a query.

Query Designer

You can execute queries both in Excel (see Section 5.2) and on the Web (see Section 5.4).

The BEx Analyzer is a tool integrated in Excel, which you can use to execute queries and design the layout of workbooks. The navigation is supported by context menus and drag-and-drop functions. This is a suitable tool for users who regularly create evaluations in SAP NetWeaver BI and know how to use Excel.

BEx Analyzer

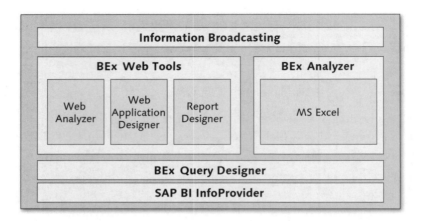

Figure 5.9 Business Explorer Suite

BEx Web Web-based reporting tools are also available, which you can use to display evaluations and analyses in the browser ranging from a simple query to comprehensive Web Cockpits.

Web Analyzer You can execute queries and query views in the Web Analyzer using flexible navigation options. You can also graphically format the data. You can save and distribute the executed analyses. You can use the saved views for SAP NetWeaver BI applications.

Web Application Designer The Web Application Designer helps you retrieve reports in the portal. You can combine queries and charts and integrate them into Web Cockpits. You can process the XHTML code directly in the Web Application Designer or use other tools. A wizard helps you create applications.

Report Designer The Report Designer enables you to create formatted reports. These reports are suitable for presentation or printing and can be converted to PDF format using the connected Adobe® server.

BEx Information Broadcasting You can use the BEx Information Broadcaster to calculate Web applications, queries, or workbooks and publish them in the portal. You can send the data as mail or print it. If the recipient is authorized to view the data online, you can also send links to the data.

[+] The Reporting Agent was previously the tool used for scheduling evaluations in the background. Information Broadcasting replaces the Reporting Agent in SAP NetWeaver 2004s BI. However, you can still use the Reporting Agent for queries and Web templates in the 3.x format.

SAP uses OLAP technology (Online Analytical Processing) to analyze data flexibly. This technology enables the formatting of large amounts of information and a multidimensional analysis from different business perspectives.

OLAP technology

The OLAP functions include the following:

▶ Navigation, with which drill-downs can be inserted, exchanged, and removed and hierarchies can be displayed with expandable nodes

▶ Filtering, which can restrict characteristics according to single values or value ranges

▶ Aggregation, which can aggregate single values according to different specifications

▶ Result-dependent selection and display, which can display or hide values depending on the result

▶ Additional functions such as using variables that make a query more flexible and support authorization checks

In the following sections, we introduce the practical uses of the Business Explorer Analyzer, BEx Query Designer, BEx Web Analyzer, BEx Report Designer, and BEx Information Broadcasting tools.

5.2 Business Explorer Analyzer

You can start the BEx Analyzer in two different ways:

▶ Starting the BEx Analyzer from the Windows Start Menu (see Figure 5.10)
The user, who has nothing to do with the administration of the BI system, does not have to log on to the SAP NetWeaver BI system but instead starts the BEx Analyzer directly from the Windows Start menu by selecting the path **Start • Programs • Business Explorer • Analyzer**. The system logon occurs as soon as the user opens any queries in Excel.

▶ Starting the BEx Analyzer from the SAP NetWeaver BI system from the SAP Easy Access menu and by selecting the **Business Information Warehouse • Business Explorer • Analyzer** path (Transaction: RRMX)

This method is useful for administrators and developers, who can use it to start the BEx Analyzer directly from the SAP NetWeaver BI system

[+]   Only transaction RRMX is still available in SAP NetWeaver 2004s BI. The path in the SAP Easy Access menu no longer exists.

[+]   If the Business Explorer tools are installed in the NetWeaver 2004s version on your PC, the programs are available in two versions: in the NetWeaver 2004s BI version and in the 3.x version. You must use the relevant tools based on the release version (see Figure 5.10). In NetWeaver 2004s, you can also use 3.x tools for queries that are still in the 3.x version if the queries were not created or changed with the new Query Designer.

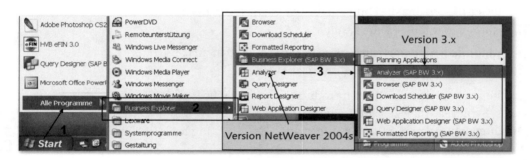

Figure 5.10 Starting the BEx Analyzer

5.2.1   BEx Analyzer Functions

After you start the BEx Analyzer, Excel starts automatically, and a security warning appears depending on the security level set for macros. You must activate the execution of macros. Without this, queries are not possible in Excel. The toolbars displayed in Figure 5.11 are subsequently available in Excel, and you can use them to execute and design queries and workbooks.

[!]   If you still have a release version 3.x system, you cannot use the new Business Explorer tools.

The functions are divided into the Analysis Toolbox and the Design Toolbox (see Figure 5.11).

BEx Analyzer (NetWeaver 2004s)

Figure 5.11 BEx Analyzer (Release SAP NetWeaver 2004s)

The following functions are contained in the *Analysis Toolbox*:

Analysis Toolbox

▶ **Opening queries and workbooks**
A workbook is an Excel file that contains one or more formatted BI queries. Workbooks can be made available to other users, be inserted into roles, or be distributed in an automated way using the BEx Information Broadcaster.

▶ **Saving queries and workbooks**

▶ **Updating data from SAP NetWeaver BI**
A connection to the BI server is established and the data is updated in the workbook. This is necessary if no one has yet logged on to the BI system.

▶ **Changing variable values**
If variable characteristic restrictions are defined, these can be changed. The query is then updated with the entered values.

▶ **Extras**
Extras encompass the functions for executing the query in the browser, starting the Report Designer, and calling the Query Designer.

▶ **Global settings**
Here, you can define the workbook template and the behavior of the BEx Analyzer when Excel is started.

▶ **System information**
You can display information about the SAP NetWeaver BI server.

▶ **Application help**
This function calls the help for the Business Explorer.

The *Design Toolbox*, which is specifically intended for customizing the layout, contains the following functions:

Design Toolbox

▶ **Design mode**
You can toggle between analysis and design mode. The BEx Analyzer switches automatically between these two modes, depending on the function you select. You can use this button to manually switch between modes.

[!] To execute the design mode, the Trust Access to Visual Basic Projects option must be active. In Excel, you will find this option on the **Trusted Publishers** tab under the macro security settings.

▶ **Inserting an analysis table**
The analysis table is the design item used the most. It displays the query result and enables you to navigate using OLAP functions.

▶ **Inserting a navigation area**
The navigation area provides access to all characteristics and structures of the query. It enables you to restrict filter values and provides OLAP functions.

▶ **Inserting a filter area**
This function displays the current filter values.

▶ **Inserting a button**
This function enables you to add buttons for your own commands such as switching between views or between a table and graphic, for example.

▶ **Inserting a drop-down box**
You can use this function to select filter values using drop-down value lists.

▶ **Inserting a checkbox group in the workbook**
You can also create checkboxes for setting filters.

▶ **Adding a radio button group in the workbook**
Similarly, you can execute the filtering of values using a group of radio buttons.

▶ **Inserting the list of conditions**
This function specifies all conditions with the current status and enables you to activate or deactivate these conditions.

▶ **Inserting the list of exceptions**
With this function, you can display all exceptions and activate and deactivate them.

▶ **Inserting text**
This function allows you to display text-based information such as InfoProviders, global filters, authors, or the last time data was loaded.

▶ **Inserting messages into a workbook**
You can specify the types of messages you want to be displayed.

▶ **Workbook settings**
You can use this function to define the workbook settings, for example, an automatic update after you open the workbook. You can specify a password to protect the workbook.

The BEx Analyzer functions are available in a toolbar in Release SAP BW 3.x (see Figure 5.12).

BEx Analyzer (SAP BW 3.x)

Figure 5.12 BEx Analyzer (Release SAP BW 3.x)

The toolbar functions in the sequence shown in Figure 5.12 are as follows:

▶ Open queries, workbooks, or views

▶ Save queries, views, and workbooks

> You can save the current navigation status of the query as a view. Enter a technical name for this in the Technical Name field and a description of the view in the Text field. This global view is now available to every user.
>
> You can also save a view as a jump target in workbooks to be able to jump back and forth between navigation statuses. This view is now available within the workbook and makes it easier for you to navigate.

View

▶ Update the data from SAP NetWeaver BI

▶ **Back**
The last navigation step is undone.

▶ **Change**
You can change the query in the local view or in the global definition. However, from a functional point of view, changing the query in the local view is very restricted. You can also execute the functions using normal navigation options.

Call the Query Designer described in Section 5.3 to make changes in the global definition. You require corresponding authorization to do this. After you save your changes, they become globally effective for all users.

▶ **GoTo**
If jump targets (that is, views) are defined in a workbook with different navigation statuses, you can use this button to go back and forth between the jump targets.

▶ **OLAP functions for active rows**
You can use this button to execute the OLAP functions described in Section 5.1.3. The functions provided always refer to the field where the cursor is positioned at the time. You can access the same functions by placing the cursor on the required field and right-clicking to call the context menu.

[+] You can use the **Tools** button to deactivate calling the OLAP functions using the right-click mouse button. In this case, the usual Excel context menu will appear instead.

▶ **Format**
You can use the format functions to adapt the font, patterns, alignment, and borders. The function is applied to the field where the cursor is positioned and incorporates related fields. For example, if you select a personnel area that is used as a characteristic in the row drill-down and you change the font, the font is subsequently changed for all personnel areas.

▶ **Layout**
The layout function enables you to integrate graphics and maps. You should use the functions available in the SAP system to integrate graphics. In contrast to the Excel functions, the reference to the data is retained, which means the graphic can be adapted automatically when you perform navigation steps. The Excel graphic would lose the reference to the data during the navigation.

▶ **Tools**
This button offers the following functions: You can execute the current query in the browser, call the Query Designer, insert additional queries into the current worksheet, or use the SAP sheet protection function for the worksheet.

▶ **Settings**

The settings include managing workbook templates, displaying information about the SAP NetWeaver BI server, and activating the OLAP functions using the right-click mouse button.

The SAP sheet protection allows you to assign a password, without which you can no longer make any changes to the worksheet. Although you can continue to use the navigation options, you cannot execute any function that changes the layout. This includes all the functions of the **Layout** and **Format** buttons that are locked by this. In addition, you cannot input and format the Excel fields around the query.

SAP sheet protection

▶ **Help**

Use this function to call the online help for the Business Explorer.

5.2.2   Working with the BEx Analyzer

Click the **Open** button and select the **Open Query** function to execute a query. Then log on to the SAP NetWeaver BI system and choose a query from the **Open** dialog box displayed in Figure 5.1. The following areas are available to help you find the correct query:

Opening a query

▶ **Find**

This option enables you to search for a query based on the technical name or description.

▶ **History**

The history provides a list of the last queries used.

▶ **Favorites**

You can assign queries to your favorites by right-clicking to select a query and choosing the **Add to Favorites** option.

▶ **Roles**

The Roles area provides queries that are assigned in the user role.

▶ **InfoAreas**

InfoAreas are used to classify objects in SAP NetWeaver BI. Each InfoCube is assigned to an InfoArea. The queries are arranged under the relevant InfoCube, as shown in Figure 5.13.

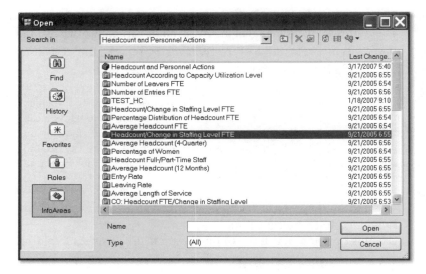

Figure 5.13 Opening a Query

Select a query and choose **Open** to start it.

If variable characteristics are defined in the query, the window displayed in Figure 5.14 appears, where you can select values or available variants.

You can save your selections as variants or press the **Personalize Variables** button in the upper right-hand corner of the window to initialize the provided variables with fixed default values. This is useful if you always have to start this query using the same criteria since the next time you call the query, you do not have to enter all the details again and the query starts immediately. Once you have started the query, you can change the variables by selecting the **Change variable value** button or remove the personalization again.

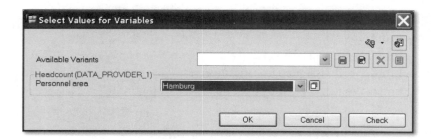

Figure 5.14 Selecting Values for Variables

▶ The query starts once you confirm the prompt (see Figure 5.15). In the new SAP NetWeaver 2004s design, three buttons are displayed in the upper area of the screen:

▶ **Chart/Table**
A graphic containing the displayed data is generated in the background. You can use this button to toggle between the graphic and the table.

▶ **Filter**
You can use this button to display the filter values.

▶ **Information**
This button displays a screen with information such as the InfoProvider and technical name.

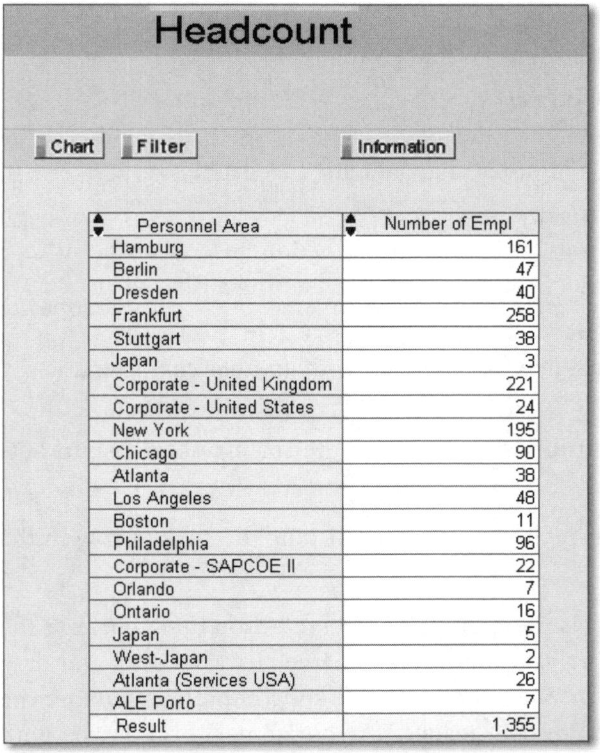

Headcount

Chart	Filter		Information

Personnel Area	Number of Empl
Hamburg	161
Berlin	47
Dresden	40
Frankfurt	258
Stuttgart	38
Japan	3
Corporate - United Kingdom	221
Corporate - United States	24
New York	195
Chicago	90
Atlanta	38
Los Angeles	48
Boston	11
Philadelphia	96
Corporate - SAPCOE II	22
Orlando	7
Ontario	16
Japan	5
West-Japan	2
Atlanta (Services USA)	26
ALE Porto	7
Result	1,355

Figure 5.15 Query in the BEx Analyzer

5.2.3 Navigation in the Query

You can use context menus, which you activate by right-clicking, to navigate in the query (see Figure 5.16):

▶ **Back**
This option undoes the last navigation step.

▶ **Back to the start**
This function undoes all navigation steps and returns the query to its initial status.

▶ **Retain filter value**
The selected row is set as a filter value.

▶ **Select filter value**
The dialog box is opened to select filter values.

▶ **Delete filter**
This option deletes the set filter value.

▶ **Filter and drill-down**
This function sets the value of the current row from the filter value and inserts an additional characteristic as a drilldown.

▶ **Drill down vertically**
Like the previous function, this function inserts an additional characteristic as a drill-down, without setting a filter value.

▶ **Replace ... with**
The current drill-down is replaced with another characteristic.

▶ **Sort ...**
You can use this option to arrange the sorting according to key, text, or result.

You can also sort the information by clicking the small arrow in the table header.

Navigating by drag and drop
The navigation is also supported by drag-and-drop functions. Use the **Filter** button to activate the display of free characteristics and drag (as shown in Figure 5.17) the employee subgroup directly under the **Number of Employees** header. A horizontal drill-down with employee subgroups is subsequently inserted.

Figure 5.16 OLAP Functions

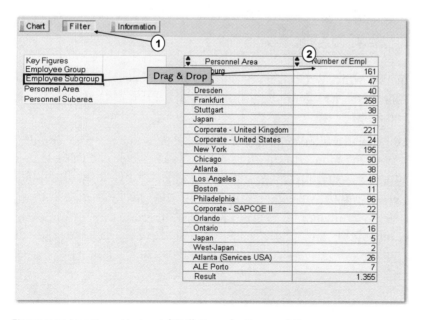

Figure 5.17 Inserting a Horizontal Drill-Down by Drag-and-Drop

5.2.4 Filtering Characteristics

To filter characteristics, activate the **Filter** button (see Figure 5.18) and right-click to select the required filter object. In the context menu, use the **Select Filter Value** option to call the window for selecting values (Figure 5.19).

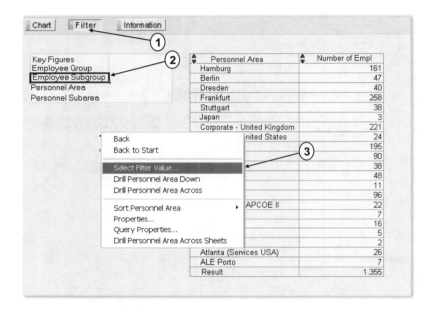

Figure 5.18 Filtering Characteristics

In this window (see Figure 5.20), you can select single values or value sets or exclude them from selection. You can save the values you select as favorites.

Filtering by drag and drop You can also filter by drag and drop. Select a characteristic and drag it with the mouse to the filter area. The characteristic value is then adopted as the filter. If you drag the object beneath the filter area, the characteristic value is excluded from the selection.

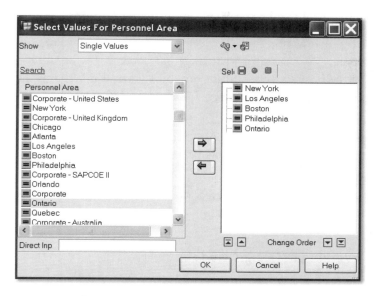

Figure 5.19 Selecting Filter Values

5.2.5 Graphical Display of Data

Parallel to the displayed table, a graphic that adapts to the navigation in the table is dynamically created in the background. You can use the **Chart** button to switch to the graphic. Numerous functions for formatting the graphic are provided on the right-hand margin of the window. You can also access these functions by right-clicking the graphic objects.

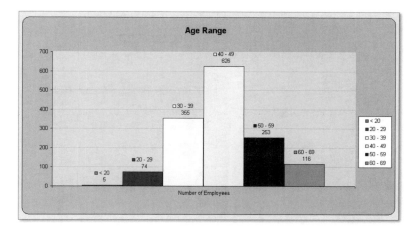

Figure 5.20 Graphical Display in the BEx Analyzer

A large number of format functions are available for formatting the graphic. These include:

- **Chart type**
  With this function, you can use different vertical bar charts, pie charts, and line charts. You can also save user-defined chart types.

- **Formatting data series**
  You can use this option to choose colors, patterns, and labels and to change the layout of individual elements.

- **Diagram options**
  These options enable you to select the axes, titles, legends, colors, and patterns of the background.

5.2.6 Working in Design Mode

The Business Explorer provides new options for designing workbooks in design mode on SAP NetWeaver 2004s. Some of the functions already known from Version 3.x are better supported, but new functions such as the option to define buttons or insert drop-down boxes and radio buttons have also been added.

Figure 5.21 shows a checkbox group as an example of inserting an item in design mode. Select the area where you want to place the item and choose the button for inserting a checkbox.

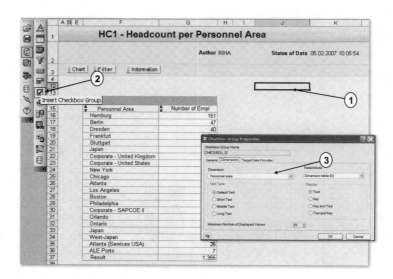

Figure 5.21 Inserting a Checkbox Group in Design Mode

In the window displayed in Figure 5.22, select the required dimension, to which the item should refer (in this case, the **Personnel Area**), and the target DataProvider, to which the selection refers. The result is displayed in Figure 5.23.

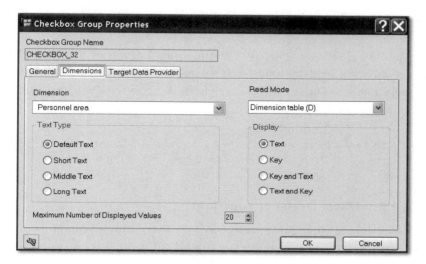

Figure 5.22 Properties of the Checkbox Group

Personnel Area	Number of Empl		
Hamburg	161		
Berlin	47		
Dresden	40	☑ Active	
Frankfurt	258		
Stuttgart	38	☐ External	
Japan	3		
Corporate - United Kingdom	221	☐ Inactive	
Corporate - United States	24		
New York	195		
Chicago	90	Submit	Clear
Atlanta	38		
Los Angeles	48		
Boston	11		
Philadelphia	96		
Corporate - SAPCOE II	22		
Orlando	7		
Ontario	16		
Japan	5		
West-Japan	2		
Atlanta (Services USA)	26		
ALE Porto	7		
Result	1,355		

Figure 5.23 Filtering by Checkbox Group

When you have processed the queries and graphics, you can save the completed workbook on the BI server, integrate it into roles, and

Saving workbooks

send it through Information Broadcasting. You can also make the workbooks available offline. You only need to log on to the BI server when you want to update the data.

5.3 BEx Query Designer

The BEx Query Designer is a Windows application of the Business Explorer for creating queries. You can use the queries you create with the BEx Query Designer in the BEx Analyzer, Web Analyzer, and formatted reporting.

[+]   Each query is based on exactly one InfoProvider and can only process key figures and characteristics that are contained in this InfoProvider.

5.3.1 Query Designer Functions

You also start the Query Designer from the Windows menu. However, you can also start it directly from the BEx Analyzer by selecting the **Extras** button and the **Create New Query** function.

Modeling a query involves defining rows and columns, assigning fixed and variable filter values, and displaying exception values. As shown in Figure 5.24, the window consists of the following areas:

▶ **InfoProvider**
The selected InfoProvider is displayed here with key figures and dimensions. To select these, use the mouse to drag them to the Rows or Columns area. The available structures are also provided.

▶ **Rows/Columns**
You design the query in the Rows and Columns areas and can see the defined rows and columns in the Preview area.

▶ **Filter**
The Filter area appears behind the Rows/Columns area. You can access it by selecting the tab at the bottom of the screen. You define fixed and variable characteristic values as well as default values here. For example, you could assign the status of employment a fixed value of 3 (meaning active) or define the Personnel Area characteristic as a variable, which results in a selection window appearing when you start the query.

▶ **Properties**

The Properties area on the right displays the properties of the active object. You can also set the properties here. This includes the setting options for displaying characteristics and key figures.

▶ **Tasks**

The Tasks area is also located on the right of the screen and can be displayed by selecting the tab at the bottom of the screen. Functions that are related to the active object are provided here, but they are also available in the toolbar.

▶ **Messages**

Errors and warning messages are displayed in the lower part of the screen. Error messages and notes are provided here for correction purposes.

▶ **Where-used list**

The where-used list is located in the same part of the screen, which you can call using a tab.

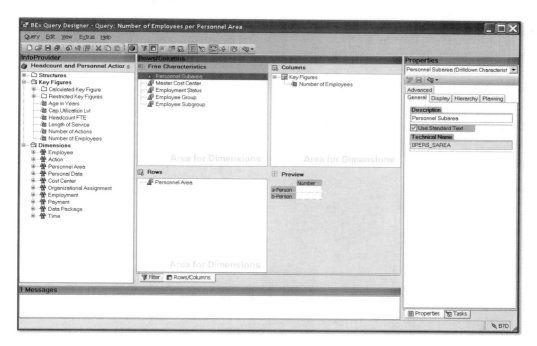

Figure 5.24 Query Designer

The toolbar is divided into the **Standard** (see top level of Figure 5.25) and **View** (bottom level) areas. You use the **View** area to control the areas of the screen. For example, you can display the **Exceptions** area of the screen, which is not active immediately after you start the Query Designer. The **Standard** area contains functions such as **Create New Query**, **Open**, and **Save**.

Figure 5.25 Query Designer Toolbar (Release SAP NetWeaver 2004s)

Query Designer (SAP BW 3.x) For comparison purposes, Figure 5.26 shows Release 3.x of the Query Designer. The window areas are fixed. The InfoProvider is displayed in the left area, whereas the area for modeling the query is displayed on the right-hand side. Above this is the definition area for filters.

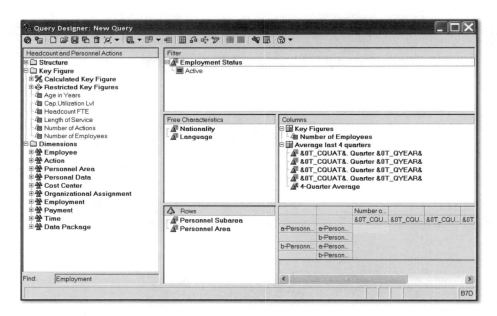

Figure 5.26 Query Designer (Release SAP BW 3.x)

5.3.2 Creating Queries

To illustrate the functions of the Query Designer, we will now use examples in which we will create queries.

> **Query: headcount**
>
> ► You want to display the number of active employees separated by personnel areas.
>
> ► You also want to be able to drill down according to employee subgroup and length of service. Use Number of Employees as the key figure in the Headcount and Personnel Actions InfoCube.

To create a new query, start the Query Designer from the Windows Start menu and select the **New Query** button. In the **Select InfoProvider** window (see Figure 5.27), choose the required InfoProvider and select **Open**. The **Find** and **History** functions and the structured area of the **InfoAreas** are available to help you find the InfoProvider you require. You will find the InfoProvider in the **InfoAreas** by selecting the **Human Resources • Personnel Administration** path.

Creating the query

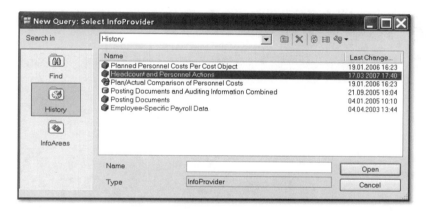

Figure 5.27 Selecting an InfoProvider

The existing characteristics and structures are now available in the **InfoProvider** area (see Figure 5.24), and you can drag these to the **Rows/Columns** area bydrag and drop.

Drag the **Number of Employees** key figure with the mouse to the **Columns** area. Open the **Personnel Area** dimension by clicking the [+] in front of the dimension, and drag the **Personnel Area** characteristic contained here to the **Rows** area. This defines the structure of the simple query, which you can see in the **Preview** area.

Enabling
variable navigation
To enable variable navigation according to employee subgroup and length of service, open the **Employment** dimension and drag **Employee Subgroup** and **Length of Service** to the **Free Characteristics** area. The **Rows/Columns** area is displayed in Figure 5.28.

Now switch to the **Filter** area and drag the **Employment Status – Active** and **Employee Group – Active** characteristic values to the **Characteristic Restrictions** area (see Figure 5.29). Open the characteristic values under the **Employment Status** and **Employee Group** characteristics for this and select the values. This defines a fixed restriction of these characteristics that cannot be changed in the query.

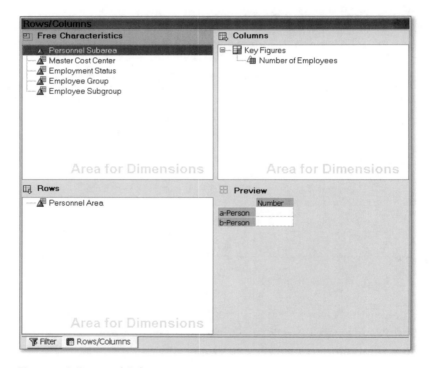

Figure 5.28 Rows and Columns

To enable users to enter the evaluation period using variable values, select **Current Date** from the **Calendar Day** characteristic from the **Time** dimension and drag it to the **Characteristic Restriction** area, as shown in Figure 5.30.

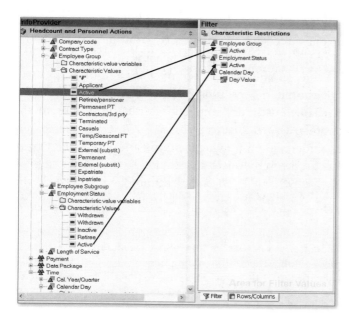

Figure 5.29 Restricting Characteristics

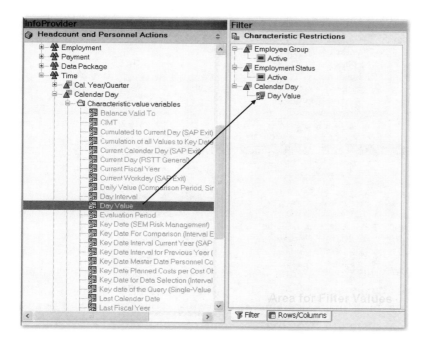

Figure 5.30 Variable Restriction of Characteristics

5.3.3 Variables

Variables are only filled with values at the runtime of the query. Variables are most commonly used to specify manual values. The characteristic value variable is also used to check authorizations (see Section 5.8). Select the folder with the characteristic variables under the required characteristic and drag this with the mouse to the required area of the screen (Figure 5.31).

[Ex]
Proceed as follows if you want to include the employee subgroup as a variable for selection when the query is started: Open the Employment dimension and the Employee Subgroup characteristic underneath it by clicking [+]. The folder for characteristic variables is located under Employee Subgroup.

Right-click **Characteristic Variables** and select **New Variable**. Call the variable **Employee Subgroup** and then drag this variable with the mouse to the Characteristic Restriction area. This ensures that the selection query for the employee subgroup occurs when you start the query.

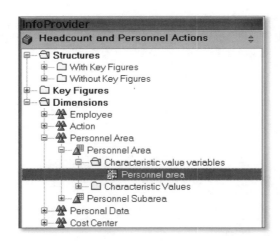

Figure 5.31 Characteristic Value Variables

5.3.4 Structures

Creating structures from key figures or characteristics
You can group key figures and characteristics in structures. The structure forms the basic framework for an axis of the table. You can use a maximum of two structures, one of which must be a key figure structure. When you use two structures, a table with fixed cells is generated.

Structures are saved in relation to the InfoProvider and can also be used in other queries. Therefore, when you change structures, you should always check in which queries these structures are contained.

> **Query: average age**
>
> You want the query to display the average age of employees. The average age is calculated from the total age, divided by the number of employees.
>
> The key figure does not exist in the InfoCube but is calculated.

There are two ways in which you can create a calculated key figure, as illustrated in Figure 5.32 and Figure 5.33. A calculated key figure does not exist in the InfoCube, but is usually calculated from other key figures. These can be the average age, for example, which is calculated by dividing the **Age** key figure by the number of **Employees** or a currency translation. You can create a new key figure by right-clicking the **Calculated Key Figure** folder. The formula editor provides numerous calculation options for this purpose.

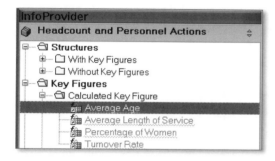

Figure 5.32 Calculated Key Figure

You can also display the calculation of the average age using a structure. As shown in Figure 5.34, this structure consists of three columns, of which the two grayed-out columns are not displayed in the query. They are simply used for the calculation. The average age is calculated by dividing the two key figures.

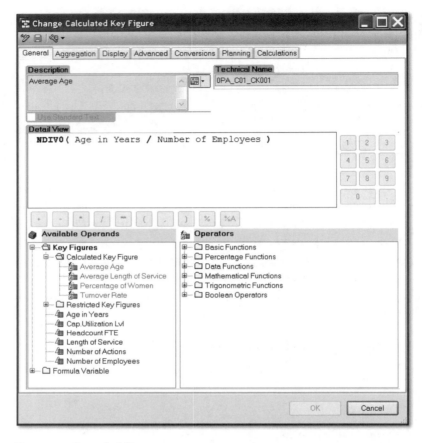

Figure 5.33 Formula Editor

Figure 5.34 Structure with Key Figures

The structure displayed in Figure 5.35 only consists of selections. The rows of the query are determined by strictly selected personnel areas.

Figure 5.35 Structure with Selections

5.3.5 Hierarchies

SAP ERP HCM contains different hierarchies such as those for the organizational structure or the business event catalog.

Navigation in hierarchies

You can transfer a part of these hierarchies into the BI system and use them there for navigating in evaluations.

Characteristics that you can display in hierarchies enable you to drill down and navigate in subordinate levels (see Figure 5.36). The following hierarchies exist in the standard content of SAP ERP HCM:

▶ Organizational structure

▶ Cost center hierarchy

▶ Age of employees

▶ Employment level

▶ Qualifications catalog

▶ Business event catalog

Organizational unit	Average Age
▪ Result	44.3064
▼ Executive Board ·	44.9232
▶ Operations	40.0306
▶ Sales	45.8462
▼ Human Resources	46.8989
▶ Labor Relations	48.1218
▶ Payroll Administration	46.0000
▶ Workforce Planning	41.4000
▶ HR Information Systems	42.3494

Figure 5.36 Hierarchy

5.3.6 Exceptions

Highlighting values in queries

You can use exceptions to select values in queries (see Figure 5.37). You can use several shades of color to highlight values, for example, as *positive* using different shades of green, or as *negative* using shades of red. This enables you to recognize exceptional cases that may require action.

Select the **Exception** button to activate the section of the screen in the Query Designer. Right-click in this area and select **New Exception**. You can create several AlertLevels with the **New** button and assign these different levels, from **good** to **critical** to **poor**.

Table	
	Average Age
Hamburg	44.1963
Berlin	50.4894
Dresden	48.4500
Frankfurt	47.7984
Stuttgart	50.0976
Paris	
Chicago	45.9778

Figure 5.37 Displaying Exceptions

5.3.7 Conditions

Hiding rows

Conditions allow you to hide rows that do not match the selected criteria. For example, you can create an evaluation where only organizational units that exceed a defined threshold value are displayed. All other organizational units are hidden.

In the Query Designer, select the **Condition** button to activate the section of the screen that is not previously displayed. Right-click in this area and select **New Condition**. Now double-click on this condition, at which point the screen shown in Figure 5.38 is displayed. Select **New**, enter your condition in the fields under the screen, and then transfer the condition.

You can enter several conditions, all of which need to be met for a row to be displayed.

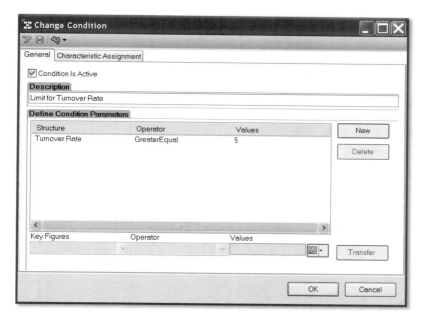

Figure 5.38 Creating a Condition

5.4 BEx Web Analyzer

The BEx Web Analyzer facilitates ad hoc evaluations based on queries, query views, and InfoProviders. The integration into the SAP NetWeaver Portal allows you to save queries in the BEx Portfolio or in your favorites.

Figure 5.39 shows the BEx Web Analyzer after you start it in the Portal. In the upper margin, you have the **My Portfolio** and **BEx Portfolio** functions, where you can save and retrieve evaluations you have performed.

Figure 5.39 Starting the BEx Web Analyzer

Here's another example:

Ad hoc evaluation: FTE statistics

In an evaluation in the BEx Web Analyzer, you want the number of FTEs to be displayed based on employee subgroups.

Click **New Evaluation** and select the **InfoProvider** type, as shown in Figure 5.40. The areas **Find**, **History**, **Favorites**, **Roles**, and **InfoArea** are available for selecting the InfoProvider. Select the **Headcount and Personnel Actions** InfoProvider, which you can find using the search function, for example. Select the row and click on **OK**.

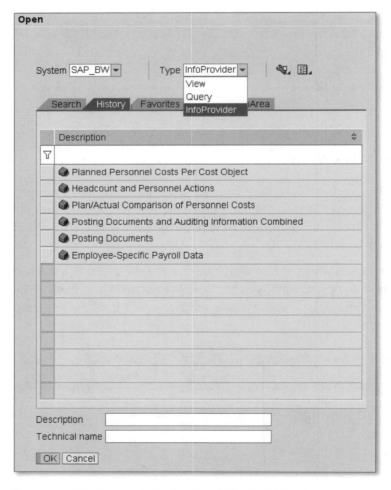

Figure 5.40 Selecting an InfoProvider for Ad Hoc Evaluation

All the key figures of the InfoCube are displayed, and you must restrict these to the **Headcount FTE**. To do this, select the **Select Filter Value** function by right-clicking on **Key Figures** in the navigation area on the left-hand side. Select the key figure, as shown in Figure 5.41, and transfer this by clicking on **OK**.

In the next step, insert the vertical drill-down by employee subgroup. To do this, right-click the **Employee subgroup** characteristic and select the path displayed in Figure 5.42.

Figure 5.43 shows the result of the ad hoc evaluation. You can use the **Save As** function to save this evaluation in your own portfolio, the BEx portfolio, or your favorites.

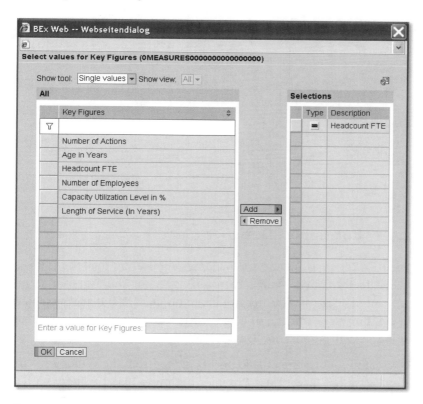

Figure 5.41 Restricting Key Figures

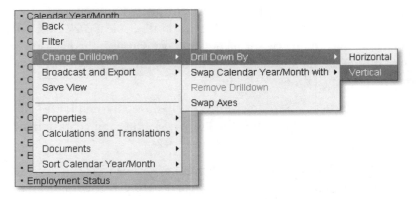

Figure 5.42 Vertical Drill-Down by Employee Subgroup

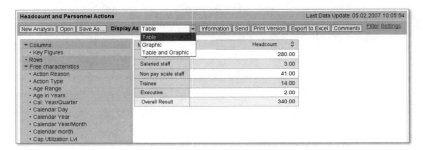

Figure 5.43 Ad Hoc Evaluation

5.5 BEx Report Designer

The BEx Report Designer is a Windows application that you can use to create formatted reports to format data for online reports and printing. The reports created are based on queries and are presented in the browser. You can also use formatted reports as a Web item with the Web Application Designer.

To create a report, open the Report Designer from the Windows Start menu. Use the **Insert Data Provider** button to insert a query with a headcount evaluation. The result could look like the one displayed in Figure 5.44.

You can send the result through the BEx Information Broadcaster (**Send** button) or convert it to PDF for printing (**Print Version** button).

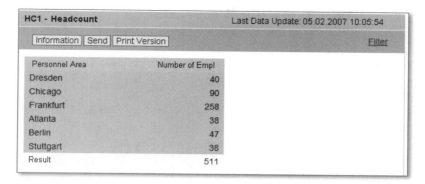

Figure 5.44 Report Example

You can change the PDF output to landscape format by selecting the **Report • Page Setup** menu options (see Figure 5.45).

The Report Designer provides different format functions that you can access from the **Format** menu. For example, you can format individual cells and files with fonts, font colors, and so on. You can use the **Extra • Portal Theme** menu option to select available style sheets for the formatting.

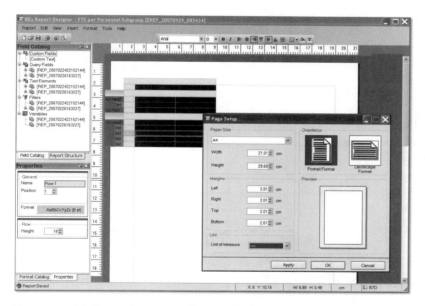

Figure 5.45 BEx Report Designer – Changing the Format

5.6 BEx Information Broadcaster

The BEx Information Broadcaster enables you to distribute queries, Web templates, query views, reports, and workbooks. The following options are available for distributing BI contents:

- Sending them by email as a link, PDF document, Excel file, or HTML file
- Printing them in the PS or PCL format or as a PDF
- Sending them to the portal as a link, PDF document, Excel file, or HTML file

As shown in Figure 5.46, you can select an **object type** (such as the report created in Section 5.5) and either maintain the settings manually to send the contents or use the Wizard.

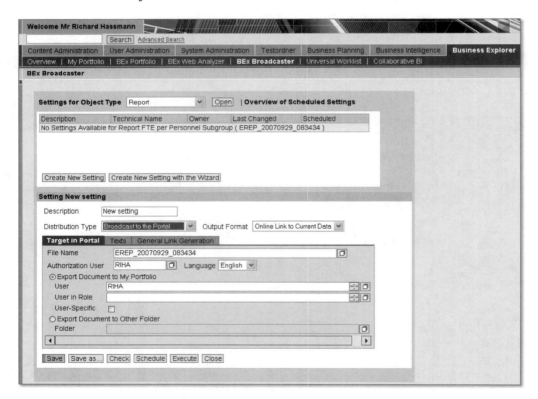

Figure 5.46 BEx Information Broadcaster

The wizard guides you through the settings in four steps.

The first step involves selecting the distribution type and output format, as shown in Figure 5.47. In the following example, we select **Send Email** as the **Distribution Type**.

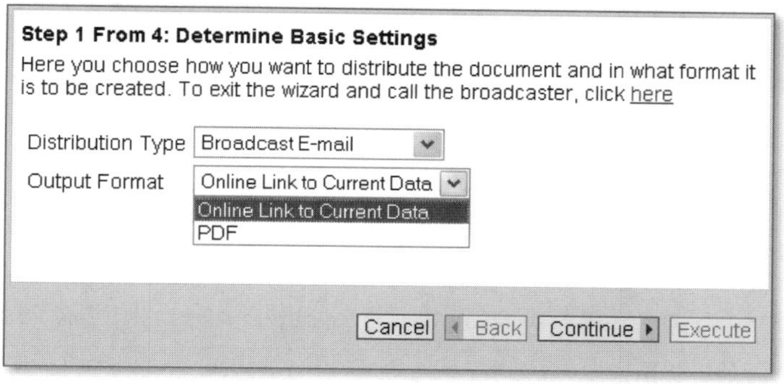

Step 1 From 4: Determine Basic Settings

Here you choose how you want to distribute the document and in what format it is to be created. To exit the wizard and call the broadcaster, click here

Distribution Type   Broadcast E-mail

Output Format   Online Link to Current Data
Online Link to Current Data
PDF

Cancel   ◀ Back   Continue ▶   Execute

Figure 5.47 Broadcasting Wizard – Basic Settings

In step 2 (see Figure 5.48), you can enter the email address, reference line text, and message for the recipient.

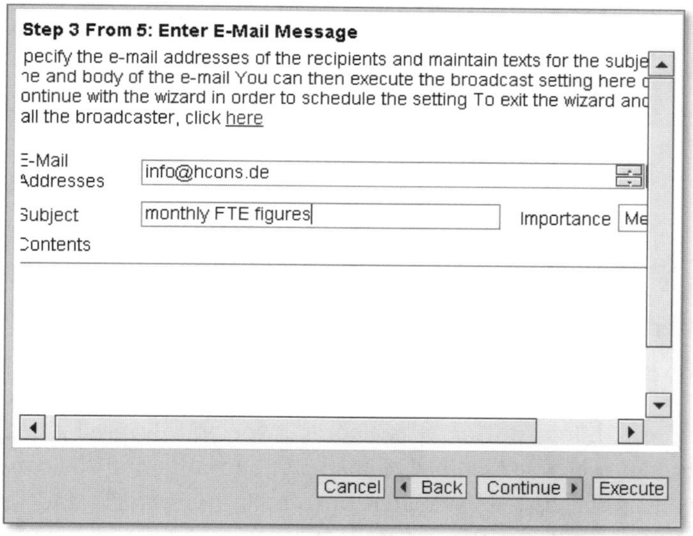

Step 3 From 5: Enter E-Mail Message

pecify the e-mail addresses of the recipients and maintain texts for the subje
ne and body of the e-mail You can then execute the broadcast setting here
ontinue with the wizard in order to schedule the setting To exit the wizard and
all the broadcaster, click here

E-Mail
Addresses   info@hcons.de

Subject   monthly FTE figures   Importance   Me

Contents

◀   ▶

Cancel   ◀ Back   Continue ▶   Execute

Figure 5.48 Broadcasting Wizard – Entering an Email Message

In step 3, you can specify a technical name and a description under which the settings are saved before you define the scheduling details in step 4 (see Figure 5.49).

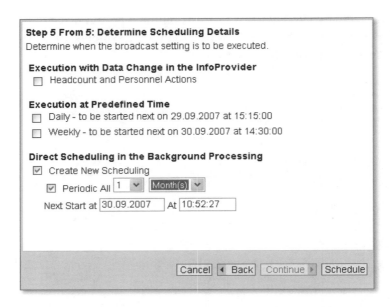

Step 5 From 5: Determine Scheduling Details
Determine when the broadcast setting is to be executed.

Execution with Data Change in the InfoProvider
☐ Headcount and Personnel Actions

Execution at Predefined Time
☐ Daily - to be started next on 29.09.2007 at 15:15:00
☐ Weekly - to be started next on 30.09.2007 at 14:30:00

Direct Scheduling in the Background Processing
☑ Create New Scheduling
  ☑ Periodic All [1 ▾] [Month(s) ▾]
  Next Start at [30.09.2007] At [10:52:27]

[Cancel] [◀ Back] [Continue ▶] [Schedule]

Figure 5.49 Broadcasting Wizard – Defining the Scheduling Details

You can schedule the execution regularly, or this can be done automatically when data is changed.

[+] Depending on the distribution type, the options may differ from those displayed in the figures here.

5.7 Standard Content

The standard Business Content provides a basis for using SAP NetWeaver BI. Although predefined solutions reduce the implementation time, you should not view them as complete solutions. The word *standard* should not be regarded as a specifically predefined solution to which changes cannot be made. The content must be considered as a model that must match business requirements and, if necessary, can also be enhanced with your own requirements. In practice, the delivered queries can only seldom be used unchanged. However, since it is relatively easy to create queries, this is only a minor problem. If InfoCubes do not provide the required content, more effort will be required to enhance the content of the InfoCubes or create new InfoCubes.

The SAP standard content consists of extractors, InfoCubes, and que- ries. The InfoCubes contain predefined key figures. Templates are also delivered for standard calculations. Web Cockpits provide tem- plates for presenting BI content in the SAP NetWeaver Portal.

Extractors, InfoCubes, and queries

5.7.1 Standard Content for HCM Modules

Standard content exists for the following HCM modules:

▶ **Personnel administration**
This includes headcount, leaving rate, entry rate, and average age.

▶ **Recruitment**
This includes the number of applications and recruiting successes.

▶ **Event management**
This includes attendances, cancellations, and resource reserva- tions.

▶ **Payroll**
This includes salary costs for each organizational unit and wage type comparison.

▶ **Time management**
This includes an overview of personnel times, time and labor data, illness rates, and CATS evaluations.

▶ **Personnel development**
This includes information about employees by qualification.

▶ **Organizational management**
This includes an overview of position and vacancies.

▶ **Compensation management**
This includes compensation evaluations and comparisons of mar- ket data with employee compensation.

▶ **Benefits**
This includes cost analyses according to benefits criteria.

▶ **Personnel cost planning**
This includes comparisons between cost projections and planned and actual comparison.

▶ **Payroll and time management**
This includes comprehensive evaluations from payroll and time management and overtime costs.

▶ **Travel management**
This includes the number of trips and expense receipts.

▶ **Pension funds**
This includes the age structure of insured employees and account balances.

New contents have been added to the following areas in Version 7.0 of the Business Content:

▶ **Learning Solution**
This evaluates learning processes and Web-based training.

▶ **Objective Settings and Appraisals**
This evaluates appraisals and the appraisal process.

▶ **Talent Management**
This evaluates talent groups or key staffing assignments, for example.

▶ **Shared Services**
This evaluates processes from the ESS and MSS areas and processes and forms, for example, the number of processes and retention periods.

▶ **Employee Interaction Center**
This evaluates the customer satisfaction overview.

5.7.2 Standard Content for Benchmarking

Comparing companies using benchmarks is common in many industries such as banking and insurance. You can simplify data retrieval by using an InfoCube that determines the data.

The SAP standard content contains an InfoCube for this with the following key figures:

▶ FTE of active employees

▶ Number of active employees

▶ FTE in the HR department

▶ Number of employees in the HR department

▶ Employee departures

▶ New employees

▶ Scheduled workday

- Leaving rate
- Leaving rate in personnel area
- Employers' leaving rate
- Employees' leaving rate
- Internal hiring rate
- External hiring rate
- Net hiring rate
- Net entry rate
- Average length of service
- Average age
- Full-time/part-time staff rate
- Salary payroll staffing factor
- Personnel area staffing factor
- Sources of recruitment rate
- Illness rate
- Training costs for each employee (FTE)
- Training costs for each hour of training
- Training hours for each employee
- Number of part-time staff
- Number of full-time staff
- Number of employees
- Employee departures

5.7.3 The Organizational Structure in the Standard Content

The organizational structure is not a pure HCM object but is used to create the purchasing and sales structure, for example. For example, in Figure 5.50, the **Organizational Unit** characteristic contains attributes from the Purchasing and Sales areas, whereas it only contains a few attributes from the HCM system, which have to be enhanced frequently here. This means these attributes are also displayed in the HCM module when you create queries.

The structures are also mixed if purchasing structures or sales structures from the customer relationship management (CRM) system and organizational structures from the HCM system are loaded. We therefore recommend that you use your own object in SAP ERP HCM, from which the nonrelevant attributes are deleted.

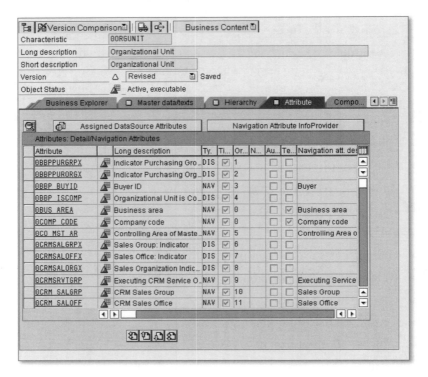

Figure 5.50 Characteristic – Organizational Unit

5.7.4 Conclusion

The standard content is a very good template for implementing SAP NetWeaver BI into the HR environment. It makes the implementation process considerably easier. Nevertheless, do not underestimate the effort required to evaluate the content and adapt and enhance it to meet business factors.

5.8   Authorizations in SAP NetWeaver BI

The basic setup of the role concept in the SAP system also applies to the BI system. Roles with menu structures and authorization profiles are assigned to the user. The user receives a menu that can contain queries, workbooks, and other objects.

Setting up the role concept

The data structures in SAP NetWeaver BI differ fundamentally from the data structures in the R/3/ERP system, which is why the authorizations cannot be transferred. There is no logical database PNP. This is why the associated authorizations cannot be used. The structural authorization is the only HR authorization that you can transfer into SAP NetWeaver BI (see Section 5.9).

Data structures

5.8.1   Specific Authorization Objects of SAP NetWeaver BI

The following list contains the most important authorization objects of SAP NetWeaver BI:

▶ S_RS_IOBJ InfoObjects

▶ S_RS_ISOUR InfoSources

▶ S_RS_ISRCM InfoSources with Direct Updating

▶ S_RS_ICUBE InfoCube

▶ S_RS_MPRO MultiProvider

▶ S_RS_ISET InfoSet

▶ S_RS_HIER Hierarchy

▶ S_RS_IOMAD Processing Master Data in the Administrator Workbench

▶ S_RS_COMP Components for the Query Definition

▶ S_RS_COMP1 Queries from Specific Owners

▶ S_RS_FOLD Display Authorization for Folder

▶ S_RS_TOOLS Authorizations for Individual Business Explorer Tools

The authorization objects enable you to restrict authorization to specific InfoCubes or queries but not to contents within an InfoCube. If you want to restrict authorization to employee subgroups or personnel areas within the InfoCube, for example, you need to perform the activities described in the following section.

You must manually create the authorization objects for reporting. You can do this for characteristics and key figures. This is necessary if authorizations are required at the level of personnel area, personnel subarea, or employee subgroup, for example.

You must enable the **Authorization relevant** option for this in the characteristic (see Figure 5.51).

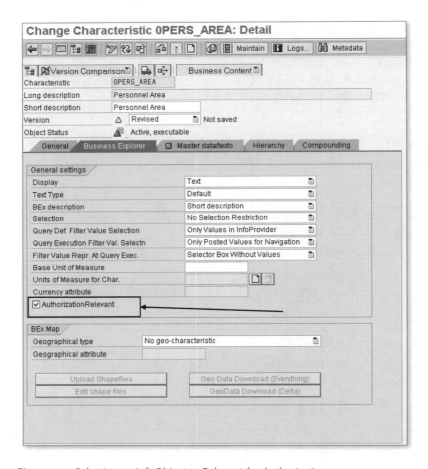

Figure 5.51 Selecting an InfoObject as Relevant for Authorization

If you have selected the characteristic, you can create an authorization object in transaction RSECADMIN, which replaces the previously used transaction RSSM in NetWeaver 2004s.

As shown in Figure 5.52, create a new authorization object and enter text in the descriptive text fields. In the **Authorization Structure** area, enter the characteristic that you previously selected as being **authorization relevant**. The authorization object is then assigned to the InfoCubes where you want the authorization check to occur. Assign the new authorization you have created to a user or role.

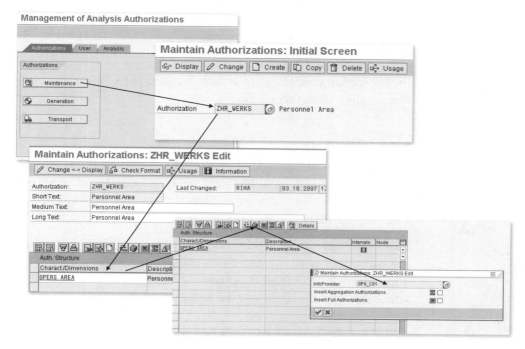

Figure 5.52 Creating an Authorization Object

5.8.2 Tools for Authorization Check

In addition to the general **Display authorization check**, which you can call from transaction SU53 or the SAP menu options **System • Utilities • Display auth. check**, SAP NetWeaver BI contains another tool for evaluating authorizations: transaction **RSECADMIN**. You can use this transaction to check the authorizations in the **Reporting** area. You can also access the transaction from the SAP Easy Access menu by selecting the **Business Explorer • Authorizations** path.

5.9   Structural Authorization

The structural authorization in SAP ERP HCM is frequently used to assign authorizations to managers. It is based on the structures of organizational management. Much time and effort would be required to create this structure in SAP NetWeaver BI. The standard content therefore has an option you can use to transfer the structure into the BI system and generate profiles from it.

In this section you will learn how to transfer the structural authorization into SAP NetWeaver BI.

5.9.1   Overview

As you can see in Figure 5.53, the structural authorizations are read using report RHBAUS00 and written into the INDX cluster. Two DataSources read this cluster and transfer the data into two DataStore InfoProviders of the BI system.

Three tables are processed in this case, namely, table T77PR, where the definitions of the authorization profiles are saved, table T77UA, which contains the user assigned to the profile, and table T77UU, which contains the users you want to extract.

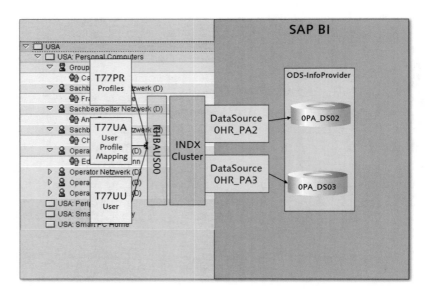

Figure 5.53 Structural Authorization in SAP NetWeaver BI

SAP NetWeaver BI contains two DataSources for the extraction: 0HR_PA2 and 0HR_PA3.

DataSource 0HR_PA2 processes the user assigned to the allowed objects.

The user is assigned to the object type and object ID here. You can process all object types.

DataSource 0HR_PA3 processes hierarchical authorizations. You process users with objects and hierarchies here.

Only the active plan version **01** is supported. DataSource 0HR_PA3 only supports the **Organizational Unit** object with the ORGEH evaluation path delivered with the Business Content. DataSource 0HR_PA2 is not time dependent but instead maps the version of the authorization during the extraction. This requires a daily extraction to have the latest version of the authorization in the BI system.

Restrictions

5.9.2 Process

Preparing the extraction:

1. To extract the user authorization, you must enter the user in table T77UU. To help you, you can use the RHBAUS02 report, which fills the table with users.

2. The RHBAUS00 report then writes the authorizations into the INDX cluster that is used for the extraction.

3. Provided that the extractors and the Business Content were already activated and set up and an InfoPackage was created, the extraction can now take place.

As described in Section 5.8.1, in the BI system you must create your own authorization object, to which you must assign the 0ORGUNIT (Organizational Unit), 0POSITION (Position), and 0EMPLOYEE (Employee) characteristics. For this purpose, these characteristics are identified as being relevant for authorization and are assigned when you create the authorization object.

Your own authorization object

You can generate the authorization profile for the structural authorization using the RSSB_GENERATE_AUTHORIZATIONS report.

You must create authorization-relevant variables in the queries that, when you call the query, perform an authorization check by using the 0ORGUNIT, 0POSITION, or 0EMPLOYEE variables that you identified as being relevant for authorization.

5.10 Critical Success Factors

SAP NetWeaver BI projects involve a lot of work and should be well planned to generate corresponding added value. This starts by defining objectives.

5.10.1 Defining Objectives

Objectives such as "We want to achieve everything that's possible!" or "With this BI system, we want to achieve what was previously achieved by evaluations" are not sufficient. To achieve a successful outcome for your company along with corresponding benefits, you should invest time and effort in preparing an SAP NetWeaver BI project.

Evaluations of Processes with Derivation of Key Figures

As a starting point, the existing processes should be evaluated. Key figures are derived from these processes to help control and evaluate the process. SAP NetWeaver BI is an evaluation tool designed to assist you in decision-making processes. Not only can the result be a fine graphical display of the development of personnel turnover rates, but it must also help you discover in which areas and the reasons why the turnover rate develops negatively so that you can define measures based on this information. The results of the evaluations must indicate whether the measures you have introduced are effective and changes have been successful.

In Section 2.1, we explain how you can derive key figures based on processes.

Defining and Verifying the Data Basis

After you have defined the key figures, you must check in which data fields of the SAP ERP HCM system the information has been saved and according to which rules it is to be read. One example is the exclusion of inactive employees from evaluations. Can this information be read from a data field such as an employee group, for example, or must this information be derived from specific absences? Another example would be determining the FTE key figure. In practice, a variety of variants are used here, ranging from reading the percentage rate directly from IT0008 (basic pay) to taking overtime and days worked into account for the calculation.

This is a crucial factor because the contents must be compared when standard extractors are checked so that you can decide whether you can use these contents unchanged.

In addition, you must specify whether the required data originate from one system or several sources. For example, this will enable data from areas of the business where an SAP system is not used to be imported by EXCEL files.

Data harmonization may be required in this case, which will have to be designed.

Defining Required Evaluations with Recipients

It is useful to define required evaluations with their recipients when planning the load cycles and authorization concept. You should also specify the form in which the evaluations are to be provided, online with Excel or in the portal or offline by email or in printed form.

5.10.2 Establishing a Project Team

To be able to use SAP NetWeaver BI effectively, expertise in the following areas is required:

Business Knowledge

Although external consultants can use their experience and workshops to help define the necessary requirements, only the employees know the company's business processes. The support of specialist departments and management is therefore required to define relevant key figures and determine necessary evaluations.

Knowledge of the Data Structures Used in SAP ERP HCM

To define and evaluate the data basis, you must determine at the level of the data fields which information is stored in a particular way. To do this, you need to be familiar with data structures and know how they are used. It's not enough to know what type of fields are available; what's important here is how you can use these fields.

Knowledge of Data Modeling in SAP NetWeaver BI

To implement the authorization concept, you need to define the structure of InfoCubes. You must check the standard content provided and enhance it, if necessary, or add your own InfoProviders to it. You need to know how to implement the authorization concept and (with large datasets) optimize performance.

Technical Expertise in SAP NetWeaver BI

You also require technical expertise to implement loading processes and organize transport systems, for example. BI objects are mainly Workbench objects; when you transport these objects, you must observe the effects on the live system.

This expertise should exist in the project team. One person can, of course, cover several areas.

5.10.3 Final Implementation Tips

If the objective is not already clearly outlined, as a basic rule you should always start with small, limited areas when using SAP NetWeaver BI. The requirements will increase automatically, and more InfoCubes can be added at any time. This option is more effective than producing a data garbage dump that no one uses.

Frequently, a BI system that can be used is already available for other SAP modules. As a result, you can start with a manageable number of evaluations to build up your initial experience, and the effort required to set up an additional system will not have to be justified.

Alternatively, a detailed project with the implementation of personnel controlling with support from SAP NetWeaver BI can be a worthwhile project, where the strengths of SAP NetWeaver BI are used with evaluation options and the wide range of variants to present key figures. However, intensive business and technical planning is required here to ensure that the project is successful.

Validating the Standard Content

You should use the standard content first. In practice, you can often use this content with small enhancements. Only if basic problems occur with the logic of the InfoCubes, must you create your own. This is, of course, also required for topics that are not covered in the standard version.

Checking the Quality of Data

Before the live operation, you should perform test runs to check the quality of the data. Initial evaluations in SAP NetWeaver BI frequently reveal poor data quality, which requires maintaining the data in the source system or correcting the extraction and transformation processes.

To enhance the standard functions, you need to create programmed customer reports for company-specific requirements. This chapter helps you optimize the implementation and maintenance effort required.

6 Customer Report

In practice, requirements are too individual and varied for all of them to be covered by the SAP standard tools: There are many industries with different collective agreements, different company sizes, and different business approaches in HR. Self-defined customer reports in these areas enhance the functions of SAP standard reports and the SAP Query, Ad Hoc Query, and SAP NetWeaver BI evaluation tools.

6.1 Defining Requirements

When does a customer report need to be developed? Three all-encompassing questions need to be answered first:

First, three questions

- What is the benefit of this report?
- How much will it cost to implement?
- Are there alternatives?

If your requirements are complex, you will instinctively be able to answer No to the question about the alternatives. This only leaves the cost–benefit analysis to help you decide whether you want to implement this development.

However, with simple evaluations in particular, you should check possible alternatives to programming. You should perform the check in the sequence displayed in Figure 6.1.

Are there alternatives?

Using SAP NetWeaver BI sets the basic course. If you are using BI, you will of course implement all requirement by using BI there.

Otherwise, you will begin looking for alternatives in the standard reporting. Does a standard report exist that could fulfill the requirements (if necessary, supported by report Customizing)? If this is not the case, you can structure the report flexibly using the SAP Query and Ad Hoc Query tools (see Chapter 4, *Queries*). If the evaluation cannot be created using these tools, the only option left is programming.

If many reports need to be programmed (for example, for redesigning HR Reporting), you should first check whether you can reduce future programming and maintenance efforts required — by developing a company-specific logical database, for instance (see Section 6.3) or implementing SAP NetWeaver BI (see Chapter 5). In terms of extensive programming work, additional topics are available that help you reduce the effort required when creating reports and subsequently maintaining them (see Section 6.2).

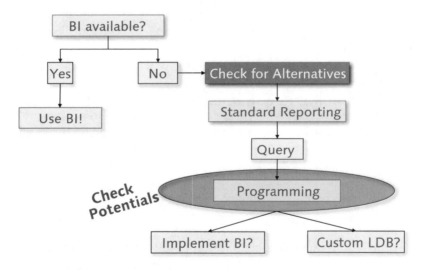

Figure 6.1 Decision Tree for Using Customer Reports

Limitations of the query

One area to consider is evaluations, which can still be mapped with the query but involve a great deal of effort to execute in practice. For example, if you require monthly statistics, whose numbers are compiled from several queries, the effort required to create this information can easily take more than one day. By programming reports that deliver these numbers at the touch of a button, you gain a day during which you can concentrate on evaluating the key figures and do not have to worry about retrieving the relevant data. The time and effort required to program these reports in several executed projects took less than five days.

6.2 Specifications for Programming

Because we can generally assume that multiple customer reports will be created for your company, we recommend that you develop a programming concept before the first programming. Programming specifications reduce the amount of programming and maintenance effort involved.

Reusable parts of the program should be integrated into function modules or classes. These can consequently be made available to many programs. However, this only works if these functions are integrated into a library and made available to programmers as documentation. If this does not happen, although each programmer looks after his own programs and uses these for his own ends, this reduces the intended benefits.

Reusability

The days of spaghetti code, where programs consisted of endless numbers of command lines, should be over. Subprograms can create a program concisely, which enables you to quickly familiarize yourself with the code. You should also observe rules for a structured program layout. This can mean that, for example, in addition to events such as START-OF-SELECTION and END-OF-SELECTION, you only allow PERFORM statements at the highest level.

Structured programming

Naming conventions help you understand the program more quickly. You should begin the names of variables, constants, and internal tables with a defined letter. The subprograms should be given mnemonic names that reflect the relevant function.

Naming conventions

In most cases, reports and other Workbench objects are created in the customer name range beginning with Z. To distinguish objects for the HCM module from other modules, for example, you can use ZHCM. To keep track of the big picture if there are many developments, it is useful to subdivide this further; for example, time management applications can begin with ZHCM_PT. Alternatively, you can also create packages. All HCM developments are frequently assigned to a Z_HCM package. You will find it easier if you define

Customer name ranges

several packages, for example, ZHCM_PT for time management developments.

[+]   SAP has defined name ranges for customers that are not used by standard objects. This prevents any conflicts between customer objects and SAP objects. These name ranges are documented in SAP Note 16466.

Documentation   Besides the documentation for users, documentation for maintaining the system, which describes the implementation, should also be available in addition to the functional specifications. This can also occur directly in the code.

6.3   Using a Company-Specific Logical Database

Shortcomings of the logical database PNPCE

▸ The logical database PNPCE and its fundamental data structures are the basis for many standard reports, InfoSets for the Query and Ad Hoc Query, and customer reports. Its shortcomings therefore reoccur in many evaluations. For example, these include:

▸ **The structure concepts in Infotype 0001 are not generally sufficient to map lower-level structures.**
Whereas Organizational Management can be layered as deeply as required in a hierarchy, the individual organizational levels are not characterized sufficiently. In addition to the department ID, the HR analyst usually requires indicators for management areas, other areas, technical sections, branch offices, teams, and so on.

▸ **The selection and aggregation options available through the personnel structure are not always sufficient.**
Apart from the employee subgroups and positions, Personnel Controlling often requires a grouping of employees based on more or less dynamic criteria such as "outside continued pay period," "maternity leave," "national service," or "on night shift on key date." It would be very time-consuming and unnecessary to change employee subgroups every time these characteristics are changed in order to make clear selections in reports.

▸ **Organizational structures with several dimensions are ignored in the selection.**
These dimensions include the matrix organization and project structure.

▶ **The logical database PNPCE only contains HCM data.**
HCM data, combined with data from Accounting, Logistics, or industry solutions, can only be evaluated outside the logical database. This requires you to have more in-depth knowledge of data structures and know-how to program the authorization check.

The most flexible and comprehensive solution is to use SAP NetWeaver BI (see Chapter 5). To optimize the performance for evaluations, BI is installed on a separate system and works with extracted datasets rather than with real-time data. In addition, the implementation of a Business Information Warehouse frequently originates from departments other than the HR department, so its use often depends on whether it is already being used in the company.

Using SAP NetWeaver BI

One alternative is the company-specific logical database (see Figure 6.2). A separate logical database can encapsulate a large portion of the company-specific logic, which means it does not have to be reprogrammed for every report.

Company-specific logical database

Time				
Key date(s)	01.09.2007			

Projection				
Projection mode	☐ OM at date	01.09.2007		

Organizational Management				
Code		to		⇨
Kind of organizational unit		to		⇨
Another Kind of org. unit		to		⇨
Group network		to ·		⇨
Group		to		⇨
Division		to		⇨
Subsidiary company inland		to		⇨
Subsidiary company abroad		to		⇨
Business area		to		⇨
Place of Service		to		⇨
Cost center		to		⇨
Organizational unit		⇨		
☑ Evaluate org. structure				

Employee				
Personnel number		to		⇨
Company code		to		⇨
Personnel area		to		⇨
Personnel subarea		to		⇨
Employee group		to		⇨
Employee subgroup		to		⇨
Payroll area		to		⇨
Cost center		to		⇨
Job Key		to		⇨
Gender	○ male	○ female	⦿ All	

Figure 6.2 Sample Selection Screen of a Company-Specific Logical Database

Advantages of a
separate logical
database The advantages of programming a separate logical database are as follows:

- **You can use defined and coordinated key figures in all reports.**
  This primarily ensures consistency in the reports and encourages confidence in the report results.

- **You can compare the reports against each other.**
  Due to the uniform data source, the results between the reports can be compared, and the results of reprogrammed reports can be validated more quickly.

- **You can flexibly define your own selection and aggregation criteria.**
  An employee's affiliation to an aggregation level can be determined at runtime based on dynamic criteria. The selection is no longer only restricted to organizational units. For example, you can maintain additional criteria on the organizational unit in a separate infotype and use it as selection criteria and aggregation levels (see Figure 6.2).

- **The authorization concept is flexible.**
  Access to reports is not restricted by the structural organization and the check performed on personnel master data. You can also assign employees to VIP levels based on different criteria. Depending on the target group, you can also design the selection screen, choice of fields, and the option to change the layout of a report.

- **You can reduce the number of reports.**
  Based on the described flexibility of the authorization concept, you can create several variants using just one report for a flexible employee list, thereby fulfilling several requirements. No programming knowledge is required to create variants. Personnel Controlling is completely flexible and can immediately process new queries itself. For example, variants of this employee list can include Anonymous employee list," "Severely challenged employees," "Overview of semiretirements," "Age-related retirements," and so on.

- **You can reduce the effort required for programming reports.**
  Since the data and calculations are already processed in the logical database, new reports can be created more efficiently.

▶ **You can reduce the maintenance effort required.**
Since the processing and calculations only take place once and do not have to be repeated in every program, you can make adjustments considerably more quickly, and these are also applied to all the reports based on this logical database. In addition, this increases the security and data quality in the reports.

The reasons why this method is so seldom used are as follows:

Why customer logical databases are so seldom developed

▶ This option is not well known.

▶ The workload required to develop a separate logical database is overestimated.

▶ The additional evaluations are developed on an individual basis as required, and therefore the potential to consolidate them is overlooked.

▶ It is easier to obtain a small budget several times for specific requirements than a somewhat bigger budget for a one-time investment in the future.

▶ Users do not want to take on the workload involved in initially having to define a full Personnel Controlling concept and, consequently, a clean structure.

Even if these reasons are often difficult to overcome, in our experience it is worth the effort. You must have previously clarified that the standard solution is inadequate in some places and that several reports need to be programmed.

The following reasons for using a separate logical database are as follows:

Reasons for using a logical database

▶ Employee groups and subgroups are not suitable for reporting.

▶ Complex personnel change statistics are required.

▶ Users constantly need aggregations at defined organizational levels that cannot be mapped using organizational criteria from Infotype 0001 and the neutral concept of the organizational unit in Organizational Management.

▶ Employee data must be combined with data from cross-HCM modules or external sources of data.

▶ The standard authorization concept for reporting is inadequate.

6.4   Critical Success Factors

If the first reports are programmed, new requirements quickly follow. The option to be able to implement almost every requirement individually is tempting.

Reporting is often postponed and poorly planned in implementation projects. This means lists are suddenly expected shortly before or sometimes only after the system has gone live, which no one had thought of beforehand. Operational panic erupts, and the required customer reports are produced in a minimum amount of time. As a result, the reports are not adequately documented, no programming guidelines are specified, and the requirements cannot be evaluated correctly. The only important thing is that the reports are made available quickly.

The implementation effort required is also frequently estimated insufficiently and without due thought. This is due to a reluctance to face the relevant costs. Who willingly says to his IT manager, I need programmers for 100 days' programming of customer reports."? It is easier to request 10 days here for one evaluation and 15 days there for another evaluation. This procedure cannot take into account concepts such as developing a separate logical database (see Section 6.3) or customer-specific function modules or classes that provide functions that can be used in many reports.

Therefore, the following points should be included in the planning:

▸ **Requirements should be defined and the implementation should be planned at an early stage.**
The requirements should be defined as functional specifications. The more complicated the requirement, the more necessary a description of the required evaluation. This will make the implementation process easier, because the programmer gets a clear overview of what is required. Improvements do not have to be repeatedly made, and (in a worse-case scenario) program components do not have to be completely renewed. The functional specifications can be enhanced for future requirements or release upgrades and are important documentation for maintaining the system.

▸ **The scope should be view in its entirety.**
If there are larger programming projects, they should be viewed

in their entirety. Using reusable code in the form of function modules and classes can greatly reduce the development work and the future maintenance effort required.

▶ **Maintenance of the reports should be planned.**
Release upgrades, Unicode conversions, and changes in the processes require adjustments in the programs. To reduce this maintenance effort, consider the points mentioned: Providing programming and documentation guidelines makes the maintenance of programs independent of individual users and helps them still be able to understand the programming at a later stage. Using function modules and classes provides functions that can be used in many programs. It is therefore sufficient for you to adapt the function just once, instead of having to change each program.

PART III
Reporting in HCM Modules

In the third part of this book, we give you an overview of the standard evaluations and their possible uses in the individual HCM modules. We explain their strengths and weaknesses in each case. You will also become familiar with the SAP NetWeaver BI standard content for each HCM module.

This introduction will give you an initial overview of what you can expect from the following chapters relating to standard reporting in HCM modules and how you can use the chapters efficiently.

7 Introduction to Part III

Standard evaluations are tools that are delivered by SAP and are available to the user for reporting purposes at no additional cost or effort. However, these tools cannot fulfill all the specific requirements of the user. They do not claim to be custom-made but are considered to be "off-the-rack" tools. Like fashion, while these tools meet the necessary requirements, users may not find them suitable for modern and contemporary outputs. Whereas in the past the output of a formatted list was sufficient, nowadays the user requires an output that he can adapt to suit his own requirements and that must also contain graphical formatting of the data.

In the third part of this book, we give you an overview of the standard evaluations and their possible uses in SAP ERP HCM. Since the modules in the data structure and the requirements differ considerably in parts, we will differentiate by modules here. We will show you the strengths and weaknesses of evaluations in relevant modules. Because more than 200 standard evaluations are available in SAP Human Resources Management, in the following chapters we will only discuss some selected reports that reflect the possibilities and weaknesses of standard reporting.

The reports (*evaluation* and *list* are also synonyms) presented here are executable programs that read data from the database and evaluate it without making any changes to the database.

Some of the reports presented here are created and generated using the SAP Query. You will recognize these reports by the ABAP program name that begins with AQZZ and by the missing documentation in the selection screen of the report. The documentation for

SAP Query reports

189

these reports is available in the SAP library under **SAP ERP Central Component** • **Human Resources** • **Reporting in Human Resources** in the corresponding HCM modules.

Standard reports

The standard reports are available in the SAP Easy Access menu in the infosystems of the individual HCM modules or in the HCM information system (**Personnel** • **Infosystem** • **Reports**). The HCM standard reports are also bundled in the SAP Easy Access menu in the cross-application infosystems. In the next chapters, we only describe the path for the individual HCM modules.

SAP NetWeaver BI

Since SAP NetWeaver BI is a special type of evaluation, each chapter for the individual modules contains its own subchapter, where the HCM Business Content is discussed. The Business Content of SAP Human Resources (HCM) enables you to access predefined business standard reports and key figures very easily. You can use the HCM Business Content to perform evaluations directly, present other views, and evaluate the data. The HCM Business Content is available in the SAP menu of SAP NetWeaver BI under the path **Business Information Warehouse** • **Modeling** • **Data Warehousing Workbench: BI Content**.

Displaying queries

You can use the Query Designer to output the existing queries in Excel or directly on the Web. To display a query on the Web, click the **Display Query on Web** button in the Query Designer. Figure 7.1 shows the **Number of Positions** query in Internet Explorer®. For more detailed information about this query, refer to Chapter 9, *Organizational Management*.

To output a query in Excel (see Figure 7.3), you must start the Analyzer in the Business Explorer. Like the Query Designer, you will find this in the start menu of your operating system, as shown in Figure 7.2 for Windows XP.

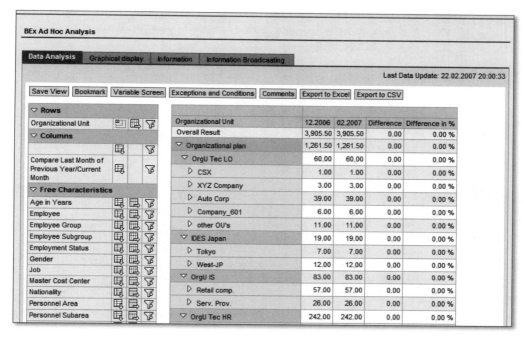

Figure 7.1 Displaying a Query on the Web

Figure 7.2 Start Menu in Windows XP (Business Explorer)

Figure 7.3 shows the **Number of Positions** query, as displayed in Figure 7.1, in an Excel file.

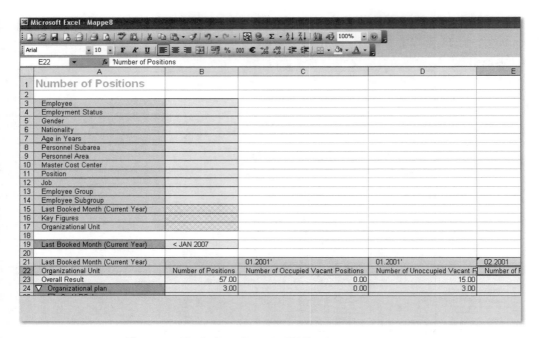

Figure 7.3 Displaying a Query in MS Excel

Modules in Part III of this book   In the following chapters, we will introduce reporting in the following HCM modules in more detail:

- ▶ Personnel Administration (Chapter 8)
- ▶ Organizational Management (Chapter 9)
- ▶ Recruitment (Chapter 10)
- ▶ Payroll (Chapter 11)
- ▶ Personnel Time Management (Chapter 12)
- ▶ Personnel Development (Chapter 13)
- ▶ Benefits (Chapter 14)
- ▶ Training and Event Management (Chapter 15)
- ▶ Personnel Cost Planning (Chapter 16)

Personnel Administration reports consist of evaluations for individual employees, employees within the organizational units, and the logging of changes to employee data.

8   Personnel Administration

Personnel administration is the basis for all other processes in Personnel Management. It is composed of all tasks ranging from the employment through to the resignation of an employee. Reporting supports the varied range of administration tasks, to which the reporting of a company also belongs. In the SAP Easy Access menu, the reporting is divided according to employee data, organizational data, and document creation. In relation to employee data, reporting such as the HR master data sheet, for example, is created for each employee. In terms of organizational data, the user can use reports to create evaluations within the organizational units or the entire company. One such report is the headcount change. Infotype changes and report starts are logged when you create a document. This supports the auditing security of the SAP system.

You can access the Personnel Administration reporting in the SAP Easy Access menu by selecting the path **Human Resources • Personnel Management • Administration • Info System • Reports**. The **Reports** path is divided into **Employees, Organizational Data, Documents,** and other country dependences reports.

SAP Easy Access path

8.1   Employee-Related Reports

Employee-related reports evaluate the personal data of employees such as educational details, date of birth, actions, and information about when an employee started or left employment.

8.1.1   Flexible Employee Data

The Flexible Employee Data report displays up to a maximum of 20 of 92 fields for a key date from the personal and organizational data of one or more employees. This report does not have the flexibility of an SAP Query, because you can only add new fields by adapting the report.

To be able to start this reporting, you do not have to have authorization to use all information types that can be evaluated using this report. You can check the authorization based on the selected fields.

You can only start the report if you have selected at least one field from the field selection. To do this, click on the **Field selection** button under **Additional data** (see Figure 8.1). Select your fields for the list here. You must also select the **Personnel Number**. The fields under **Selection** are not automatically transferred to the list display.

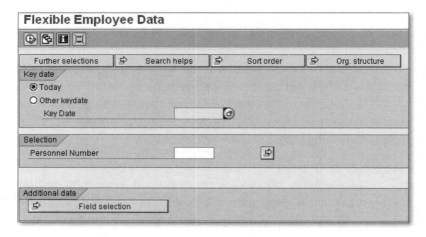

Figure 8.1 Flexible Employee Data Selection Screen

ALV grid control   The reporting result is displayed as a list in the ALV grid control format (see Figure 8.2).

[Ex]   In the ALV grid control, you can no longer add fields that you did not previously also transfer into the field selection. You must also select the relevant plain text in the field selection for many indicators such as the cost center.

Flexible Employee Data

Key date: 10.07.2007

Personnel Number	Last Name	Personnel Area	Cost Center
00109553	Gasson	Atlanta	0000009515
00109554	Miller	Atlanta	0000009515
00109555	Johnson	Atlanta	0000009515
00109556	Smoltz	Atlanta	0000009510
00109557	Maddux	Atlanta	0000009510
00109558	Millwood	Atlanta	0000009510

Figure 8.2 Flexible Employee Data List

8.1.2 HR Master Data Sheet

The HR Master Data Sheet report creates the HR master data sheet for one or more employees. The data is displayed as an ABAP list, which means there are also limitations to how this list is displayed and printed. Only normal or bold face type is possible, and only one font type can be printed. To see what an HR master data sheet looks like when you use SAPscript, you can start the RPLSTMC0 report, which is the HR master data sheet for Switzerland.

The HR master data sheet uses data from the following internal info- Infotypes types for printing:

- Actions (0000)
- Organizational assignment (0001)
- Personal data (0002)
- Addresses (0006)
- Planned working time (0007)
- Basic pay (0008)
- Bank details (0009)
- Recurring payments and deductions (0014)
- Contract components (0016)
- Next of kin/contact person (0021)
- Education (0022)
- Date specifications (0041)

You control the display of the HR master data sheet in the **Print one/more page(s)** field of the selection screen. This field is predefined with MZHA in the standard system. You can use this entry to display the HR master data sheet over several pages, if necessary. The master data sheet is displayed on one page for all other entries. Correspondingly less data is then also printed.

When you use the XP02 standard form, you must not make any changes to the tables of the form control (see Figure 8.3). However, this is rarely the case, since bonuses outside the basic pay mean you have to maintain the wage types to be printed in the **Form-Related Control of Wage Types** (V_T512E) table. Note that this form is language dependent. It currently only exists in country version 01 for Germany and should be copied to the corresponding country version in advance. However, you can print this form beforehand as a test. To do this, enter 01 for Germany in the **Country grouping** field on the selection screen.

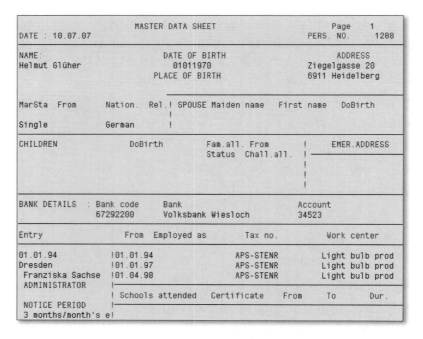

Figure 8.3 Extract from the HR Master Data Sheet

When you develop your own form, you must maintain the following tables/views:

- Form-Related Control of Wage Types (V_T512E)
- Form Background (V_T512P)
- Information in Fixed Positions (V_T512Q)
- Form Windows (V_T512F)

The views maintenance is not available in a coherent form in the IMG of Customizing. Instead, maintain the views using the enhanced table maintenance in the menu (**System • Services • Table maintenance • Extended table maintenance**) in transaction SM30. We do not recommend maintaining this form in transaction PE51, the HR form editor, because it suggests displaying data fields that cannot be displayed in the HR master data sheet.

8.1.3 Date Monitoring

The Date Monitoring report evaluates the **Monitoring of Tasks** (0019) infotype. In addition to the selection options of the logical database PNP, you can filter data through the **Task, Reminder date, Task type,** and **Processing indicator** fields of infotype 0019. The **Personnel Administrator** from the **Organizational Assignment** information type is also available.

The following fields are displayed depending on the selection:

Fields of the report

- Task
- Reminder date
- Processing indicator (numeric value)
- Processing indicator (text)
- Task type (numeric value)
- Task type (text)
- Personnel number
- First name
- Last name
- Remarks (line 1 to 3)

> The date monitoring is a report generated through the SAP Query. It has replaced the Date Monitoring report (RPPTRM00) with Release 4.6C. You can therefore no longer go directly from the list into the Monitoring of tasks infotype for processing purposes.   **[!]**

197

As is the case in every generated SAP Query, you are offered a variety of output options in the selection screen (see Figure 8.4). These options are otherwise only available in the output in the ALV grid. The selection ranges from the List Viewer to the storage of data in a local file.

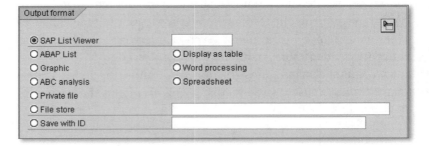

Figure 8.4 Output Options of the Date Monitoring Report

8.1.4 Education

The Education report creates an evaluation of the education of your employees based on the data in the infotype of the same name (0022). You can use this report, generated from an SAP Query, to filter employees across cost centers, education, school diploma, school type, and branch of study. The following data are output in the report:

► Personnel number

► First name

► Last name

► School type text

► School diploma text

► Education text

► User department

► Institute/location

► Cost center

With the exception of the cost center, no additional organizational data about the employee is available in this report for outputting.

8.1.5   Time Spent in Pay Scale Group/Level

The Time Spent in Pay Scale Group/Level report (RPLTRF10) displays the assignment to wage level and the time spent in pay scale group/level of the individual employees. You can further restrict the selected employees to pay scale areas, types, groups, and levels.

The report outputs the names of the employees in a table, together with the following data from the **Basic pay** infotype (0008):

► Personnel number

► Name of employee

► Pay scale area, type, group, level

► Date as of which the individual employee appears in the current assignment

► Time spent in pay scale group/level in years and months

> You cannot use this report to determine missing infotype basic pay for an   **[+]**
> employee. Use the Assignment to Wage Level report for this purpose (see
> Section 8.2.3).

You can use the RPLTRF10 report (**Human Resources · Personnel Management · Administration · Information System · Reports · Employees · Defaults for Pay Scale Reclassification** in the SAP Easy Access menu) to display default values for the next pay scale reclassification for the individual employees. However, this only makes sense if your collective agreement provides a reclassification when a certain age has been reached, or following a particular time spent in pay scale group/level for a pay scale group. You can use the Pay Scale Reclassification According to Age or Pay Scale Membership Period report (RPITUM00) to achieve an automatic pay scale reclassification when an employee has reached a certain age or after a particular time spent in the pay scale group/level for a pay scale group.

8.1.6   List of Maternity Data

The List of Maternity Data report creates a list of saved maternity cases and related absences. The prerequisite here is that you have maintained the absence times of the maternity protection using the **Maternity protection/parental leave** infotype (0080).

In addition, you can only output a list of maternity cases that have not yet been reported to the supervisory authorities, as shown in Figure 8.5. Select the **Only display unreported cases** field for this purpose.

Personnel No.	Empl./appl.name	Personnel area	Pers. subarea	Cost Center	Start Date	End Date	Notified on	Ex.del.dt.	Ac.del.dt.	Reported on
Att./abs. type	A/A type text	Start Date	End Date							
1023 Nicole Hörter	1300	0001		2200	29.06.2006	31.12.9999	29.06.2006	20.08.2006	20.08.2006
0500	Maternity protection 09.07.2006 15.10.2006									
1024 Nicole Hörter	1300	0001		2200	20.03.2006	31.12.9999	29.06.2006	20.08.2006	20.08.2006
0500	Maternity protection 09.07.2006 15.10.2006									
0510	Maternity protection 20.03.2006 02.05.2006									
60101196 Nora Neun	DE01	1000			29.06.2006	31.12.9999	06.09.2006	20.08.2006	20.08.2006
0500	Maternity protection 09.07.2006 15.10.2006									

Figure 8.5 List of Unreported Maternity Cases

8.1.7 Employees Entered/Left the Company

Use the Entries/Leavings report to create a list of employees who have joined or left the company at a particular time. The ENTRY characteristic (rule for determining the entry date) stores information about which infotype should be used to determine the initial entry date. You can use the following infotypes to determine the date in the characteristic:

- Actions (0000)
- Organizational assignment (0001)
- Contract elements — initial entry date or entry into group (0016)
- Date specifications — specific date types (0041)

[+] If you do not determine the entry date from these infotypes, you can also use the HRPAD00_ENTRY_LEAVE Business Add-In to program an entry or leaving date that corresponds to your requirements.

If required, you can restrict these actions further in the selection screen. Under **Program selections**, you can limit the entries and leavings to a particular date. The following data is output in the standard system:

- Personnel number
- First name
- Last name
- Entry

▶ Leaving

▶ Organizational unit

▶ Name of organizational unit

The Headcount Change report in the SAP Easy Access menu **Human Resources • Personnel Management • Administration • Information System • Reports • Organizational Unit** provides additional fields for outputting the data. However, you must assign the **personnel action types** that contain the data about an employee leaving the company (see Section 8.2.1). The entry date is always displayed in this list.

8.1.8 Anniversary of Years of Service

You can use the Anniversary of Years of Service report to create a list of employees' years of service that occur over the course of a year. Under **Program selection**, you can only evaluate certain anniversaries under **Anniversary in Years**. For example, you may only want to display the employees who celebrate their 25th anniversary in this year. The list only contains the **Personnel number, Last name, First name, Entry date**, and **Years (Anniversary)** fields.

Note that this report only evaluates the **Personnel actions** (0001) infotype. An initial entry date that may occur in the **Contract elements** (0016) or **Date specifications** (0041) infotypes is ignored.

8.1.9 Power of Attorney

Use this report to evaluate the subtypes of the **Powers of attorney** infotype (0030). The comment lines are not contained in the list. The **Personnel No., Last name, First name, Power of attorney type**, and **Org. Unit** fields are output (see Figure 8.6).

Powers of attorney

Personnel No.	Last name	First name	Power of attorney	Power of attorney key	Org. Unit	Name of Organizational Unit
00070043	Grant	Nancy	General commercial power of attorney	02	50012481	Human Resources
00100241	Parker	John	Limited commercial powers of attorney	01	50000603	Compensation and Benefits - (US)
00109503	Richardson	Cathryn	P.of attorney for banking transactions	03	50020339	United Kingdom Subsidiary

Figure 8.6 Powers of Attorney List

If you do not fill the **Power of Attorney Type** program selection, the employees are also displayed without a **Powers of attorney** infotype in the list.

8.1.10 Family Members

Use this report to evaluate the subtypes of the **Next of kin/contact person** infotype (0021). The comment lines are not contained in this list. The **Personnel number, Name of Employee or Application**, and **Entry date of employee** are output from the **Personnel action infotype** (see Figure 8.7). The **Family relationship, Last name, First name**, and **Date of Birth** fields are listed for the family member. If you only want to display employees for whom the **Family Member/Dependents** infotype is maintained, you must fill the Type of **Family membership in the** program selection.

Family members

Personnel number	Name of Employee or Applicant	Family relationship	First name	Last name	Date of Birth
00000010	Herr James Bond				
00000069	Mr. Horatio Holder	Spouse	Harriet	Holder	01.01.1960
00000069	Mr. Horatio Holder	Child	Harold	Holder	01.01.1998
00000070	Miss Beryl Broughton				
00000071	Mr. Harry Hill				
00000072	Miss Freda Fish				
00000073	Mr. Colman Mustard				
00001000	Anja Müller	Spouse	Hans-Joachim	Müller	12.10.1955
00001000	Anja Müller	Child	Anna Sophie	Müller	11.11.2006
00001001	Michaela Maier				
00001002	Dipl.Kfm. Ulrike Zaucker	Spouse	Michael	Zaucker	06.04.1959
00001002	Dipl.Kfm. Ulrike Zaucker	Child	Maximilian	Zaucker	25.02.1991
00001002	Dipl.Kfm. Ulrike Zaucker	Child	Katharina	Zaucker	12.06.1993

Figure 8.7 Family Members List

8.1.11 Birthday List

Use the Birthday list report to create a list of employees' birthdays. In addition to the date of birth, the list contains the age of the employees on the current date. Figure 8.8 displays an example of a birthday list.

Birthday list

Personnel No.	Last name	First name	Entry	Leaving date	Date of Birth	Day	DoB	Year	Month	Gend.	Cost ctr	Org. Unit	Age of employee
00109202	Jamison	Michele	00.00.0000	31.12.9999	03.05.1960	03	0305	1960	05	2	9520	50024604	46
00109203	Worthington	Amy	00.00.0000	31.12.9999	14.04.1965	14	1404	1965	04	2	9520	50024604	41
00109204	Hoffman	Robert	00.00.0000	31.12.9999	07.06.1968	07	0706	1968	06	1	9520	50014498	38
00109205	Connors	Michael	00.00.0000	31.12.9999	14.04.1965	14	1404	1965	04	1	9525	50014500	41
00109206	Soprano	Anthony	00.00.0000	31.12.9999	01.09.1962	01	0109	1962	09	1	9520	50024604	44
00109207	Fox	Michael	00.00.0000	31.12.9999	01.08.1965	01	0108	1965	08	1	9520	50024598	41
00109208	Jeter	Derek	00.00.0000	31.12.9999	03.09.1973	03	0309	1973	09	1	9520	50024598	33
00109209	Iverson	Allen	00.00.0000	31.12.9999	01.09.1975	01	0109	1975	09	1	9522	50027396	31
00109210	Snow	Eric	00.00.0000	31.12.9999	03.07.1973	03	0307	1973	07	1	9522	50027396	33
00109211	McKie	Aaron	00.00.0000	31.12.9999	03.09.1975	03	0309	1975	09	1	9522	50027401	31
00109212	Lynch	George	00.00.0000	31.12.9999	04.06.1972	04	0406	1972	06	1	9522	50027401	34
00109213	Crow	Sheryl	00.00.0000	31.12.9999	20.07.1975	20	2007	1975	07	2	9522	50027396	31

Figure 8.8 Birthday List

This list enables you to sort the employees' dates of birth in different ways according to month, day, and year. You can also sort the information according to organizational unit and cost center, although a page break in the output would be useful for dividing the lists, for example, each time you change the organizational unit. This is a flaw in almost all lists that use the ALV grid. Other data about the employee such as the personnel area and the plain text for the organizational unit and cost center, for example, would also be useful here.

8.1.12 Vehicle Search List

The Vehicle Search List report creates a list of your employees' license plate numbers stored in the **Internal Data** infotype (0032). In addition to the license plate numbers, the building number, room number, and In-House Telephone Number from infotype 0032 are also listed (see Figure 8.9). You can also use these fields to further restrict the selection under **Program selections**. In addition to the personnel number and name, the payroll area, company code, and cost center are also printed.

> In this case also, if you do not enter anything in the program selections, the employees without the control data infotype are also displayed. **[+]**

Vehicle search list

Personnel No.	First name	Last name	License Plate Number	Tel.	BirNo	RoomN	Payr.area	CoCd	Cost ctr
00001025	Christine	Rottenbaum	PFM-WS 2543	6137	9	75	D2	1000	2200
00001026	Johanna	Browning	STC-RG 9865	4058	0	119	D2	1000	1000
00001027	Martin	Jost	TIQ-CU 7751	7318	0	217	D2	1000	3200
00001028	Matthias	Klocke	GKB-OJ 8259	4904	5	261	D2	1000	4120
00001029	Jan	Kubat	ELL-XT 4174	1012	17	199	D2	1000	1000
00001030	Arnim	Sachsen	QIV-EH 1404	8580	7	240	D2	1000	2100
00001031	Maria	Rauenberger	SXV-TJ 9899	523	6	65	D2	1000	2200
00001032	Martin	Beck	RIF-UO 8913	269	1	283	D2	1000	2200
00001033	Michaela	Bayerle	VDW-UU 7001	141	12	215	D2	1000	2200
00001034	Lydia	Schiffer	NO-DT 2441	6568	19	286	D2	1000	2100
00001035	Barbara	Schröder	NM-XG 9118	9663	1	69	D2	1000	2100
00001036	Walburga	Ludewig	KQL-TK 1141	8870	10	278	D2	1000	2300
00001037	Karin	Anselm	FGL-VK 9765	8834	7	106	D2	1000	2100

Figure 8.9 Vehicle Search List

8.1.13   Telephone Directory

You can use the Telephone List report to create different telephone directories of employees. You can evaluate internal and external telephone extensions and other communication types, such as email addresses, stored in the **Communication** infotype (0105) and print these as a directory.

You can also select the employees according to zip code. Under **Output data**, select the type of connections you want the system to evaluate:

▸ If you select **External Telephone Extensions**, the system always evaluates all the telephone numbers stored in the Addresses infotype (0006).

▸ Use **Internal Telephone Extensions** to select the entered telephone numbers in the Internal Data infotype (0032).

▸ Under **Internal Communications**, the system evaluates all the extensions stored in the Internal Data (0032) and Communication (0105) infotypes. You can restrict the data from the Communication infotype using the Communications selection option by entering the corresponding subtypes.

▸ If you select the Only Known Telephone Numbers field, only employees whose telephone numbers were stored in the Addresses infotype (0006) and Internal Data infotype (0032) are displayed. If you select Internal Communications, the indicator in the Only Known Telephone Numbers field is ignored in the reporting. You can use the Internal Communications selection option to restrict the internal communications by maintaining the corresponding subtypes.

▸ You can use the **With Personnel Number** selection to display the employees' personnel numbers in the list output.

▸ If you also want to output the employees' addresses, select **With Address**.

▸ If you select the **As a Directory** option, the system automatically sorts the information according to the name of the employees. The list is formatted in individual pages that you can insert into a standard telephone directory. Figure 8.10 displays an example of the telephone list output as a directory.

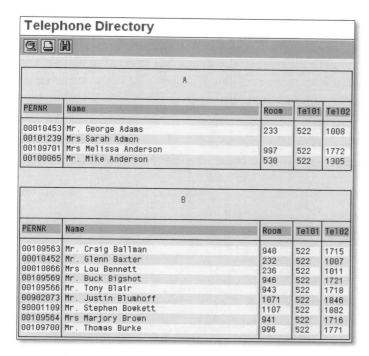

Telephone Directory

A

PERNR	Name	Room	Tel01	Tel02
00010453	Mr. George Adams	233	522	1008
00101239	Mrs Sarah Admon			
00109701	Mrs Melissa Anderson	997	522	1772
00100065	Mr. Mike Anderson	530	522	1305

B

PERNR	Name	Room	Tel01	Tel02
00109563	Mr. Craig Ballman	940	522	1715
00010452	Mr. Glenn Baxter	232	522	1007
00010866	Mrs Lou Bennett	236	522	1011
00109569	Mr. Buck Bigshot	946	522	1721
00109566	Mr. Tony Blair	943	522	1718
00902073	Mr. Justin Blumhoff	1071	522	1846
90001109	Mr. Stephen Bowkett	1107	522	1882
00109564	Mrs Marjory Brown	941	522	1716
00109700	Mr. Thomas Burke	996	522	1771

Figure 8.10 Telephone Directory

If you want an output as a directory, you must not specify a sort sequence. **[+]**

8.2 Organizational Data

The reporting that refers to organizational units such as personnel area and organizational unit provides you with an overview of the organizational data in your company, for example, in the headcount changes or salary structure.

8.2.1 Headcount Change

The Headcount Change report creates a list of personnel actions that have been performed for employees in the selected period.

Under **Program selections**, define those **action types that you want to be evaluated**. You can therefore restrict the selection to particular types of personnel actions. You can also use **Date of action** to limit the period for the actions to be evaluated if you want this period to differ from the selection period.

Displayed fields In addition to the entry date, the data of all selected actions is also displayed in the list. The entry date is determined in the same way as in the "Entries and Leavings" list (see Section 8.1.7). The following fields are displayed:

- ▶ Personnel number
- ▶ First name
- ▶ Last name
- ▶ Entry date
- ▶ Action type
- ▶ Name of action type
- ▶ Valid from date
- ▶ Organizational unit
- ▶ Name of organizational unit
- ▶ Personnel area
- ▶ Text for personnel area
- ▶ Employee subgroup
- ▶ Text for employee subgroup
- ▶ Employee group
- ▶ Text for employee group
- ▶ Cost center

8.2.2 Headcount Development

This report determines the headcount development based on the organizational unit that employees belong to within a selected payroll period. You must therefore enter details about the payroll area and payroll period under **Payroll period** in the report selection screen.

If you want to evaluate more than one period, **under Additional data** specify the **Selection periods** from to that you want to be displayed in the list. You can then use the **Key date** to determine the key date for which you want the employees to be evaluated. The **First**, **Middle**, and **Last** day of the payroll period is available here.

You can use the **Pages in sequence order** to decide whether you want to display the list output of the report on the screen or create a printable list version. You have the following options to enter data:

Maintaining a list output

▶ If you do not make an entry, you receive an interactive list with the option to output the information as an SAP business graphic. The interface for the SAP business graphic in this case allows tables with up to 31 rows. If the displayed screen list is bigger than 31 rows, a screen appears in which you are asked to reduce the dataset further by aggregating it. If you evaluate more than one year, you get a maximum of 12 months per page. You can switch between the years using the buttons for the next and previous periods.

▶ With the X parameter, you receive a printable list. If you select more than 12 months, for example, all 12 months maximum are displayed beside one another. The next periods then follow under this period.

▶ With 1, you create a list like the one created with the X parameter, but with a divider for a new period.

▶ With 2, you create a list like the one created with the X parameter, but with two dividers for a new period.

The list separates the results according to the set selections available under **Key date in period**:

▶ Personnel area

▶ Personnel subarea

▶ Employee group

▶ Employee subgroup

In Figure 8.11, a list covering a span of two years is displayed using the **Pages in sequence order parameter "X."**

If you have set the SAP XXL List Viewer parameter, the report is transferred to Microsoft Excel as a normal table or pivot table. The **Pages in sequence order** parameter must not be filled in this case.

[+]

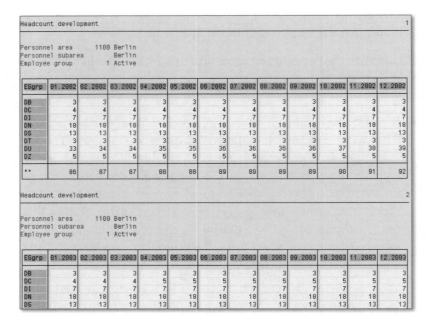

Figure 8.11 Headcount Development 2002/03 List

8.2.3 Assignment to Wage Level

The Assignment to Wage Level report (Figure 8.12) creates a list of the assignments to wage level of employees based on the **Basic Pay** infotype (0008) with the **Basic Contract** subtype (0).

Customizing

Under **Additional data**, you can enter the following details, which determine how the selected data are evaluated:

▶ Nationality

▶ Country grouping

▶ Pay scale area

▶ Pay scale type

▶ Pay scale group

▶ Pay scale level

▶ New entries in time interval

[+] You can perform the reporting on a gender-specific or generic basis.

The reporting results are displayed as a table, whereby a separate table is output for each pay scale area. The system creates a row for each pay scale type. If the selected employees belong to several pay scale areas, a table displays the grouped results after the individual tables.

The reporting contains the number of employees in the assignment to wage level, subdivided by male and female employees. The results are displayed in absolute numbers and percentages. The last column of the table shows the duration of the time spent in pay scale group/level of employees in years.

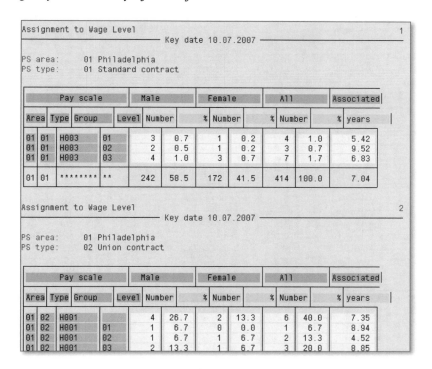

Assignment to Wage Level — Key date 10.07.2007 — 1

PS area: 01 Philadelphia
PS type: 01 Standard contract

Pay scale				Male		Female		All		Associated
Area	Type	Group	Level	Number	%	Number	%	Number	%	years
01	01	H003	01	3	0.7	1	0.2	4	1.0	5.42
01	01	H003	02	2	0.5	1	0.2	3	0.7	9.52
01	01	H003	03	4	1.0	3	0.7	7	1.7	6.83
01	01	********	**	242	58.5	172	41.5	414	100.0	7.04

Assignment to Wage Level — Key date 10.07.2007 — 2

PS area: 01 Philadelphia
PS type: 02 Union contract

Pay scale				Male		Female		All		Associated
Area	Type	Group	Level	Number	%	Number	%	Number	%	years
01	02	H001		4	26.7	2	13.3	6	40.0	7.35
01	02	H001	01	1	6.7	0	0.0	1	6.7	8.94
01	02	H001	02	1	6.7	1	6.7	2	13.3	4.52
01	02	H001	03	2	13.3	1	6.7	3	20.0	8.85

Figure 8.12 Assignment to Wage Level List

If the system cannot include personnel numbers in the reporting, it issues an error list at the end, which displays the individual personnel numbers and the reasons why they were rejected.

Error list

8.2.4 Salary According to Seniority List

The Salary According to Seniority report calculates the average annual salaries of employees, broken down by cost centers or organizational units and the seniority of the employees. The reporting performed is based on key dates because the payment dates are not standardized.

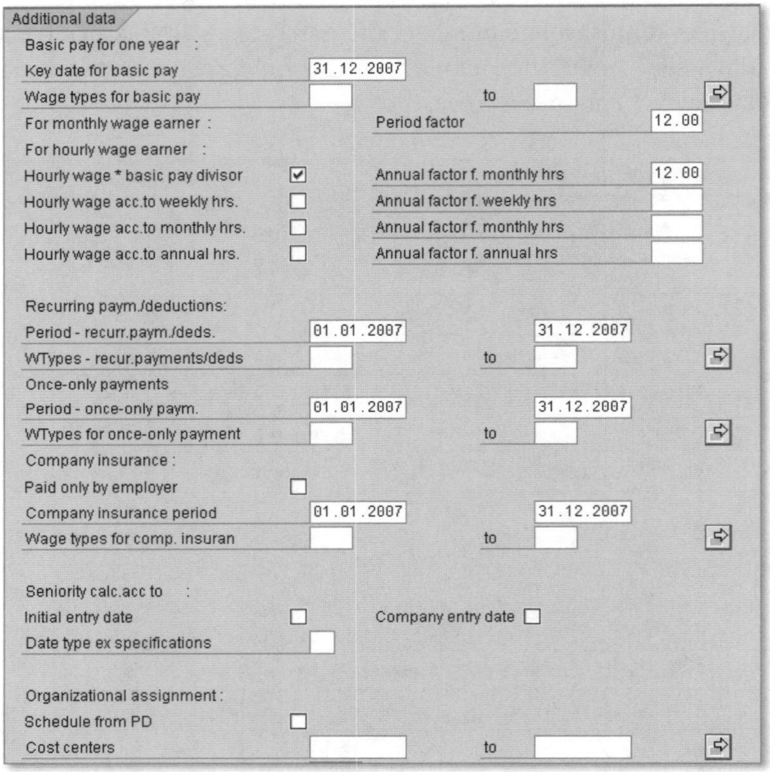

Figure 8.13 Additional Data for Salary by Seniority List

Under **Additional data** (see Figure 8.13), enter data that will provide a basis for the program run. The system provides some time values as default values, but you can overwrite these.

The entries that you include in this framework refer to the following factors:

- ▶ Payments
- ▶ Seniority

▶ Organizational assignment

▶ Currency

The list displays the average annual salaries for each cost center or organizational unit. The annual salaries are displayed within the individual lists, broken down by seniority. Each list shows the total amount of salaries in the reporting period under **Total salary** (see Figure 8.14). In addition, the average salary calculated from this total is displayed for each employee as well as the number of all evaluated employees.

Salary Information			
Seniority	Number of employees		Average salary
00	9	USD	2,211.25
01	2	USD	0.00
02	11	USD	424.24
Total salary		USD	24,567.95
Average salary per employee		USD	1,116.73
Employee(s)			22
Salary Information			

Figure 8.14 Annual Salaries by Seniority List

However, when interpreting the annual salary values, you should bear in mind that the reporting does not reflect the actual values for an employee but simply represents a projection of the values for a key date in a year.

The infotypes **Basic Pay** (0008), **Company Insurance** (0026), **Additional Payments** (0015) and **Recurring Payments/Deductions** (0014) **are** taken into account in the reporting.

The salaries for part-time employees are projected up to the annual salary for full-time work, based on the specified capacity utilization levels in the **Basic Pay** infotype (0008) so they can be compared with the salaries of full-time employees.

You can also display the result as an SAP business graphic. You can use the graphic display to compare the results for the cost centers or organizational units with each other.

8.2.5   Other Reporting for an Organizational Unit

Lists that contain information about nationality, gender, age, and seniority are additional reports you can use for an organizational unit within Personnel Administration.

▶ The Nationality report gives you a list of nationalities of your employees based on a key date, broken down according to gender. In the selection, you can define which country is to apply as the domestic country for the reporting. You can also specifically identify EU members.

▶ The Gender Sorted by Age report creates statistics about the age of your employees, broken down by gender.

▶ The Gender Sorted by Seniority report creates statistics about your employees according to their seniority, broken down by gender. In the selection, you can restrict the seniority to be evaluated.

8.3   Documents

The reporting in the Documents area supports the auditing security within Personnel Administration. The auditing is supported by printing the logged changes in the data of the information types and of the logging of report starts.

8.3.1   Logged Changes in Infotype Data

The Logged Changes in Infotype Data report (Figure 8.15) displays all changes in the infotypes that have been created using the infotype log creation . In addition to the infotypes for the master data, the infotype log creations for the payroll and time management infotypes are also evaluated.

Customizing   To ensure the infotype log creation of the infotypes, you must perform the following actions in the Customizing of the IMG (**Personnel Management • Personnel Administration • Tools • Revision • Set Up Change Document**):

1. For **Infotypes to be Logged**, you must enter those infotypes for which you want changes to be automatically logged.

2. For **Field Group Definition**, define the fields within an infotype that you want to be logged. You can combine several fields into a **field group**. All fields of a field group are regarded as a unit for the infotype log creation and are logged together.

3. For **Field Group Characteristics**, you let the system know which field groups you want to be logged. You must also specify here whether you want the document to be entered as a long-term document (**L**) or a short-term document (**S**).

SAP does not deliver any entries for this purpose in the standard system. **[+]**

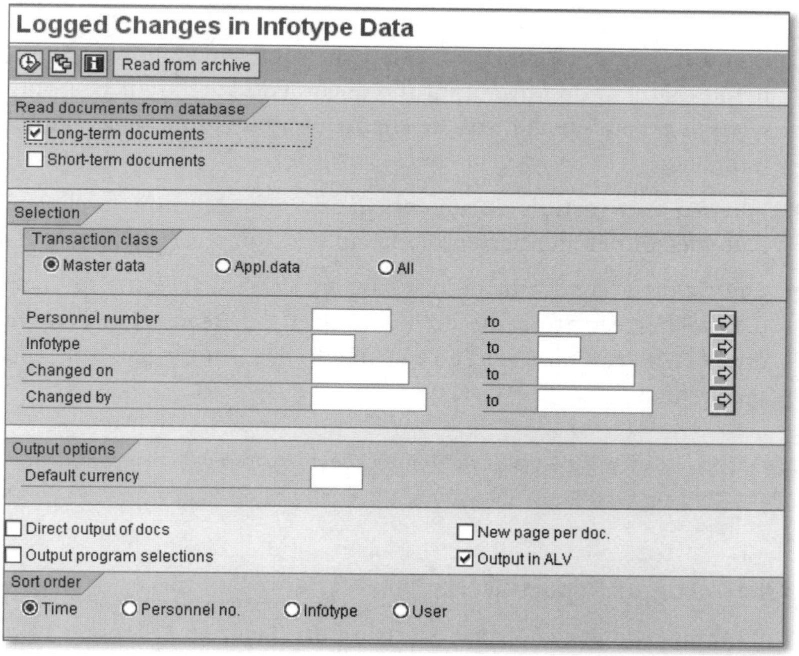

Logged Changes in Infotype Data

Read from archive

Read documents from database
☑ Long-term documents
☐ Short-term documents

Selection

Transaction class
◉ Master data   ○ Appl.data   ○ All

Personnel number		to		⇨
Infotype		to		⇨
Changed on		to		⇨
Changed by		to		⇨

Output options
Default currency

☐ Direct output of docs   ☐ New page per doc.
☐ Output program selections   ☑ Output in ALV

Sort order
◉ Time   ○ Personnel no.   ○ Infotype   ○ User

Figure 8.15 Logged Changes in Infotype Data Selection Screen

The following data selection and display options are available in the selection screen of this report:

Data selection and display

▸ You can use the Read documents from the database option to decide which document types you want to display.

▸ Long-term documents are used for auditing purposes to be able to retrospectively determine what, when, and by whom data was were changed, deleted, or added.

▸ Short-term documents are used, for example, to connect external systems to the SAP system. Consequently, you can evaluate short-term documents using customer-specific programs to supply an external system with change data.

▸ You can use the transaction class to select whether you only want to display HR master data or applicant master data or both. You can also filter the data by personnel number, infotype, change date, and user name.

▸ You can output the data as an ALV grid control or as a normal list. If you have more than one infotype in your selection, we recommend that you do not output the documents directly if you only want to get an overview of the changes for one or more personnel numbers.

▸ You can only sort the documents in advance according to change date, personnel number, infotype, and user name.

▸ The report reads from the database by default. If you also want data to be read from the archive, select the **Read from archive** option. You can then start a reporting both from the database and the archive.

[+]   An archive can only be displayed if it has been created using archive management (transaction SARA).

8.3.2 Log of Report Starts

Customizing You can use the Log of Report Starts report (Figure 8.16) to get a list of all report starts that you requested in the selection screen. To ensure that report starts can be logged, the following prerequisites must be met:

▸ The reports to be logged must use the logical database PNP.

▸ In the Customizing of the IMG (**Personnel Management · Personnel Administration · Tools · Revision · Log Report Starts**), you included the report in the HR Report Attributes table (V_T599R) and selected the **Record at start required** option.

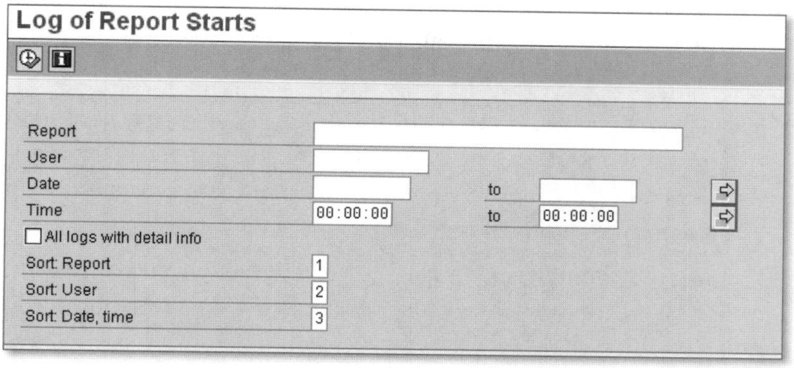

Figure 8.16 Log of Report Starts Selection Screen

In addition to the start date and time, the users and content of the parameters and selection options that were used to start the report are logged. If you have not selected **All logs with detail info**, an overview list is displayed first. To subsequently obtain details about a report, select the row and request the details by choosing **Select**.

You can delete the logs from the report starts using report RPUPROTU, if   [+]
required.

8.4   SAP NetWeaver BI Standard Content

Access the InfoCubes and ODS objects for Personnel Administration under the **InfoProviders by InfoAreas** option in the Data Warehousing Workbench of the Business Content. In the middle part of the screen (see Figure 8.17), the personnel administration objects are contained in the **Human Resources • Personal Administration** InfoArea. The **Headcount** and **Headcount and Personnel Actions** InfoCubes are available here. This InfoArea also contains the **Employee – Education** ODS object.

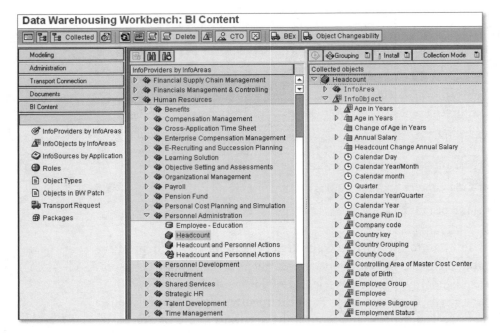

Figure 8.17 BI Standard Content for Personnel Administration

In the right-hand area of the Workbench, the content of a selected InfoCube is displayed under **Collected objects**. Drag the selected object with the mouse to the **Collected objects**. When you open the **InfoObject** folder, all characteristics and key figures for the object are displayed.

8.4.1 Headcount InfoCube

Infotypes The characteristics of the **Headcount** InfoCube contain data from the following Infotypes:

- Actions (0000)
- Organizational assignment (0001)
- Personal data (0002)
- Addresses (0006)
- Basic pay (0008)

However, not all fields of the infotypes are contained here. For example, the street is missing for the address; you can only extend this data by making enhancements to the standard system. The

Employee and **Person** characteristics are available for the employee. The **Employee** characteristic contains the organizational data. The **Person** characteristic provides the personal data for the employee, such as nationality, age, and gender.

You can also select calculated (derived) characteristics, such as age, for the characteristics from the infotypes of the HR master data.

The following hierarchies are created for the characteristics:

▶ Organizational units

▶ Cost centers

▶ Age of employees

▶ Employment level

Characteristic hierarchies

The following characteristics are available as time characteristics:

▶ Calendar day

▶ Calendar year/month

▶ Calendar month

▶ Quarter

▶ Calendar year/quarter

▶ Calendar year

Time characteristics

The calculation for the key figures is available in the update rules (see Figure 8.18).

Update rules					
Status	Key Figures		Ty.	Srce Fields	
◇	Number of Actions		✖		▲ ▼
☐	Number of Employees	⇐	🗎	Employee	
☐	Age in Years	⇐	🗎	Age	
☐	Capacity Utilization Level in %	⇐	🗎	Capacity utilization lev	
☐	Headcount FTE	⇐	🗎	Workforce Share	
☐	Length of Service (In Years)	⇐	🗎	Seniority	

Figure 8.18 Update Rules for the Key Figures

These do not always correspond to the calculation base for your own company. Because some of the key figures occur within programmed includes (routines), knowledge of the ABAP programming language is necessary to make changes (see Figure 8.19).

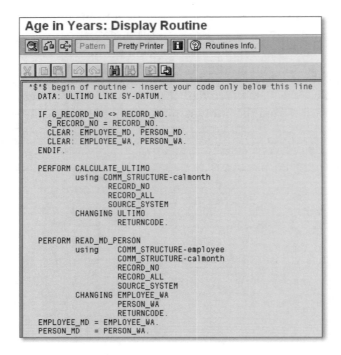

Figure 8.19 Routine for the Age Calculation

Key figures of the InfoCube The following key figures are available in the **Headcount** InfoCube:

▶ Age in years

▶ Annual salary

▶ Number of employees

▶ Headcount FTE

▶ Length of service (in years)

8.4.2 Headcount and Personnel Actions InfoCube

This InfoCube corresponds in many parts to the **Headcount** Info-Cube. However, it contains other characteristics such as the action reason and action type, age range (derived characteristic), and contract type.

Key figures of the InfoCube This InfoCube contains the following key figures:

▶ Number of actions

▶ Age in years

▶ Annual salary

▶ Number of employees

▶ Headcount FTE

▶ Employment level

▶ Length of service (in years)

Like the calculation for the headcount FTE, you do not need any programming knowledge to calculate the employment level. These calculations have been created using the formula editor (see Figure 8.20).

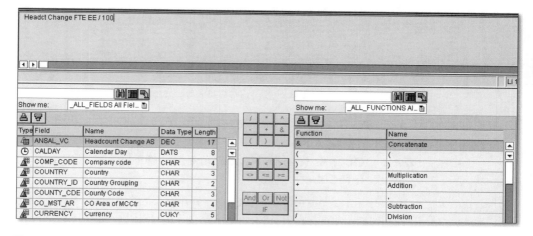

Figure 8.20 Determining the Employment Level in the Formula Editor

8.4.3   Employee – Education ODS Object

The ODS object for employees' education (see Figure 8.21) contains information from the **Education** (0022) infotype. The employee data is stored in the Employee characteristic which, in addition to the name, contains the employee's organizational data such as personnel area, organizational unit, position, and salary group. The hierarchies already mentioned in Section 8.4.1 are also used. The course fees are stored as a key figure in this object.

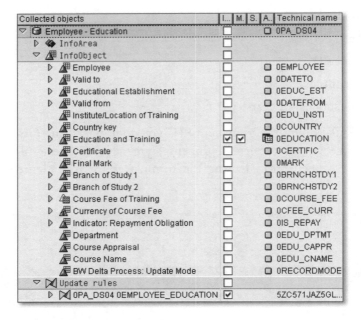

Collected objects	I...	M.	S.	A.	Technical name
▽ 🗃 Employee - Education	☐			☐	0PA_DS04
▷ 🔷 InfoArea	☐				
▽ 🖽 InfoObject	☐				
▷ 🖽 Employee	☐			☐	0EMPLOYEE
▷ 🖽 Valid to	☐			☐	0DATETO
▷ 🖽 Educational Establishment	☐			☐	0EDUC_EST
▷ 🖽 Valid from	☐			☐	0DATEFROM
🖽 Institute/Location of Training	☐			☐	0EDU_INSTI
▷ 🖽 Country key	☐			☐	0COUNTRY
▷ 🖽 Education and Training	☑	☑		📧	0EDUCATION
▷ 🖽 Certificate	☐			☐	0CERTIFIC
🖽 Final Mark	☐			☐	0MARK
▷ 🖽 Branch of Study 1	☐			☐	0BRNCHSTDY1
▷ 🖽 Branch of Study 2	☐			☐	0BRNCHSTDY2
▷ 🖽 Course Fee of Training	☐			☐	0COURSE_FEE
▷ 🖽 Currency of Course Fee	☐			☐	0CFEE_CURR
▷ 🖽 Indicator: Repayment Obligation	☐			☐	0IS_REPAY
🖽 Department	☐			☐	0EDU_DPTMT
🖽 Course Appraisal	☐			☐	0EDU_CAPPR
🖽 Course Name	☐			☐	0EDU_CNAME
🖽 BW Delta Process: Update Mode	☐			☐	0RECORDMODE
▽ ⋈ Update rules	☐				
▷ ⋈ 0PA_DS04 0EMPLOYEE_EDUCATION	☑				5ZC571JAZ5GL...

Figure 8.21 ODS Object for Education

8.4.4 Queries for the Headcount and Personnel Actions InfoCube

Queries for reporting headcounts and personnel movements are available for the InfoProviders contained in the BI content of Personnel Administration. In addition to entries and leavings, you can compare the headcount periods and evaluate the structure of the staff. You can find the queries for Personnel Administration in the Query Designer by selecting the **Open query** function. In the dialog box for selecting the queries, choose **InfoAreas** and then **Human Resources • Personnel Administration** from the tree structure. Figure 8.22 shows the Query Designer with the query for Average Headcount (4 Quarter).

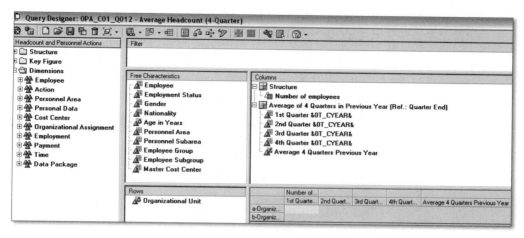

Figure 8.22 Query Designer

▶ New employees

  ▶ The Number of Entries query in the annual comparison compares the last month of the previous year with the current month and outputs the differences in absolute numbers and percentages.

  ▶ The Proportional Distribution of Entries query displays the proportional number of entries for the current calendar year in relation to the total number of entries relating to the reporting characteristics used in each case.

  ▶ The Entry Rate shows — based on the closed previous year — the number of entries relating to the average headcount.

  ▶ The Net Entry Rate shows the number of entries relating to the number of leavings for the current calendar year.

  ▶ The Headcount FTE Number of Entries query displays the number of entries for the current calendar year based on headcount FTE.

▶ Leavings

  ▶ The Number of Leavings query in the annual comparison compares the number of employees who have left the company in the last month of the previous year with the current month and outputs the differences in absolute numbers and percentages.

  ▶ The Proportional Distribution of Leavings query displays the proportional number of leavings for the current calendar year in relation to the total number of leavings relating to the reporting characteristics used in each case.

► The Leaving Rate displays — based on the closed previous year — the number of leavings relating to the average headcount.

► The Headcount FTE Number of Leavings query displays the number of leavings for the current calendar year based on headcount FTE.

► Headcount/personnel structure

► You can use the Headcount Changes query to compare the changes in the headcount of the last month in the previous year with the current month. The difference values are output in absolute numbers and percentages.

► The Average Headcount (4 Quarters) and Average Headcount (12 Months) queries display the headcount of four quarters/12 months of a year and create an average value from this data.

► The Proportional Distribution of Employees query displays the proportional distribution of employees for the last posted month of the current calendar year in relation to the total number of employees relating to the reporting characteristics used in each case. This means the proportion of employees can also be evaluated in percentages, among other things, according, for example, to gender and nationality.

► The Average Age of Employees query relates the age of the employees in years to the number of employees for the last posted month of the current calendar year.

► The Full/Part-Time Staff Headcount query shows the number of full-time and part-time staff for the last posted month of the current calendar year.

► You can use Headcount by Employment Level to output the number of employees according to the corresponding employment level in the annual comparison (last month of previous year/current year) with the absolute and percentage difference.

► The Average Length of Service query relates the length of service of employees in years to the number of employees for the last posted month of the current calendar year.

▶ Headcount FTE/personnel structure

　▷ The Headcount FTE Change query displays the headcount FTE and headcount FTE changes in the annual comparison.

　▷ Headcount Distributed Proportionally displays the proportional distribution of the headcount FTE in relation to the total headcount FTE for the last posted month of the current calendar year. This occurs depending on the reporting characteristics you use.

　▷ The Average Headcount query contains the FTE headcounts of four quarters from the previous year and calculates an average value from this data.

　▷ Headcount for the Current Year shows the headcount and headcount FTE for the last posted month of the current calendar year.

▶ Personnel movement
The Number of Personnel Actions is output in the annual comparison, restricted to the personnel action types Early Retirement/Retirement, Leaving, Organizational Reassignment, and Hiring. The last month of the previous year is compared with the current month. The difference is output in absolute and percentage values.

8.5　Conclusion

The standard reporting in Personnel Administration was replaced by queries with each new release over time. Some functions have unfortunately been lost as a result of these changes (see Section 8.1.3). In addition, the selection of reports was not noticeably increased. Since Personnel Administration corresponds to Organizational Management data in many cases, an increased integration of personnel master data with data from Organizational Management would be preferable. Therefore, only the organizational structure with organizational units is available for selecting employees, for example. An enhancement to the selection options using more flexible evaluation paths, which also covers the job, would be ideal here. This not only affects the selection but also the printing of lists, for which organizational data is missing from the master data infotypes in many cases.

The integration of customer-specific infotypes is, of course, always a topic for all standard reports of Personnel Administration. However, standard reporting often reaches its limits here and can only be adapted to meet the user's requirements by having enhancements programmed.

The BI Standard Content is much more flexible in the layout of print-outs, but expertise is also required here if you want to add data (from customer infotypes, for example). Nevertheless, a major advantage of using SAP NetWeaver BI is that you can link data, not just within the HCM system but also with Controlling and Financial Accounting.

Organizational Management provides numerous reports that you can use to obtain data for the most important issues for organizing the structure of your company.

9   Organizational Management

You can access reporting for Organizational Management in the SAP Easy Access menu by selecting the **Human Resources • Organizational Management • Info System** path. The path then divides into subfolders with the reports for organizational management, organizational unit, job, position, work center, and general reports.

SAP Easy Access path

9.1   Organizational Unit

The organizational unit (O object key) is used to form the basic framework of the organizational structure of a company. Depending on how the distribution of tasks is organized in the company, this could be departments, groups, or project teams, for example.

9.1.1   Existing Organizational Units

The Existing Organizational Units report provides a corresponding overview (Figure 9.1). You cannot restrict the selection of organizational units using an evaluation path and must instead use the **Organizational Unit** selection option.

You can use the **Standard Selection Screen** parameter to access the standard selection screen to select additional parameters. To do this, select this parameter and select **Execute**. This starts the Existing Objects report (see Section 9.5.1).

Figure 9.1 Existing Organizational Units List

The **Plan version, Object type, Start date, End date, Object status, Object abbreviation, Object name,** and **Ext.obj ID** fields are output. The **Object ID, Plan version, Historical record,** and **Object abbreviation** fields are available for display purposes in the available columns.

9.1.2 Staff Functions for Organizational Units

This report displays the staff functions of organizational units. The prerequisite here is that you must have selected the **Staff** field for the organizational unit in the **Organization and Staffing** transaction (PPOSE).

Expert mode   Create a **Staff/Department** infotype record (1003) for the relevant organizational unit in **expert mode** (transaction PO10) and select the **Staff** field. You can only restrict the **Period** in the selection screen. If you want to make other restrictions, select the **Standard selection screen** field and click **Execute**. The selection screen of the logical database PCH is subsequently displayed. You have now called the Staff Functions report (RHSTAB00). In this report, you can search for staff functions for all object types of Organizational Management. However, this usually only makes sense for positions and organizational units.

The results are output as an ALV grid. The number of organizational units with a staff function is displayed first. Select the relevant row and choose **Select**. All organizational units with staff functions are subsequently displayed with the **Object name**, **Object status name**, and **Period** fields. The **Object ID** and **Plan status** fields are available in the available columns.

9.2 Job

Jobs (C object key) are the general descriptions of functions (for example, secretary) in a company. They provide the job descriptions that apply to several positions with similar tasks and characteristics.

9.2.1 Existing Jobs

The Existing Jobs report generates a corresponding overview. You cannot restrict the selection of jobs using an evaluation path and must instead use the **Jobs** selection option. The report is similar to the Existing Organizational Units report in Section 9.1.1.

9.2.2 Job Index

The Job Index report creates a list (Figure 9.2) with the selected jobs and assigned positions including the holder. If the assigned position is not filled, the time as of when the position has been unoccupied is displayed under **Holder**. You can use the **Directly assigned persons** parameter to display the jobs of assigned persons directly.

If you want to make other restrictions, select the **Standard selection screen** field and click on **Execute**. The selection screen of the logical database PCH is subsequently displayed.

The list contains all jobs with information about the assigned position, holder, and staffing percentage of the position. The available columns contain other fields for **Job**, **Position**, and **Holder** such as the **Object ID** and **Personnel number**.

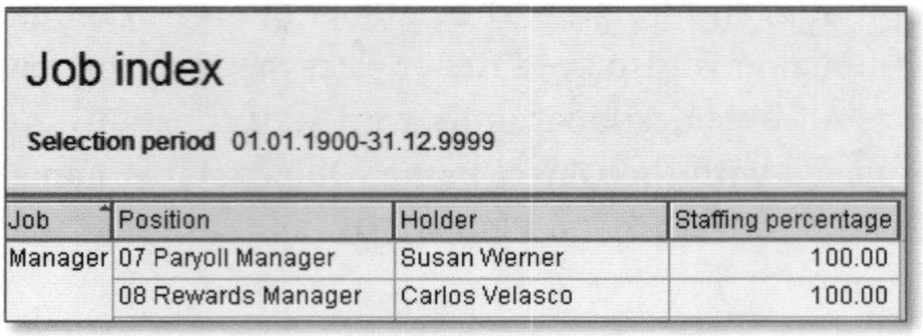

Job index

Selection period 01.01.1900-31.12.9999

Job	Position	Holder	Staffing percentage
Manager	07 Paryoll Manager	Susan Werner	100.00
	08 Rewards Manager	Carlos Velasco	100.00

Figure 9.2 Job Index List

9.2.3 Job Description

The Job Description report is a preliminary report for the general Object Description report (RHDESC20). You can select more than one job in this report. To do this, select the **Standard selection screen** field and click on **Execute**. If you have selected more than one job, a selection list of all selected jobs is displayed. Select the jobs you want to view and click on **Display selected objects**.

The SAP system displays the description for the first of the selected objects. You can navigate between the jobs using the **Previous object** and **Next object** buttons. The display in Figure 9.3 has been adapted by selecting the **Change layout** option.

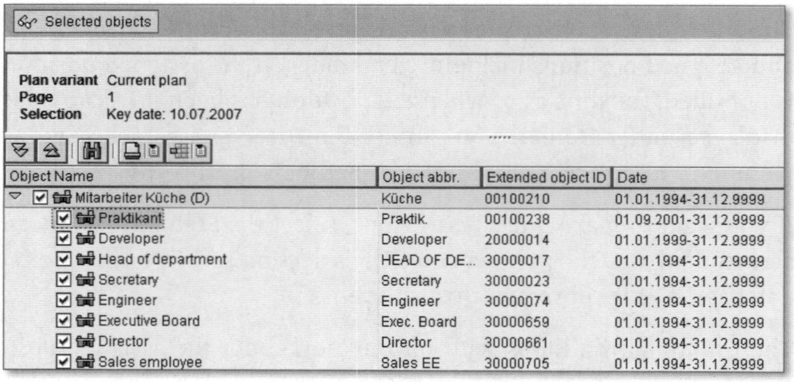

Selected objects

Plan variant Current plan
Page 1
Selection Key date: 10.07.2007

Object Name	Object abbr.	Extended object ID	Date
Mitarbeiter Küche (D)	Küche	00100210	01.01.1994-31.12.9999
Praktikant	Praktik.	00100238	01.09.2001-31.12.9999
Developer	Developer	20000014	01.01.1999-31.12.9999
Head of department	HEAD OF DE...	30000017	01.01.1994-31.12.9999
Secretary	Secretary	30000023	01.01.1994-31.12.9999
Engineer	Engineer	30000074	01.01.1994-31.12.9999
Executive Board	Exec. Board	30000659	01.01.1994-31.12.9999
Director	Director	30000661	01.01.1994-31.12.9999
Sales employee	Sales EE	30000705	01.01.1994-31.12.9999

Figure 9.3 Selection List of All Selected Jobs

The following additional functions are available in the list:

- You can use the Display infotype button to go to transaction PP01_DISP. You can display all infotypes for the job here (Figure 9.4).

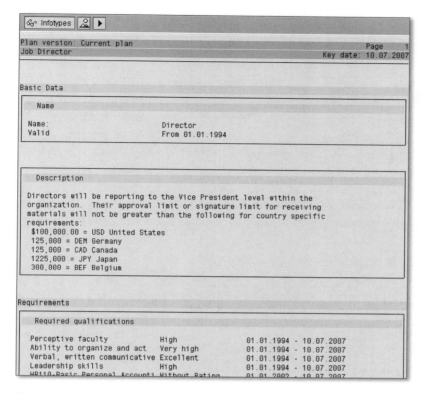

Figure 9.4 Director Job Description

▶ In the output list, you can create your own report layout (transaction OOOD) for this report by selecting **Settings • Change profiles** from the menu.

9.2.4 Complete Job Description

The Complete Job Description report (Figure 9.5) lists the specifications for jobs in terms of description, requirements profile, task profile, and resources and authorities. The description includes the following information:

▶ Description of job (infotype 1002)

▶ Requirements profile (only if you have maintained the qualifications and requirements)

▶ Activity profile

▶ If necessary, resources/authorities (infotype 1010)

[+] You can only evaluate the requirements profile of jobs if you use the Personnel Development module.

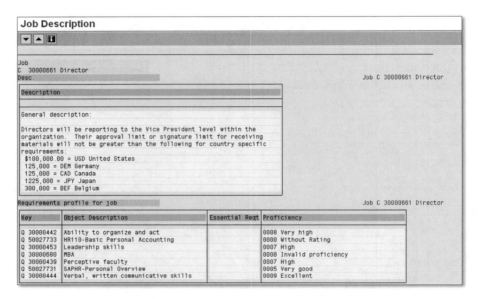

Job Description

Job
C 30000661 Director
Desc.
                                                              Job C 30000661 Director

Description

General description:

Directors will be reporting to the Vice President level within the
organization. Their approval limit or signature limit for receiving
materials will not be greater than the following for country specific
requirements:
    $100,000.00 = USD United States
    125,000 = DEM Germany
    125,000 = CAD Canada
    1225,000 = JPY Japan
    300,000 = BEF Belgium

Requirements profile for job   Job C 30000661 Director

Key	Object Description	Essential Reqt	Proficiency
Q 30000442	Ability to organize and act		0008 Very high
Q 50027733	HR110-Basic Personal Accounting		0000 Without Rating
Q 30000453	Leadership skills		0007 High
Q 30000680	MBA		0008 Invalid proficiency
Q 30000439	Perceptive faculty		0007 High
Q 50027731	SAPHR-Personal Overview		0005 Very good
Q 30000444	Verbal, written communicative skills		0009 Excellent

Figure 9.5 Complete Job Description List

9.3   Position

Positions (S object key) are the specific positions occupied by holders (employees) in a company, for example, a secretary in Purchasing.

9.3.1   Existing Positions

The Existing Positions report provides a corresponding overview. You cannot restrict the selection of positions using an evaluation path. You must instead use the **Positions** selection option for this purpose. The report is similar to the Existing Organizational Units report in Section 9.1.1.

9.3.2   Staff Functions for Positions

The Staff Functions for Positions report corresponds to the Staff Functions for Organizational Units report (see Section 9.1.2) in terms of functions and output.

9.3.3 Periods When Positions Are Unoccupied

The Periods of Unoccupied Positions report (Figure 9.6) displays the periods for each organizational unit when assigned positions are unoccupied. The unoccupied periods (in days) of positions assigned to a specific organizational unit are accumulated. You can also detail several specific organizational units for the reporting. The SBESX evaluation path is used by default for this reporting. You can use it to evaluate all positions that are assigned to the entire organizational structure or to a substructure.

Periods when positions are unoccupied per org. unit

Selection period: 01.01.2007 - 31.12.2007

Organizational unit	Position	Unocc. from	Unocc. to	New holder	Unocc. days	Average unocc. da...
New York Production Site	Assembly Worker	01.01.2007	31.12.2007		365	
		01.01.2007	31.12.2007		365	
		01.01.2007	31.12.2007		365	365
Atlanta Production Site		01.01.2007	31.12.2007		365	
		01.01.2007	31.12.2007		365	
	Production Manager	01.01.2007	31.12.2007		365	365
Los Angeles Production Site	Chemical Technician	01.01.2007	31.12.2007		365	
		01.01.2007	31.12.2007		365	

Figure 9.6 Periods of Unoccupied Positions List

If you want to introduce other restrictions or if you have to change the evaluation path, select the **Standard selection screen** field and click on **Execute**. The selection screen of the logical database PCH is subsequently displayed. This screen is also displayed if you do not enter any organizational unit and click on **Execute**.

9.3.4 Staff Assignments

The Staff Assignments report (Figure 9.7) displays the relevant staff assignments (positions and people) for one or more of the selected organizational units.

The data is reported alongside the organizational structure with the ORGEH evaluation path (organizational structure) if you have set the **Report on organizational structure** parameter.

The list contains all selected positions and people for one or more organizational units with a staffing percentage and approval and employment hours. You can either display the position holders only or the substitutes too.

Staff assignments

Key date 10.07.2007

Org. unit	Positions	Employee(s)	Chief	Staffing status	Actual working hours	Target working hours	Staffing percentage
IDES NZ	Managing Director		Chief	Unoccupied since 01.01.1994	0.00	40.00	0.00
IDES NZ	Personal Assistant to MD			Unoccupied since 01.01.1994	0.00	40.00	0.00
Sales	General Manager Sales		Chief	Unoccupied since 01.01.1994	0.00	40.00	0.00
SalesN	Sales Manager	Hillary Edward	Chief		40.00	40.00	100.00
SalesN	Sales Rep			Unoccupied since 01.01.1994	0.00	40.00	0.00
SalesN	Sales Rep			Unoccupied since 01.01.1994	0.00	40.00	0.00

Figure 9.7 Staff Assignments List

The sequence in which the positions are sorted occurs in accordance with the priority that was defined in the **Maintenance of Organizational Unit** view in the **Relationships** infotype (1001).

The actual working time is taken from the **Planned Working Time** infotype (0007) of the employee, and the planned working time is taken from the **Work Schedule** infotype (1011) of Organizational Management. The display of weekly working time in hours is predefined. If you want the data to be displayed for each day, month, or year, switch to the extended selection by choosing the **Standard selection screen** parameter. Enter the display you want here (for example, **D** for day) with the **Basis for Working Time** parameter.

The available column for the layout contains other columns for displaying data such as the object ID of the position, personnel number, effective working time, and effective staffing percentage.

9.3.5 Position Description

The Position Description report is a preliminary report for the general Object Description report (RHDESC20). You can select more than one position in this report. To do this, select the **Standard selection screen** field and click **Execute**. Section 9.2.3 contains more descriptions. In addition to the job description, the integration into the organizational structure and the associated job description are output.

9.3.6 Vacant Positions

You can use the Vacant Positions report to display positions that are identified as being vacant in the **Vacancy** infotype (1007) on a key date. A vacant position is a position that does not have a holder for a particular period of time and is specifically identified as being vacant. The PLSTE evaluation path (overview of positions along organizational structure) is set by default.

The period of the vacancy and the staffing status are displayed in the list. The staffing status contains information about whether the position is still occupied and how long or since when it has been vacant.

You can use the **Succession Planning** button to get a list of the selected vacant positions that contains suggestions indicating which employees are suitable successors for the position.

9.3.7 Obsolete Position

You can use this report to display positions that are identified as being obsolete in the **Obsolete** infotype (1014) for a specific key date. An obsolete position is a position that is removed at a particular time. The PLSTE evaluation path (overview of positions along organizational structure) is set by default, so the organizational unit is used to search for obsolete positions.

The list displays the date on which a position is obsolete. If the position is still occupied, you can use the **Career planning** button to create a career planning proposal for the holder.

Career planning

9.3.8 Complete Position Description

The Complete Position Description report creates a description for one or more positions similar to the Complete Job Description report (see Section 9.2.4).

The description includes the following information:

▶ Description of the position from infotype 1002

▶ Staffing, that is, a list of holders of the position

▶ Reports to/direct reports of the position

▶ Special activity profile of the position

▶ If necessary, special requirements profile (only if you use the Personnel Development module)

▶ Job that describes the position

▶ Activity profile of the job

▶ Requirements profile of the job

▶ Work center assigned to the position

▶ Organizational integration of position

You can use the **Object description** function to display additional information such as **Resources/Authorities**.

9.3.9 Authorities and Resources

This report lists all positions with the authorities and resources specified for them. To report authorities and resources, you must have maintained the subtypes of the **Resources/Authorities** infotype (1010) for the positions.

You must enter all organizational units for whose positions you require the reporting. You can also use the **Authorities/Resources** selection option to restrict the subtypes to be evaluated.

If you select the **Standard selection** parameter and select **Execute**, you go to the selection screen of the logical database PCH. You can print the position holders here (Figure 9.8). To do this, select the **Display staffing** parameter.

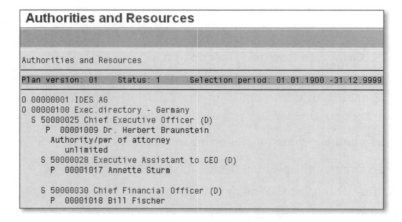

Figure 9.8 Authorities/Resources List with Position Holders

9.3.10 Planned Labor Costs

You use the Planned Labor Costs report to determine the planned compensation per position for one or more organizational units.

The **Planned Compensation** infotype (1005) must be maintained for the positions of the relevant organizational units or at least for the jobs in question. The standard evaluation path is SOLLBE, which encompasses organizational units, positions, and jobs.

If the system does not find a Planned Compensation infotype (1005) record for the positions using the standard evaluation path, the report does not output an amount when the standard evaluation path is used.

[+]

The report outputs the amount for the position of the relevant job with the following logic:

Output logic of the report

1. The system checks whether there is a **Planned Compensation** infotype (1005) for the corresponding job (the time constraint of the jobs allows several records of the **Planned Compensation** infotype for a key date).

2. If the system finds a record, it checks whether there is an Account Assignment Features infotype (1008) for the position or organizational unit.

3. If the system finds a record, it checks whether there is a personnel area and personnel subarea in this infotype.

4. If a personnel area and personnel subarea have been maintained, the system checks whether there is a **Planned Compensation** infotype (1005) for the pay scale type and pay scale area.

5. If there is a record, the report outputs the amount from this infotype.

6. If the system does not find a corresponding record of the **Planned Compensation** infotype (1005), the report determines the average value from the amounts of all available records of the **Planned Compensation** infotype (1005) for the job.

When you exit the table, you go to the related error log.

If you select the **Standard selection** parameter and choose **Execute**, you go to the selection screen of the logical database PCH. Note that the logic for determining the amount changes with an evaluation path without jobs.

[+]

9.4   Work Center

The work center (A object key) is the organizational unit that represents a suitably equipped physical area where work is performed.

9.4.1   Existing Work Centers

The Existing Work Centers report provides a corresponding overview. You can restrict the selection of work centers using an evaluation path in the **Maintain work centers** selection option. The report is similar to the Existing Organizational Units Report in Section 9.1.1.

9.4.2   Authorities and Resources

The Authorities and Resources report lists these for all work centers. To report authorities and resources, you must have maintained the subtypes of the **Resources/Authorities** infotype (1010) for the work centers. This report corresponds to the Authorities and Resources for Position report described in Section 9.3.9.

9.4.3   Restrictions/Health Examinations

The **Human Resources · Organizational Management · Info System · Work Center** path in the SAP Easy Access menu still contains two subfolders for restrictions and health examinations. They contain the following reports, which are only described briefly here:

▶ The Work Centers with Restrictions in an Organizational Unit report evaluates the Restrictions infotype (1006) along an organizational structure.

▶ You can use the Single Work Centers with Restrictions report to evaluate the Restrictions infotype (1006) for individual work centers.

▶ The Single Work Centers with Health Examinations in an Organizational Unit report evaluates the Health Examinations infotype (1009) along an organizational structure. The health exclusion (0001) and examination (0002) subtypes are evaluated.

▶ The Single Work Centers with Health Examinations report evaluates the Health Examinations infotype (1009) for individual work

centers. The health exclusion (0001) and examination (0002) subtypes are also evaluated here.

9.5 General Remarks

You can start the following reports irrespective of the object types of
organizational unit, job, and so on. You can use them flexibly for all
object types, including customer-specific object types.

9.5.1 Existing Objects

The Existing Objects report provides a corresponding overview. You
can call this report from other reports such as the Existing Organizational Unit (see Section 9.1.1) and Transactions reports. The list contains all objects, each with information about the validity period, status, name, and extended object ID. The **Object ID**, **Plan version**,
Historical record, and **Object abbreviation** fields are still available
for display purposes in the available columns.

9.5.2 Structure Display

The Structure Display report displays an extract from an organizational structure in accordance with the specified initial object and
evaluation path.

A structure tree that displays the assignments of the organizational
objects to each other is output. The hierarchy levels are illustrated by
corresponding indentations in the tree structure.

> In Basis Release 6.20, the tree is output using a tree control. However, if   **[+]**
> you want the classic output to be displayed as an ABAP list, you can
> branch to this display using the Classic Output parameter. Alternatively,
> you can call the RHSTRU00_OLD report directly. Figure 9.9 shows the
> output using the ABAP tree control.

You can go to the corresponding transaction for displaying or maintaining infotypes by selecting the **Edit • Information** or **Edit • Maintenance transaction** menu options. To do this, you must first select
from the tree the object to be displayed or maintained. Click the row
icon for this to make sure the whole row is selected.

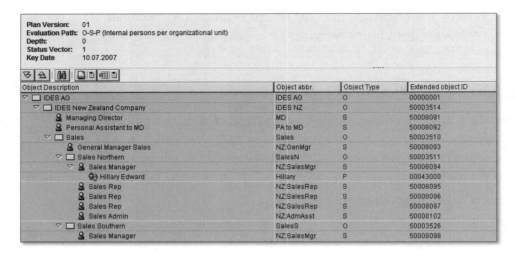

Plan Version:	01			
Evaluation Path:	O-S-P (Internal persons per organizational unit)			
Depth:	0			
Status Vector:	1			
Key Date	10.07.2007			

Object Description	Object abbr.	Object Type	Extended object ID
▽ ☐ IDES AG	IDES AG	O	00000001
▽ ☐ IDES New Zealand Company	IDES NZ	O	50003514
Managing Director	MD	S	50008091
Personal Assistant to MD	PA to MD	S	50008092
▽ ☐ Sales	Sales	O	50003510
General Manager Sales	NZ:GenMgr	S	50008093
▽ ☐ Sales Northern	SalesN	O	50003511
▽ Sales Manager	NZ:SalesMgr	S	50008094
Hillary Edward	Hillary	P	00043000
Sales Rep	NZ:SalesRep	S	50008095
Sales Rep	NZ:SalesRep	S	50008096
Sales Rep	NZ:SalesRep	S	50008097
Sales Admin	NZ:AdmAsst	S	50008102
▽ ☐ Sales Southern	SalesS	O	50003526
Sales Manager	NZ:SalesMgr	S	50008098

Figure 9.9 Structure Tree with O-S-P Evaluation Path

[+] The logical database PCH does not normally perform a recursion check. You cannot create a recursion using the standard tools, so this should not occur. Nevertheless, recursions can take place due to data inconsistencies or automatic modifications with reports. You can use the Recursion parameter to activate the check to determine these recursions.

9.5.3 Displaying and Maintaining Infotypes

The Display and Maintain Infotypes report (RHDESC00) provides an overview of all available infotypes including the status (transaction PP01_DISP – display objects) within a plan variant for one or more objects. You can also edit the (parameter-controlled) infotypes provided.

If you have set the **With All National Infotypes** parameter, you can display and edit all infotypes, both international and national. If you have not set this parameter, the international infotypes and only the national ones for the country that you selected using the country code are displayed.

9.5.4 Starting HR Reporting

You can use the Start HR Reporting report to start different reports for a number of personnel numbers that result from the structures of an organizational plan.

The program goes through the Organizational Management database in accordance with the specified selection criteria and collects personnel numbers, provided type P (Person) objects are contained in the selected set of objects.

The HR master data reporting specified in the **PA reporting** parameter is then started using these personnel numbers.

This allows you to start each reporting of HR master data using a quantity of personnel numbers and in the personnel number sorting that results from an HR planning structure (organizational structure or similar).

In addition to the known selection criteria (see Figure 9.10) of the logical database PCH, you must specify the ABAP name of the PA reporting. You can also fill the following parameters as an option:

▶ In the Report variant, enter the variant that you want to use to start the report. You must have previously saved this variant for the report.

▶ If you set the Extended personnel selection parameter, you go to the selection screen of the report specified under PA reporting after you start the report. You can make more selections here.

▶ If you do not set the Sort by Personnel Number parameter and the Extended personnel selection parameter is also initial, the PA reporting is started on the personnel planning database in accordance with the sorting. If the Extended personnel selection parameter is not initial, the Personnel Number selection option on the selection screen of the report is filled by the logical database PNP. Otherwise, the data is always output in ascending order according to the value of the personnel number.

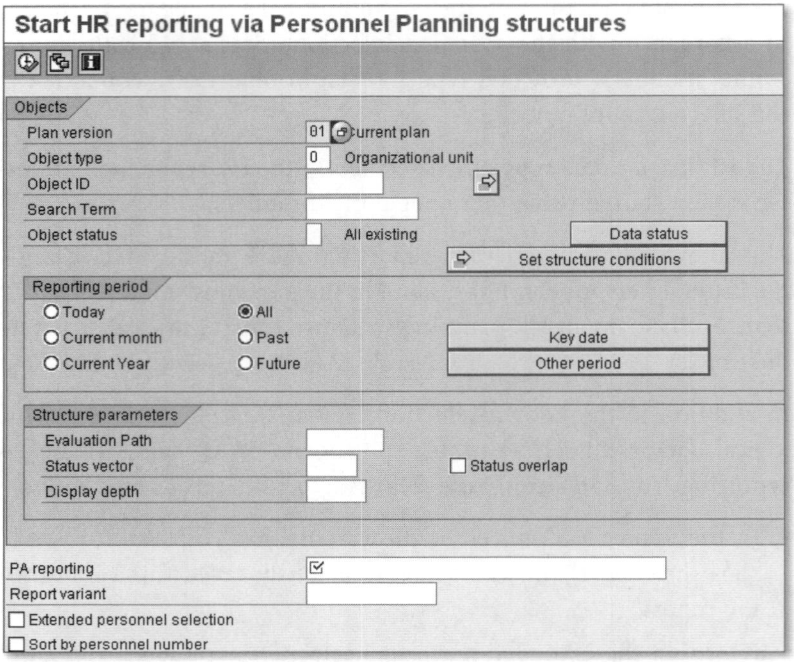

Figure 9.10 Start HR Reporting Selection Screen

9.6   SAP NetWeaver BI Standard Content

The BI Standard Content of Organizational Management contains the **Staffing Assignments** InfoCube.

9.6.1   Staffing Assignments InfoCube

The **Staffing Assignments** InfoCube contains all movement data transferred from the HCM system for staffing assignments in the company. The **Staffing Assignments** InfoSource is used to provide the data in the InfoCube. The InfoCube contains both the master data for the employee and information from the infotypes of the position such as limitations of the position or management functions of the position by the A/B012 relationship with the organizational unit.

[»]   In the BI Content of Organization Management, the structural authorization is also contained in the **HR Structural Authorizations – Hierarchy and HR Structural Authorizations – Values** ODS objects (see Figure 9.11).

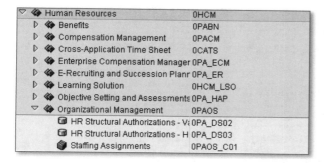

Figure 9.11 BI Standard Content for Organizational Management

The InfoCube contains hierarchies for the organizational unit, cost centers, and ages of the employees. Note that the **Age in Years** characteristic shows the age of an employee at the end of the period.

A person can be listed as an employee several times. To be able to differentiate between the employment relationships (Employee characteristic) and the real persons (Person characteristic), the person is an attribute of the employee.

[+]

This InfoCube contains the following general key figures:

Key figures of InfoCube

- Number of Occupied Positions
- Number of Unoccupied Positions
- Number of Vacant Unoccupied Positions
- Occupied Positions FTE
- Unoccupied Positions FTE
- Vacant Unoccupied Positions FTE
- Number of Occupied Vacant Positions
- Occupied Vacant Positions as FTE
- Number of Positions
- Positions as FTE
- Span of Control of a Position

The structure and calculation of the key figures are contained in the update rules for the InfoCube (see Figure 9.12).

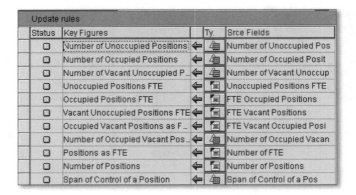

Figure 9.12 Update Rules for the Staffing Assignments

The *Full-Time Position* or *Full-Time Equivalent* (*FTE*) is provided as an additional attribute for the position. The full-time position relates the planned working time of the position to the standard working time in the organizational unit to which the position is assigned. The inheritance logic of the general working time of the organizational unit is also taken into account. If the standard working time is 40, for example, and the planned working time specified for the position is 20 hours per week, this corresponds to the value of a full-time position of 0.5. If no particular working time is specified for the position, it corresponds by definition to the value of a full-time position of 1.

The **Calendar year, Calendar year/month, Calendar year/quarter, Calendar month, quarter**, and **Last posted month** (current calendar year) are available as time-based dimensions for the reports.

Several structures or templates that contain the key figure combined with specific invoicing rules are delivered with the InfoCube. These templates enable you to easily access frequently required reporting structures (for example, comparison of previous year and current year) with absolute and percentage differences in the result values.

[+]   In the update rules, fields are read from the master data tables and written into the InfoCube as characteristics. You therefore need to load and activate the master data before the InfoSources.

9.6.2 Queries for the Staffing Assignments InfoCube

The Organizational Management queries evaluate positions and their numbers, functions, and vacancies. The following queries are available in the BI Content:

▶ The Vacant Positions per Job query displays the number of positions for each job in the entire organizational structure per calendar month over a period of a calendar year.

▶ The Vacant Positions in Annual Comparison query contains the number of vacant unoccupied positions for each organizational unit in the annual comparison. You can use this query to evaluate the relevant absolute and relative differences in the number of vacant unoccupied positions, for example.

▶ For the last posted month of the current calendar year for each organizational unit, the Positions Overview query contains the number of the following:

  ▹ Occupied positions

  ▹ Unoccupied positions

  ▹ Vacant unoccupied positions

  ▹ Occupied vacant positions

▶ The Proportional Distribution of Vacant Positions query displays the number of vacant unoccupied positions for each organizational unit for the last posted month of the current calendar year. The percentage, which constitutes the calculated number of the total result of vacant unoccupied positions available in all of the organizational units, is also calculated.

▶ The Number of Temporary Positions query outputs the number of full positions available for the last posted month of the current calendar year. This query also displays how many of these positions span an object period that ends before 31.12.9999.

▶ The Number of Positions query determines the number of full positions available for the last posted month of the current calendar year and how many of these positions are occupied and vacant or unoccupied and vacant.

▶ The Number of Positions with Management Function query is available to determine the total number of positions and the number of positions with management functions for the last posted month.

- ▸ The Staff Positions query determines the number of staff positions for the last posted month.

- ▸ The Vacant Positions overview displays a list of the number of vacant and as yet unoccupied positions.

- ▸ The Positions as Full-Time Positions: Occupied, Vacant, Unoccupied query displays the occupied positions, unoccupied positions, vacant unoccupied positions, and occupied vacant positions that are available for each organizational unit. The positions are converted into full-time positions.

- ▸ The Number of Full-Time Positions in the Annual Comparison query compares the number of full-time positions for the last posted month of the previous year with the number of full-time positions for the last posted month of the current calendar year. The absolute and relative difference between these two numbers is also displayed.

- ▸ The Quarterly Comparison of Vacant Positions (Full-Time) query displays the vacant unoccupied positions — shown as full-time positions — for each organizational unit.

9.7   Conclusion

The standard reporting of Organizational Management already meets many requirements for the user. The selection screen of the logical database PCH enables you to also extend the reporting very flexibly on other object types, in addition to the standard object types for organizational unit, job, and position. This also applies to customer-specific object types. To do this, you only need to maintain corresponding evaluation paths and add these to the selection screen.

In this case, however, as in Personnel Administration, customer-specific infotypes can only be integrated into the reports by means of programmed enhancements.

You can use the BI Standard Content to extend the options for reporting Organizational Management data considerably. Regrettably, however, the data and queries available deal almost exclusively with the positions and their changes. Other (in particular, customer-specific) object types can, unfortunately, only be reported using enhancements and separate extractors.

Recruitment reports contain statistical evaluations or lists about applicants, vacancies, and job advertisements.

10   Recruitment

You can use Recruitment reports to create statistical evaluations or lists about applicants, vacancies, and job advertisements.

Most reports use the logical database for applicant master data (PAP). For this, note that entering a key date in the **Receipt of Application** field means that only the applications that were specifically entered on this key date are selected. The date entered in the **key date for data selection** field results in only data records for an applicant that are valid on the specified key date being selected.

Logical database PAP

You can access Personnel Administration reporting in the SAP Easy Access menu by selecting the path **Human Resources · Personnel Management · Recruitment · Info System · Reports**. The path then divides into the **Applicants, Vacancies**, and **Job Advertisements** subfolders. These subfolders contain the reports for Recruitment.

SAP Easy Access path

10.1   Applicants

You can use the reports that refer to applicant data to create different lists about applicant data. For example, you can output a variable applicant list entirely according to your reporting requirements or specifically defined lists sorted according to applicant name, for instance. The Planned Activities report provides administrative support. The personnel officer responsible can use this report to create a worklist of the applicant activities still to be processed.

10.1.1   Variable Applicant List

The Variable Applicant List report displays up to a maximum of 20 from 60 fields from the applicant data on a key date. You define the data to be displayed in the selection screen using the **Field Selection** button. To ensure that the report can start, you must select at least one field to display. The fields from the selection screen of the logical database for the applicant master data (PAP) are not automatically transferred into the list. The reporting results are subsequently displayed as a list in the format of an ALV grid control.

10.1.2 Applicants by Name

Short profile The Applicants by Name report outputs a list of names of all applicants who correspond to the conditions specified in the selection screen. The applicant number, applicant name, current applicant status, and start date of the applicant status are output. In the output, you can use the **Short profile** button to display a short profile of an applicant selected in the list, as shown in Figure 10.1.

```
Mr.
Peter Petersen
AA
11111 AA


Date of Birth:    01.01.1965
Gender:           Male
Nationality:      German
Letter language:  English

Actions:
  Action: Enter additional data,
          valid from 14.02.1996
  Status: In process

Application(Activities):
  on 14.02.1996 , Advertisment 00000111 from 10.01.1996
                  in New York Times
      - Receipt scheduled on 14.02.1996 , at 00.00 Uhr.
    Vacancy: Robotics Specialists Pump
      - Interview appt finished on 14.02.1996 , at 00.00 Uhr.
    Responsible: Sebastian Schulz
    Vacancy: Robotics Specialists Pump
      - Interview inv. scheduled on 14.02.1996 , at 00.00 Uhr.
    Vacancy: Robotics Specialists Pump
```

Figure 10.1 Short Profile of an Applicant

If you started the report by selecting the **Human Resources • Personal Management • Recruitment • Applicant Master Data • Bulk Processing • Applicants by Name** path in the SAP Easy Access menu, other interactive functions are available for you to use to maintain the applicant data. These can include changing the master data, additional data, or overall status.

10.1.3 Applicants by Actions

The Applicants by Actions report outputs a list that displays which applicant actions were performed for each applicant. The list contains the **Applicant number**, **Applicant name**, **Action performed**, **Applicant status**, and **Personnel officer responsible** fields.

Like in the Applicants by Name report, other functions are available for maintaining the applicant data when you start the report from the SAP Easy Access menu **Human Resources • Personnel Management • Recruitment • Applicant Master Data • Bulk Processing • Applicants by Actions**.

10.1.4 Education of Applicants

The Education of Applicants report provides information about the education and further education of applicants. The output list also contains two statistics:

▶ Statistic I is an accumulation of all applicants who each have the same school type, school diploma, branch of study, and education.

▶ Statistic II is an accumulation of all applicants who have the same school type and school diploma.

10.1.5 Applications

The Applications report outputs a list of all applications. In the output, you can use the **Short profile** button to display a short profile of an applicant selected in the list. The list contains the following information:

▶ Applicant number

▶ Name of applicant

▶ Date of receipt of the application

▶ Job advertisement or unsolicited applicant group to which the application refers

Like in the Applicants by Name report, other functions are available for maintaining the applicant data when you start the report from the SAP Easy Access menu **Human Resources • Personnel Management • Recruitment • Applicant Master Data • Bulk Processing • Applications**.

10.1.6 Applicant Statistics

The Applicant Statistics report covers several reporting levels. In the first reporting level, you receive information about the number of applicants per applicant status, and when you double-click an applicant status, a list of the relevant applicants is displayed.

Applicant status (overall)	Number
In process	133
On hold	7
Rejected	8
To be hired	24
Contract offered	4
Offer rejected	0
Invite	3
Total	179

Applicant Statistics

Key date 10.07.2007

Figure 10.2 Applicant Statistics (Reporting Level 1)

You can use the **Activities Statistics** function (Figure 10.3) to display the status of planned and completed activities per activity type for each applicant status listed. To do this, select an applicant status from the list and click on the **Activities Statistics** button. In the next selection screen that appears, select the activities that you want to be evaluated and click on **Continue.** A list with the statistics of the selected activities is subsequently displayed.

If you double-click one of the rows in the Total columns, a list with the applicants according to the relevant activities is displayed.

```
┌─────────────────────────────────────────────────────────────────────┐
│          Activity statistics for applicant status: In process        │
│                                                                       │
│              135  Applications from   133  applicants selected        │
│                                                                       │
├────────────────┬─────────────────┬─────────────────┬──────────┬──────┤
│ of which       │ at least one    │ at least one    │ no       │total │
│ per activity type:│completed activity│planned activity│corr.activity│   │
├────────────────┼─────────────────┼─────────────────┼──────────┼──────┤
│ 001 Receipt         │      13      │      96      │     26      │ 135 │
│ 002 Transfer file   │       0      │       0      │    135      │ 135 │
│ 003 File returned   │       0      │       0      │    135      │ 135 │
│ 004 Interview inv.  │      18      │      13      │    104      │ 135 │
│ 005 Interview appt  │      15      │      19      │    101      │ 135 │
│ 006 Tel.invitation  │       1      │       0      │    134      │ 135 │
│ 007 Test invitation │       0      │       4      │    131      │ 135 │
│ 008 Test date       │       2      │       3      │    130      │ 135 │
│ 009 Appraisal       │       1      │       1      │    133      │ 135 │
│ 010 Mail contract   │       0      │       1      │    134      │ 135 │
│ 011 Rejection       │       0      │       0      │    135      │ 135 │
└────────────────┴─────────────────┴─────────────────┴──────────┴──────┘
```

Figure 10.3 Activity Statistics

When you start the report by selecting the **Human Resources • Personal Management • Recruitment • Applicant Master Data • Mass Processing • Applicant Statistics** path from the SAP Easy Access menu, the lists with the corresponding applicants also contain other functions for maintaining the applicant data.

10.1.7 Planned Activities

You can use the Planned Activities report to output a list of all planned activities that a personnel officer is to perform up to a particular time. The following information is available for the personnel officer:

▶ Name of the personnel officer

▶ Name of the applicant

▶ Planned activity

▶ Date by which the planned activity must be performed; if necessary, the date when an email was sent for this activity (the last date if there are several emails)

When you start the report by selecting the **Human Resources • Personal Management • Recruitment • Applicant Activity • Planned Activities** path from the SAP Easy Access menu, the lists with the corresponding applicants also contain other functions for maintaining the applicant data. You can then send emails to those responsible for the activity or set the planned activities to Completed.

10.2 Vacancy

A company's workforce requirements are represented in the *Recruitment* module by vacancies. A *vacancy* is a position to be occupied fully or partially, which is maintained by a line manager or relevant personnel officer responsible. Reports based on vacancies provide you with lists containing data about vacancies and existing vacancy assignments. The prerequisite in this case is that the integration for personnel planning is active and the vacancies have been maintained in personnel planning.

10.2.1 Vacancy Assignments

You can use this report to output a list of all vacancy assignments with the following information:

▶ Name of applicant

▶ Overall status of applicant

▶ Vacancy to which the application refers

▶ Applicant status for this vacancy

You can also display a short profile for the applicant here. To do this, choose an applicant and select the **Short profile** button.

Other functions are available for maintaining the applicant data when you start the report from the SAP Easy Access menu **Human Resources • Personnel Management • Recruitment • Applicant Master Data • Bulk Processing • Vacancy Assignment.**

10.2.2 Vacancies

You can use the Vacancies report to display a list of all vacancies created in personnel planning. The list contains the following information:

▶ Activity

▶ Start date

- End date
- Line manager
- Abbreviation of personnel officer
- Staffing status
- Indicator as to whether the vacancy was maintained in Organizational Management
- Information about whether a requirements profile was maintained

This report contains the following additional functions for the individual vacancies:

Other functions in the report

- You can display information about the vacancy and the requirements profile.
- You can search for suitable candidates.
- You can print the applicant statistics, applicant list, and position description.

In addition, you can maintain vacancy assignments by selecting the **Edit • Maintain Vacancy Assignments** option from the menu.

10.3 Job Advertisements and Recruitment Instruments

You can use the reports for job advertisements to create lists for published job advertisements or for recruitment instruments used (media, Internet, and so on) and report this information accordingly.

10.3.1 Job Advertisements

This report outputs all the "job advertisements" contained in the selection criteria. The following selection criteria are available for this purpose:

- Job advertisement
- Recruitment instrument
- Publication date
- End of job advertisement
- Vacancy

You receive information for the following contents:

▸ Number of the job advertisement

▸ Publication date of the job advertisement

▸ Recruitment instrument used for the job advertisement

▸ Vacancies published in the recruitment instrument

▸ Status of the vacancies

▸ Number of applications for each job advertisement

The output list (see Figure 10.4) contains functions for displaying the job advertisement and vacancy as well as applicant statistics.

Job Adverts

Public.date	Expiration	Advert	Name of instrument	Start Date	Position (Short Text)	St	App.
18.11.2004	18.12.2004	354	Estado de São Paulo	01.01.2004	Secretary	vac.	0
01.11.2004	31.12.9999	356	USA South	01.11.2004	SCS Administrative Associ	vac.	0
01.11.2004	31.12.2004	355	USA South	11.02.2004	SCS Administrative Associ	vac.	0
01.11.2004	31.12.2004	355	USA South	17.05.2005	SCS Administrative Associ	occ.	0
01.11.2004	31.12.2004	355	USA South	18.08.2005	SCS Administrative Associ	vac.	0
01.10.2004	31.12.2004	353	RH Recruiting	01.01.2002	RH Human Resources Genera	vac.	0
01.10.2004	31.12.2004	353	RH Recruiting	01.01.2002	RH Payroll Specialist	vac.	0
01.01.2004	31.12.2004	352	USA South	01.01.2002	RH Payroll Generalist	vac.	0
01.01.2004	31.12.9999	351	USA West	01.01.2004	SCS Administrative Associ	vac.	2
01.01.2004	31.12.9999	351	USA West	11.02.2004	SCS Administrative Associ	vac.	2
01.01.2004	31.12.9999	351	USA West	17.05.2005	SCS Administrative Associ	occ.	2
01.01.2004	31.12.9999	351	USA West	18.08.2005	SCS Administrative Associ	vac.	2
20.05.2003	31.12.9999	347	USA South	01.01.2003	Production Worker	vac.	0
19.05.2003	31.12.9999	345	USA South	01.01.2003	Chief Financial Officer	vac.	0
19.05.2003	31.12.9999	345	USA South	01.06.2003	Chief Financial Officer	vac.	0
02.05.2003	01.06.2003	344	USA NorthEast	01.01.2003	Resource Clerk	vac.	5
02.05.2003	01.06.2003	344	USA NorthEast	01.01.2003	Enrollment Clerk	vac.	5
02.05.2003	01.06.2003	344	USA NorthEast	01.01.2004	Enrollment Clerk	vac.	5
02.05.2003	01.06.2003	344	USA NorthEast	01.01.2003	Booking Clerk	vac.	5
02.05.2003	31.12.9999	343	USA NorthEast	16.11.2000	Sr. Performance Managemen	vac.	0
02.05.2003	31.12.9999	343	USA NorthEast	01.01.2004	Sr. Performance Managemen	vac.	0
01.01.2003	31.12.2003	350	USA South	01.01.2003	Sales Manager	vac.	0

Figure 10.4 Job Advertisements List

10.3.2 Recruitment Instruments

You can use this report to evaluate the effectiveness of the recruitment instruments used. The output list contains the following information:

▸ Recruitment instrument

▸ Number of job advertisements published using this recruitment instrument

▶ Number of applicants who have applied in response to these job advertisements

▶ Overall costs for all job advertisements published using this recruitment instrument

▶ Job advertisement costs for each application received (the value output here is the result from the total costs of all job advertisements in a recruitment instrument, divided by the number of applicants)

The output list (see Figure 10.5) contains other functions you can use to receive additional information about the recruitment instrument and job advertisement. You can also call the applicant statistics and an applicant list.

Other functions in the report

| Instrument | Evaluate advert | Applicant statistics | Applicant list |

Evaluate Recruitment Instruments

Instrument	Number of adverts	Number of applications	Total cost		Cost per application	
Jornal Interno	0	0	0.00		0.00	
FAZ	3	15	0.00	XXX	0.00	XXX
New York Times	3	103	2,253.50	USD	21.88	USD
Le Monde	0	0	0.00		0.00	
AA Frankfurt	0	0	0.00		0.00	
Encontre Aqui	2	7	1,253.50	DEM	179.07	DEM
PA	1	0	2,300.00	DEM	0.00	DEM
Aamt Stuttgart	0	0	0.00		0,00	
La Guardian	0	0	0.00		0.00	
Quiosque Empregado	1	3	0.00	USD	0.00	USD
Chicago Tribune	1	1	0.00		0.00	
DePaul University	0	0	0.00		0.00	
Marquette University	0	0	0.00		0.00	
U of I	0	0	0.00		0.00	
Internet Connection	0	0	0.00		0.00	
Reforma	0	0	0.00		0.00	
Excelsior	0	0	0.00		0.00	
Agencia de Empleos	0	0	0.00		0.00	
Boston Globe	1	2	500.00	USD	250.00	USD
Boston University	0	0	0.00		0.00	
Boston College	0	0	0.00		0.00	
Northeastern Univer	0	0	0.00		0.00	

Figure 10.5 Recruitment Instruments List

10.4   SAP NetWeaver BI Standard Content

The BI Standard Content of personnel planning contains the **Applications and Applicant Actions** InfoCube.

10.4.1 Applications and Applicant Actions InfoCube

The **Applications and Applicant Actions** InfoCube contains all the data for applications and applicant actions uploaded from the HCM system. The **Applicants, Applications,** and **Applicant Actions** InfoSources are used to provide the data in the InfoCube.

General key figures

The InfoCube contains the following general key figures (see Figure 10.6):

- ▶ Number of Applicants
- ▶ Number of Applications
- ▶ Number of Actions
- ▶ Age in Years

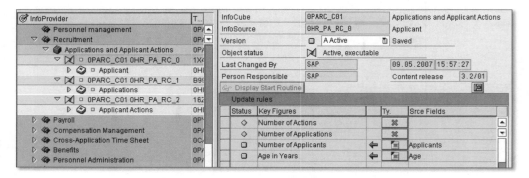

Figure 10.6 General Key Figures for Recruitment Update Rule

Restricted key figures

Restricted key figures are also provided. The restricted key figures are derived from the key figures of the InfoCube using a filter on one or more characteristics of the InfoCube. This consequently results in the following restricted key figures:

- ▶ Number of applicants with the To be Hired status
- ▶ Number of applicants with the Contract Offered status
- ▶ Number of applicants with the Offer Rejected status
- ▶ Number of unsolicited applicants
- ▶ Number of applications in response to a job advertisement

In the update rules, many fields are read from the master data tables up to the period end and written into the InfoCube as characteristics. You therefore need to load and activate the master data before the InfoSources. **[!]**

Calendar day, **Calendar year/month**, **Calendar year/quarter**, and **Calendar year** are available as time-based dimensions for the reporting.

You can use the Recruitment queries to evaluate the data for applications, applicants, advertising, and hirings or rejected contracts.

Due to the InfoSources that SAP provides, we only recommend certain reporting for each InfoSource. For example, it makes sense to include reporting based on applications in the Applications InfoSource, but not reporting based on applicant actions. **[+]**

10.4.2 Queries for the Applications and Applicant Actions InfoCube

The following queries are contained in the BI Standard Content:

▸ Applications

  ▹ The Number of Applications with Master Data query in the annual comparison shows the absolute and percentage difference of the current year compared to the previous year. This query contains data about the applications such as the applicant, overall status of the applicant, and applicant group.

  ▹ The Proportional Distribution of Applications with Master Data query contains the proportional distribution of applications for the current calendar year in relation to the overall number of applications.

  ▹ The Average Number of Applications query displays the average number of applications based on the last four quarters.

  ▹ The Applications to Applicants Ratio query determines the ratio of applications to applicants.

▸ Applicants

  ▹ The Number of Applicants with Master Data query displays the number of applications with master data including absolute and percentage differences. The last month of the previous year is compared with the last posted month of the current calendar year.

► In addition to displaying the average age of applicants, the Average Age of Applicants query displays other data about the applicants such as the overall status of the applicant, gender, and nationality.

► The Average Number of Applicants query displays the average number of applicants based on the last four quarters.

► Advertising

► The Number of Applications Relating to Advertising query provides an annual comparison (current year/previous year) with absolute and percentage differences for applications relating to advertising. Some of the InfoObjects you can use to report the relevant data include Job advertisement, Media, and "Recruitment instrument.

► You can use the Number of Applications Per Job Advertisement with Costs query to obtain the number of applications for each job advertisement with the corresponding costs for each job advertisement for the current calendar year.

► The Proportional Distribution of Applications Based on Advertising query gives you a report for the current calendar year, which displays the proportional distribution of applications related to advertising. Additional reporting characteristics such as recruitment instrument, medium, and unsolicited applicant group are available for the reporting.

► You can use the Unsolicited Applications and Applications in Response to Job Advertisements query to obtain the number of unsolicited applications and applications in response to job advertisements for the current calendar year.

► The Rate of Unsolicited Applications query contains the number of applicants, unsolicited applications, and applications in response to job advertisements for the current calendar year as well as the rate of unsolicited applications.

► Hirings/employment contracts

► You can use the Hirings/Offered/Rejected Contracts query to display the number of all applicants as well as applicants with the To Be Hired status, Contract Offered status, and Offer Rejected status for the last posted month of the current calendar year.

▶ The Annual Comparison of Hirings/Offered/Rejected Contracts query is available for comparing the current year with the previous year for hirings and contracts. The absolute and percentage differences are displayed.

▶ The Proportion of Number of Applicants/Hirings query calculates the proportion of the number of applicants for hirings from the number of applicants and number of applicants with the To Be Hired status.

▶ The Proportion of Number of Offered/Rejected Contracts query calculates the proportion of contracts offered compared to those rejected based on the number of applicants with the Offer rejected status and those with the Contract offered status.

10.5 Conclusion

The standard reports and the BI Standard Content already meet a great deal of the user's requirements for reports in the *Recruitment* module. It is unfortunately also the case here that integration with other SAP system modules is only feasible with SAP NetWeaver BI. In this context too, customer-specific infotypes or additional information from standard infotypes are only possible by way of programmed enhancements in the reports.

This chapter describes the standard reports used for payroll processes. This description does not include any details about legal reporting requirements.

11 Payroll

The following sections provide an overview of the standard reports that are available for payroll processes. You can find the reports in the SAP Easy Access menu via the following path: **Human Resources • Payroll • <Continent> • <Country> • Information System**.

SAP Easy Access path

Country-specific, legally required reports such as statements of contributions paid or the identification of severely handicapped persons are not treated in this book. You can find detailed information about these types of reports as part of the respective country-specific payroll documentation in the SAP Library.

[+]

11.1 Remuneration Statement

The remuneration statement provides an overview of the payments and deductions for each employee per payroll run. The statement is primarily intended to provide employees with all relevant information regarding their income.

11.1.1 Remuneration Statement (Standard Version)

The standard version of the Remuneration Statement report provides the results of a payroll run in an ABAP list. That list is designed in a very simple way and doesn't allow for much redesign.

What you can do, though, is include personal or general notifications from the **Notifications** infotype (0128) in addition to the payroll data as additional information in the remuneration statement. You can define the format, structure, and contents of the remuneration statement forms in Payroll Customizing (**Payroll • Payroll: USA • Forms • Remuneration Statement • Set up remuneration statement**).

In the selection screen (see Figure 11.1), you must select the payroll period and payroll area for which you want to print the remuneration statement. You can also select one or multiple personnel numbers.

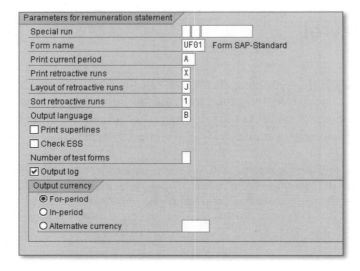

Figure 11.1 Selection Screen for Remuneration Statement

Parameters for remuneration statement

In addition, you can specify general parameters for the remuneration statement in the selection screen. The following parameters are available:

▶ **Form name**
This field contains the four-digit alphanumeric identifier for the form you previously defined in Customizing.

▶ **Print current period**
This parameter controls whether or not a form for the current payroll period is printed. Here you can enter the following values:

  ▷ A: The system always prints a form for the current payroll period.

  ▷ D: The system prints a form for the current payroll period only if a retroactive run has already been printed or if a change has occurred compared to the previous period for the wage type that's specified in Table T512E and identified accordingly in the DIFAR field.

- ▶ F: The system prints a form for the payroll period only if the output appears in a form window.
- ▶ Z: The system prints a form for the payroll period only if a customer-specific condition is met. For this purpose, you must integrate a CHECK_PRINT_MOD routine with the relevant condition in the RPCEDSZ9 include.
- ▶ Print retroactive runs
- ▶ Layout of retroactive runs
- ▶ Sort retroactive runs
- ▶ Output language
- ▶ Print superlines
- ▶ Check ESS ·
- ▶ Output log

You may enter data in the special run fields only for off-cycle payroll runs. The output currency section allows you to define the currency in which you want to output the remuneration statement.

11.1.2 Remuneration Statement with HR Forms

The remuneration statement with HR forms enables you to include graphics and use different fonts and font formats in the output of the statement. To do that, SAP provides sample forms. For the United States, you should select the SAP_PAYSLIP_US sample form (see Figure 11.2).

To be able to print the remuneration statement using this transaction, you must first set up and generate a form in the HR Forms Workplace (Transaction HRFORMS).

You can enter the Customizing settings for the remuneration statement with HR forms in the IMG via **Payroll • Payroll: USA • HR Forms Workbench**.

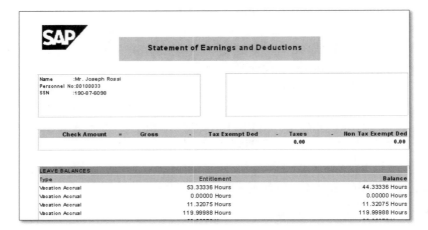

Figure 11.2 Sample Remuneration Statement with HR Forms

The following three options are available to print the selected form:

▶ **Print without variant**
If you do not specify any variant in the selection screen (see Figure 11.3), the system displays the report selection screen of the form in which you can enter additional selection conditions and output parameters, such as the printing of retroactive runs. You have defined the parameters previously in Customizing. Figure 11.4 shows an example of additional parameters.

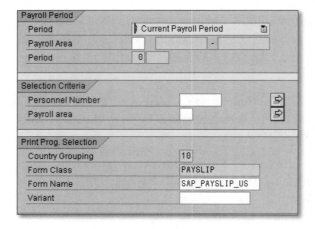

Figure 11.3 Selection Screen for Calling the Remuneration Statement with HR Forms

▶ **Print with variant**

If you have already created a variant, you can select it by pressing the (F4) key and directly start the print run.

▶ **Print with customer-specific transaction**

You can create a customer-specific transaction, that is, a copy of the standard transaction, in which you can use the parameters to define the type of printout you require. Refer to the documentation of the standard transaction for further details on this topic.

Form-specific Settings		
☐ Suppress Statistics		
Archive Forms	Do Not Archive	▤
☐ Form in Language of Employee		

Figure 11.4 Form-Specific Settings

11.2   Reports for Infotypes and Payroll Results

The reports for infotypes and payroll results of employees greatly support the daily work of the members of the payroll department. The following reports represent only a small fraction of the many reports in the standard version, which are used to provide employees, the company, and external authorities with the relevant information.

11.2.1   Payroll Journal

The Payroll Journal report contains selected, detailed payroll data for multiple employees, which has been created during a specific period or during a selected payroll period. For example, you can use the payroll journal to identify errors that occurred during the payroll run, or you can use it for totaling the payroll data of an organizational unit. In addition, you can use the payroll journal as an additional detailed controlling instrument for auditing purposes.

> The payroll journal should not be used as a basis for harmonizing financial accounting and controlling data. For this purpose, you must use the relevant reconciliation reports.

[+]

The payroll journal can be structured according to your requirements. You can find comprehensive information on how to set up the individual components of the payroll journal in the Implementation Guide via **Payroll • Payroll: USA • Forms • Payroll Journal • Payroll Journal**.

The output layout can be designed by entering the relevant information in the **Additional data** and **Print format** sections in the selection screen (see Figure 11.5).

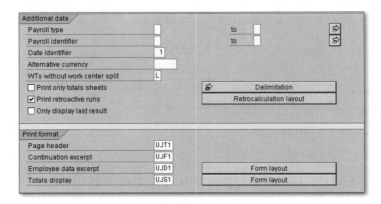

Figure 11.5 Formatting Parameters for the Payroll Journal

Output control The following options for outputting the payroll journal are available in the **Additional data** section:

▶ **Date identifier**
The date identifier defines which date type is relevant for the decision as to whether or not a payroll result lies within the specified period.

　▶ 01: Payday

　▶ 02: Date of the payroll run

　▶ 03: Period end date

If the program is executed for only one payroll period, this field will be ignored.

▶ **WT without work center split**
This parameter allows you to define the way in which wage types that aren't stored in accordance with the work center split will be used in the analysis:

　▶ F: Assignment to first work center/basic reference period

　▶ L: Assignment to last work center/basic reference period

- Space: No assignment

- **Print only totals sheets**
  If this option is checked, the system displays only totals but no employee data excerpts. The **Delimitation** button next to this field enables you to define the totals levels, such as the company code, personnel area, and cost center.

- **Print retroactive runs**
  This parameter allows you to define whether or not you want the system to print retroactive runs. The **Retrocalculation layout** button next to the parameter enables you to control the type of retroactive calculation printout as well as the way in which the wage types are sorted for printing.

- **Only display last result**
  If this field is activated, the system displays only the last payroll result for the selected period for each personnel number. If the field is not checked, the system displays all payroll results for the selected period.

To create the payroll result, the system analyzes the payroll data records whose in-period ranges within the specified period. Retroactive accounting differences that may have occurred for a specific payroll period are analyzed in the payroll journal in conjunction with the payroll period in which the retroactive calculation occurred. The selected payroll results are listed sequentially in the form in accordance with the in-period view. Figure 11.6 shows the output of a payroll journal in accordance with the parameters shown in Figure 11.5.

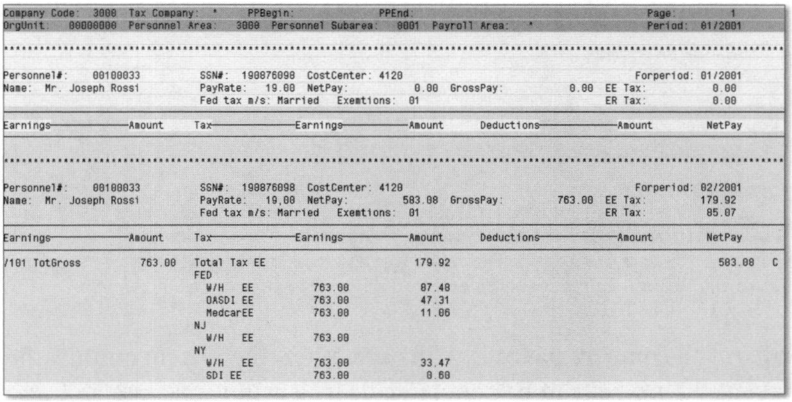

```
Company Code:  3000  Tax Company:  *     PPBegin:                PPEnd:                          Page:        1
OrgUnit:   00000000  Personnel Area:   3000  Personnel Subarea:   0001  Payroll Area:   *         Period:  01/2001

*****************************************************************************************************************

Personnel#:     00100033          SSN#:  190876098  CostCenter: 4120                          Forperiod: 01/2001
Name:  Mr. Joseph Rossi           PayRate:   19.00  NetPay:            0.00  GrossPay:        0.00  EE Tax:        0.00
                                  Fed tax m/s: Married   Exemtions:  01                         ER Tax:        0.00

Earnings----------Amount    Tax----------Earnings----------Amount    Deductions----------Amount        NetPay

*****************************************************************************************************************

Personnel#:     00100033          SSN#:  190876098  CostCenter: 4120                          Forperiod: 02/2001
Name:  Mr. Joseph Rossi           PayRate:   19,00  NetPay:          583.08  GrossPay:      763.00  EE Tax:      179.92
                                  Fed tax m/s: Married   Exemtions:  01                         ER Tax:       85.07

Earnings----------Amount    Tax----------Earnings----------Amount    Deductions----------Amount        NetPay

/101 TotGross       763.00  Total Tax EE                    179.92                                 583.08   C
                            FED
                              W/H   EE        763.00         87.48
                              OASDI EE        763.00         47.31
                              MedcarEE        763.00         11.06
                            NJ
                              W/H   EE        763.00
                            NY
                              W/H   EE        763.00         33.47
                              SDI EE          763.00          0.60
```

Figure 11.6 Output of a Payroll Journal

11.2.2 Wage Type Reporter

The Wage Type Reporter report analyzes wage types on the basis of the payroll results for a specific period. The data used for this process originate exclusively from Tables RT (Result Table) and WPBP (Work Place Basic Pay).

The **Selection** group box provides the standard selection fields of the logical database, PNP. In these fields, the selection according to organizational criteria does not necessarily have to correspond to a selection according to payroll results for the selected organizational unit. Especially with regard to retroactive master data changes, there may be differences. It is useful to include objects that have been searched for in the object selection.

The **Payroll Period** group box allows you to enter the period for which you want to analyze the wage types. This period may contain more than one payroll month. You can limit the payroll period to be analyzed by clicking on the **Payroll Interval** button. In addition, you can run and display a comparison between regular payrolls. Furthermore, you can restrict the data to be displayed via the absolute and percentage deviation of amount and number. Figure 11.7 shows the selection based on the payroll period.

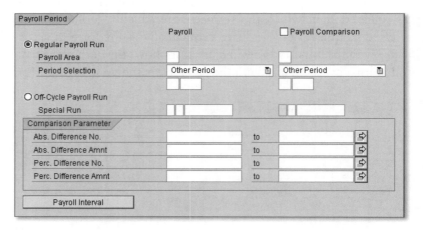

Figure 11.7 Payroll Comparison Selection

When you compare payrolls with each other, the system outputs the data of the payrolls to be compared as well as the absolute and percentage deviations between number and amount in the list.

If you activate the **In-Period Payroll View** or **For-Period Payroll View** field in the **Define Period** group box, the list is created in the selected view.

If you activate the **In-Period Payroll View**, the system selects all results that were created within the selected period. Note that the period end date is the decisive criteria for the period assignment. In the above example, a payroll for December 2006 would be included in February 2006, whereas a February 2006 payroll would not be included in May 2006.

If you activate the **For-Period Payroll View**, the system selects all results that were created for the selected period. Note that here the payment date of the period is the decisive criteria for the period assignment. In this case, a payroll for December 2006 would not be included in February 2006, whereas a February 2006 payroll would be included in May 2006.

If you do not specify any wage type in the **Other Selection** group box, the system selects all wage types that are contained in the result table (RT) for the selected payroll result. Apart from that, you must specify here whether you want the system to display archived data and records containing zero values as well.

The **Object Selection** function enables you to define which objects should be displayed as columns in the list and which objects you want to aggregate. The selected objects are then output as columns in the list and aggregated across the nonselected objects.

The **Output** group box allows you to specify whether you want to create the wage type list using the SAP List Viewer, the ALV Grid Control, or Microsoft Excel. Figure 11.8 shows the output of the list as an ALV Grid Control.

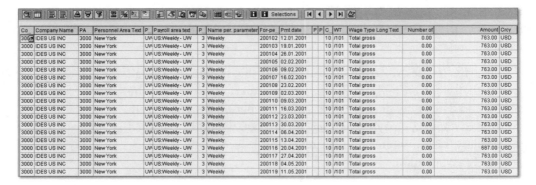

Figure 11.8 Output of the Wage Type Reporter Report (ALV Grid Control)

11.2.3 Displaying Payroll Results

The Display Payroll Results report displays the payroll results that pertain to one or multiple personnel numbers.

The screen shown in Figure 11.9 is divided into the following areas: **Selection**, **Selected Employees**, and **Payroll Results**.

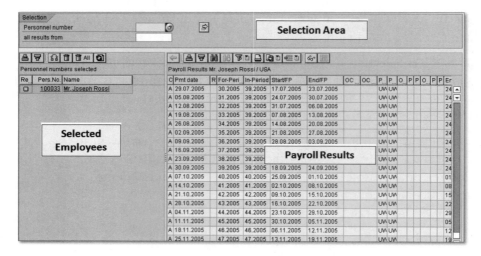

Figure 11.9 Display Payroll Results Screen

In the **Selection** area, you must enter the personnel numbers in the **Personnel number** field whose payroll results you want to display; then select **Copy**. If you enter a date in the **all results from** field, the system displays all payroll results whose beginning of the for-period or end of the in-period is included in the specified period.

The system displays the selected personnel numbers in the **Selected Employees** area. The default setting for the display of selected personnel numbers is the formatted name from the **Organizational Assignment** infotype (0001). If you want to display the sortable names from the **Personal Data** infotype (0002), You must select the **First name and last name** function. An icon in the **Res.** column indicates whether or not results exist for the selected period.

▶ ◉ : Results are available for the selected period.

▶ ◧ : No results are available for the selected period.

▶ ◈ : No authorization to display available results.

To display the payroll results for a personnel number that's contained in the list, you must highlight the personnel number. The system will then display the available payroll results in the right-hand area of the screen. To remove personnel numbers from the list, you must highlight them and select **Delete** or **Delete all**.

If you want to format the list of payroll results according to your own requirements, you can set up and store your own default layout. This way you can always display the results in the same layout when you run the report. The system contains predefined layouts for different countries that contain the relevant country-specific fields. If you don't store any personal default layout, the system will always choose the relevant country-specific layout.

The overview of the payroll results provides general information about how up-to-date the results are as well as about the in-period and the for-period.

The status indicator in the first column contains information about the age of a payroll result. The indicator can have three different values:

▶ **Value A**
The payroll result was created during the last payroll run and is therefore up to date.

▶ **Value P**
The payroll result was replaced by a new record during the course of a retroactive calculation. It is therefore the predecessor of the current record.

▶ **Value O**

The payroll result was replaced by at least two retroactive calculations. Therefore the record is neither up to date nor is it the predecessor of the current record.

To display the tables for a payroll result, you must highlight the payroll result and select **Display Overview**. The system then displays an overview of all payroll result tables that are relevant for the country of the respective employee (see Figure 11.10) as well as the number of records per table.

WPBP	Work Center/Basic Pay	1
RT	Results Table	65
RT_	Results Table (Collapsed Display)	65
CRT	Cumulative Results Table	114
BT	Payment Information	1
VO	Variable Assignment	1
PCALAC	Status info. for subsequent programs	1
ABC	Cumulation of Absence Classes	1
VERSION	Information on Creation	1
PCL2	Update information PCL2	1
VERSC	Payroll Status Information	1
TAX	Employee tax details	3
TAXR	Residence and unemployment tax details	4
TAXPR	Tax proration table	1
TCRT	Cumulated tax results	526
NAME	Name of Employee	1
ADR	Address	1
PERM	Personal Characteristics	1
MODIF	Modifiers	1

Figure 11.10 Tables for a Payroll Result

You can also display the tables that do not contain any records for the selected payroll result. To do that, you must select **Tables • Empty Tables • Display** from the menu.

It is possible to highlight multiple rows in the overview. To do this, hold down the ⌈Ctrl⌋ key and select the respective table. Then select **Display Contents**. The system then displays the **Tables/Field strings of payroll result** screen that contains the records of the selected tables for the respective payroll results (see Figure 11.11).

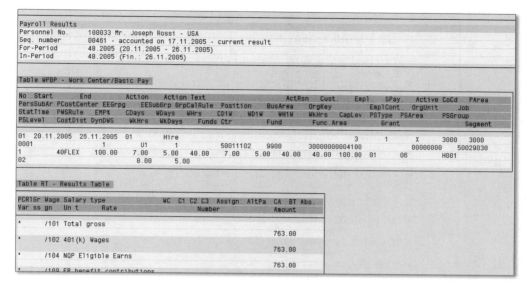

Figure 11.11 Contents of Tables WPBP and RT

You can save this selection before exiting the program by selecting the **Save Selected Entry** function. If you have already stored a selection of tables for a specific payroll result, you can directly go to the display of these selected tables by using the **Display Content** function in the payroll results overview.

From there, you can also navigate to the maintenance and personnel master data displays. To do that, select **Goto • HR Master Data • Display or Goto • HR Master Data • Maintain**.

Furthermore, you can include loan wage types in the display by selecting **Tables • Loans • Display**. The report replaces the Print Loan Results report (RPCLSTO).

11.2.4 Garnishment Details Report

The Garnishment Details Report provides a comprehensive list of employees whose wages are garnished, as well as garnishment-related information for each employee from payroll results.

The Garnishment Details Report draws garnishment-related data from payroll results and displays per employee (see Figure 11.12):

- ▸ Employee name and personnel number
- ▸ Garnish document date
- ▸ Internal and sequence numbers
- ▸ Garnishment document start and release dates
- ▸ Document number (issued by the authority)
- ▸ Document originator state
- ▸ Garnishment status (for example, active or pending)
- ▸ Garnishment amount (see the following note)
- ▸ Garnishment amount taken during the specified payroll period
- ▸ Garnishment initial balance
- ▸ Garnishment category (for example, creditor)
- ▸ Priority
- ▸ Remaining balance to be paid
- ▸ Total for the specified organizational entity

Garnishment Details Report									
Company - 3000 IDES US INC			Garnishment Details Report				Page No. - 1		
Pay Area -							Run Date - 09.09.2007		
Pay Per. - 00.		-					Run Time - 12:05:43		
Pay Date -							Report ID - RPCGRNU0		
Employee Name	Employee ID	Document Date / Internal N. Seq.N.	Start / Release Date	Document Number	Orig. St. State	Gar. Amount Taken	Initial Balance	Gar. Cat. Gar. Pri.	Remaining Balance
Mr. Randy Gordon	00100142	15.05.1999 0002 01	16.05.1999 00.00.0000	151653423	CA 1	250.00		CS 101	
		15.05.1999 0002 01	16.05.1999 00.00.0000	151653423	CA 1	250.00		CS 101	
		15.05.1999 0002 01	16.05.1999 00.00.0000	151653423	CA 1	250.00		CS 101	
		15.05.1999 0002 01	16.05.1999 00.00.0000	151653423	CA 1	250.00		CS 101	

Figure 11.12 Garnishment Details Report Output

[+]   The garnishment amount is the amount scheduled to be taken, or calculated during a payroll run, according to the terms outlined in the garnishment order. This amount could be reduced if an employee's disposable net income is not sufficient to cover the whole garnishment amount.

11.2.5 US Workers' Compensation Summary Report

To access this report from the Personnel management menu choose **Administration · Info system · Reports · Administration · US Worker's compensation · US Worker's compensation report**.

The US Workers' Compensation Summary report provides you with a summary of the workers' compensation information for a given organizational unit, as well as detailed workers' compensation information per employee. This information serves as a basis for calculating workers' compensation insurance premiums. The report only calculates Workers' Compensation wages and premiums per pay date.

In the **Other Selections** box on the selection screen (see Figure 11.13), you can enter the tax authority for which the workers' compensation amount should be calculated. If entered, the workers' compensation amount is calculated for this tax authority only; otherwise, the amount is accumulated for all tax authorities (including Federal) and reported.

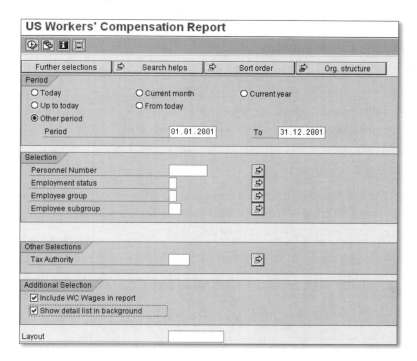

Figure 11.13 Selection Screen of the US Workers' Compensation Summary Report

In the **Additional Selection** box on the selection screen, you can choose to include workers' compensation wage information in the report. You can also choose to include detailed information when the report is run in the background.

> Before running the report you need to make the appropriate settings in the IMG (**Personnel Administration** • **Organizational Data** • **Workers' Compensation**)

This report reads data defined for your employees and/or organizational units defined in the *Workers' Compensation chapter* of the *Personnel Administration Implementation Guide* under *Organizational Data*. You can also make workers' compensation code assignments and other settings using the WC State and Code PD infotype for organizational units and the WC State, Code, Attribute PD infotype for positions.

The report includes summary information in SAP List Viewer form for the following:

▶ Workers' compensation state

▶ Workers' compensation code

▶ Total number of employees per workers' compensation code within the group of selected employees

▶ Total workers' compensation wage of all employees per workers' compensation code

▶ Total workers' compensation premiums due for the group of selected employees

The SAP List Viewer function allows you to filter data according to a wide range of criteria. You can also view further details by selecting a line and selecting the **Choose details** function.

11.3 SAP NetWeaver BI Standard Content

The standard BI content for payroll (see Figure 11.14) contains the following InfoCubes:

▶ Employee-Specific Payroll Data

▶ Posting Documents

▶ Auditing Information on Postings Relevant to Cost Accounting

▶ MultiCube (Time and Payroll Data)

Collected objects	I	M	S	A	Technical n	Elevated object's assc
▽ 🕸 Payroll	☐				☐ 0PY	
▷ 🕸 InfoArea	☐					
▽ 🗇 InfoCube	☐					
▷ 🗇 Employee-Specific Payroll Data	☐				☐ 0PY_C02	Uses : 0PY [AREA]
▷ 🗇 Posting Documents	☐				☐ 0PY_PP2	Uses : 0PY [AREA]
▷ 🗇 Auditing Information on Postings Relevant to Cost Accou	☐				☐ 0PY_PPC01	Uses : 0PY [AREA]
▷ 🗇 Auditing Info on Postings for Position Budgeting and Co	☐				☐ 0PY_PPC02	Uses : 0PY [AREA]
▷ 🏬 InfoObject Catalog	☐					
▽ 🕸 MultiProvider	☐					
▽ 🕸 HR MultiCube (Time and Payroll Data)	☐				☐ 0PY_MC02	Uses : 0PY [AREA]
▷ 🕸 InfoArea	☐					
▽ 🗇 InfoCube	☐					
▽ 🗇 Time and Labor	☐				☐ 0PT_C01	Sends data to : 0PY_M
▷ 🕸 InfoArea	☐					
▷ 🖽 InfoObject	☐					
▷ 🖾 Update rules	☐					
🗇 Employee-Specific Payroll Data	☐				☐ 0PY_C02	Sends data to : 0PY_M
▷ 🖽 InfoObject	☐					
▽ 🗐 DataStore Object	☐					
▷ 🗐 Auditing Information and Payroll Data	☑	☑			🗔 0PY_PP_C1	Uses : 0PY [AREA]
▷ 🗐 Posting Documents	☑	☑			🗔 0PY_PP_C2	Uses : 0PY [AREA]
▷ 🗐 Posting Documents and Auditing Information Combined	☑	☑			🗔 0PY_PP_C3	Uses : 0PY [AREA]

Figure 11.14 Standard BI Content for Payroll

11.3.1 Employee-Specific Payroll Data InfoCube

The **Employee-Specific Payroll Data** InfoCube contains wage types with country-specific grouping with key figures **Amount** and **Number**. However, it does not contain the **Amount/Unit** field, which often leads to the situation that no hourly rate, normally stored in this field, is available. The country grouping characteristic allows you to use the InfoCube on an international basis.

Unfortunately, this InfoCube does not differentiate between a for-period view and an in-period view, which is a commonly used procedure in payroll. Therefore, you cannot use this InfoCube to create controlling reports, which usually require the use of the in-period view. This type of report must be executed on the basis of the **Posting Documents** or **Auditing Information on Postings Relevant to Cost Accounting** InfoCubes. Figure 11.15 shows the InfoCube with dimensions and key figures.

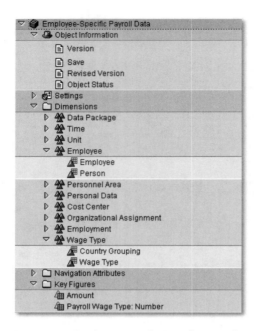

Figure 11.15 Employee-Specific Payroll Data InfoCube

The **Employee-Specific Payroll Data** InfoCube enables you to create a large number of different wage type reports. Figure 11.16 shows an annual overview of gross payments per cost center. SAP NetWeaver BI enables you to easily carry out tasks that were only possible by using a payroll account in standard SAP R/3 or SAP ERP versions. Compared to standard reporting, an InfoCube containing a small number of queries provides a multitude of options.

Table		1st Quarter 2006	2nd Quarter 2006	3rd Quarter 2007	4th Quarter 2006	4th Quarter 2007
Master Cost Center		Amount	Amount	Amount	Amount	Amount
1000/#	1000/Not assigned	173,056.05 EUR	18,452.25 EUR		13,307.64 EUR	0
1000/1000	Corporate Services	38,517.12 EUR		3,847.46 EUR		
1000/1110	Executive Board	265,741.56 EUR	16,270.67 EUR	8,753.32 EUR	19,508.85 EUR	
1000/1200	Cafeteria	8,262.92 EUR		9,262.06 EUR		56,571.22 EUR
1000/1210	Telephone	3,847.46 EUR	70,725.12 EUR	218,581.47 EUR		10,305.62 EUR
1000/1220	Motor Pool	8,753.32 EUR	6,161.06 EUR	132,980.81 EUR		5,045.58 EUR
1000/1230	Power	9,262.06 EUR				101,071.44 EUR
1000/2100	Finance & Admin.	218,581.47 EUR	10,560.00 EUR		10,560.00 EUR	36,438.46 EUR
1000/2200	Human Resources	132,980.81 EUR	37,097.13 EUR		41,816.88 EUR	
1000/2300	Procurement	70,725.12 EUR		70,725.12 EUR		56,571.22 EUR
1000/3100	Motorcycle Sales	6,161.06 EUR		6,161.06 EUR		10,305.62 EUR
1000/4240	Paint/Solvent Prod.	20,894.75 EUR	10,400.64 EUR		12,378.03 EUR	5,045.58 EUR
1000/4290	Prod. Elevators/Turb	56,571.22 EUR	30,411.23 EUR	56,571.22 EUR	35,946.15 EUR	36,438.46 EUR
1000/4295	Elevator Assembly	10,305.62 EUR	6,810.75 EUR	10,305.62 EUR	8,087.62 EUR	56,571.22 EUR
1000/4296	Turbine preassembly	5,045.58 EUR		5,045.58 EUR		10,305.62 EUR
1000/4297	Turbine fin. assmbly	101,071.44 EUR		101,071.44 EUR		5,045.58 EUR
1000/4300	Plant Maintenance	36,438.46 EUR		36,438.46 EUR		101,071.44 EUR
1000/4400	Quality Assurance	37,160.94 EUR	13,708.95 EUR		16,262.69 EUR	36,438.46 EUR
1000/4500	R & D	43,144.82 EUR	12,049.77 EUR		14,435.80 EUR	
1000/6230	Laptop GR 02	16,910.64 EUR				
1000/30200	1000/30200	165,750.69 EUR	40,748.25 EUR		70,748.25 EUR	
1000/AC040	production AC040	8,800.00 EUR				
Overall Result		2,425,276.26 EUR	196,509.64 EUR	265,741.56 EUR	243,051.91 EUR	1,701,071.44 EUR

Figure 11.16 Wage Type Report – Annual Overview

11.3.2 Posting Documents InfoCube

The **Posting Documents** InfoCube contains the posting document including account assignment and posting information (see Figure 11.17). The data are based on the document lines of the HR document. You cannot carry out a drill-down by wage types or employees, which can be done using the **Auditing Information and Payroll Data** InfoCube.

Table		TotGross	BaseWage	EE taxes	ER share	Transfer
1st Quarter 2006	Amount	2,425,276.26 EUR	473,911.56 EUR	428,426.80 EUR	483,492.27 EUR	1,492,080.86 EUR
2nd Quarter 2006	Amount	196,509.64 EUR	35,426.64 EUR	29,078.93 EUR	32,984.84 EUR	129,052.95 EUR
3rd Quarter 2006	Amount	176,372.95 EUR	35,426.64 EUR	25,198.26 EUR	29,257.64 EUR	117,241.81 EUR

Figure 11.17 Posting Documents InfoCube

11.3.3 Posting Documents and Auditing Information Combined InfoCube

The **Posting Documents and Auditing Information Combined** InfoCube enables the presentation and analysis of personnel costs per employee. You can analyze the posting document from payroll in conjunction with the auditing information on employees and wage types. This allows you to create reports on posted personnel costs, which had previously only been possible by using customer-specific reports.

11.3.4 Time and Payroll Data MultiCube

The **Time and Payroll Data** MultiCube combines the contents of the **Time and Labor** and **Employee-Specific Payroll Data** InfoCubes to analyze time data and the associated costs together in one query (see Figure 11.18).

[+]

Unfortunately, this MultiCube contains all the weaknesses of the Info-Cubes it is based on. A particular disadvantage is that it doesn't contain the Amount/Unit field, especially because it is typically applied in the context of overtime costs or illness costs.

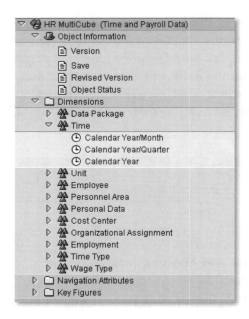

Figure 11.18 Time and Payroll Data MultiCube

11.3.5 Queries for InfoCubes in Payroll

Queries for the Employee-Specific Payroll Data InfoCube

The **Employee-Specific Payroll Data** InfoCube contains the following queries:

▶ **Wage Type Analysis**
You can display wage type amounts by wage type, currency, master cost center, and period.

▶ **Quarterly Wage Types Overview**
This query presents the last four quarters in separate columns. The rows contain the wage types, which were previously selected in the selection screen.

▶ **WEB: My Cost Center Current Personnel Costs and YTD**
Presentation of the personnel costs for an employee's cost center in the portal.

▶ **WEB: My Cost Center Quarterly Personnel Costs**
Presentation of personnel costs of an employee's cost center per quarter.

► **Wage Type Comparison Personnel Areas**
This query compares wage types of different personnel areas or personnel subareas with each other. The period is designed as a free characteristic. The organizational criteria can also be selected according to your requirements.

► **Wage Types Overview US**
This query provides a quarterly overview of central wage types from U.S. payroll.

► **Wage Types Overview Germany**
This query provides a quarterly overview of selected wage types from German payroll (see Figure 11.19).

► **Annual Wage Types Overview**
This query provides an annual total for the current year as well as an annual total for the previous year. It specifies a difference as well as a percentage deviation. The selection screen enables you to select wage types.

► **Quarterly Wage Types Overview**
This query provides a quarterly overview of any wage type.

The **Employee-Specific Payroll Data** InfoCube can be used in many situations. The queries listed here should be regarded as examples and may be complemented by company-specific queries.

		1. Quart	2. Quart	3. Quart	4. Quart
Account		Amount	Amount	Amount	Amount
Salaries and wages p	CACA/176000	-960,652.57 CAD	-1,379,302.35 CAD	-1,229,842.27 CAD	-1,450,207.76 CAD
Salaries and wages p	CACA/176001	-64,622.42 CAD	-89,717.23 CAD	-78,288.14 CAD	220,769.40 CAD
Federal Income Tax W	CACA/176100	-424,326.57 CAD	-603,012.35 CAD	-505,656.79 CAD	-632,125.43 CAD
Federal Income Tax W	CACA/176101	-119,630.92 CAD	-105,892.18 CAD	-36,522.36 CAD	-13,225.52 CAD
Federal Income Tax W	CACA/176102	-81,597.74 CAD	-77,224.88 CAD	-27,280.70 CAD	-11,987.59 CAD
Social Security Cont	CACA/176200	-34,962.65 CAD	-46,612.74 CAD	-41,004.05 CAD	-48,653.64 CAD
Social Security Cont	CACA/176201	-17,300.26 CAD	-14,105.06 CAD	-3,420.46 CAD	-3,001.04 CAD
Social Security Cont	CACA/176202	-2,002.27 CAD	-2,674.14 CAD	-2,357.75 CAD	-2,711.97 CAD
Federal Income Tax W	CACA/176203	-160.35 CAD	-177.53 CAD	-88.53 CAD	-44.10 CAD
Federal Income Tax W	CACA/176204	-4,004.28 CAD	-5,347.94 CAD	-4,715.14 CAD	-5,423.59 CAD
Employees' Saving Pl	CACA/176401	-7,906.34 CAD	-11,026.03 CAD	-9,641.36 CAD	-9,843.45 CAD
Social Security Cont	CACA/176401	-3,027.88 CAD	-4,174.18 CAD	-3,652.06 CAD	-3,735.10 CAD
Social Security Cont	CACA/176402	-28,467.99 CAD	-40,253.83 CAD	-33,708.50 CAD	-34,169.80 CAD
Social Security Cont	CACA/176407	-5,175.20 CAD	-7,762.80 CAD	-6,469.00 CAD	-6,467.80 CAD
Social Security Cont	CACA/176408	-48,080.05 CAD	-67,683.85 CAD	-58,072.30 CAD	-58,856.85 CAD
Social Security Cont	CACA/176419	-705.29 CAD	828.76 CAD	184.20 CAD	199.55 CAD
Federal Income Tax W	CACA/176501	-119.60 CAD			

Figure 11.19 Wage Types Overview Germany Query

Query for the Posting Documents InfoCube

Only one query is available for the **Posting Documents** InfoCube: the Posting Documents (Quarterly) query (see Figure 11.20).

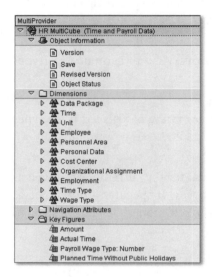

Figure 11.20 Posting Documents (Quarterly)

Queries for the Posting Documents and Auditing Information Combined InfoCube

The Posting Documents and Auditing Information Combined Info-Cube is the basis for the planned/actual comparison in personnel cost planning. It contains the following queries:

▶ WEB: Personnel Costs of the Current Fiscal Year (uarters)

▶ WEB: Personnel Costs of the Previous Posting Period

▶ Employee-Specific Payroll and Posting Information

▶ WEB: Personnel Costs of the Current Fiscal Year

Queries for the Time and Payroll Data MultiCube

▶ **Annual Overview of Illness Hours and Costs**
The number of illness hours is taken from the reporting time type, whereas the costs originate from wage type /841 in Payroll. Both values are specified as limited key figures and are compared in a structure that consists of columns for previous year values and the creation of differences.

▶ **Overtime Hours and Costs (Web Cockpit)**

This query contains four views: Current overtime costs (no drill-down), Current overtime costs, Current overtime costs and previous months, and Overtime costs for four quarters.

▶ **Illness Hours and Costs (Web Cockpit)**

This query contains four views: Current illness costs (no drill-down), Current illness costs, Current illness costs and previous months, Illness costs for four quarters.

▶ **Annual Overtime Overview**

This query provides the overtime hours and costs for the current and previous years as well as the difference in an absolute amount and percentage.

▶ **Overtime: Overview of Hours and Costs**

This query presents the costs and hours in separate columns.

The queries must be customized according to the specific requirements, particularly those related to overtime. Limited key figures must be specifically defined for each individual company. Figure 11.21 shows the definition of the **Annual Overtime Overview** query with limited key figures.

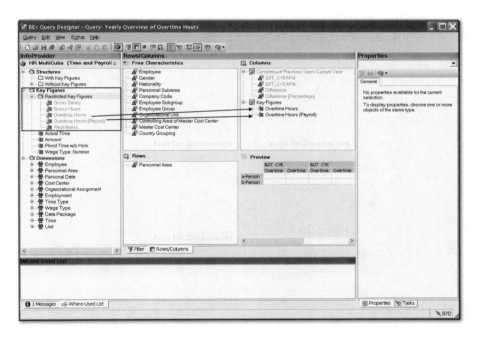

Figure 11.21 Annual Overtime Overview Query

11.4 Conclusion

From the point of view of someone working in the Payroll department, the number of lists for reconciliation and analysis purposes cannot be high enough. However, the standard reports provided by SAP meet a large part of the reporting requirements. Unfortunately, the combination of payroll data and time management data, especially in order to analyze the costs of absence times, for example, is only available in the standard BI content.

Personnel Time Management reports provide information on employees' work schedules, attendances and absences, and time accounts.

12   Personnel Time Management

Personnel Time Management supports you with executing all the HR processes involved in the planning, recording, and evaluation of employees' work performance and absence times.

Standard reports provide time administrators and time supervisors with information on employees' time and labor data and free time quotas.

To access the Personnel Time Management reports, open the SAP Easy Access menu path **Human Resources · Time Management · Administration · Information System · Report Selection**. The reports are contained here under the headings Work Schedule, Attendance, Absence, and Leave Information.

SAP Easy Access path

12.1   Work Schedule

The work schedule reports contain information on the target values for employees' work schedules and on the various working time models that are defined using the work schedule. They give you a multiple-employee overview of all the most important of these target values for specific dates. You can also use these reports to obtain an overview of daily work schedules based on certain criteria.

12.1.1   Personal Work Schedule

The Personal Work Schedule report creates a multiple-employee overview of all the main target values for employees' work schedules (see Figure 12.1) for specific dates over any period.

Cluster B2   If you check the **Read from Cluster** box, the data of the B2 cluster are used as a basis when the personal work schedule data are read. In this case, a daily work schedule that is dynamically created by the time report is displayed.

You can also restrict the data selection period using the selection screen in other ways. For example, you can display the working time target values only for the days on which the employee in question was active. Because Inactive and Pensioned Employees also still have a **Planned Working Time** infotype, you have to fill this parameter. To do this, select the corresponding parameter from the **Display periods** group.

Pers.No.	Name	Date	Day	DWS	DV	Daily WS text	Va	Text	Grp	Start	End	PiHrs	HCi	DT	Day type text	Personal WS	Description	HCr	Text
00010960	Mr. Frank Fredericks	19.07.2007	TH	NORM		Normal Days			10	08:00	17:00	8.00	0		Work/paid	NORM	Normal work schedule	US	Public holiday calendar USA
		20.07.2007	FR	NORM		Normal Days			10	08:00	17:00	8.00	0		Work/paid	NORM	Normal work schedule	US	Public holiday calendar USA
		21.07.2007	SA	FREE		Off			10			0.00	0		Work/paid	NORM	Normal work schedule	US	Public holiday calendar USA
		22.07.2007	SU	FREE		Off			10			0.00	0		Work/paid	NORM	Normal work schedule	US	Public holiday calendar USA
		23.07.2007	MO	NORM		Normal Days			10	08:00	17:00	8.00	0		Work/paid	NORM	Normal work schedule	US	Public holiday calendar USA
		24.07.2007	TU	NORM		Normal Days			10	08:00	17:00	8.00	0		Work/paid	NORM	Normal work schedule	US	Public holiday calendar USA
		25.07.2007	WE	NORM		Normal Days			10	08:00	17:00	8.00	0		Work/paid	NORM	Normal work schedule	US	Public holiday calendar USA
		26.07.2007	TH	NORM		Normal Days			10	08:00	17:00	8.00	0		Work/paid	NORM	Normal work schedule	US	Public holiday calendar USA
		27.07.2007	FR	NORM		Normal Days			10	08:00	17:00	8.00	0		Work/paid	NORM	Normal work schedule	US	Public holiday calendar USA
		28.07.2007	SA	FREE		Off			10			0.00	0		Work/paid	NORM	Normal work schedule	US	Public holiday calendar USA
		29.07.2007	SU	FREE		Off			10			0.00	0		Work/paid	NORM	Normal work schedule	US	Public holiday calendar USA
		30.07.2007	MO	NORM		Normal Days			10	08:00	17:00	8.00	0		Work/paid	NORM	Normal work schedule	US	Public holiday calendar USA
		31.07.2007	TU	NORM		Normal Days			10	08:00	17:00	8.00	0		Work/paid	NORM	Normal work schedule	US	Public holiday calendar USA
00010961	Mrs Anne Henning	01.07.2007	SU	FREE		Off			10			0.00	0		Work/paid	NORM	Normal work schedule	US	Public holiday calendar USA
		02.07.2007	MO	NORM		Normal Days			10	08:00	17:00	8.00	0		Work/paid	NORM	Normal work schedule	US	Public holiday calendar USA
		03.07.2007	TU	NORM		Normal Days			10	08:00	17:00	8.00	0		Work/paid	NORM	Normal work schedule	US	Public holiday calendar USA
		04.07.2007	WE	NORM		Normal Days			10	08:00	17:00	8.00	1	1	TimeOff/paid	NORM	Normal work schedule	US	Public holiday calendar USA
		05.07.2007	TH	NORM		Normal Days			10	08:00	17:00	8.00	0		Work/paid	NORM	Normal work schedule	US	Public holiday calendar USA

Figure 12.1 Personal Work Schedule Report Output

You have the following options in the report output:

▶ Display detailed information on the daily work schedule (see Section 12.1.2) or the target working time (0007) of an employee, for example.

▶ Find out how many, if any, time infotype records were recorded for an employee on a particular day. The infotypes Attendances (2001), Absences (2002), Substitutions (2003), Availability for Work (2004), and Overtime (2005) are taken into account. You also have the option to display detailed information on the employees' time infotype records.

Error list   ▶ Display a report of all errors that have occurred, such as Customizing errors (see Figure 12.2). This report contains the error message type (for example, a red icon means "Error"), the personnel number of the employee for whom the error occurred, and the error text.

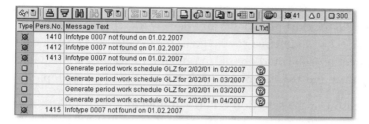

Figure 12.2 Error Report

> Very irritatingly, a message window opens for every personnel number **[+]**
> with errors before the report is output, and you then have to confirm the
> message for each person. For example, if the **Automatic generation** field
> in the Customizing of the work schedule rules (view V_T508A) contains an
> M, and the work schedule has not yet been generated, the message about
> generating a (monthly) work schedule is displayed in this message win-
> dow for every personnel number.

12.1.2 Daily Work Schedule

The Daily Work Schedule report creates an overview in the form of a   Customizing
table control of all the daily work schedules that correspond to certain criteria (see Figure 12.3). You can use this table to check the
daily work schedules that you created in the Customizing, for example. This table displays the content of the view V_T550A.

Grpg	Daily work schedule	Variant	Daily WS text	Start Date	End Date	
	1010H		10 hour day	01.01.1990	31.12.9999	
	1010H	A	10 hour day	01.01.1990	31.12.9999	
	1010HR		10 HR w/o brk.	01.01.1990	31.12.9999	
	1012H		12 hour day	01.01.1990	31.12.9999	
	1012H	A	12 hour day	01.01.1990	31.12.9999	
	108E		Early shift 8h	01.01.2002	31.12.9999	
	108L		Late shift 8h	01.01.2002	31.12.9999	
	109E		Early shift 9h	01.01.2002	31.12.9999	
	109L		Late shift 9h	01.01.2002	31.12.9999	
	109X80		9x80 Flex	01.01.1990	31.12.9999	
	109X80	A	9x80 Flex	01.01.1990	31.12.9999	
	10AWS1		Altern day 1	01.01.1992	31.12.9999	

Figure 12.3 Daily Work Schedule Report

In the selection criteria, restrict the personnel subarea grouping for
the daily work schedule (**Personnel subarea grouping** field) or the ID
of the daily work schedule (**Daily work schedule** field).

The long text of the daily work schedule, as well as the ID, is output in this table. All the existing variants for a daily work schedule are also displayed. Select an individual row to go to the detailed screen of a daily work schedule. You could do this to obtain information on the target working time and the assigned work break schedule, for example.

You can also use the selection criteria in the table to further restrict the display of the daily work schedule. If, for example, you only want to see daily work schedules with less than eight target hours, select **Selection • By Contents** from the menu. A dialog box then opens that contains more selection criteria. Select the ones you require (such as target working hours) and click on **Next**. You then enter your restrictions in the next selection screen.

When you print the content of the table, all data on the daily work scheduled are printed. You can also adapt the content of the list to your requirements; to do this, choose **Settings • Layout • Change** in the list.

It is also possible to email the list or to export it to Excel or Word for further processing.

12.2   Absences and Attendances

The reports on absences and attendances provide an overview of times and dates on which employees either did not work due to absence or were present at work or performed a specially assigned activity.

12.2.1   Attendance/Absence Data – Overview

The Attendance/Absence Data – Overview report enables managers to collapse and expand employees' absence and attendance data in accordance with various criteria. For example, they can run reports based on absences only, attendances only, or individual attendance and absence types. They can also display the leave data of employees in a particular personnel area, expanded, for example, by personnel subarea and employee.

Besides the usual selection options for the PNP database, the selection screen (see Figure 12.4) also contains the following list formatting and display options:

▶ Select employees without attendances and absences.

▶ Specify which attendances and absences you want to include in the report.

▶ Use the **Grouping by org. assignment** button to specify which organizational data are included in the report output in the form of columns. The personnel area and personnel subarea are preset. If you click this button, a window opens in which you can select further organizational data. These data are then added to the list in the form of columns in the order that you specify.

▶ Click the **Data to display** button to specify which additional data you want to add to the report output in the form of columns. The following columns are preset: attendances and absences in hours, target hours, attendance and absence hours as a percentage of target times, attendances and absences in days, target days, attendance and absence days as a percentage of target days, and number of attendance and absence records.

▶ Expand the data in the entry list to get an initial idea of the data basis (for example, if you only need a summary of the data based on organizational assignment and absences).

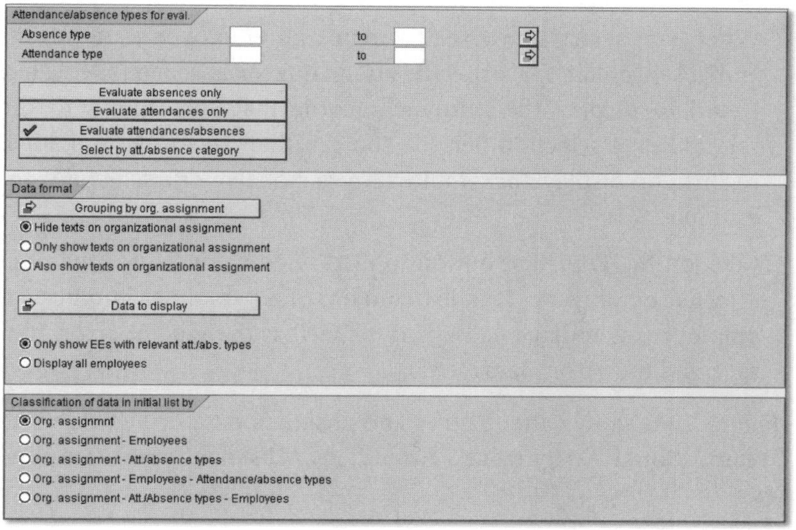

Figure 12.4 Attendance/Absence Data Selection Screen

Output control

You can switch between different views in the **Attendance/Absence Data – Overview** report output. For example, you can adapt the layout of the report output in accordance with your requirements.

▶ Select **Change view** to switch from the employee-based to the attendance/absence-based data view.

▶ Select **Expand all** to display all data.

▶ Select **Expand · Collapse** to show or hide the data in a row.

▶ Select **Layout** to switch between two different layouts.

▶ Select **Detail** (not to be confused with **Details**, the magnifying-glass icon) to choose between various detailed views. However, you will not have access to this button if you have collapsed the display to the organizational assignment level. The following detailed views are available:

Table T554S

▶ When you select a row that contains collapsed data for attendance and absence, select **Detail** to open the **Display attendance/absence data: detail** view (Table T554S).

▶ When you select a row that contains collapsed data for each employee, select **Detail** to open the **Display attendance/absence data: calendar** view (see Section 12.2.2).

▶ When you select a row that contains an employee's attendance and absence data for a specific attendance or absence type, select **Detail** to display the infotype records that correspond to the selected data selection period. You can then go to the individual records or display the employee's personal work schedule, for example.

▶ Click on the **Error list** button to display an error list for the non-selected employees. This list contains the personnel numbers of employees who have had errors, as well as the type of error message and the error message text.

Figure 12.5 shows attendances and absences data drilled down to **Organizational Assignment · Attendance/Absence types · Employees**.

Attendance/Absence Data: Overview

Period: 01.01.1997 - 31.12.2003
Statistics not complete
2 Error during evaluation

PA	Subarea	A/AType	Att./abs. type text	Pers.No.	Employee/app.name	Hrs	PInd hrs	Hrs/pInd	Days	Plan.days	Days/pInd	No.records
		****	****	****	****	1,097,75	472,427,25	0.23 %	147.32	64,248.00	0.23 %	56
1200		****	****	****	****	1,097,75	472,427,25	0.23 %	147.32	64,248.00	0.23 %	56
1200		****	****	****	****	1,097.75	472,427.25	0.23 %	147.32	64,248.00	0.23 %	56
1200		0340	Paid leave of abs < 1 day	****	****	2.00		0.00 %	0.32		0.00 %	1
1200		0340	Paid leave of abs < 1 day	00001288	Helmut Glüher	2.00	10,906.25	0.02 %	0.32	1,511.00	0.02 %	1
1200		0100	Leave w. quota d. (days)	****	****	184,75		0.04 %	25.00		0.04 %	5
1200		0100	Leave w. quota d. (days)	00001288	Helmut Glüher	15.50	10,906.25	0.14 %	2.00	1,511.00	0.13 %	1
1200		0100	Leave w. quota d. (days)	00001290	Heiner Kunze	84.00	10,906.25	0.77 %	12.00	1,511.00	0.79 %	2
1200		0100	Leave w. quota d. (days)	00001291	Jan-Peter Wunderlich	85.25	10,906.25	0.78 %	11.00	1,511.00	0.73 %	2
1200		0200	Illness with certificate	****	****	539.00		0.11 %	74.00		0.12 %	2
1200		0200	Illness with certificate	00001288	Helmut Glüher	500.25	10,906.25	4.59 %	69.00	1,511.00	4.57 %	1
1200		0200	Illness with certificate	00001293	Juri Heller	38.75	10,906.25	0.36 %	5.00	1,511.00	0.33 %	1
1200		0800	Attendance hours	****	****	372.00		0.08 %	48.00		0.07 %	48

Figure 12.5 Attendance/Absence Data Report

12.2.2 Attendance/Absence Data – Calendar View

The Attendance/Absence Data – Calendar View report allows you to display attendances and absences for each employee in a calendar or list format. You can also output statistics and a legend for each employee.

Besides the usual selection options for the PNP database, the selection screen also contains the following formatting and display options for the calendar view:

Output control

▶ To select the attendances and absences using the attendance/absence type, select the **Attendance/absence type** field and check the box to specify that you want to select attendances and absences. You then have the option to restrict your report to individual attendances and absences.

▶ To select the attendances and absences using the attendance/absence category, select the **Attendance/absence category** field and check the box to specify that you want to select attendances and absences.

▶ In the calendar view, you can specify the periods into which you want to subdivide the person selection period when creating the calendar view. You can specify the period using the selection screen only.

▶ The list view outputs all days that you specified in the data selection period. You can restrict the output to the actual days of the required attendances and absences.

▶ Click on the **Display organizational assignment** button to specify which organizational data are displayed in the page header of the report output. The personnel area and personnel subarea are pre-set. If you click on this button, a window opens in which you can select further organizational data. These data are then output in the order of your choice in the page header.

▶ If you check the Generate **Statistics** field, monthly statistics are output when monthly or weekly periods are selected. If you select a different period, statistics are output for the period in question. The statistics cumulate the hours that come under a specific attendance or absence type — in any one month, for example — and output the percentage of the target number of hours that these hours represent. Attendances or absences with previous day assignments belong to the period in which the previous day falls.

▶ If you selected **Display Legend**, every page of the calendar view displays a legend of the selected attendances and absences (ID plus attendance or absence type).

Additional symbols Attendances and absences are displayed in the report output in the form of their attendance or absence category (ID). The ID is output in lowercase letters in the case of partial-day attendances and absences. Besides the IDs are specified in the Customizing, the following additional symbols can also be used:

▶ The symbol ? means no ID is specified in the Customizing for the corresponding attendance or absence type.

▶ The symbol / indicates an employee's inactive days.

▶ The symbol < means that an attendance or absence that occurred on the following day is assigned to this day marked by this symbol (previous day assignment).

▶ The symbol * means multiple attendances or absences occurred on this day.

▶ Public holidays are marked in red in the calendar.

To view detailed information on attendances and absences in the calendar, double-click on the corresponding ID. This takes you to the display for the relevant infotype record. If both attendances and absences occurred on a particular day, you have to specify in a dialog box the infotype record that you want to open.

You can go to the multiple-employee view (see Section 12.2.3) from both the calendar view (see Figure 12.6) and the list view. The multiple-employee view can be displayed for any period on which you have positioned the cursor. To use this function, click on the **Multiple employee view** button. If the cursor is positioned elsewhere in the report output, the last-selected period or the last month is displayed.

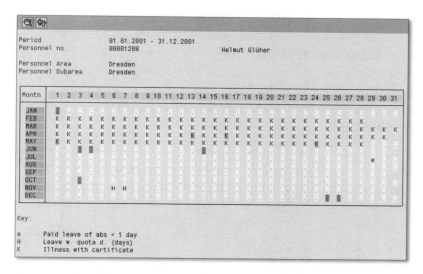

Figure 12.6 Monthly Calendar View

The multiple-employee view function is not available if you have selected the weekly display option for the calendar view. **[+]**

12.2.3 Attendance/Absence Data – Multiple-Employee View

The Attendance/Absence Data – Multiple-Employee View report shows the attendances and absences in each month for each employee (see Figure 12.7). The selection period corresponds to one month; in other words, the report reports on the exact month in which the key date lies. You can also run reports based on absences only, attendances only, or individual attendance and absence types, for example.

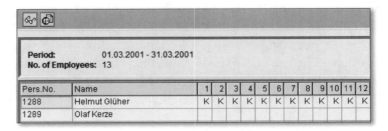

Figure 12.7 Multiple-Employee View of Attendance/Absence Data

The various attendances and absences are displayed in the report as IDs. Besides the IDs specified in the Customizing, the symbols *****, **?**, **<**, and **/** can also be used. The meanings of these additional IDs are the same as in the **Attendance/Absence Data – Calendar View** report (see Section 12.2.2).

From the multiple-employee view, you can go to the infotype that corresponds to the attendance or absence in question. In the case of errors, you can display a list of the employees for whom the errors occurred.

12.2.4 Attendance Check

The Attendance Check report creates a list of the employees who at a specific point in time were either present, absent with reason, absent without a reason, or arrived late. You can also create a report of employees who should have been at work according to their personal work schedule, but were neither present nor absent with reason.

This report is based on time events recorded in a time recording system and on the infotypes **Absences** (2001) and **Attendances** (2002).

Time events   If your company uses time recording devices, the time events have to be loaded into the SAP system before the report starts. If you use time event types that mean both **Clock-in entry** and **Clock-out entry** (such as **Clock-in entry** or **clock-out entry**), the pair formation has to have been set in the time evaluation function. These time events can be reported on only in conjunction with another time event (Figure 12.8).

Pers.No.	Empl./appl.name	Stat.	Status text	TET	Meaning	Time	Planned wo	A/AType	AttAbsTxt
10967	Mrs Ellen Olbright	1	At work	P10	Clock-in	07:45:46	08:00-17:00		
10968	Mr. Alan Parker	1	At work	P10	Clock-in	07:45:21	08:00-17:00		
10969	Mrs Jessica Tendy	1	At work	P10	Clock-in	07:49:49	08:00-17:00		
70128	Mr. Rolf Lissie	5	Full-day Absent			00:00:00	08:30-17:00	0240	Vacation

Figure 12.8 Absence Report

The status of an absence is determined as follows:

Determining absence status

1. Based on the last posting before the time that the report was run, the system determines whether the employee is present, doing off-site work, or on a break. If you activated the **Evaluate work schedule** field, the last posting is also used to check whether the employee arrived **Late** or **Late based on normal working time** or whether there is a core time violation.

2. If the employee is not present according to the last posting, the system checks whether the employee is present (2001) or absent (2002). The attendance status is then set to either **Partial-day attendance**, **Partial-day absence**, **Full-day attendance**, or **Full-day absence**.

3. If there are no attendance or absence data and you want to report on the daily work schedule, the system checks whether the employee in question should have been present in accordance with his daily work schedule. The attendance status may be set to **Missing** or **Missing based on normal working time**.

By specifying the **Hours before report time**, you determine the maximum number of hours that may elapse between the last posting and the point in time at which the report is run. Only these postings are taken into account in the report.

If the **Report on work schedule** field is activated, the report also outputs employees who should have been working at the time at which the report was run, in accordance with their personal work schedule, but were neither present nor absent with reason.

In the case of employees with the status **Time Management 0 (No time evaluation)**, status **Time Management 7 (Time evaluation without Payroll integration)** or status **Time Management 9 (Time evaluation of planned time)** for whom there are no attendance or absence data in the specified time period, it is assumed that they were in attendance in accordance with their daily work schedule. Employees with the status **Time Management 8 (External services)** for whom there is no attendance or absence data in the evaluation period are not included in the report.

Daily work schedules that include midnight correctly recognize whole-day absences only if the **Evaluate work schedule** field is activated. If all you want is a report on the employees who were present, leave the **Evaluate work schedule** field empty, as calculating the daily work schedule consumes quite a lot of computing power.

12.2.5 Graphical Overview of Attendance/Absence

The report Graphical Overview of Attendances/Absences creates a planning table that graphically represents employees' attendances and absences (see Figure 12.9). It also allows you to report on locked records.

In the graphic, attendances are displayed in yellow, absences in red, locked attendances in blue, and locked absences in green.

The report can also contain various time periods such as a day or a week. You can modify the granularity of the time period interactively in the graphic, and you can adapt the layout of the graphic. For example, you can modify the color assignments or the grid density.

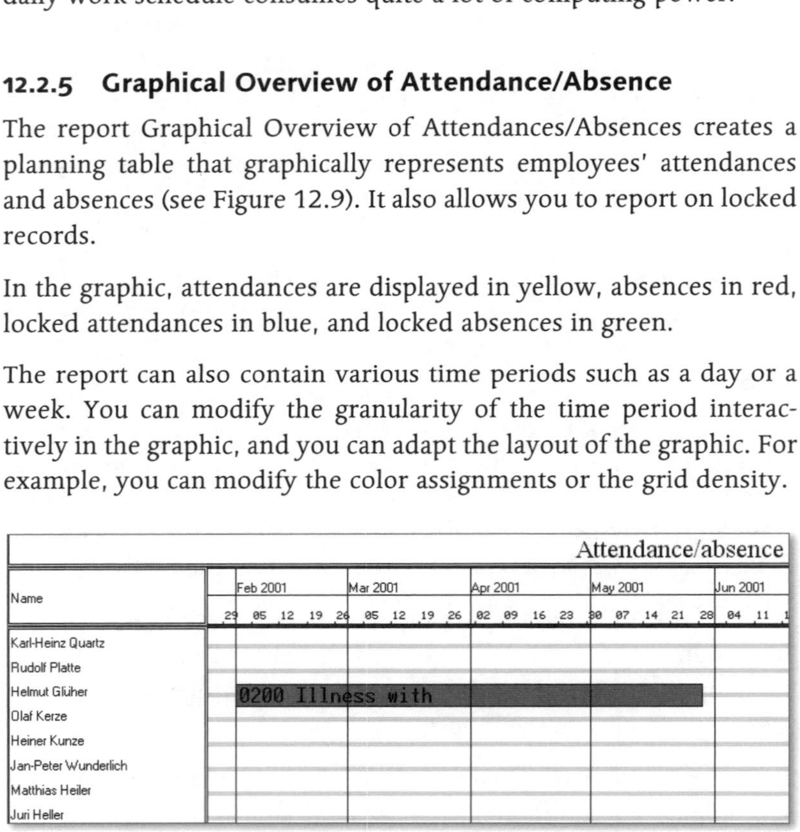

Figure 12.9 Graphical Overview of Attendance/Absence with Calendar Week as Time Unit

In the graphic, you can click on a particular attendance or absence to go to the corresponding infotypes or click on the name of an employee to go to the **Display time data** function.

12.3 Time Accounts

The reports for displaying and reporting on time accounts output the results calculated in the time evaluation function (RPTIME00) (such as time balances, time wage types, and error messages). They also provide information on employees' absence quotas.

12.3.1 Time Statement

The Time Statement report creates an overview of the results calculated by the time evaluation function, such as time balances and time wage types per employee. You can use this report to check the time evaluation results, for example, or to send time statements to employees for their information. The time statement self-service application enables employees to view up-to-date information on their time balances and time wage types via the Internet or intranet.

To be able to create a time statement, you have to have run the Time Evaluation (RPTIME00) report on the time data of the employees in question; in other words, you have to have stored this data in cluster B2.

Time Evaluation report

On the time statement selection screen, you can specify what form you want to use to output the time statement. This can be either a standard form or one of your own that you created previously in the Customizing (**Personnel Time Management • Time Evaluation • Reports and Worklist • Time Statement Form**).

The standard template forms are listed in Table 12.1.

Description	Content
TF00	Report of the most important time balances for each day
TF01	Report of the most important time balances for each day, letter header with address, additional information
TF02	Report of the most important time balances for each day, letter header with address, additional information with a sophisticated interface design

Table 12.1 Template Forms in the Time Statement Report

Description	Content
TFL1	Overview report of cumulated time balances
TFL2	Overview report of cumulated time balances. Can be output only under certain conditions; for example, the flexitime excess/deficit is output only if it is <0 (this condition is specified in the Customizing).

Table 12.1 Template Forms in the Time Statement Report (cont.)

[+]   The time balance overview within the time account reports uses this report with the form TFL1.

The time data and the time balances and time wage types determined by the time report are output for each day, as shown in Figure 12.10. If the time statement covers a full period for which the Payroll run has already been completed, a totals overview is output of the balances calculated for the report period, as well as the day balances.

```
                         Time statement list
Printed on : 26.07.2007                                    Page :   1

Employee      : 00001288 Helmut Glüher
Administrator : Marianne Uhr

Personnel area    : 1200        Personnel subarea  :
Employee group    : 1          Employee subgroup  : DK
Cost center       : 4260        Position           : 50011534   WS rule : M3-3

            Evaluation period from  01.01.2001 to  31.01.2001


                         Individual results

Day Text        ITer OTer  Start End   rec.  Plnd   Skel.   Flex  OTime  DWS

01  Nw Yrs Day            05:11 14:30  9.33  7.75   7.75   0.00  0.00   F-11
    Day off
    Normal hours                      7.75
    Holiday bonus 100%                9.33
02  Tu                   05:25 14:27  9.04  7.75   7.75   0.00  0.29   F-11
    Normal hours                      7.75
    Overtime bonus 25%                0.29
03  We                   05:11 14:17  9.09  7.75   7.75   0.00  0.34   F-11
    Normal hours                      7.75
    Overtime bonus 25%                0.35
04  Th                   05:11 14:20  9.14  7.75   7.75   0.00  0.39   F-11
    Normal hours                      7.75
    Overtime bonus 25%                0.39
```

Figure 12.10 Extract from a Time Statement (TF02)

You can also use the Printout of **Recalculation** parameter to output a time statement for periods for which a time statement was triggered in the time evaluation. To set the maximum earliest retroactive accounting period, go to **Human Resources • Time Management • Administration • Settings • Earliest Recalculation for the Time Statement** in the SAP Easy Access menu.

To also output a time statement for employees who have experienced an error in their time evaluation, check the **Include employees with errors** parameter.

Branch to time data info on the selection screen can be used to specify whether users can go to the time data records from the report screen.

You can also create summarized views of the report results, such as weekly totals and collapsed time wage types (in other words, a time wage type is displayed only once per day on the time statement). Use the **Parameters for List Layout** to specify this.

It is also possible to specify an **Output language** for the time statement. This could be the employee's native language, for example.

The SAP extension HRPTIM04 can be used to modify the information in the cluster B2 tables before it is output.   [+]

12.3.2 Cumulated Time Evaluation Results

The Cumulated Time Evaluation Results report creates a list of day balances (Table ZES), as shown in Figure 12.11, cumulated balances, or the time wage types (Table ZL) in the cluster B2. You can use this report to check which balances per organizational unit were created, for example. You can also restrict the balances or wage types that are included in the report using the **Selection criteria**.

This report is also used to check value limits, which you can set in the Customizing for individual time types or time wage types. However, for this to be possible, you have to activate the **Take account of value limits (hours)** parameter in the selection screen. Define the value limits for the individual time types and time wage types in the **LIMIT** characteristic (hourly value limits for cumulated balances).

Day balances

Data select. period 01.01.2001 - 31.01.2001

Pers.No.	Name	Period	Current Date	TmType	Time type descript.	≣ Number
1288	Helmut Glüher	200101	01.01.2001	0600	Absence on public holiday	7.75
1288	Helmut Glüher	200101	01.01.2001	0120	Fill time Absence	7.75
1288	Helmut Glüher	200101	01.01.2001	0100	Fill time	7.75
1288	Helmut Glüher	200101	01.01.2001	0020	Absence	7.75
1288	Helmut Glüher	200101	01.01.2001	0003	Skeleton time	7.75
1288	Helmut Glüher	200101	01.01.2001	0500	Break	1.00
1288	Helmut Glüher	200101	01.01.2001	0002	Planned time	7.75
1288	Helmut Glüher	200101	02.01.2001	0043	Overtime basic/time off	0.29
1288	Helmut Glüher	200101	02.01.2001	0410	Time off from overtime	0.29
1288	Helmut Glüher	200101	02.01.2001	0040	Overtime worked	0.29

Figure 12.11 Day Balances Report

This characteristic is subdivided into the following three subcharacteristics:

▶ LIMIE: hourly value limits for day balances

▶ LIMIS: hourly value limits for cumulated balances

▶ LIMIZ: hourly value limits for time wage types

You can set the value limits in accordance with organizational and wage-related criteria, such as the personnel area or pay scale type. To make the required settings for the value limits, go to the Customizing for time evaluations (**Time Management • Information System • Set Value Limits for Cumulated Evaluation Results**).

In this report, you also have the option to graphically output the data. To do this, choose **Go To • Graphic** in the report.

12.3.3 Display Time Accounts

Time evaluation The Display Time Accounts report creates an overview of selected, up-to-date time balances for each employee (see Figure 12.12). The time balances in question are calculated in the time evaluation (RPTIME00). You can use this report as an alternative to the time statement (see Section 12.3.1) if you want quick information about individual employees' latest time balances, for example. Define the balances that you want displayed in the Customizing (**Time Management • Time Evaluation • Time Evaluation Settings • Define Time**

Types). You have to enter "1" (Storage) in the **Store for time accounts** field in the time types definition.

Time Accounts				
PersNo.	Name of employee or applicant	Tm...	Time type descript.	Number
00001288	Helmut Glüher	0002	Planned time	6.25
		0003	Skeleton time	6.25
		0005	Flextime balance	15.00
		0050	Productive hours	7.25
		0110	Fill time Attendance	6.25
		0410	Time off from overtime	198.66
00001299	Sabine Frantz	0002	Planned time	135.25
		0003	Skeleton time	135.25
		0005	Flextime balance	15.00
		0050	Productive hours	153.25
		0110	Fill time Attendance	135.25

Figure 12.12 Display of Time Balances in Time Accounts

If your company uses time recording devices, some of the balances displayed are the balances that are downloaded to these devices.

> The status of the balances displayed is that of the last error-free run of the [+]
> Time Evaluation report (RPTIME00).

12.3.4 Display Absence Quota Information

The Display Absence Quota Information report creates an overview of employees' **Absence quotas** (Infotype 2006), based on various criteria.

You can use the **Settings · Display Variant · Current** menu in the report output to add more fields with information on employees' organizational assignments and absence quotas. Figure 12.13 shows the standard format of the report.

Pers.No.	Name	Quota	Unit	Σ Entitlement	Σ Used	Σ Compensated to key da	Σ Total remain.
1800	Dorothee Kroll	Leave (Days)	Days	30.00000	13.00000	0.00000	7.00000
1800	Dorothee Kroll	Leave (Hours)	Days	12.00000	0.00000	0.00000	12.00000
1809	Friedrich Neubauer	Leave (Days)	Days	30.00000	16.00000	0.00000	14.00000
1907	Dr. Heinz Chef	Leave (Days)	Days	30.00000	15.00000	0.00000	15.00000
1911	Gerhard Keller	Leave (Days)	Days	30.00000	15.00000	0.00000	15.00000
1912	Jürgen Jansen	Leave (Days)	Days	30.00000	18.00000	0.00000	12.00000
1951	Renate Rainers	Leave (Days)	Days	30.00000	0.00000	0.00000	30.00000
1952	Nadja Rogerts	Leave (Days)	Days	30.00000	0.00000	0.00000	30.00000
1960	Eva Jagoda	Leave (Days)	Days	30.00000	0.00000	0.00000	30.00000
1961	Gudrun Heilmann	Leave (Days)	Days	30.00000	0.00000	0.00000	30.00000
1962	Frauke Gunthert	Leave (Days)	Days	30.00000	0.00000	0.00000	30.00000
1963	Hiltrud Christiansen	Leave (Days)	Days	30.00000	0.00000	0.00000	30.00000

Figure 12.13 Absence Quotas Display

In the selection criteria for this report, you can restrict the absence quotas that are included in the report. You can also select which quota types, which time units, and which deduction periods are to be made available.

You can also output quota statuses for the future and the past, as well as current quota statuses. To do this, specify a key date for the deduction and a key date for the entitlement in the selection screen. This data is then used as follows in the report:

If a selected employee has an absence quota that is available for reporting, the following things happen:

▸ His entitlement to this quota is calculated on the key date, giving the value of the entitlement.

▸ The deduction, remainder, and compensation of this quota are calculated on the key date, giving the value of the deduction.

You can perform an extrapolation of future quota statuses so that, for example, the employees can be informed about their expected leave entitlements. If the key dates (entitlement or deduction) for a selected employee are greater than or less than the **Recalculation date for PDC** in the **Payroll Status** infotype (0003), activating the extrapolation has the effect that the time evaluation (RPTIME00 run in simulation mode) is triggered for this employee.

[Ex] For example, you can output a report at the end of the year that reports on the remaining entitlement and compensation for every employee.

You can restrict the employee selection as follows for the output:

▸ **All selected employees**
Employees without selected absence quotas are included in the output list.

▸ **Only employees with selected absence quota records**
The output list contains only employees to whom at least one of the selected quota records can be assigned. You can further restrict the selection, as follows:

  ▹ Only employees with entitlement

  ▹ Only employees with remaining entitlement

▶ Only employees with deductions

▶ Only employees with consumption

You can also specify an interval for every selection within which the remaining entitlement is to lie, for example, employees with a remaining entitlement of at least 10 days. If conditions are placed on the quota entitlement and the remaining quota, only employees who fulfill both conditions at the same time are output.

12.3.5 Display Time Evaluation Messages

The Display Time Evaluation Messages report creates a list of messages that were output in the time evaluation process (Figure 12.14). To do this, the report reads the ERROR table from Cluster B2. This report is located under **Human Resources · Time Management · Administration · Time Evaluation · Time Evaluations Messages**.

It returns useful results only if the employees in question participate in time evaluation and if the time evaluation report (RPTIME00) has run for the required period.

Time evaluation

You can use additional selection criteria, such as the category or number of the message type, to restrict the list of selected messages in the selection screen.

The messages (in the form of the message category number and the long text of the message) are color-coded as follows in the report output:

▶ A message that is a note has a gray background (no message type).

▶ For messages with message type 1, the message type and the message text have a yellow background.

▶ A message that makes a recalculation necessary has a pink background (message type F).

▶ A message that causes the time evaluation process to terminate has a dark red background (message type E).

In the time evaluation schema, the message types are either created within rules with the COLER operation or are technical errors, such as those that occur within pair formation. The message types in question have the following meanings:

Message types

- ▶ E: Time evaluation is terminated for the current employee.

- ▶ F: Processing proceeds as normal; the recalculation indicator is set so that the current day is calculated again in the next evaluation run.

- ▶ I: Processing proceeds as normal; the recalculation indicator is not set. The message remains in cluster B1 until it is confirmed by the message processing process.

- ▶ Otherwise: Time evaluation proceeds as normal; the message is a note.

MessTy	Message long text	PersNo	Empl./appl.name	CD	Logical date
42	Flextime excess	1912	Jürgen Jansen	WE	31.01.2001
08	At work despite day type "1"	1951	Renate Rainers	MO	01.01.2001
42	Flextime excess	1951	Renate Rainers	WE	31.01.2001
08	At work despite day type "1"	1952	Nadja Rogerts	MO	01.01.2001
42	Flextime excess	1952	Nadja Rogerts	WE	31.01.2001
42	Flextime excess	1960	Eva Jagoda	WE	31.01.2001
42	Flextime excess	1961	Gudrun Heilmann	WE	31.01.2001
42	Flextime excess	1962	Frauke Gunthert	WE	31.01.2001
08	At work despite day type "1"	5169	Manfred Effenberg	MO	01.01.2001
70	Unapproved overtime exists	5169	Manfred Effenberg	MO	01.01.2001

Figure 12.14 List of Error Messages from the Time Evaluation Process

The column set of the ALV Grid contains more fields relating to the list output. These include information on organizational assignment, daily work schedules, and additional error message data, among other things.

12.3.6 Display Time Evaluation Results (Cluster B2)

The Display Time Evaluation Results report enables you to display the content of cluster B2 from the time evaluation report (RPTIME00) on a per-employee and per-period basis.

This report is located under **Human Resources • Time Management • Administration • Tools • Tools Selection • Cluster • Display Time Evaluation Results (Cluster B2)** in the SAP Easy Access menu.

Choose **List of personnel numbers and periods** in the list format to open the report output, which displays an overview of the selected personnel numbers and periods. Choose the **Select** function to open an overview of the tables in cluster B2, which includes information on the number of entries created per period (see Figure 12.15). You have the following options here:

▶ Place the cursor on a table and select the **Select** function to display detailed information on the table entries.

▶ Select the **All tables** function to output a list of all entries of all tables in a period. This function is useful if you want to output the report for the purposes of a detailed error analysis.

▶ The **Detailed description of all table entries** function has the same purpose as the **All tables** function when you make a selection via the list of personnel numbers and periods.

▶ The Archived Data Group window enables you to specify whether nonarchived clusters only, archived clusters only, or both should be displayed. Note that the runtime of the report can increase if you choose to display archived data.

Group Table Name	Name	Number of entries
Basic data and work schedule		
WPBP	Basic data	1
PSP	Personal work schedule	33
Balances, wage types and quota transactions		
ZES	Time balances for each day	195
SALDO	Cumulated time balances	10
ZKO	Time quotas	35
ZL	Time wage types	130
ALP	Different payment	0
C1	Cost dist.	0
VS	Variable balances	0
CVS	Accrued variable balances	0
FEHLER	Messages	0
KNTAG	Work bridging two calendar days	1
Automatic accrual of absence quotas		
QTACC	Absence quota generation	17
QTBASE	Base entitl.	17
QTTRANS	Transfer pool	0
URLAN	Leave accrual	0
Time pairs and time tickets		
PT	Time pairs	18

Figure 12.15 Overview of Tables in Cluster B2 for an Employee in a Single Period

For explanations of the tables in cluster B2, see the SAP Library under **SAP** **[+]** **ERP Central Component · Time Management · Time Evaluation · Appendix · Clusters · Tables in Cluster B2.**

12.4 SAP NetWeaver BI Standard Content

BI standard content in Personnel Time Management contains both data from the time management infotypes and data from the time evaluation process (cluster B2). Unfortunately, some time management infotypes are not included, such as Availability for work (2004), Time transfers (2012), and Substitutions (2003). Therefore, although substitutions are contained in actual time, the substitution type, such as reduced working hours, can also be relevant.

12.4.1 Time and Labor Data InfoCube

The Time and Labor Data InfoCube is part of the SAP NetWeaver BI standard content for Personnel Time Management. Time and labor data in the HCM system is divided up by time types for reporting, regardless of the source of the data (such as database table or function module). These time types have to be defined in the HCM Customizing. To enable queries and key figures with business significance to be output in a report, the standard contains predefined time types with fixed semantics (see Table 12.2).

Time Type	Description
00000001	Leave
00000002	Illness
00000003	Target time (work schedule time evaluation)
00000004	Overtime
00000005	Productive time
00000009	Target time based on personal work schedule

Table 12.2 Predefined Time Types in the BI Standard Content

Customizing You maintain the time types in the Customizing of the HCM system under **Time Management · Information System · Settings for Reports · Employee Time and Labor Data · Define Reporting Time Types** (see Figure 12.16).

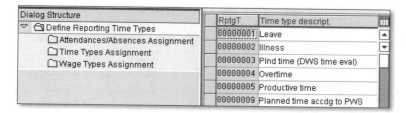

Figure 12.16 Define Report Time Type

Assignments of HCM time management data to time types and additional customer-specific time types are both freely definable in the SAP Time Management system. The time management information types **Absences** (2001), **Attendances** (2002) and **Employee remuneration information** (2010) as well as **Time evaluation results** (cluster B2) are all possible sources. Figure 12.17 shows the definitions of Leave.

Dialog Structure						
▽ ☐ Define Reporting Time Types	RptgTmType	00000001	Leave			
☐ Attendances/Absences Assignment						
☐ Time Types Assignment	Attendances/Absences Assignment					
☐ Wage Types Assignment	G	P	A/A	AttAbsTxt	Hrs	Day	PHrs	PD

G	P	A/A	AttAbsTxt	Hrs	Day	PHrs	PD
00	10	0100	Paid leave	☑	☑	☑	☐
01	01	0100	Leave w. quota d. (days)	☑	☑	☑	☐
01	10	0100	Paid leave	☑	☑	☑	☐
01	10	0101	Vacation	☑	☑	☑	☐
01	10	0110	PTO/Floating Holiday	☑	☑	☑	☐
01	10	0600	Maternity Leave	☑	☑	☑	☐
10	10	0100	Paid leave	☑	☑	☑	☐

Figure 12.17 Definition of Leave Time Type

Time type 00000009 (Planned time accdg to PWS) is an exceptional case; the source of the data records for this type is always the personal work schedule. There is no equivalent database object for this type in ERP; instead, the personal work schedule is always created dynamically at runtime.

Personal work schedule

The InfoCube saves cumulated monthly time data in units of days and hours. Hourly values (Overtime) and daily values (Leave) are required for reporting purposes.

In principle, the extractor in HCM allows daily totals to be transferred. However, this InfoCube is designed for key figure reports for which the monthly totals are sufficient. The figures are further compressed to form quarterly and annual key figures by an automatic process in the InfoCube.

If an employee changes his assignment within a month in the SAP ERP HCM system (for example, if he changes to a new master cost center) and if the associated InfoObject is contained as a characteristic in an InfoCube, the times are distributed across the individual areas on a per-day basis and, correspondingly, are output separately in the report under the characteristic values.

Cost distribution   The data from the Cost distribution infotype are also available, as are the Different cost assignment data and the activity allocation data for attendances/absences and substitutions (see Figure 12.18).

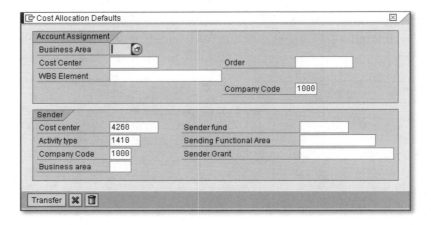

Figure 12.18 Activity Allocation in Personnel Time Management

Hierarchies   The following hierarchies can be used with the characteristics:

▶ Organizational units

▶ Cost centers

Time character-   The following characteristics can be used as time characteristics:
istics

▶ Calendar day

▶ Calendar year or month

▶ Calendar year or quarter

▶ Calendar year

The following key figures are contained in the Time and Labor Data InfoCube:

▸ Wage type amount for payments

▸ Actual time

▸ Time affecting accounts

▸ Target time based on personal work schedule

▸ Target time without public holidays

The wage type amount is calculated using a valuation basis that is explicitly specified in the HCM system in the time data recording function, multiplied by the actual hours. If the calculation basis is not specified, this field is not populated in the HCM system by default. You can populate or modify this field in a customer extension of the extractor of the 0HR_PT_2 InfoSource. The actual time is primarily a container for the attendance/absence hours or days of the infotypes Absences (2001) and Attendances (2002).

The restricted key figures are also available. These are derived from the key figures of the InfoCube by means of a filter on one or more characteristics of the InfoCube. Thus, illness hours are derived from the value of the **Actual times** key figure, for example. In this case, the conditions *Unit of measure = Hours* and *Time type = Illness* have to be fulfilled, as otherwise, the result will be 0 illness hours. You may have to adapt the formulation of the condition in the customer system to the Instances InfoObjects and their semantics. In particular, the filter values for the Hours and Days units will differ from the pre-set filter values. Only when consistent conditions have been formulated in accordance with the InfoCube data that has been loaded into the system can the queries return correct key figures.

Besides the master data from the infotypes, the InfoSources of the Time and labor data InfoCubes provide the following data:

▸ **Times from personal work schedule**
The key figures Planned time from personal work schedule and Planned time without public holidays are available here. They are taken from the report time type 00000009 (Planned time based on work schedule). Different cost assignment is not available here.

▶ **Personnel actual times**

The key figures of this InfoSource contain the actual times, the time affecting accounts, and the amount from the different calculation basis. The times are taken from the corresponding report time types, while the different amount used as a calculation basis is taken from the different payment for attendances/absences, substitutions, and employee remuneration information (see Figure 12.19). These data are stored in cluster B2 in Table ALP.

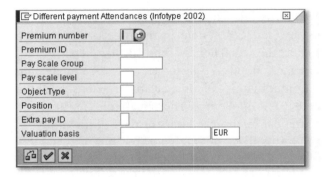

Figure 12.19 Different Payment for Attendances

▶ **Quota transactions**

Quota transactions contain the data from the infotypes Leave Entitlement (0005), Absence Quotas (2006), and Attendance Quotas (2007). The key figures contain the entitlement, consumption, inflow, expiry, and compensation for leave or quotas.

12.4.2 Reports for the Time and Labor Data InfoCube

The Personnel Time Management reports include the key figures for time and labor data, such as the illness and overtime rates, and a period comparison of time and labor data.

▶ Time and labor data key figures

▶ The Productivity Rate report is used to compare employees' actual working time with their planned working times in one quarter. The quarter view contains the current quarter and the last quarter, plus the previous three quarters.

▶ The Illness Rate report compares employees' absences due to illness with the target times in one quarter. This report outputs the illness rate as a percentage, as well as the target hours and illness hours.

▸ The Overtime Rate report compares employees' overtime hours with the target times in one quarter. This report outputs the absolute value of the hours and the overtime rate as a percentage value of the target hours.

▸ The Leave per Target report compares the absence times due to leave taken by employees with the target time in one quarter.

> This report is based on the actual time and not on the time that is subtracted from the leave account, which may be different. **[+]**

▸ The Leave Taken per Effective Full-Time Equivalent report is used to compare the leave days taken by each employee with the planned working times in one quarter. The leave days are compared to the target time in units of full-time equivalents (FTEs), and the result is a key figure that represents the leave days taken by an effective FTE in that quarter per organizational unit.

▸ In the Leave Taken per Effective Full-Time Equivalent report, the time affecting accounts, rather than the actual time (as in the Leave per Target report), is used as the basis for calculating the leave days. The efficiency of an employee is calculated based on the ratio of target hours in the quarter to a quarter of the yearly working time of an FTE. For example, if the yearly working time of an FTE is 2,000 hours, a target time of 1,800 hours gives a value of 0.9 FTE units.

▸ Overviews of time and labor data

▸ The Annual Comparison of Cost Centers Debits report is used to compare selected time types in a year with the times in the previous year. An external hierarchy is the only row characteristic that can be assigned to the cost center from which the relevant personnel costs have been debited.

▸ The Monthly History of Time and Labor Data report displays selected time and labor data within a year on the basis of one month. However, you can also select the row characteristics to collapse the data to quarters and to years. Personnel area and

Calendar year/month are used as selection variables. The time types displayed are illness hours, productive hours, overtime, and target hours.

▶ The Time and Labor Data Overview Compared to Previous Year report enables you to sort the time and labor data of a year by time types and to compare these data to the target working time and the times of the previous year. The current year is compared to the previous year, and the difference is output both as an absolute value and as a percentage.

▶ Time and labor data expressed as FTEs

The Time and Labor Data Expressed as FTEs report compares the target time, productive time, and overtime in a year with the values of the previous year. The times are expressed as FTE units; that is, the number of hours is compared to the yearly working time of an FTE. The yearly working time of an FTE is stored in the Business Information Warehouse; the default value is 2,000 hours. For example, if the yearly working time of an FTE is 2,000 hours, a target time of 1,000 hours gives a value of 12.70 mm FTE units.

12.5   Conclusion

The standard time management reports should be regarded as only a basis for other reports on time management data. It is recommended that data such as personal working time, absence quotas, and attendances/absences be linked in a report. Currently, the standard reports serve only as a vehicle for figures and data that are then merged in MS Excel tables, for example.

Unfortunately, the BI standard content does not provide much more in the way of a comprehensive reporting concept. You will usually have to make adaptations in the Customizing in order to transfer the data to the BI system. Experience has shown that this is still usually insufficient, and you still have to program your own extractors in the HCM system.

The reports described in this chapter support systematic personnel development in a company.

13 Personnel Development

The Personnel Development component allows company owners to systematically align personnel development with company objectives, while simultaneously taking employee expectations into account. Many standard reports are available with Personnel Development, which you can use to perform statistical evaluations based on employee or organizational data.

You can access these reports from the SAP Easy Access menu via **Human Resources · Personnel Management · Personnel Development · Information System · Reports**.

SAP Easy Access path

13.1 Profiles

The profile reports provide Personnel Development Managers with tools for comparing the profiles of a position with the profile of an employee, for example.

13.1.1 Profile Matchup

The Profile Matchup report allows you to compare the qualifications and requirements of objects (persons, applicants, jobs, positions, and so on). The required and existing proficiency of each qualification is taken into account in the report. You can, for example:

▶ Compare the qualifications of an employee with the requirements of the position currently held by the employee

▶ Determine the degree to which one or more persons are suited to a position

▶ Identify persons who are overqualified or underqualified for a position

- Identify suitable applicants for a vacant position
- Identify appropriate training options for people
- Check the current level of qualification within an organizational unit
- Determine the training requirements within an organizational unit

The following options are available for selecting the objects to be included in a profile matchup:

- The objects to be included are specified individually.
- The profile matchup is executed directly from the profile of a person/user or of a position for the current position the person holds or for the person who currently holds the position.
- The profile matchup is executed for all persons in an organizational unit and the positions they currently hold.

Figure 13.1 shows the selection screen for the profile matchup with the following selection options:

- Select objects for which the qualifications are to be included in the profile matchup.
- Select objects for which the requirements are to be included in the profile matchup.
- Restrict the selection to qualification deficits (where the proficiency of the qualification held is lower than the proficiency required).

Training and event management

- Determine training proposals. In this case, the Training and Event Management component must also be used.
- Select a key date for the evaluation.

Training proposals

Figure 13.2 shows the output of a profile matchup with a training proposal. If you click on the icon in the **Training proposals** column, an overview of the training proposed for the required qualification is displayed.

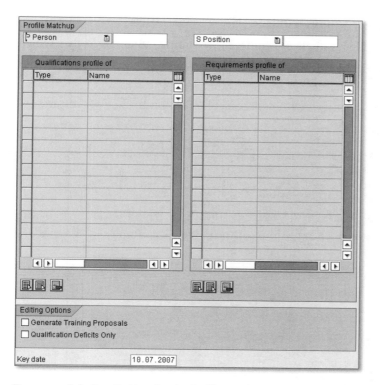

Figure 13.1 Selection Options for the Profile Matchup

	Name	Object type	Qualification	Essential Reqt	Required	Existing	Difference	Training
	PC technician: standard skills	Person	Knowledge of Excel	☐	Adequate	Do(es) Not Exist	4	
	PC technician: standard skills	Person	Knowledge of Excel	☐	Adequate	Do(es) Not Exist	4	
	PC technician: standard skills	Person	Knowledge of Excel	☐	Adequate	Do(es) Not Exist	4	
	PC technician: standard skills	Person	Knowledge of Excel	☐	Adequate	Do(es) Not Exist	4	
	PC technician: standard skills	Person	Knowledge of Excel	☐	Adequate	Do(es) Not Exist	4	
	PC technician: standard skills	Person	Knowledge of Excel	☐	Adequate	Do(es) Not Exist	4	
	PC technician: standard skills	Person	Knowledge of Lotus Notes	☐	Adequate	Do(es) Not Exist	4	
	PC technician: standard skills	Person	Knowledge of Lotus Notes	☐	Adequate	Do(es) Not Exist	4	

Figure 13.2 Output of the Profile Matchup with Training Proposal

13.1.2 Profiles of an Organizational Unit

The Profiles of an Organizational Unit report allows you to perform a profile matchup for a selected organizational unit. The benefit of accessing the profile matchup in this way is that all objects in the organizational unit, including jobs, positions, and persons, are included in the selection (see Figure 13.3 in Section 13.1.3).

13.1.3 Profile Evaluation

The Profile Evaluation report allows you to generate a list, which provides an overview of the profiles of any persons, positions, and so on. The selection screen for profile evaluation is shown in Figure 13.3.

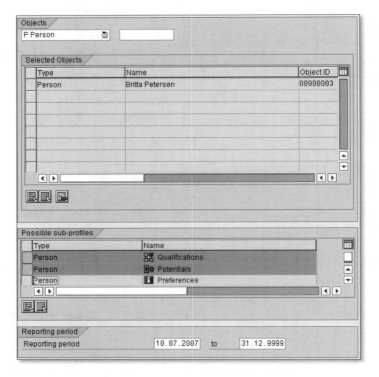

Figure 13.3 Selection Screen for Profile Evaluation

The following functions are provided:

Functions of profile evaluation

- ▶ You can evaluate any number of planning objects, such as persons or positions.
- ▶ You can evaluate planning objects belonging to various object types at the same time.
- ▶ You can specify which subprofiles you want to display for each object type, for example, qualifications, potential, and dislikes for a person.
- ▶ By changing the selection period, you can perform evaluations for the past, present, or future.

13.2 Qualifications

The reports for qualifications in Personnel Management help personnel development managers systematically search for the qualifications of company employees. They can also use these reports to
search for suitable employees, for example, for a vacant position.

13.2.1 Searching for Qualifications

The Search for Qualifications report allows you to search for objects
(such as persons) with specific qualifications. You can specify the
exact proficiencies required for each qualification and define criteria
to restrict the search to certain objects (Figure 13.4). You can also
check for people's availability.

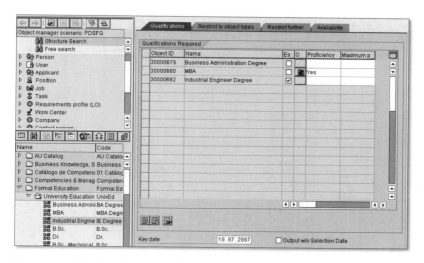

Figure 13.4 Selection Options for the Search for Qualifications Report

The following selection options are available during searches for
qualifications. First, you can select the qualifications for which
objects are to be found. You can select the qualifications in one of the
following ways:

Selection options

▶ You can select individual qualifications from the qualifications catalog.

▶ You can use the qualifications and requirements profiles of any
objects as templates and edit these as required.

▶ You can call up the search from the structural display of an organizational unit.

When you select an object, its qualifications and requirements are copied directly into the search. These qualifications and requirements comprise the following elements:

▶ The proficiency of each qualification

▶ Whether the qualification is essential (an essential requirement)

▶ Optional restriction of the search to certain object types (for example, persons and users only or applicants only)

▶ Optional restriction of the search according to additional criteria (based on the selected object types), for example, persons at a certain organizational level or in a certain personnel area

▶ Optional restriction of the hit list to persons available for a certain number of days in a planning period

▶ The user-specific settings determine whether alternative qualifications are taken into account

You can save the complete search template as a variant and use it again for future searches (Figure 13.5).

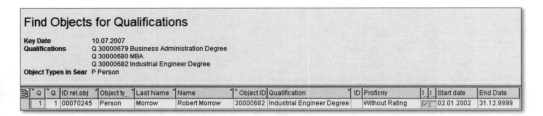

Figure 13.5 Result of the Search for Qualifications Report

13.2.2 Expired Qualifications

Career Planning The Expired Qualifications report shows all planning objects in an organizational unit that have qualifications that have expired in the evaluation period. The resulting list supplies information about the planning objects and the qualifications that have expired or are due to expire (and their validity periods) and displays training proposals for renewing these qualifications. For each planning object, you can navigate to the profile display and to Career Planning.

13.3 Other Reports

In this section, we describe two more reports as examples of the many other reports available for Personnel Development. These reports are used to evaluate appraisals and to compare the requirements of positions with the qualifications of the persons currently holding those positions.

13.3.1 Appraisal Evaluations

This report allows you to manage, find, and evaluate all appraisals created using the appraisal system in Personnel Development (Figure 13.6). You can use the powerful search function to specify various combinations of selection criteria to define complex search variants and perform differentiated database searches.

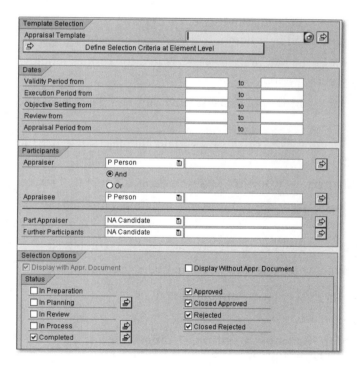

Figure 13.6 Appraisals Selection Screen

You can choose from a wide range of evaluation and display options in the resulting list (see Figure 13.7). In Change mode, you can also access and edit the appraisals directly.

Number	Appraisal Document Name	App.Document Type	Type	Appraiser Name	Type	Appraisee Name	App. Stat
1	Performance Goal Setting	Appraisal Document	Person	Mr. Mark Taylor	Person	Mrs Patricia Otto	Completed
1	Managers Appraisal of Employee 2003	Appraisal Document	Person	Mrs Patricia Otto	Person	Mr. Jonathan Meyers	Completed
1	Performance Goal Setting	Appraisal Document	Person	Mr. Tom Peterson	Person	Mr. Michael Hire	Completed
1	Managers Appraisal of Employee 2003	Appraisal Document	Person	Mr. Jack Kincaid	Person	Mr. Michael Roth	Completed
1	Performance Goal Setting	Appraisal Document	Person	Mr. Peter Trautmann	Person	Harvey Stevens	Completed
1	Performance Goal Setting	Appraisal Document	Person	Mr. Tom Peterson	Person	Mrs Michelle O'Connor	Completed
1	Performance Goal Setting	Appraisal Document	Person	Mr. Thomas McNamara	Person	Douglas Darwin	Completed
1	Performance Goal Setting	Appraisal Document	Person	Mr. William Brabazon	Person	Mrs Aileen Band	Completed
1	Managers Appraisal of Employee	Appraisal Document	Person	Mr. Thomas McNamara	Person	Mrs Sue Benoy	Completed
1	Performance Goal Setting	Appraisal Document	Person	Mr. John Silvan	Person	Mrs Jennifer Gibson	Completed
1	Performance Goal Setting	Appraisal Document	Person	Mr. Jack Kincaid	Person	Mr. Rick Smolla	Completed
1	Managers Appraisal of Employee	Appraisal Document	Person	Mrs MaryEllen Wells	Person	Mr. Mike Anderson	Completed
1	PC4YOU: Zielvereinbarungen 2003	Appraisal Document	Person	Buster Keaton	Person	Ruth Cabrera	Completed

Figure 13.7 Extract from the Appraisals List

You can use this report in various ways, for example:

▶ To determine whether an employee was appraised in a certain period

▶ To determine which employees in an organizational unit have been appraised and by whom

▶ To determine which appraisals were created for various employees for a specific period

▶ To determine which appraisers created appraisals for a specific period

▶ To find all appraisals created by a certain appraiser for a specific period

▶ To identify persons who have achieved a specific appraisal result

▶ To find all appraisals created in an organizational unit for the last appraisal period

▶ To determine which appraisals have not yet been completed

▶ To determine which appraisals have not been approved

You can also evaluate objects without appraisals.

13.3.2 Profile Matchup: Positions/Holders for an Organizational Unit

The Profile Matchup: Positions/Holders for an Organizational Unit report is used to compare the requirements of all positions in the specified organizational units with the qualifications of the persons currently holding these positions. In the output (see Figure 13.8), you can select the menu option **Goto • Table** to navigate to the display of the list in the ALV Grid.

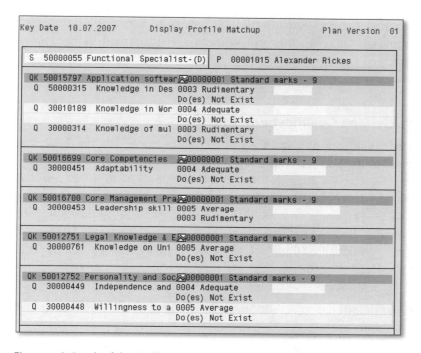

```
Key Date  10.07.2007      Display Profile Matchup          Plan Version  01

  S   50000055 Functional Specialist-(D)  P  00001015 Alexander Rickes

 QK 50015797 Application softwar 00000001 Standard marks - 9
   Q  50000315   Knowledge in Des 0003 Rudimentary
                                   Do(es) Not Exist
   Q  30010189   Knowledge in Wor 0004 Adequate
                                   Do(es) Not Exist
   Q  30000314   Knowledge of mul 0003 Rudimentary
                                   Do(es) Not Exist

 QK 50016699 Core Competencies   00000001 Standard marks - 9
   Q  30000451   Adaptability     0004 Adequate
                                   Do(es) Not Exist

 QK 50016700 Core Management Pra 00000001 Standard marks - 9
   Q  30000453   Leadership skill 0005 Average
                                   0003 Rudimentary

 QK 50012751 Legal Knowledge & E 00000001 Standard marks - 9
   Q  30000761   Knowledge on Uni 0005 Average
                                   Do(es) Not Exist

 QK 50012752 Personality and Soc 00000001 Standard marks - 9
   Q  30000449   Independence and 0004 Adequate
                                   Do(es) Not Exist
   Q  30000448   Willingness to a 0005 Average
                                   Do(es) Not Exist
```

Figure 13.8 Result of the Profile Matchup for Positions and Holders

If the **Training proposals** parameter was selected on the selection screen, a training proposal is also shown in the list (see Figure 13.9). If you click on the icon next to the training proposal, a dialog box opens where you can book the relevant event. Click on the **Junior Management – Sales** development plan to navigate from the list to **individual development planning**.

Training proposals

```
QK 50015797 Application softwar 00000001 Standard marks - 9
  Q  50000315   Knowledge in Des 0003 Rudimentary
                                 Do(es) Not Exist
                                 D  50014024 Powerful Presentations
  Q  30010189   Knowledge in Wor 0004 Adequate
                                 Do(es) Not Exist
                                 D  50010526 Text processing with MSWord
                                 D  50013689 Computer Literacy
```

Figure 13.9 Training Proposal for the Profile Matchup

13.4 SAP NetWeaver Standard BI Content

The standard BI Content for Personnel Management provides an overview of the employee qualifications and of the proficiency required for each qualification. Information about the number of appraisals and evaluations of appraisals is also provided. The **Qualifications** and **Appraisals** InfoCubes in the BI Content are used for this purpose.

13.4.1 The Qualifications InfoCube

Qualifications

The Qualifications InfoCube contains transaction data for employee qualifications. It includes the general key figures Number of Employees, Number of Qualifications, and Proficiency. In addition, selected master data from the Actions (0000), Organizational Assignment (0001), Personal Data (0002), and Basic Pay (0008) infotypes are available in the characteristics. Of course, all relevant data about employee qualifications are also provided by this InfoCube. This includes:

▶ Proficiency

▶ Qualification

▶ Qualification group

▶ Alternative qualification

▶ Scale

You can use **calendar year/month**, **calendar year/quarter**, **calendar month**, **quarter**, or **calendar year** as time dimensions for the evaluations.

13.4.2 The Appraisals InfoCube

Appraisals

The Appraisals InfoCube contains the transaction data for appraisals and allows you to evaluate all appraisals created with the appraisal system in Personnel Development. It includes the general key figures Number of Criteria Valuations and Number of Appraisals. In addition to the time dimensions available for qualifications, calendar day can be used here. This InfoCube (see Figure 13.10) contains the following characteristics in addition to the data about the employee (the **Person** characteristic is an attribute of the **Employee** characteristic):

- ▶ Flag: Unevaluated
- ▶ Applicant
- ▶ Appraisal
- ▶ Appraisee
- ▶ Appraiser
- ▶ Type of Appraisee
- ▶ Type of Appraiser
- ▶ Appraisal Criterion
- ▶ Creation Date of Appraisal
- ▶ Criteria Group 1
- ▶ Criteria Group 2
- ▶ Rating
- ▶ Appraisal Model
- ▶ Appraisal Status

This InfoCube also provides information about events and qualifications.

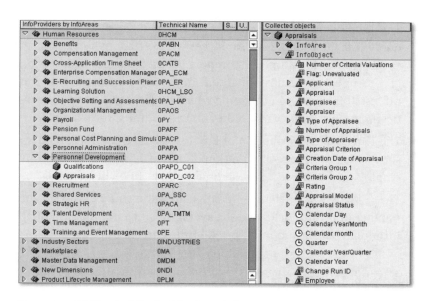

Figure 13.10 BI Standard Content for Appraisals

13.4.3 Queries for the Personnel Development InfoCubes

The following queries are included in the standard BI Content:

Queries for the Qualifications InfoCube

▸ The Annual Comparison of Qualifications per Employee query allows you to evaluate how qualifications have changed from one year to the next, for example. All employees with certain qualifications are included. The last month of the previous year is compared with the current month. The differences between the two are shown as both absolute and percentage values.

▸ If you want to find out which qualifications and how many qualifications are held by employees in various organizational units, use the Qualifications per Employee by Organizational Unit query. This query provides an overview of the number of employees with certain qualifications in each organizational unit in the company for the last month posted.

▸ The Proficiency of a Qualification per Employee query, meanwhile, shows the number of employees who had certain qualifications and proficiencies in the last month posted.

▸ The Employees by Qualification Group per Organizational Unit query lists the number of employees with certain qualifications in each organizational unit. The report is based on the qualification groups in each organizational unit in the last month posted. You can use this report to determine which qualification groups/qualifications exist in the various organizational units, for example.

▸ The Percentage Distribution of Employees for Qualification query shows the percentage distribution of the qualifications held by the employees compared with the total number of qualifications.

▸ The Average Proficiency per Qualification query shows the number of proficiencies and the average proficiency for each qualification in the last month posted in the current calendar year.

Queries for the Appraisals InfoCube

▸ The Number of Evaluations per Scale query shows the number of evaluated appraisal criteria, based on a scale, and the corresponding proficiencies. You can use this query to find out which appraisal criteria received better evaluations than others, for example.

▶ The Annual Comparison of Appraisal Evaluations query shows you the frequency with which better evaluations than others were awarded. This query outputs the percentage and absolute difference in frequency of the evaluated appraisal criteria between the last month of the previous year and the current month.

13.5 Conclusion

The standard reporting options in the area of Personnel Development are very extensive and should cover most requirements of personnel development managers. However, the standard BI Content is also an essential tool, in particular, for reports relating to employee appraisals.

Benefits play an important role with regard to the retention of employees in an enterprise. For this reason, reports on employees' feedback and on costs are essential. This chapter provides an overview of the reporting options in the area of benefits.

14 Benefits

The benefits a company offers to its employees are supposed to make it more attractive and help to retain the employees. The HCM module enables you to define and manage complex benefit packages. The reports allow for an analysis of the available programs and demonstrates how frequently these programs are used. In addition, you can use the reports to analyze costs and provide the employees with additional information to support them in selecting a specific program.

You can reach the reports relating to benefits via the following SAP Easy Access Menu path: **Personnel · Personnel Management · Benefits · Information System · Reports**.

14.1 Participation

These reports display employees who are already participating in a benefits program or are eligible to take part.

14.1.1 Eligible Employees

The report shows all employees who are eligible for a special benefit plan on a specific date, as shown in Figure 14.1.

Eligible Employees

Eligible Employees

Key date 01.01.2004
Benefit area 10 USA

Benefit plan text	Pers.No.	Name	Entry	G	Last name	Birth date	First name	1st PG	2.PG	1st ProgrGroup. Text	2nd ProgrGroup. Text
Company Dental Plan	109052	Mr. Smith Emmitt	01.04.2001	M	Emmitt	04.08.1977	Smith	HRLY	FULL	Hourly Employees	Full time
	109053	Mr. Jada Pinkett	01.04.2001	M	Pinkett	09.04.1972	Jada	HRLY	FULL	Hourly Employees	Full time
	109054	Mrs Pamela MaAfee	01.04.2001	F	MaAfee	07.07.1956	Pamela	HRLY	FULL	Hourly Employees	Full time
	109055	Mrs Jane Jenkins	06.06.1996	F	Jenkins	08.04.1962	Jane	SAL	FULL	Salaried Employees	Full time
	109056	Mr. Daniel Fouts	01.01.1996	M	Fouts	19.07.1936	Daniel	HRLY	FULL	Hourly Employees	Full time
	109057	Mr. Troy Aikman	01.01.1996	M	Aikman	08.08.1969	Troy	HRLY	FULL	Hourly Employees	Full time
	109058	Mrs Toni Braxton	08.04.1996	F	Braxton	08.04.1967	Toni	HRLY	FULL	Hourly Employees	Full time
	109101	Mr. Douglas Dougherty	01.06.1996	M	Dougherty	08.09.1950	Douglas	SAL	FULL	Salaried Employees	Full time
	109151	Mrs Kellie Fishpaw	20.09.1999	F	Fishpaw	31.12.1968	Kellie	HRLY	FULL	Hourly Employees	Full time
	109152	Mr. Gary Johnston	20.09.1999	M	Johnston	17.03.1963	Gary	HRLY	FULL	Hourly Employees	Full time
	109153	Mrs Connie Cook	05.12.1997	F	Cook	24.08.1969	Connie	HRLY	FULL	Hourly Employees	Full time
	109201	Mr. Steven Chambers	01.01.1996	M	Chambers	07.05.1950	Steven	SAL	FULL	Salaried Employees	Full time
	109202	Mrs Michele Jamison	14.03.1996	F	Jamison	03.05.1960	Michele	SAL	FULL	Salaried Employees	Full time
	109203	Mrs Amy Worthington	05.07.1997	F	Worthington	14.04.1965	Amy	HRLY	FULL	Hourly Employees	Full time
	109204	Mr. Robert Hoffman	24.09.1996	M	Hoffman	07.06.1968	Robert	SAL	FULL	Salaried Employees	Full time
	109205	Mr. Michael Connors	01.01.1996	M	Connors	14.04.1965	Michael	HRLY	FULL	Hourly Employees	Full time
	109206	Mr. Anthony Soprano	02.01.2000	M	Soprano	01.09.1962	Anthony	SAL	FULL	Salaried Employees	Full time
	109207	Mr. Michael Fox	26.01.2001	M	Fox	01.08.1965	Michael	SAL	FULL	Salaried Employees	Full time
	109208	Mr. Derek Jeter	24.10.2000	M	Jeter	03.09.1973	Derek	SAL	FULL	Salaried Employees	Full time

Figure 14.1 List of Eligible Employees

14.1.2 Participation

As shown in Figure 14.2, the report shows all employees who are participating in a special benefit plan.

Participation

Participation

Period 01.01.2004 - 31.12.2004
Benefit area 10 USA

Benefit plan text	Pers.No.	Name	Entry	Part.date	Start	End	Last name	G	First name	Birth date	1st PG	2.PG	1st ProgrGroup. Text	2nd ProgrGroup. Text
Company Dental Plan	109405	Mr. Ernie Edwards	01.01.1996	01.01.1998	01.01.1998	31.12.9999	Edwards	M	Ernie	01.04.1950	SAL	FULL	Salaried Employees	Full time
	109551	Mrs Ethel Palm	15.01.1999		15.07.2001	31.12.9999	Palm	F	Ethel	20.10.1952	SAL	FULL	Salaried Employees	Full time
	109552	Mr. Tom Glavin	01.01.1996	01.01.1998	01.01.1998	31.12.9999	Glavin	M	Tom	01.04.1950	SAL	FULL	Salaried Employees	Full time
	109553	Mr. Roy Gasson	15.02.2000	15.04.2000	15.04.2000	31.12.9999	Gasson	M	Roy	15.11.1945	SAL	FULL	Salaried Employees	Full time
	109554	Mrs Virginia Miller	18.02.1996	01.03.1999	01.03.1999	31.12.9999	Miller	F	Virginia	18.03.1965	HRLY	FULL	Hourly Employees	Full time
	109556	Mr. John Smoltz	15.01.2000	15.03.2000	15.03.2000	31.12.9999	Smoltz	M	John	13.06.1972	SAL	FULL	Salaried Employees	Full time
	109557	Mr. Gregory Maddux	01.02.2000	01.04.2000	01.04.2000	31.12.9999	Maddux	M	Gregory	20.10.1970	SAL	FULL	Salaried Employees	Full time
	109558	Mr. Kevin Millwood	15.12.1999	15.02.2000	15.02.2000	31.12.9999	Millwood	M	Kevin	17.03.1973	SAL	FULL	Salaried Employees	Full time
	109560	Mr. Charlie Finance	15.07.2001		15.07.2001	31.12.9999	Finance	M	Charlie	13.11.1965	SAL	FULL	Salaried Employees	Full time
	109562	Mrs JoAnn Hughes	10.08.2000	18.08.2000	18.08.2000	31.12.9999	Hughes	F	JoAnn	25.07.1972	SAL	FULL	Salaried Employees	Full time
	109563	Mr. Craig Ballman	01.04.2001	10.05.2001	10.05.2001	31.12.9999	Ballman	M	Craig	03.05.1960	HRLY	FULL	Hourly Employees	Full time
	109567	Mr. Dennis Miller	01.04.2001		01.03.2002	31.12.9999	Miller	M	Dennis	15.12.1968	HRLY	FULL	Hourly Employees	Full time
	109602	Mrs Vickie Jones	01.05.2001	01.05.2001	01.05.2001	31.12.9999	Jones	F	Vickie	20.07.1956	SAL	FULL	Salaried Employees	Full time
	109603	Mr. James Christopher	01.05.2001	01.05.2001	01.05.2001	31.12.9999	Christopher	M	James	20.07.1948	SAL	FULL	Salaried Employees	Full time
	109604	Mrs Marie Riddley	01.05.2001	01.05.2001	01.05.2001	31.12.9999	Riddley	F	Marie	23.06.1946	HRLY	FULL	Hourly Employees	Full time
	109605	Todd Michaels	06.09.2000	08.09.2000	02.05.2001	31.12.9999	Michaels	M	Todd	12.02.1965	SAL	FULL	Salaried Employees	Full time
	109606	Mrs Terry Walden	06.09.2000	06.09.2000	06.09.2000	31.12.9999	Walden	F	Terry	12.03.1977	HRLY	FULL	Hourly Employees	Full time

Figure 14.2 List of Participants

14.1.3 Changes of Benefits Elections

As shown in Figure 14.3, this report shows all changes, especially new enrollments, terminations, or changes in the employees' election of a plan over a certain period.

Changes in Benefits Elections

Changes in benefit elections
——— Evaluation period 01.01.2004 to 31.12.2004 ———

Provider Name of Provider Name	Plan Pers.no.	PlanName From	To	Changed	Total changes By	Reason/Details
00000000	PEN1	Standard Pension Plan			4	
Mr. James Keith	00100067	08.06.2004	31.12.2004	08.06.2004	HEATWOLE	First enrollment in plan type PENS
Mr. James Keith	00100067	08.06.2004	31.12.2004	08.06.2004	HEATWOLE	Participation terminated
Chris Nixon	00108014	01.01.2004	31.12.2004	25.02.2004	HENLEY	First enrollment in plan type PENS
Chris Nixon	00108014	01.01.2004	31.12.2004	25.02.2004	HENLEY	Participation terminated

——— Evaluation period 01.01.2004 to 31.12.2004 ———

Provider Name of Provider Name	Plan Pers.no.	PlanName From	To	Changed	Total changes By
List contains no data					

Figure 14.3 Changes in Benefits Election

14.1.4 Change of Eligibility Status

This report shows employees who are no longer eligible for the plan in which they are participating (see Figure 14.4).

The reason can be:

- The plan has been removed.
- They have moved within the organization to an area in which the plan is not applicable.
- They no longer fulfill the requirements of the plan.

Change of eligibility status

Change of eligibility status

Period 01.01.2004 - 31.12.2004
Benefit area

Benefit plan text	Pers.No.	Name	Changed on	Text	Plan	Start	1st PG	End	2.PG	1st ProgrGroup. Text	2nd ProgrGroup. Text
Dependent Life	109306	Shamus Higgins	01.01.2004	No entry for program groupings SAL/FULL / plan LIF1	LIF1	16.04.1999	SAL	31.12.9999	FULL	Salaried Employees	Full time
	109358	Mr. Oliver Wendell Douglas	01.01.2004	No entry for program groupings SAL/FULL / plan LIF1	LIF1	01.01.1998	SAL	31.12.9999	FULL	Salaried Employees	Full time
	109362	Mr. Samuel Drucker	01.01.2004	No entry for program groupings SAL/FULL / plan LIF1	LIF1	22.04.1998	SAL	31.12.9999	FULL	Salaried Employees	Full time
	109367	Mr. Newt Kiley	01.01.2004	No entry for program groupings SAL/FULL / plan LIF1	LIF1	01.01.1998	SAL	31.12.9999	FULL	Salaried Employees	Full time
	109405	Mr. Ernie Edwards	01.01.2004	No entry for program groupings SAL/FULL / plan LIF1	LIF1	01.01.1998	SAL	31.12.9999	FULL	Salaried Employees	Full time
	109552	Mr. Tom Glavin	01.01.2004	No entry for program groupings SAL/FULL / plan LIF1	LIF1	01.01.1998	SAL	31.12.9999	FULL	Salaried Employees	Full time
	109750	Mr. Mario Andretti	01.01.2004	No entry for program groupings SAL/FULL / plan LIF1	LIF1	01.01.1998	SAL	31.12.9999	FULL	Salaried Employees	Full time
Gastos por Servicios Dentales	320011	Hernández Alanis María del Pila	01.01.2004	New benefit area MX	DENT	17.01.2000	EMPL	31.12.2004	ESTD	Empleados Adtivos.	
	320016	Toledano Ibarra María del Carm	01.01.2004	New benefit area MX	DENT	01.02.2000	EJEC	31.12.2004	ESTD	Ejecutivos	
Health Care Account	100201	Mr. Dan Young	01.01.2004	No entry for program groupings EXEC/FULL / plan HCAR	HCAR	15.02.2000	EXEC	31.12.9999	FULL	Executives	Full time
HMO	100224	Mr. John Valentine	01.01.2004	No entry for program groupings EXEC/FULL / plan MED2	MED2	01.01.1998	EXEC	31.12.9999	FULL	Executives	Full time
	100350	Mr. Kurt Surls	01.01.2004	No entry for program groupings EXEC/FULL / plan MED2	MED2	16.08.1997	EXEC	31.12.9999	FULL	Executives	Full time
	109255	Mrs Vicki Dromey	01.01.2004	Employee's zip code lies outside the permitted group	MED2	01.01.1999	HRLY	31.12.9999	FULL	Hourly Employees	Full time
Life Plan - Step Limits	100119	Mrs Erica Carr	01.01.2004	No entry for program groupings HRLY/FULL / plan LSTP	LSTP	01.01.1998	HRLY	31.12.9999	FULL	Hourly Employees	Full time
	100169	Mr. Jack Jackson	01.01.2004	No entry for program groupings SAL/FULL / plan LSTP	LSTP	01.01.1997	SAL	31.12.9999	FULL	Salaried Employees	Full time
	100172	Mr. David Hunter	01.01.2004	No entry for program groupings HRLY/FULL / plan LSTP	LSTP	01.01.1998	HRLY	31.12.9999	FULL	Hourly Employees	Full time
	100238	Mrs Viola S. Gains	01.01.2004	No entry for program groupings SAL/FULL / plan LSTP	LSTP	17.06.1997	SAL	31.12.9999	FULL	Salaried Employees	Full time
	100319	Mr. Michael Daverson	01.01.2004	No entry for program groupings SAL/FULL / plan LSTP	LSTP	01.01.1998	SAL	31.12.9999	FULL	Salaried Employees	Full time
	108060	Ms. Emma Ward	01.01.2004	No entry for program groupings SAL/FULL / plan LSTP	LSTP	01.01.2002	SAL	31.12.2005	FULL	Salaried Employees	Full time
	109252	Mr. John Benton	01.01.2004	No entry for program groupings SAL/FULL / plan LSTP	LSTP	01.02.1996	SAL	31.12.9999	FULL	Salaried Employees	Full time
	109359	Mr. Mister Haney	01.01.2004	No entry for program groupings SAL/FULL / plan LSTP	LSTP	22.04.1998	SAL	31.12.9999	FULL	Salaried Employees	Full time
	109362	Mr. Samuel Drucker	01.01.2004	No entry for program groupings SAL/FULL / plan LSTP	LSTP	22.04.1998	SAL	31.12.9999	FULL	Salaried Employees	Full time
Long Term Disability	100067	Mr. James Keith	08.06.2004	No entry for program groupings SAL/FULL / plan LTD	LTD	08.06.2004	SAL	31.12.2004	FULL	Salaried Employees	Full time
	100083	Mr. Jack Kincaid	01.01.2004	No entry for program groupings SAL/FULL / plan LTD	LTD	01.01.2004	SAL	31.12.9999	FULL	Salaried Employees	Full time
	100134	Mr. Tom Peterson	01.01.2004	No entry for program groupings SAL/FULL / plan LTD	LTD	01.01.1999	SAL	31.12.9999	FULL	Salaried Employees	Full time
	100152	Mrs Joanne Pawlucky	01.01.2004	No entry for program groupings SAL/FULL / plan LTD	LTD	16.04.1999	SAL	31.12.9999	FULL	Salaried Employees	Full time
	100226	Mr. Matthew Black	01.01.2004	No entry for program groupings SAL/FULL / plan LTD	LTD	01.01.2000	SAL	31.12.9999	FULL	Salaried Employees	Full time
	100228	Mrs Karen Altobelli	01.01.2004	No entry for program groupings SAL/FULL / plan LTD	LTD	01.01.2000	SAL	31.12.9999	FULL	Salaried Employees	Full time
	100229	Mr. Jerry Wagner	01.01.2004	No entry for program groupings SAL/FULL / plan LTD	LTD	01.01.2000	SAL	31.12.9999	FULL	Salaried Employees	Full time

Figure 14.4 Change of Eligibility Status

14.1.5 Changes in General Benefits Information

The report detects manual changes, where default values have been overwritten in the benefits Infotype 0171 (see Figure 14.5).

The report identifies mismatches between the default values that have been defined in Customizing and the values that are actually stored in the infotype. The reason for the mismatch can be that the values were manually overwritten by a user during data maintenance or during a change of Customizing settings.

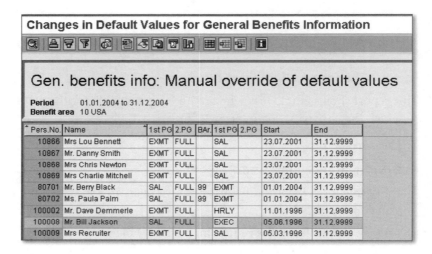

Figure 14.5 Changes in General Benefits Information

14.2 Costs and Contribution

The following reports analyze the costs of the benefits programs.

14.2.1 Health Plan Costs

This report shows the employee and employer costs of a specified health plan (Figure 14.6).

Health Plan Costs

Health Plan Costs
Key date 31.12.2004
Benefit area 10 USA

Period text	Benefit plan text	Pers.No.	Name	Option text	Dep.coverage text	EE Cost	ER Credit	Provider Cost	Curr.
Bi-weekly	Company Dental Plan	100067	Mr. James Keith	Standard Dental Option	Self + Family	14.66	3.46	18.12	USD
		100124	Mr. Hubert Laws	Standard Dental Option	Self	2.73	3.46	6.19	USD
		100136	Mr. Jeff Larsen	Standard Dental Option	Self	2.73	3.46	6.19	USD
		100227	Mr. George Metzger	Standard Dental Option	Self + Spouse	8.15	3.46	11.62	USD
		100318	Mr Christopher Bender	Standard Dental Option	Self	2.73	3.46	6.19	USD
		108021	Ms. Andrea Rene	Standard Dental Option	Self	2.73	3.46	6.19	USD
		108022	Mr. Andrew Robert	Standard Dental Option	Self + Child	8.15	3.46	11.62	USD
		108023	Ms. Angela Rae	Standard Dental Option	Self + Spouse	8.15	3.46	11.62	USD
		108046	Tami Smithington	Standard Dental Option	Self	2.73	3.46	6.19	USD
		108047	Sherral Polman	Standard Dental Option	Self	2.73	3.46	6.19	USD
		108062	Ms. Carol Harris	Standard Dental Option	Self	2.73	3.46	6.19	USD
		109056	Mr. Daniel Fouts	Standard Dental Option	Self	2.73	3.46	6.19	USD
		109057	Mr. Troy Aikman	Standard Dental Option	Self + Family	14.66	3.46	18.12	USD
		109058	Mrs Toni Braxton	Standard Dental Option	Self	2.73	3.46	6.19	USD
		109701	Mrs Melissa Anderson	Standard Dental Option	Self + Spouse	8.15	3.46	11.62	USD
		109702	Mr. Charles Parrish	Standard Dental Option	Self	2.73	3.46	6.19	USD
		700798	Colleen Caplice	Standard Dental Option	Self	2.73	3.46	6.19	USD
		700799	Katrina Parzyck	Standard Dental Option	Self	2.73	3.46	6.19	USD
		700800	Andrea Stork	Standard Dental Option	Self	2.73	3.46	6.19	USD
		10190822	Harvey Stevens	Standard Dental Option	Self + Spouse	8.15	3.46	11.62	USD
	Company Dental Plan					105.56	69.20	174.81	USD
	HMO	100124	Mr. Hubert Laws	Standard HMO	Self	15.23	67.11	82.34	USD
		100318	Mr Christopher Bender	Standard HMO	Self	15.23	67.11	82.34	USD
		109056	Mr. Daniel Fouts	Standard HMO	Self	15.23	67.11	82.34	USD
	HMO					45.69	201.33	247.02	USD

Figure 14.6 Health Plan Costs

14.2.2 Insurance Plan Costs

This report shows the employee and employer costs of a specified insurance plan (Figure 14.7).

Insurance Plan Costs

Insurance Plan Costs
Key date 31.12.2004
Benefit area 10 USA

Period text	Benefit plan text	Pers.No.	Name	Option	Insurance option text	EE Cost	ER Credit	Provider Cost	Ins. Coverage	Curr.
Bi-weekly	AD&D	100067	Mr. James Keith	1IND	Individual	0.19	0.13	0.32	50,000.00	USD
		100227	Mr. George Metzger	1IND	Individual	0.11	0.07	0.18	28,000.00	USD
		108021	Ms. Andrea Rene	1IND	Individual	0.16	0.11	0.27	41,000.00	USD
		108022	Mr. Andrew Robert	1IND	Individual	0.18	0.13	0.31	48,000.00	USD
		108023	Ms. Angela Rae	1IND	Individual	0.14	0.09	0.23	36,000.00	USD
		108047	Sherral Polman	1IND	Individual	0.26	0.18	0.43	67,000.00	USD
		108062	Ms. Carol Harris	1IND	Individual	0.20	0.14	0.34	52,000.00	USD
	AD&D					1.24	0.85	2.08		USD
	Company Life Insurance Plan	100067	Mr. James Keith	1X	1X Salary	0.00	0.92	0.92	50,000.00	USD
		100124	Mr. Hubert Laws	1X	1X Salary	0.00	0.70	0.70	38,000.00	USD
		100136	Mr. Jeff Larsen	1X	1X Salary	0.00	1.26	1.26	68,000.00	USD
		100227	Mr. George Metzger	1X	1X Salary	0.00	0.52	0.52	28,000.00	USD
		100240	Mrs Lisa Felix	1X	1X Salary	0.00	0.92	0.92	50,000.00	USD
		108021	Ms. Andrea Rene	1X	1X Salary	0.00	0.76	0.76	41,000.00	USD
		108022	Mr. Andrew Robert	1X	1X Salary	0.00	0.89	0.89	48,000.00	USD
		108023	Ms. Angela Rae	1X	1X Salary	0.00	0.66	0.66	36,000.00	USD
		108046	Tami Smithington	1X	1X Salary	0.00	0.78	0.78	42,000.00	USD
		108047	Sherral Polman	1X	1X Salary	0.00	1.24	1.24	67,000.00	USD
		108062	Ms. Carol Harris	1X	1X Salary	0.00	0.59	0.59	32,000.00	USD
		109056	Mr. Daniel Fouts	1X	1X Salary	0.00	0.59	0.59	32,000.00	USD
		109057	Mr. Troy Aikman	1X	1X Salary	0.00	0.74	0.74	40,000.00	USD
		109058	Mrs Toni Braxton	1X	1X Salary	0.00	1.61	1.61	87,000.00	USD
		109701	Mrs Melissa Anderson	1X	1X Salary	0.00	0.76	0.76	41,000.00	USD
		109702	Mr. Charles Parrish	1X	1X Salary	1.14	1.14	1.14	41,000.00	USD
		700798	Colleen Caplice	1X	1X Salary	0.00	0.59	0.59	32,000.00	USD
		700799	Katrina Parzyck	1X	1X Salary	0.00	0.59	0.59	32,000.00	USD
		700800	Andrea Stork	1X	1X Salary	0.00	0.39	0.39	21,000.00	USD
	Company Life Insurance Plan					1.14	15.65	15.65		USD

Figure 14.7 Insurance Plan Costs

14.2.3 Savings Plan Contributions

This report shows the employee and employer costs of a specified savings plan (Figure 14.8).

Savings Plan Contributions

Savings Plan Contributions

Key date 31.12.2004
Benefit area 10 USA

Period text	Benefit plan text	Pers.No.	Name	≈ EE pre-tax	≈ EE post-tax	≈ EE total contr.	≈ ER total contr.	Curr.
Bi-weekly	401K Savings Plan	100087	Mr. James Keith	113.62	0.00	113.62	113.62	USD
		100124	Mr. Hubert Laws	142.40	0.00	142.40	85.44	USD
		100136	Mr. Jeff Larsen	208.21	0.00	208.21	156.16	USD
		100209	Mr. Timmy Tabasco	314.93	0.00	314.93	314.93	USD
		100227	Mr. George Metzger	53.84	0.00	53.84	53.84	USD
		108022	Mr. Andrew Robert	92.00	0.00	92.00	92.00	USD
		108062	Ms. Carol Harris	24.00	0.00	24.00	24.00	USD
		108064	Mr. Jacob Simone	43.20	0.00	43.20	43.20	USD
		109056	Mr. Daniel Fouts	122.80	0.00	122.80	78.68	USD
		109057	Mr. Troy Aikman	152.00	0.00	152.00	91.20	USD
		109058	Mrs Toni Braxton	300.03	0.00	300.03	200.02	USD
		109701	Mrs Melissa Anderson	157.68	0.00	157.68	94.61	USD
		10190822	Harvey Stevens	88.00	0.00	88.00	88.00	USD
	401K Savings Plan			∗ 1,812.71 ∗	0.00 ∗	1,812.71 ∗	1,430.70	USD
	Pension Plan	109702	Mr. Charles Parrish	0.00	0.00	0.00	0.00	USD
	Pension Plan			∗ 0.00 ∗	0.00 ∗	0.00 ∗	0.00	USD
	Standard Pension Plan	100067	Mr. James Keith	0.00	0.00	0.00	189.36	USD
		108062	Ms. Carol Harris	0.00	0.00	0.00	120.00	USD
		108064	Mr. Jacob Simone	0.00	0.00	0.00	216.00	USD
	Standard Pension Pls.			∗ 0.00 ∗	0.00 ∗	0.00 ∗	525.36	USD
Bi-weekly				∗∗ 1,812.71 ∗∗	0.00 ∗∗	1,812.71 ∗∗	1,956.06	USD

Figure 14.8 Savings Plan Contributions

14.2.4 FSA Contributions

This report shows estimated employee and employer contributions to specified flexible spending accounts (FSAs) per pay period (Figure 14.9).

FSA Contributions

FSA Contributions

Key date 31.12.2004
Benefit area 10 USA

Period text	Benefit plan text	Pers.No.	Name	≈ EE total contr.	≈ ER total contr.	Curr.
Bi-weekly	Dependent Care	108022	Mr. Andrew Robert	3.83	0.00	USD
	Dependent Care			∗ 3.83 ∗	0.00 ∗	USD
	Health Care Account	100227	Mr. George Metzger	115.07	0.00	USD
		100240	Mrs Lisa Felix	76.71	0.00	USD
		108062	Ms. Carol Harris	19.18	0.00	USD
	Health Care Account			∗ 210.96 ∗	0.00 ∗	USD
Bi-weekly				∗∗ 214.79 ∗∗	0.00 ∗∗	USD
Monthly	Dependent Care	100111	Mrs Bianca Ramos	291.67	0.00	USD
		100113	Mrs Barbara Kent	70.00	0.00	USD
		100135	Mrs Debbie Davis	191.67	0.00	USD
		100173	Mrs Yvette Williams	47.92	0.00	USD
	Dependent Care			∗ 601.26 ∗	0.00 ∗	USD
	Health Care Account	100112	Mr. John Williams	116.67	0.00	USD
		100113	Mrs Barbara Kent	39.58	0.00	USD
		100114	Mr. Braden Washington	50.00	0.00	USD
		100115	Mr. Jonathan Tyler	141.67	0.00	USD
		100135	Mrs Debbie Davis	66.67	0.00	USD
		100173	Mrs Yvette Williams	79.17	0.00	USD
		100201	Mr. Dan Young	41.67	0.00	USD
		100249	Mr. Jonathan Smith	233.33	0.00	USD
	Health Care Account			∗ 768.76 ∗	0.00 ∗	USD
Monthly				∗∗ 1,370.02 ∗∗	0.00 ∗∗	USD

Figure 14.9 FSA Contribution

14.2.5 Stock Purchase Plan Contributions

This report shows employee and employer contributions for specified stock purchase plans on a specified date (Figure 14.10).

Stock Purchase Plan Contributions

Stock Purchase Plan Contributions

Key date   01.01.2000
Benefit area   10 USA

Period text	Benefit plan text	Pers.No.	Name	EE pre-tax	EE post-tax	EE total contr.	ER total contr.	Curr.
Bi-weekly	Stock Purchase Plan	100227	Mr. George Metzger	0.00	43.08	43.08	0.00	USD
Semi-monthly		100134	Mr. Tom Peterson	0.00	99.12	99.12	0.00	USD
		100152	Mrs Joanne Pawlucky	0.00	462.96	462.96	0.00	USD
		100226	Matthew Black	0.00	65.00	65.00	0.00	USD
		100228	Mrs Karen Altobelli	0.00	25.00	25.00	0.00	USD
		100229	Mr. Jerry Wagner	0.00	91.80	91.80	0.00	USD
		100230	Mrs Jennifer Esposito	0.00	15.00	15.00	0.00	USD
		100239	Mr. Mark Taylor	0.00	600.00	600.00	0.00	USD
		109551	Mrs Ethel Palm	0.00	320.00	320.00	0.00	USD

Figure 14.10 Stock Purchase Plan Contributions

14.2.6 Costs/Contributions for Miscellaneous Plans

This report shows employee and employer contributions for a specified miscellaneous plan on a specific date.

14.2.7 Vesting Percentages

This report shows the vesting percentages for plans with contributions according to the vesting rules defined in Customizing (Figure 14.11). This report must be run when an employee leaves the company in order to determine the amount contribution to which the employee is entitled.

> For retirement plans that use a calculation process to determine vesting   **[+]**
> services, the report reads the latest vesting percentage from the retirement plan valuation results Infotype 0565. If this infotype is not available, the percentage is zero.

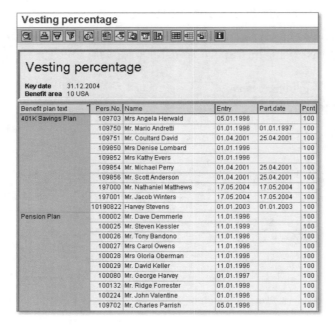

Figure 14.11 Vesting Percentages

14.2.8 Contribution Limit Check

During enrollment, the system automatically checks the defined limits and only allows employees to choose contributions that range within these limits. When different contribution rules become valid, an employee's contributions becomes invalid. The report detects the employees who must change their contributions.

14.3 Statistics

Finally, there are some statistical reports that provide the user with information on the potentials of benefits plans that may be analyzed.

14.3.1 Employee Demographics

This report summarizes age and gender and indicates whether the employee is a smoker or nonsmoker (Figure 14.12). This is required for health insurance purposes.

Employee Demographics

Demographic Employee Data: Overview

Employees :	Evaluation date 22.08.2007 840 selected 840 evaluated 0 rejected (see list of errors)
Benefit area :	10 USA
1st Program group :	EXEC Executives EXMT HRLY Hourly Employees SAL Salaried Employees
2nd Program group :	FULL Full time FULL Full time FULL Full time PART Part time

Age Ran	Gender	Number of Employees	Percentage of Employees	Number of Smokers	Percent of Smokers	No. of Non-Smokers	Per. of Non-Smokers
1 - 19	Total	1	0.12	0	0.00	1	100.00
	Female	1	100.00	0	0.00	1	100.00
	Male	0	0.00	0	0.00	0	0.00
20 - 24	Total	3	0.36	0	0.00	3	100.00
	Female	1	33.33	0	0.00	1	33.33
	Male	2	66.67	0	0.00	2	66.67
25 - 29	Total	25	2.98	0	0.00	25	100.00
	Female	15	60.00	0	0.00	15	60.00
	Male	10	40.00	0	0.00	10	40.00
30 - 34	Total	64	7.62	0	0.00	64	100.00
	Female	29	45.31	0	0.00	29	45.31
	Male	35	54.69	0	0.00	35	54.69
35 - 39	Total	160	19.05	0	0.00	160	100.00
	Female	70	43.75	0	0.00	70	43.75
	Male	90	56.25	0	0.00	90	56.25
40 - 44	Total	132	15.71	0	0.00	132	100.00
	Female	59	44.70	0	0.00	59	44.70
	Male	73	55.30	0	0.00	73	55.30
45 - 49	Total	271	32.26	0	0.00	271	100.00
	Female	128	47.23	0	0.00	128	47.23
	Male	143	52.77	0	0.00	143	52.77
50 - 54	Total	103	12.26	1	0.97	102	99.03
	Female	54	52.43	0	0.00	54	52.43
	Male	49	47.57	1	0.97	48	46.60
55 - 59	Total	51	6.07	11	21.57	40	78.43
	Female	12	23.53	0	0.00	12	23.53
	Male	39	76.47	11	21.57	28	54.90

Figure 14.12 Demographics Statistics

14.3.2 Benefit Election Analysis

The report shows percentage changes in plan participation and indicates the eligibility for benefits plans offered by the company (Figure 14.13).

Benefit Election Analysis

Percentage changes between 01.01.2004 and 31.12.2004

Sel. benefit areas: 1
Sel. benefit plans: 17

Description	Text	Eligible EEs	Participation	Scal. particip.
USA	401K Savings Plan	1.33	1.76	0.43
	AD&D	1.95	7.14	5.19-
	Dependent Care	1.33	0.00	1.33-
	Company Dental Plan	1.32	4.08	2.76
	Health Care Account	1.36	0.00	1.36-
	Dependent Life	1.95	0.00	1.95-
	Company Life Insurance Plan	1.33	2.52	1.19
	Supplementary Life Insurance	1.36	1.41	0.05
	Spousal Life	1.09	0.00	1.09-
	Long Term Disability	1.95	0.00	1.95-
	Standard Medical Plan	1.32	5.16	3.84
	HMO	1.92	0.00	1.92-
	Non Qualified Savings Plan	0.00	0.00	0.00
	Standard Pension Plan	1.95	0.00	1.95-
	Pension Plan	0.00	0.00	0.00
	Pension Plan (DB)	0.00	0.00	0.00
	Stock Purchase Plan	1.95	0.00	1.95-

Figure 14.13 Benefits Election Analysis

333

14.3.3 Enrollment Statistics

This report counts enrollments that have been made per day during a series of days (Figure 14.14).

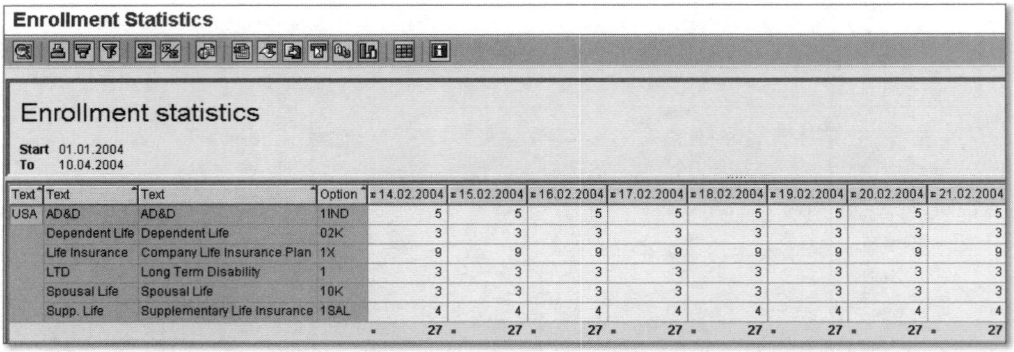
Enrollment Statistics

Enrollment statistics

Start 01.01.2004
To 10.04.2004

Text	Text	Text	Option	14.02.2004	15.02.2004	16.02.2004	17.02.2004	18.02.2004	19.02.2004	20.02.2004	21.02.2004
USA	AD&D	AD&D	1IND	5	5	5	5	5	5	5	5
	Dependent Life	Dependent Life	02K	3	3	3	3	3	3	3	3
	Life Insurance	Company Life Insurance Plan	1X	9	9	9	9	9	9	9	9
	LTD	Long Term Disability	1	3	3	3	3	3	3	3	3
	Spousal Life	Spousal Life	10K	3	3	3	3	3	3	3	3
	Supp. Life	Supplementary Life Insurance	1SAL	4	4	4	4	4	4	4	4
				27	27	27	27	27	27	27	27

Figure 14.14 Enrollment Statistics

14.4 SAP Netweaver BI Standard Content

In addition to the standard reports, SAP NetWeaver BI provides a powerful tool to analyze benefits plans. For this purpose, the standard content provides an InfoCube containing a large number of key figures and navigation criteria.

14.4.1 The Benefits InfoCube

The following key figures are provided by the InfoCube (Figures 14.15 and 14.16):

- Age in Years
- Capacity Utilization Level in %
- Employees – Pre Tax Deductions – Bonus
- Employees – Post Tax Deductions – Bonus
- Employees – Pre Tax Deductions
- Employees – Post Tax Deductions
- Number of Eligible Employees
- Employer Expenses – Bonus
- Employer Credits

- ▶ Employer Costs
- ▶ Employer Contributions
- ▶ Number of Participating Employees
- ▶ Provider Costs
- ▶ Imputed Income

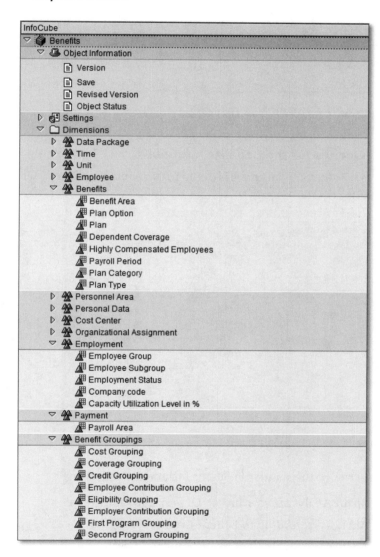

Figure 14.15 Dimensions of the Benefits InfoCube

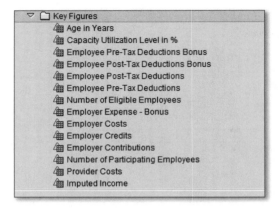

Figure 14.16 Key Figures of the Benefits InfoCube

14.4.2 Queries for the Benefits InfoCube

Figure 14.17 shows an an analysis of the participants based on different benefits criteria.

Participation Analysis According to Benefits Criteria									
Author SAP				Status of Data 09.09.2005 12:22:56					
Filter	Information								
1st Program Grouping	2nd Program Grouping	Executives Full time	Executives Result	Hourly Employees Full time	Hourly Employees Part time	Hourly Employees Result	Salaried Employees Full time	Salaried Employees Result	Overall Result
Plan Type									
401K	Number of Participating EEs	2.000	2.000	41.000		41.000	126.000	126.000	169.000
401K	No. of Eligible EEs	15.000	15.000	256.000		256.000	486.000	486.000	757.000
401K	Percentage Participation (in %)	13.3333	13.3333	16.0156		16.0156	25.9259	25.9259	22.3250
AD&D	Number of Participating EEs			13.000		13.000	81.000	81.000	94.000
AD&D	No. of Eligible EEs			256.000		256.000	486.000	486.000	742.000
AD&D	Percentage Participation (in %)			5.0781		5.0781	16.6667	16.6667	12.6685
Dental	Number of Participating EEs	3.000	3.000	57.000	4.000	61.000	135.000	135.000	199.000
Dental	No. of Eligible EEs	15.000	15.000	256.000	6.000	262.000	486.000	486.000	763.000
Dental	Percentage Participation (in %)	20.0000	20.0000	22.2656	66.6667	23.2824	27.7778	27.7778	26.0813
Dependent Care	Number of Participating EEs	0.000	0.000	1.000		1.000	48.000	48.000	49.000
Dependent Care	No. of Eligible EEs	15.000	15.000	256.000		256.000	486.000	486.000	757.000
Dependent Care	Percentage Participation (in %)	0.0000	0.0000	0.3906		0.3906	9.8765	9.8765	6.4729
Dependent Life	Number of Participating EEs			5.000		5.000	49.000	49.000	54.000
Dependent Life	No. of Eligible EEs			256.000		256.000	486.000	486.000	742.000
Dependent Life	Percentage Participation (in %)			1.9531		1.9531	10.0823	10.0823	7.2776
Health Care	Number of Participating EEs			3.000		3.000	65.000	65.000	68.000
Health Care	No. of Eligible EEs			256.000		256.000	486.000	486.000	742.000

Figure 14.17 Participant Analysis Query

Other queries of the standard content include the following:

▸ Participant Analysis According to Organizational Criteria

▸ Cost Analysis According to Benefit Criteria

▸ Cost Analysis According to Organizational Criteria

14.5 Conclusion

Numerous reporting options are available in the benefits area, which meet all the relevant requirements.

With its many key figures and navigation attributes, the InfoCube provides a wide range of reporting options.

Depending on the respective business requirements, the few existing standard queries can be complemented with customer-specific ones.

The reports in Training and Event Management enable extensive evaluations for business events, attendances, and resources.

15 Training and Event Management

The reports for business events, attendances, and resources in Training and Event Management provide you with tools that allow you to quickly obtain extensive information, for example, about employee training costs, details of business events or attendees, or the resources required to execute a business event.

You access these reports from the SAP Easy Access menu under **Human Resources • Training and Event Management • Information System • Reports**. This folder is divided into various subfolders containing the reports for attendances, business events, and resources. These reports are described in detail in this chapter.

SAP Easy Access path

Alternatively, you can start the reports for Training and Event Management from the dynamic information menu. You can find this in the SAP Easy Access menu under **Human Resources • Training and Event Management • Information System**. When you start the dynamic information menu, an overview of business event groups and types is displayed as shown in Figure 15.1.

Dynamic information menu

You can access the individual Training and Event management reports for attendances, business events, and resources from the **Information** menu. Figure 15.2 shows the reports available for participation (i.e., attendances).

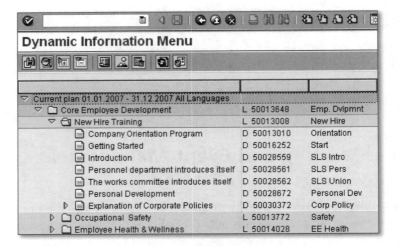

Figure 15.1 Dynamic Information Menu with Business Event Groups and Types

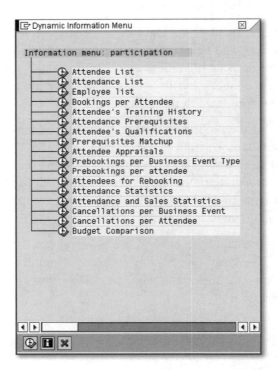

Figure 15.2 Dynamic Information Menu – Participation

15.1 Attendances

The reports for attendances provide key information about attendees in Training and Event Management. For example, they support business event schedules with attendee lists and help administrators with Training and Event Management tasks by providing lists of attendees to be rebooked, and they provide an information basis for canceling business events.

15.1.1 Attendee List

The Attendee List report generates a list of internal and external attendees for business events. You can use selection parameters to specify the reporting period and to determine whether attendees with normal bookings, essential bookings, and/or waiting-list bookings are to be included in the attendee list generated by the report. If you enter a valid location, the report will only take data relating to this event location into account. The list that is generated provides information about the business event period, the attendees, the booking date, and, if required, details of fees. Figure 15.3 shows an extract from an attendee list.

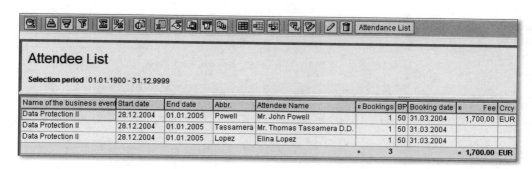

Figure 15.3 Attendee List

You can press the **Attendance List** button to navigate to the Attendance List report for a selected business event (see Figure 15.5).

15.1.2 Attendance List

The Attendance List report generates a list of all attendees of a business event, with a column for signatures. You can use this list during the event itself to check who actually attended and to determine who is to receive attendance confirmation notifications.

The output consists of a list of attendees, with each line specifying the name of one attendee and his organizational assignment and providing space for a signature (see Figure 15.4). Note that when you print the list:

- Participants on the waiting list are not shown.
- No object IDs are shown.
- n lines are output for an N.N. (unnamed) booking with n persons.

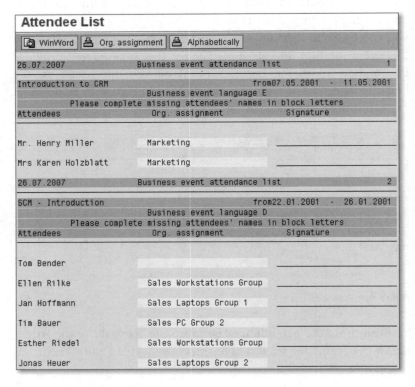

Figure 15.4 Attendee List Output

You can also execute the following functions from the list screen:

▶ Press the **WinWord** button to download the attendance list into Microsoft Word (see Figure 15.5).

▶ Sort the attendees' last names alphabetically.

▶ Sort attendees alphabetically by organizational assignment.

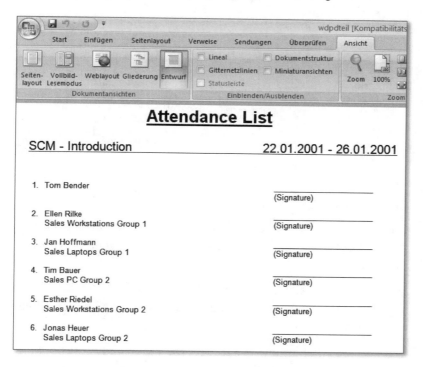

Figure 15.5 Attendance List (Microsoft Word)

15.1.3 Employee list

The Employee List report generates a list of employees in an internal (**Organizational unit** object type) or external organizational structure (of the **Company**, **Customer**, or **Interested Party** object type). This report is useful, for example, when replacing attendees of N.N. bookings of a company. An example is shown in Figure 15.6.

Org. assignment	EE abbr.	Employee name	Start date	End Date
FAG Canada Inc.	Smith	Susann Smith	01.01.1994	31.12.9999
Deutsche Bank Luxembourg	Sauer	Michaela Sauer	01.01.1994	31.12.9999
Deutsche Bank Luxembourg	Dupont	Michael Dupont	01.01.1994	31.12.9999
Editions Nathan	Fröhlich	Heike Fröhlich	01.01.1994	31.12.9999
South African Airways	Leeson	Brian Leeson	01.01.1999	31.12.9999
South African Airways	Vollmond	Berta Vollmond	01.01.1994	31.12.9999
South African Airways	Wrangler	Lisa Wrangler	01.01.1995	31.12.9999
BMW Limited	Meyer	Klaus Meyer	01.01.1994	31.12.9999
Learning Dynamics Canada	Matthews	Sheila Matthews	01.01.1997	31.12.9999
Learning Dynamics Canada	Johnston	Kit Johnston	01.01.1997	31.12.9999
Learning Dynamics Canada	Grant	Kalvin Grant	01.01.1997	31.12.9999
Learning Dynamics Canada	George	Heather George	01.01.1997	31.12.9999
McBer & Associates	Robinson	Nancy Robinson	11.01.1999	31.12.9999
McBer & Associates	Ryan	Robert Ryan	03.10.1997	31.12.9999
McBer & Associates	Thomas	Jennifer Thomas	03.10.1997	31.12.9999
Southern Alberta Institute of Technology	Rankin	Lorne Rankin	01.01.1997	31.12.9999
Southern Alberta Institute of Technology	Cobb	Bill Cobb	01.01.1997	31.12.9999
MultiHexa	Julie	Binoche Julie	01.01.1990	31.12.9999

Figure 15.6 Employee List

15.1.4 Bookings per Attendee

The Bookings per Attendee report generates a list of business events that are booked for an internal or external attendee (an individual or a group).

You can use the following selection parameters to specify the reporting period and reporting object and to determine which data is to be included in the report:

▶ If you select a business event type, the report only lists bookings for events of this type.

▶ With the **With employee bookings** parameter, the report shows the bookings for the individual employees in an N.N. booking for group attendees (company, organizational unit, customer, or interested party attendee types).

▶ If you select the **Without employee bookings** parameter, the report only displays the booking for the organizational unit as a whole, rather than for the individual attendees, in the case of a group booking.

Figure 15.7 shows an extract from a booking list.

Abbr.	Attendee Name	Business event	Start date	End date	∑ Bookings	BP	Booking date	∑	Fee	Crcy
Smith	Mr. Edward Smith	Bus Ethics	26.11.2001	26.11.2001	1	50	31.05.2002		250.00	USD
Daverson	Mr. Michael Daverson	First Aid	31.01.2001	01.02.2001	1	50	10.11.2001		500.00	USD
Palm	Mrs Ethel Palm	Leadership	09.04.2001	10.04.2001	1	50	04.09.2001		550.00	USD
Glavin	Mr. Tom Glavin	Leadership	01.08.2001	02.08.2001	1	50	26.07.2001		550.00	USD
Miller	Mrs Virginia Miller	Leadership	09.04.2001	10.04.2001	1	50	04.09.2001		550.00	USD
Maddux	Mr. Gregory Maddux	Leadership	02.03.2001	03.03.2001	1	09	02.08.2001		550.00	USD
Cox	Mrs Barbara Cox	Leadership	09.04.2001	10.04.2001	1	50	04.09.2001		550.00	USD
Jones	Mr. Andrew Jones	Leadership	09.04.2001	10.04.2001	1	50	04.09.2001		550.00	USD
Hughes	Mrs JoAnn Hughes	Leadership	09.04.2001	10.04.2001	1	50	04.09.2001		550.00	USD
Jones	Mr. Larry Jones	Leadership	01.08.2001	02.08.2001	1	50	26.07.2001		550.00	USD
Bigshot	Mr. Buck Bigshot	Leadership	01.08.2001	02.08.2001	1	50	26.07.2001		550.00	USD
Lauran	Mr. Ralph Lauran	Leadership	09.04.2001	10.04.2001	1	50	04.09.2001		550.00	USD

Figure 15.7 Bookings per Attendee List

15.1.5 Attendee's Training History

This report shows the training history of an internal or external attendee. The output consists of a list of all the training events already attended by the relevant attendee or for which the attendee is booked.

The list includes, for example, the names and locations of the events and the fees involved (see Figure 15.8).

Abbr.	Attendee Name	Event	Event type	Bus. event	Start date	End date	∑ Days	∑	Hours	∑	Fee	Crcy
Riedel	Esther Riedel	☑	☐	SCM_Intro	22.01.2001	26.01.2001	5		34.00		200.00	EUR
Rilke	Ellen Rilke	☑	☐	SCM_Intro	22.01.2001	26.01.2001	5		34.00		200.00	EUR
Ryan	Mr. Michael Ryan	☑	☐	Bus Ethics	02.10.2001	02.10.2001	1		8.00		2.700.00	USD
Ryan	Mr. Michael Ryan	☑	☐	Qual. Mgt.	31.01.2001	09.02.2001	6		40.00		800.00	USD
Schröder	Roland Schröder	☑	☐	Selling	04.04.2001	05.04.2001	2		15.00		1,500.00	DEM
Schröder	Roland Schröder	☑	☐	Safety.Trng	02.01.2001	23.01.2001	4		16.00		450.00	CAD
Schäfer	Robert Schäfer	☑	☐	Selling	04.10.2001	05.10.2001	2		15.00		1,500.00	DEM
Smith	Mr. Edward Smith	☑	☐	Bus Ethics	26.11.2001	26.11.2001	1		8.00		250.00	USD
Smith	Mr. James Smith	☑	☐	Qual. Mgt.	30.11.2001	09.12.2001	6		40.00		800.00	USD
Smith	Mr. James Smith	☑	☐	Bus Ethics	26.11.2001	26.11.2001	1		8.00		250.00	USD
Smith	Mrs Brenda Smith	☑	☐	Bus Ethics	02.10.2001	02.10.2001	1		8.00		250.00	USD
Sombat	Mrs Amy Sombat	☑	☐	Bus Ethics	02.10.2001	02.10.2001	1		8.00		250.00	USD

Figure 15.8 Training History List

15.1.6 Attendance Prerequisites

The Attendance Prerequisites report generates a list of the prerequisites for attending the events of one or more event types. These prerequisites may be previous attendance at events of a certain type or certain qualifications (such as IT skills, knowledge of HCM, etc.). Figure 15.9 shows the prerequisites for attending an event entitled "Management Techniques."

Business event type	Event type	Qual.	Prerequisite	Qual.start	End date
Management Techniques	☑	☐	Business Ethics	01.01.1995	31.12.9999
Business English	☑	☐	General English	01.01.1995	31.12.9999
Technical English	☑	☐	General English	01.01.1995	31.12.9999
Business French	☐	☑	French Language	01.01.1994	31.12.9999
Business French	☑	☐	General French	01.01.1995	31.12.9999

Figure 15.9 Attendance Prerequisites List

15.1.7 Attendee's Qualifications

The Attendee's Qualifications report generates a list of events of a specific event type attended by the attendee and a list of the attendee's qualifications, that is, knowledge, skills, and expertise.

The list (see Figure 15.10) contains information about the type of events attended, valid qualifications and their depreciation meters, and expired qualifications and their depreciation meters. Expired qualifications are displayed with a dark background.

[+] The list only displays event types of events that have taken place up to the key date specified. Waiting list bookings are not taken into account.

If the attendee has been awarded the same qualification more than once (for example, because he has attended several events of the same type), the report only shows the most recent of these qualifications.

```
26.07.2007                    Attendee's qualifications                              1

 Person                 Ms. Emma Ward
 Selection period       01.01.1900  -  31.12.9999
 Key date               26.07.2007

 NOTE: Expired qualifications are displayed with    a dark background.
```

Business event type	Validity period	Depreciation meter
First Aid	01.04.2005 - 01.04.2005	1 Year
OSHA Safety Refresher Training	23.06.2005 - 23.06.2005	6 Months
Communication with customers	20.07.2005 - 22.07.2005	

Qualification	Validity period	Depreciation meter
Knowledge of Excel	04.07.1946 - 31.12.9999	
First Aider Training	04.07.1946 - 31.12.9999	1 Year
Presentation Software	01.01.1994 - 31.12.9999	
Knowledge of Powerpoint	01.01.1994 - 31.12.9999	
Communication Skills	01.01.2002 - 31.12.9999	
Initiative	01.01.2002 - 31.12.9999	
Concern for Effectiveness	01.01.2002 - 31.12.9999	
Sociability	01.01.2002 - 31.12.9999	
Adaptability	01.01.2002 - 31.12.9999	
Ability to organize and act	01.01.2002 - 31.12.9999	
Teamwork	01.01.2004 - 31.12.9999	
Business Ethics	27.01.2005 - 31.12.9999	

Figure 15.10 Attendee's Qualifications Report

15.1.8 Attendance Statistics

The Attendance Statistics report generates attendance statistics for all events of the selected event types.

You can use the following selection parameters to specify which data is to be output:

▶ **Language**
Here you can enter a language key if you want to output statistics relating to events with a certain event language.

▶ **Catalog**
If you select this parameter, the statistics only show events that can still be booked.

▶ **Locked only**
Only locked events are shown in the statistics.

▶ **With historical records only**
The report only shows statistics for events with historical records.

▶ **Business event location**
The report only shows statistics for events taking place at the selected location.

▶ **Status**
The report only shows statistics for events with this status.

▶ **External only**
The report only shows statistics for external events.

▶ **Canceled only**
The report only shows statistics for canceled events. Figure 15.11 shows an extract from an attendance statistics report.

Depending on the layout settings, the list screen may contain the following information:

▶ Business event name

▶ Business event date

▶ Business event language

▶ Total number of attendees

▶ Number of bookings

▶ Number of waiting-list bookings

▶ Indicators for locked, canceled, historical events, and events that have been followed up

▶ Indicator for firmly booked events

▶ Indicator for external (Ext) events

Business event type	Business event	Start date	End date	L	≡ Number of Bookings	≡ Number on waitlist	Lock flag	Delete flg	Hist.	Follow-up	FB	Ext
Data Protection I	Data Protect	05.01.2004	09.01.2004	EN	3	0	☐	☐	☐	☐	☑	☐
Data Protection I	Data Protect	12.01.2004	16.01.2004	EN	3	0	☐	☐	☐	☐	☑	☐
Data Protection I	Data Protect	26.01.2004	30.01.2004	EN	3	0	☐	☐	☐	☐	☑	☐
Data Protection I	Data Protect	09.02.2004	13.02.2004	EN	3	0	☐	☐	☐	☐	☑	☐
Data Protection I	Data Protect	23.02.2004	27.02.2004	EN	3	0	☐	☐	☐	☐	☑	☐
Data Protection I	Data Protect	01.03.2004	05.03.2004	EN	3	0	☐	☐	☐	☐	☑	☐
Data Protection I	Data Protect	08.03.2004	12.03.2004	EN	3	0	☐	☐	☐	☐	☑	☐
Data Protection I	Data Protect	22.03.2004	26.03.2004	EN	3	0	☐	☐	☐	☐	☑	☐
Data Protection I	Data Protect	01.04.2004	05.04.2004	EN	1	0	☐	☐	☐	☐	☑	☐
Data Protection I	Data Protect	05.04.2004	09.04.2004	EN	3	0	☐	☐	☐	☐	☑	☐
Data Protection I	Data Protect	29.04.2004	03.05.2004	EN	2	0	☐	☐	☐	☐	☑	☐
Data Protection I	Data Protect	17.05.2004	21.05.2004	EN	3	0	☐	☐	☐	☐	☑	☐

Figure 15.11 Attendance Statistics

Additional functions on the list screen

You can also execute the following functions from the list screen:

▶ Display the attendee list

▶ Display the firmly booked and canceled events

▶ Follow up events

15.1.9 Cancellations per Business Event/Attendee

You can use two different reports in relation to the cancellation of events, namely the Cancellations per Business Event and Cancellations per Attendee reports.

The Cancellations per Business Event report generates a list of business events that have been canceled by attendees for the selected business event groups, types, and/or business events in the selection period (see Figure 15.12). Any cancellation fees charged are also shown.

The Cancellations per Attendee report generates a list of business events cancelled by one or more attendees and contains the same information as the Cancellations per Business Event report.

Cancellations per Business Event

Selection period 01.01.1900 - 31.12.9999

American Dollar

Bus. event	Start date	End date	Attendee Name	Organizational Assignment	≡ Canceled	≡	Fee	COCr	Reason canceled
HR - 010	29.07.1996	02.08.1996	1 N.N.	Arrowspace US-SANFRANCISCO	1		240.00	USD	
HR - 100	29.07.1996	31.07.1996	1 N.N.	Arrowspace US-SANFRANCISCO	1		260.00	USD	
HR - 100	05.08.1996	07.08.1996	1 N.N.	Arrowspace US-SANFRANCISCO	1		200.00	USD	
HR - 100	05.08.1996	07.08.1996	1 N.N.	Suffix Manufacturin US-PHILADELPHIA	1		260.00	USD	
HR 070	08.12.1997	12.12.1997	Michael Maier	Exec.directory - Germany	1		126.94	USD	
HR 010	14.12.1998	18.12.1998	Hannelore Eisner	Accounts Payable (D)	1		126.94	USD	
HR 010	14.12.1998	18.12.1998	Hannelore Eisner	Accounts Payable (D)	1		126.94	USD	
First Aid	03.01.2001	09.04.2001	Marita Kleinert	SB register department	1				
First Aid	01.07.2001	07.10.2001	2 N.N.	Personnel Training (D)	2				Supervisor rejects booking request
First Aid	01.07.2001	07.10.2001	Dieter Berger	Becker Berlin DE-Berlin	1		62.07	USD	

Figure 15.12 List of Cancellations per Business Event

15.2 Business Events

The reports for business events provide key information about business events to support administrators in various tasks, for example, reserving resources for an event or event date.

15.2.1 Business Event Demand

The Business Event Demand report shows the number of required and planned business event dates for each business event type. You can run the report for a planning year or for individual quarters of a planning year. You can determine the demand for the business event dates to be planned by event language and event location separately. The list that is output (see Figure 15.13) contains information about the business event type, location, and language, as well as the existing demand and the demand already covered.

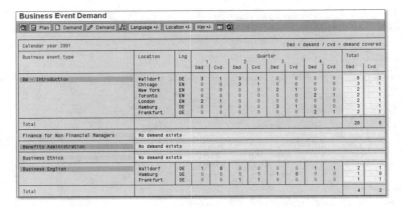

Figure 15.13 Business Event Demand List

[+]

If event dates are scheduled in a quarter, but no demand exists, these dates are not output.

Additional functions on the list screen

You can also execute the following functions from the list screen:

▶ Display existing event dates for the event types

▶ Plan event dates

▶ Create demands or change existing demands

▶ Split the display by event languages

▶ Split the display by event locations

▶ Navigate to the display of the list in the ALV Grid

15.2.2 Business Event Information

The Business Event Information report provides extensive detailed information about business event dates, including the location, instructor, room, telephone number of the room, course owner, places available, and duration. An example is provided in Figure 15.14. In addition to providing a quick overview of all relevant event information, this report can also be used to help you determine, for example, which events still need to be firmly booked or followed up or which events are currently locked.

You can use the following selection options to determine the event dates to be displayed:

▶ Only firmly booked/Only planned

▶ No historical record/Only hist. record

▶ Not canceled/Only canceled

▶ Not locked/Only locked

▶ Only available/Only reserved

▶ Only internal/Only external

▶ Not followed up/Only followed up

Business Event name	Start date	End date	L	Name Business Event Location	Building	Room	Telephone no.	≈ No. places	≈ Essential	≈ Normal	≈ Waitlist	≈ Days	≈ Hours	Name Instructor
First Aid	01.01.2001	02.01.2001	EN	Training Center Los Angeles				8	0	0	0	2	15.00	
Crane Operation	02.01.2001	02.01.2001	DE	Training Center Walldorf				10	0	0	0	1	8.00	Manfred Effenberg
Electrical Maintenance	02.01.2001	02.01.2001	EN	Training Center Philadelphia				18	0	0	0	1	8.00	Achmed Scholl
Selling Training	02.01.2001	03.01.2001	EN	Training Center Philadelphia				15	0	0	0	2	15.00	Dr. Herbert Brauns
Communication Course	02.01.2001	03.01.2001	EN	Training Center Philadelphia				15	0	0	0	2	15.00	Michaela Sauer
Company Orientation Program	02.01.2001	02.01.2001	EN	Chicago Training Center				30	0	0	0	1	2.00	
Management Techniques	02.01.2001	03.01.2001	EN	Training Center Philadelphia				15	0	0	0	2	15.00	Heike Fröhlich
Management Techniques	02.01.2001	03.01.2001	DE	Training Center Walldorf				20	0	0	0	2	15.00	Martin Beck
Safety Training	02.01.2001	23.01.2001	DE	Training Center Walldorf				8	0	12	0	4	16.00	Klaus Meyer
Business Philosophy	02.01.2001	02.01.2001	DE	Training Center Walldorf				10	0	0	0	1	3.00	Karin Anselm
Text processing with MSWord	03.01.2001	04.01.2001	DE	Training Center Walldorf				12	0	0	0	2	15.00	Anja Müller
First Aid	03.01.2001	09.04.2001	DE					20	0	0	0	8	32.00	Klaus Meyer
Management Techniques	03.01.2001	04.01.2001	DE	Training Center Walldorf				10	0	0	0	2	15.00	Hans Dampf
General French	03.01.2001	20.02.2001	DE	Training Center Walldorf				10	0	0	0	20	152.00	Martina Boffelli
Customer needs detect and wake	03.01.2001	05.01.2001	DE					10	0	0	0	3	18.00	
Introduction to Meetings	03.01.2001	03.01.2001	DE	Training Center Walldorf				18	0	0	0	1	3.00	Karin Anselm
Press Control	03.01.2001	03.01.2001	DE	Training Center Walldorf				20	0	0	0	1	8.00	Manfred Effenberg
H2S Alive	04.01.2001	04.01.2001	EN	Alberta Training Centre				9	0	0	0	1	8.00	
Coaching Workshop	04.01.2001	05.01.2001	EN	Training Center Los Angeles				5	0	0	0	2	15.00	Heather George

Figure 15.14 Business Event Information List

15.2.3 Business Event Dates

Attendee list

The Business Event Dates report shows the business event dates for the selected date types. You can navigate directly from the list screen to the attendee list of a selected business event by pressing the **Attendee** button in the toolbar.

> Events that have been canceled, locked, followed up, or historically recorded are not shown in this report.

[+]

The list output (see Figure 15.15) includes, for example, information about the event type name, the number of event dates, the event dates, and the event location.

Business Event Dates

Selection period: 01.01.1900 - 31.12.9999
Language   English

Business event type	Start date	End date	Location	L	Business event	± No.
General English	04.01.1999	08.01.1999	Philadelphia	EN	Gen. English	1
General English	22.02.1999	26.02.1999	Philadelphia	EN	Gen. English	1
General English	05.04.1999	09.04.1999	Philadelphia	EN	Gen. English	1
General English	17.05.1999	21.05.1999	Philadelphia	EN	Gen. English	1
General English	05.07.1999	09.07.1999	Philadelphia	EN	Gen. English	1
General English	16.08.1999	20.08.1999	Philadelphia	EN	Gen. English	1
General English	04.10.1999	08.10.1999	Philadelphia	EN	Gen. English	1
General English	29.11.1999	03.12.1999	Philadelphia	EN	Gen. English	1
General English	13.04.2005	31.05.2005	Chicago	EN	Gen. English	1
General English	06.06.2005	24.07.2005	Atlanta	EN	General Engl	1
						± 10

Figure 15.15 Business Event Dates List

15.2.4 Resources Not Yet Assigned per Business Event

You use the Resources Not Yet Assigned per Business Event report to generate a list of resource types that are still required for each event, in other words, resource types for which no resources have been assigned.

The list screen (see Figure 15.16) of the report shows, for example, the event name, the name of the required resource type, the reservation period of the resource type, and the number of the reservations and their times.

Resources Not Yet Assigned per Business Event

Selection Period 01.01.1999 - 31.12.2003

Business event	Resource type	Start date	End date	Start Time	End time	± No. hours
Adv.Electron	Instructor	10.01.2000	10.01.2000	10:00:00	17:00:00	7.00
Adv.Electron	Instructor	11.01.2000	11.01.2000	09:00:00	17:00:00	8.00
BW Intro	Instructors	06.01.2003	06.01.2003	10:00:00	17:00:00	7.00
BW Intro	Instructors	07.01.2003	09.01.2003	09:00:00	17:00:00	24.00
BW Intro	Room/rooms	07.01.2003	09.01.2003	09:00:00	17:00:00	24.00
BW Intro	Room/rooms	10.01.2003	10.01.2003	09:00:00	12:00:00	3.00
BW Intro	Instructors	24.02.2003	24.02.2003	10:00:00	17:00:00	7.00
BW Intro	Instructors	25.02.2003	26.02.2003	09:00:00	17:00:00	16.00
BW Intro	Instructors	14.04.2003	14.04.2003	10:00:00	17:00:00	7.00
BW Intro	Instructors	15.04.2003	16.04.2003	09:00:00	17:00:00	16.00
BW Intro	Instructors	02.06.2003	02.06.2003	10:00:00	17:00:00	7.00
BW Intro	Instructors	03.06.2003	04.06.2003	09:00:00	17:00:00	16.00
BW Intro	Room/rooms	23.07.2003	23.07.2003	09:00:00	17:00:00	8.00
BW Intro	Room/rooms	27.10.2003	27.10.2003	10:00:00	17:00:00	7.00
BW Intro	Room/rooms	28.10.2003	29.10.2003	09:00:00	17:00:00	16.00
BW Intro	Room/rooms	17.12.2003	17.12.2003	09:00:00	17:00:00	8.00
BW_Intro	Room/rooms	17.02.2003	17.02.2003	10:00:00	17:00:00	7.00
Bus Ethics	Room/rooms	02.01.2003	02.01.2003	09:00:00	17:00:00	8.00
Bus Ethics	Room/rooms	02.04.2003	02.04.2003	09:00:00	17:00:00	8.00

Figure 15.16 Resources Not Yet Assigned per Business Event List

15.3   Resources

The reports for resources in Training and Event Management provide support for administrators, for example, by providing information about the resources not yet assigned for each resource type. They also provide graphical information about resource assignments.

15.3.1   Resource Equipment

The Resource Equipment report shows the resources with which another resource is equipped, for example, a projector screen in a training room. It lists the objects of type R (equipment, such as a projector screen) that are assigned to objects of type G (resources, such as a training room).

Figure 15.17 shows an extract from a resource equipment list. It shows, for example, the resource, the equipment, the quantity of equipment, and the equipment period.

Resource	Equipment	Start date	End date	⹂ Number
Training room Johannesburg - Toronto	Terminals	01.01.1994	31.12.9999	12
Training room Sydney - Berlin	Terminals	01.01.1994	31.12.9999	12
Training room Singapore - Hamburg	Terminals	01.01.1994	31.12.9999	12
Training room Tokyo - Dresden	Terminals	01.01.1994	31.12.9999	12
Training room Moscow - London	Terminals	01.01.1994	31.12.9999	12
Training room Toronto - Frankfurt	Terminals	01.01.1994	31.12.9999	12
Training room Madrid - Montreal	Terminals	01.01.1994	31.12.9999	14
Training room Milan - New York	Terminals	01.01.1994	31.12.9999	14
Training room Freiburg - Walldorf	Terminals	01.01.1994	31.12.9999	8
Atlanta Room 2	Terminals	01.01.1994	31.12.9999	14
Training room Copenhagen - Chicago	Terminals	01.01.1994	31.12.9999	8
Training room Duesseldorf - Los Angeles	Terminals	01.01.1994	31.12.9999	6
Training room México - Mexico	Terminals	01.01.1994	31.12.9999	14
Training room 1 - Philadelphia	Terminals	01.01.1999	31.12.9999	12
Training room 2 - Philadelphia	Terminals	01.01.1999	31.12.9999	12
Training room 3 - Philadelphia	Terminals	01.01.1999	31.12.9999	12
Training room 4 - Walldorf	Terminals	01.01.2001	31.12.9999	8

Figure 15.17 Resource Equipment List

15.3.2   Instructor Information

The Instructor Information report provides information about the instructor activities of individual persons in Training and Event Management. The list generated (see Figure 15.18) shows, for example, the instructor name, the business event ID, the date of the first and last day of the event, the number of event days, the event duration per day in hours, and the overall event duration in hours.

Res.type	Resource	Name	Start date	End date	Start Time	End time	Days	No. hours
Instructor	Karin Anselm	Introduction to Meetings	04.01.2001	04.01.2001	09:00:00	12:00:00	1	3.00
Instructor	Karin Anselm	Business Philosophy	31.01.2001	31.01.2001	09:00:00	12:00:00	1	3.00
Instructor	Karin Anselm	Introduction to Meetings	15.02.2001	15.02.2001	09:00:00	12:00:00	1	3.00
Instructor	Karin Anselm	Introduction to Meetings	19.02.2001	19.02.2001	09:00:00	12:00:00	1	3.00
Instructor	Karin Anselm	Business Philosophy	02.03.2001	02.03.2001	09:00:00	12:00:00	1	3.00
Instructor	Karin Anselm	Introduction to Meetings	03.04.2001	03.04.2001	09:00:00	12:00:00	1	3.00
Instructor	Karin Anselm	Introduction to Meetings	04.04.2001	04.04.2001	09:00:00	12:00:00	1	3.00
Instructor	Karin Anselm	Business Philosophy	06.04.2001	06.04.2001	09:00:00	12:00:00	1	3.00
Instructor	Karin Anselm	Introduction to Meetings	16.05.2001	16.05.2001	09:00:00	12:00:00	1	3.00
Instructor	Karin Anselm	Introduction to Meetings	17.05.2001	17.05.2001	09:00:00	12:00:00	1	3.00
Instructor	Karin Anselm	Introduction to Meetings	02.07.2001	02.07.2001	09:00:00	12:00:00	1	3.00
Instructor	Karin Anselm	Business Philosophy	04.07.2001	04.07.2001	09:00:00	12:00:00	1	3.00
Instructor	Karin Anselm	Introduction to Meetings	05.07.2001	05.07.2001	09:00:00	12:00:00	1	3.00
Instructor	Karin Anselm	Business Philosophy	31.07.2001	31.07.2001	09:00:00	12:00:00	1	3.00
Instructor	Karin Anselm	Introduction to Meetings	16.08.2001	16.08.2001	09:00:00	12:00:00	1	3.00

Figure 15.18 List of Instructor Information

15.3.3 Resource Reservation

The Resource reservation report shows the reservation of resources belonging to a selected resource type within a specified period. Based on the period split selected, the table generated is displayed as an hourly, daily, or weekly period split. Figure 15.19 shows the resource reservation of an employee in a weekly period split.

Including or exluding business events

As well as selecting the period split, you can also include or exclude firmly booked and/or planned business events. In addition, you can restrict the data selection by business event type, event location, and the minimum reservation per resource. Finally, if you select **Day** as the period split, you can also choose to show days off in the list.

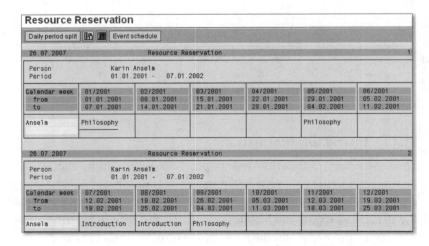

Figure 15.19 Resource Reservation of an Employee in a Weekly Period Split

The table generated by the report contains information such as the resource type name, the weekday/date/time (depending on the period split selected), the resource name, and the short name of the business event.

You can also change the period split selected in the list itself. If you choose **Edit** in the menu bar, you can switch between the display of single and multiple reservations for a resource. In addition, you can choose **Graphic** to switch to a graphical view of the resource reservation.

If you place the cursor on an event in the basic list and choose **Attendee List**, the attendee list for this event is displayed in a dialog box. If you choose **Schedule**, the time schedule of the event is shown.

15.4   SAP NetWeaver Standard BI Content

The standard BI Content for Training and Event Management contains the three InfoCubes Training and Event Management, Professional Training Provider, and Resource Reservation (see Figure 15.20).

Figure 15.20 Standard BI Content for Training and Event Management

15.4.1   The Training and Event Management InfoCube

The Training and Event Management InfoCube contains the transaction data for bookings and cancellations. The Attendance and Cancellation InfoSources supply this InfoCube with data.

The InfoCube contains the following general key figures:

▶ Number of cancellations

▶ Number of attendances

▶ Cancellation fee

▶ Attendance fee

▶ Business event duration in hours

▶ Business event duration in days

▶ Business event costs

In addition, calculated key figures (for example, Average Cancellation Fee, Total Bookings) and restricted key figures are provided, that is, key figures that depend on certain characteristics (for example, Billed Attendance Fees, Number of Internal Attendees).

You can use calendar day, calendar year, calendar year/quarter, and calendar year/month as time dimensions for the evaluations.

The Training and Event Management InfoCube contains characteristics from the employee master data (for example, name, personnel area, organizational unit, and master cost center), as well as the following data from Training and Event Management:

▶ Attendee

▶ Attendee type

▶ Attendance fee

▶ Cancellation fee

▶ Canellation date

▶ Reason for attendance cancellation

▶ Fee indicator

▶ Document status

▶ Business event

▶ Business event costs

▶ Business event group

▶ Business event type

▶ Company

▶ External person

The Attendee Type characteristic, for example, allows you to distinguish between internal and external attendees and to obtain information about each. This hinges on which attendee types you have defined as internal or external.

A person can be defined as an employee more than once. To allow you to distinguish between the employment relationship (Employee characteristic) and real persons (Person characteristic), the person is defined as an attribute of the employee.

[+]

This InfoCube contains hierarchies for the Business Event Group, Business Event Type, Business Event, Organizational Unit, and Master Cost Center InfoObjects. In Training and Event Management, the hierarchical display only shows business event groups for which event dates with bookings exist.

15.4.2 The Professional Training Provider InfoCube

The Professional Training Provider InfoCube contains the transaction data for bookings and cancellations, without the employee master data. It also contains characteristics and general key figures for business events, which are also found in the Training and Event Management InfoCube.

15.4.3 The Resource Reservation InfoCube

The Resource Reservation InfoCube contains the transaction data for resources (see Figure 15.21). The Resource Reservation InfoSource supplies this InfoCube with data. This InfoCube provides general key figures for the reservation duration in days and hours and for the resource costs. In addition to the data relating to events in the Business event characteristic, it also contains the following objects for resources:

▶ Resource

▶ Object type of resource

▶ Resource type

▶ Availability indicator resource type

▶ Resource costs

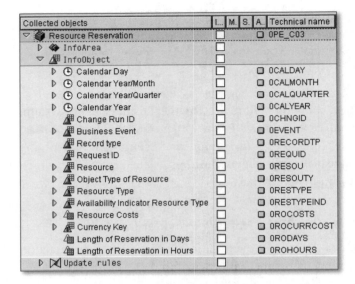

Collected objects	I...	M.	S.	A.	Technical name
▽ 🌐 Resource Reservation	☐			☐	0PE_C03
▷ ◈ InfoArea	☐				
▽ 📋 InfoObject	☐				
▷ 🕐 Calendar Day	☐			☐	0CALDAY
▷ 🕐 Calendar Year/Month	☐			☐	0CALMONTH
▷ 🕐 Calendar Year/Quarter	☐			☐	0CALQUARTER
▷ 🕐 Calendar Year	☐			☐	0CALYEAR
📋 Change Run ID	☐			☐	0CHNGID
▷ 📋 Business Event	☐			☐	0EVENT
📋 Record type	☐			☐	0RECORDTP
📋 Request ID	☐			☐	0REQUID
▷ 📋 Resource	☐			☐	0RESOU
▷ 📋 Object Type of Resource	☐			☐	0RESOUTY
▷ 📋 Resource Type	☐			☐	0RESTYPE
▷ 📋 Availability Indicator Resource Type	☐			☐	0RESTYPEIND
▷ 📦 Resource Costs	☐			☐	0ROCOSTS
▷ 📋 Currency Key	☐			☐	0ROCURRCOST
📦 Length of Reservation in Days	☐			☐	0RODAYS
📦 Length of Reservation in Hours	☐			☐	0ROHOURS
▷ ⊠ Update rules	☐				

Figure 15.21 Content of the Resource Reservation InfoCube

You can use calendar day, calendar year, calendar year/quarter, and calendar year/month as time dimensions for the evaluations.

There is only one query for resource reservation in the standard system. The Annual Comparison of Resource Costs query shows the resource costs in the current year compared with those from the previous year. The differences are shown as both absolute and percentage values. The Availability Indicator characteristic shows the resources divided into various categories, namely instructor, room, material, and other resources.

15.4.4 Queries for the Training and Event Management InfoCube

The standard system contains the following queries for Training and Event Management:

▸ The Number of Attendances and Cancellations query shows the number of attendances and cancellations for each business event group, as well as the sum total of both, in other words, the total number of bookings, for the current calendar year.

▸ The Training Duration query shows the duration of business events in days and hours for the current year at the level of business event group. In addition, the business event duration in days and hours is shown as a percentage of the overall duration of all business events.

▶ The Annual Comparison of Bookings query shows the number of bookings. It is composed of the sum total of all attendances and cancellations in the current year compared with the previous year. The differences are also shown as both absolute and percentage values.

▶ The Annual Comparison of Revenues query provides an overview of the revenue (i.e., event fees minus event costs) earned by a business event organizer for the events in an event group in the current year compared with the previous year. The total fees can be regarded as event turnover in this case.

▶ The Fees for Attendances and Cancellations query shows the fees for attendances and cancellations for each business event group compared with the previous year. The changes are shown as both absolute and percentage values.

▶ The Fee Rate query lists the average event fees in the current year compared with the previous year. It evaluates the average cost of the training activities in each business event group.

▶ The Fee Distribution by Internal and External Bookings query shows the distribution of fees, broken down by settlement type. It indicates which attendance and cancellation fees were billed externally and which were billed internally in the current year.

▶ The Attendance and Cancellation Rate query compares the values of the current year with those from the previous year. The Attendance per Cancellation key figure indicates the number of attendances included in a cancellation and thus gives the ratio of attendances to cancellations. The cancellation rate shows the cancellations as a percentage of the total number of bookings.

▶ The Annual Comparison of Business Event Costs query compares the business event costs incurred in the current year with those from the previous year. The differences are shown as both percentage and absolute values.

▶ The Training and Education Based on Organizational Assignment query shows the number of bookings for each organizational unit. The sum total of all attendances and cancellations in the current year is compared with the previous year. The differences are shown as both absolute and percentage values.

▶ The Training and Education Based on Target Group query indicates which bookings were made for each position in the current year compared with the previous year. The data are broken down by occupational group.

▶ The Training and Education Fees Based on Organizational Assignment" query compares the training and education fees incurred by each organizational unit in the current year with those incurred in the previous year.

▶ Finally, the Training and Education Fees Based on Target Group query compares the training and education fees incurred in the current year by various occupational groups for each position with those incurred in the previous year.

15.5   Conclusion

Very extensive standard reporting options are available for Training and Event Management with the reports for attendances, resources, and business events. However, the standard BI Content is also a very useful tool, in particular, for providing a detailed overview of the costs of business events or training activities.

The reports available for personnel cost planning and simulation are used to support both strategic personnel management and the overall strategy of an enterprise.

16   Personnel Cost Planning

Personnel Cost Planning enables you to plan the development of employees' salaries and wages as well as ancillary payroll costs over time. The option to simulate different planning scenarios allows you to analyze possible effects for the enterprise. You can use Personnel Cost Planning and Simulation only if you also use Organizational Management.

You can access Personnel Cost Planning reporting in the SAP Easy Access menu by selecting the path **Human Resources • Personnel Management • Personnel Cost Planning • Information System • Reports**.

SAP Easy Access path

16.1   Data Basis

Among the reports are four SAP queries under Data Collection, which show the cost items for each **employee**, **position**, **job**, and **organizational** unit that was generated during the data collection process. These SAP queries utilize the logical database PCH and hence the structure of the Organizational Management module for selection purposes. In addition, the Program Selections provide the following options for further limiting the list output:

Logical database PCH

► Data basis (subtype)

► Data collection method

► Cost item

► Vacancy identifier (for positions only)

► Vacancy status (for positions only)

▶ Pay scale type, pay grade type, and pay grade region (for organizational unit only)

▶ Full-time equivalents (FTEs) (for organizational units only)

16.2 Cost Plans

The following reports are available in the *Cost plans* area:

▶ The Plan Data report shows the result of a cost planning run.

▶ The Planned Cost Comparison report enables you to compare two personnel cost plans with each other and to specifically identify the deviations that exceed the default percentage specified in the selection screen. The values shown in Figure 16.1 are based on a maximum deviation of 10%.

▶ The "Task List Changes" report displays the changes made by the line managers or the personnel cost planner during detailed planning.

▶ The Original Documents report allows you to view the original documents generated by the SAP system during the release of cost plans. As a prerequisite, you must first release the personnel cost plans for which you want to view original documents.

Cost Object	Crcy	∑	Amount Plan	∑	Amount Ref	Percentage	∑	Difference	Tolerance
World Class Enterprises	USD		209,222.04		201,821.99	3.67		7.400.05	○○○
Human Resources	USD		793,519.82		547,688.50	44.89		245,831.32	◉○○
Finance	USD		478,198.03		286,497.70	66.91		191,700.33	◉○○
Production	USD		17.158,153.05		16,575,724.60	3.51		582,428.45	○○○
Production Unit 1	USD		397,240.34		383,626.47	3.55		13,613.87	○○○
Production Unit 2	USD		403,147.20		389,279.69	3.56		13,867.51	○○○
Services	USD		2,253,152.28		1,677,520.93	34.31		575,631.35	◉○○
	USD	▪	**21,692,632.76**	▪	**20,062,159.88**			▪ **1,630,472.88**	

Figure 16.1 Planning Data Comparison Output

The list output allows you to switch between the views for statistical key figures and primary cost documents. In addition, you can replace incorrect account assignments for nonposted document line items. To do that, select **Edit • Change Account Assignment** from the output menu.

16.3   SAP NetWeaver BI Standard Content

The reporting and analysis process for Personnel Cost Planning and Simulation is carried out in the SAP NetWeaver BI Standard Content. Therefore, it is an essential requirement to implement SAP NetWeaver BI when implementing Personnel Cost Planning if you haven't done so yet. The only alternative would involve complex programming work in the HCM system.

The Personnel Cost Planning and Simulation section contains the following InfoCubes (see Figure 16.2):

▶ Personnel Cost Plans

▶ Planned Personnel Costs per Cost Object

▶ Plan/Actual Comparison of Personnel Costs

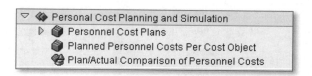

Figure 16.2 BI Standard Content for Personnel Cost Planning

16.3.1   The Personnel Cost Plans InfoCube

The Personnel Cost Plans InfoCube contains completed planning runs of Personnel Cost Planning (see Figure 16.3). The way in which the data are analyzed depend on the selected view (**Account Assignment Object/Organizational Unit**) in Personnel Cost Planning while the InfoCube retrieves the data from the cost plan.

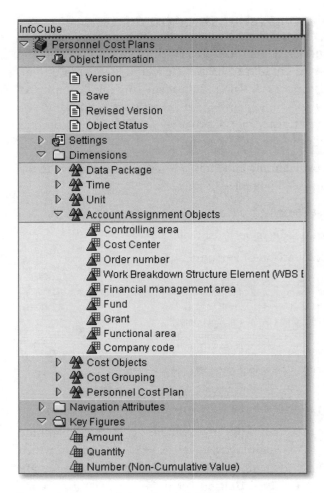

Figure 16.3 Personnel Cost Plans InfoCube

16.3.2 The Planned Personnel Costs per Cost Object InfoCube

The Planned Personnel Costs per Cost Object InfoCube carries out a planning simulation (see Figure 16.4). In doing so, it extracts the data basis of the cost objects and derives cost items. For this reason it is mandatory to define a planning context and scenario for the extraction process.

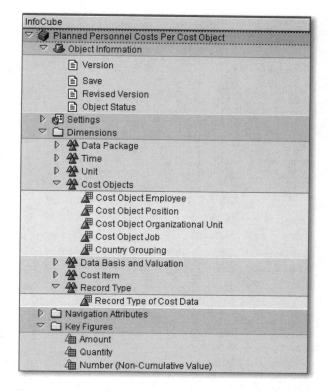

Figure 16.4 Planned Personnel Costs per Cost Object InfoCube

16.3.3 The Plan/Actual Comparison of Personnel Costs MultiCube

This plan/actual comparison is one of the most frequently used analysis tools of SAP NetWeaver BI in the HR environment. The Multi-Cube links data from the Personnel Cost Plans and Planned Personnel Costs per Cost Object InfoCubes with the auditing information about postings relevant to cost accounting, that is, the CO-relevant part of the posting document from Payroll (see Figure 16.5).

What's missing here is the possibility to carry out comparisons at the G/L account level. To be able to do that, you need to add a customer-specific extension and the account. The symbolic account provided can often not be used as a comparison object. Planning frequently requires details that aren't needed for posting the payroll data, which is why separate symbolic accounts are created during the planning process.

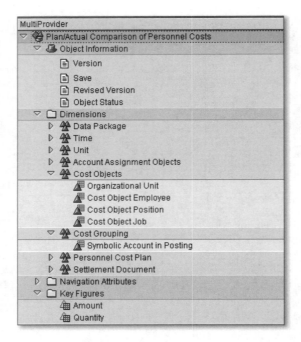

Figure 16.5 Plan/Actual Comparison of Personnel Costs MultiCube

16.3.4 Queries for the Personnel Cost Planning InfoCubes

Queries for the Personnel Cost Plans InfoCube

The Personnel Cost Plans InfoCube contains the following queries:

▶ The query Personnel Cost Plans Comparison (organizational view) enables you to compare two selectable cost plans and to view the difference and percentage of deviation in the organizational view.

▶ The query Personnel Cost Plans Comparison (account assignment view) compares the plans in the account assignment view.

▶ The query Personnel Cost Plan Analysis (organizational view) allows you to analyze the cost plan based on organizational unit criteria by quarters.

▶ The query Personnel Cost Plan Analysis (account assignment view) (see Figure 16.6) differs from the aforementioned query in that it uses the cost centers as navigation criteria.

Which query you can use depends on the view you select in Personnel Cost Planning.

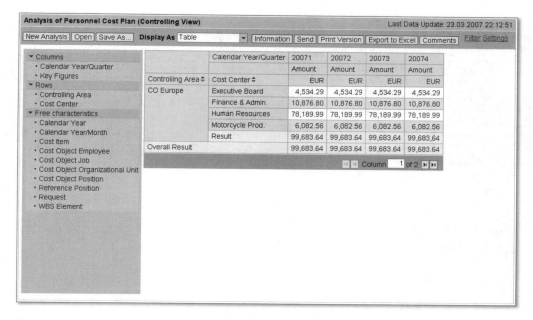

Figure 16.6 Personnel Cost Plan (Account Assignment View)

Queries for the Planned Personnel Costs per Cost Object InfoCube

The Planned Personnel Costs per Cost Object InfoCube contains the following queries:

▶ Planned Costs per Position

▶ Planned Costs per Job

▶ Planned Costs per Organizational Unit

▶ Planned Costs/Quantities per Employee

▶ Planned Costs per Employee

Queries for the Plan/Actual Comparison of Personnel Costs MultiCube

The Plan/Actual Comparison of Personnel Costs MultiCube contains the following queries:

▶ Plan/Actual Comparison (organizational view)

▶ Plan/Actual Comparison (account assignment view) (see Figure 16.7)

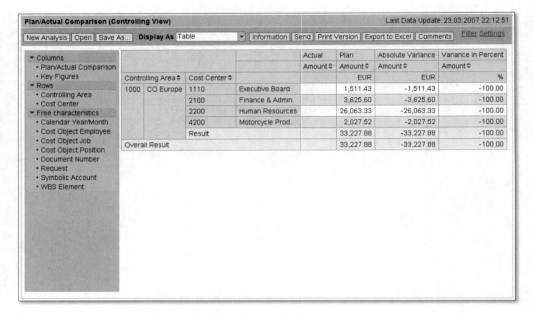

Figure 16.7 Plan/Actual Comparison

16.4 Conclusion

The analyses for Personnel Cost Planning are predominantly carried out in SAP NetWeaver BI Standard Content since the majority of reports provided in the HCM system date back to the time before the Personnel Cost Planning module was comprehensively revised for Release 4.7 Enterprise. For this reason, these reports are not useful to perform comprehensive reporting tasks in Personnel Cost Planning. If you haven't implemented an SAP NetWeaver BI system for Personnel Cost Planning yet, you must do so to avoid complex programming work in the HCM system.

PART IV
Retrieving Reports

The fourth and last part of this book provides an overview of the tools that enable you to make reports and analyses from the SAP ERP-HCM system and from SAP NetWeaver BI available to users. These tools include the report tree, the Human Resource Information System (HIS), the Manager's Desktop, and the SAP Net-Weaver Portal including the Manager Self-Service (MSS).

The area menu enables you to create your own folder structure for reports and to make this folder structure available to users as part of their user menus. The area menu thus replaces the report tree.

17 Area Menu

Prior to SAP ERP Release 4.6A you could only integrate transactions in area menus. Now you can also include reports in area menus, which was previously only possible in report trees.

The area menu allows you to structure all customer reports, standard reports, and queries you use in a separate menu tree (see Figure 17.1). This menu tree may consist of different submenus (for each user group, for example).

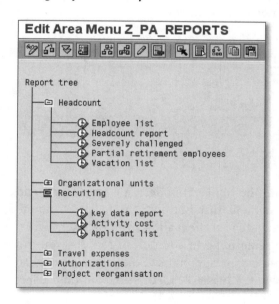

Edit Area Menu Z_PA_REPORTS

Report tree
- Headcount
  - Employee list
  - Headcount report
  - Severely challenged
  - Partial retirement employees
  - Vacation list
- Organizational units
- Recruiting
  - key data report
  - Activity cost
  - Applicant list
- Travel expenses
- Authorizations
- Project reorganisation

Figure 17.1 Area Menu for Reporting

The area menu or submenu is assigned to a user by means of a role, which has the following advantages: Users have structured access to the reports they need and can execute them directly from within the user menu by double-clicking on them. In addition, employees in Personnel Controlling who usually have no access to role maintenance are enabled to maintain parts of the user menu. The area menu thus represents a clear and easy-to-use maintenance interface for these employees, which allows them not only to define their own folder structure, but also to maintain the texts of transactions by themselves. To integrate an area menu in a role, all the authorization administrator needs is the name of the area menu.

Creating an area
menu

First you must create a new area menu:

1. Select the following path from the SAP Easy Access menu: **Tools** • **ABAP Workbench** • **Development** • **Other Tools** • **Area Menus** (or select Transaction SE43).

2. Enter a new name for the area menu (starting with Y or Z) in the input field and click on the **Create** button.

3. In the next screen, enter a description for the area menu (representing the top-level node) and confirm this by clicking Enter (see Figure 17.2).

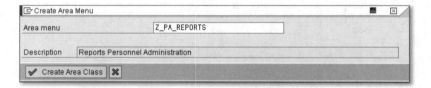

Figure 17.2 Creating an Area Menu

4. Position the mouse on the top-level node of the area menu and select **Add Entry as Subnode** (fifth button from the left) from the toolbar. The screen that displays next allows you to enter several menu options at the same time. In addition to reports, you can insert transactions, folders, or references to other area menus. To insert a report, click on the **Insert Report** button and then select the relevant report type (see Figure 17.3).

If no transaction code is available yet for the report or query, the system will generate it. By clicking on the **Display other options** button you can also define your own transaction code and description.

To add new folders to the area menu, you should specify a text without a transaction code. This type of entry is automatically interpreted
as a folder. You can also insert multiple references to other area
menus in an area menu and thus create a menu that consists of several submenus. To do that, check the **Reference to a menu** checkbox
in the **Add New Entries** dialog and enter an area menu name under
Transaction code · menu.

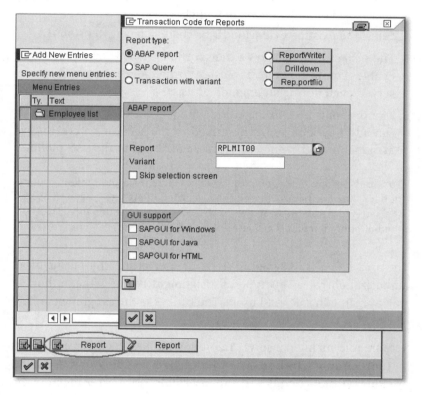

Figure 17.3 Integrating a Report in the New Area Menu

Another option to extend the area menu or to create is to integrate
other menus, such as a role menu. To do that, go to **Edit · Import ·
Other Menu**.

You can change, reassign, or delete the entries at any time at a later
stage. If you want to do that, select the relevant menu entry and click
on the respective button in the toolbar. You can also apply this action
to multiple menu entries by using the **Select** button.

Once you have saved the menu, you should carry out a check to make sure no endless loops exist. To do that, click on the **Check menus for endless structures** button.

Extending the SAP menu

You can also edit areas in the SAP menu.

1. In the area menu maintenance section (Transaction SE43), call a standard area menu via the input help and select **Change**.

2. Select **Extend** in the dialog that opens.

3. Select the existing extension ID or create a new extension ID.

4. The system then displays a transport dialog. This transport dialog enables you to generate a transport order; all changes will be preserved even during an upgrade process.

5. The system is now in the editing mode for area menus. Here you can add new entries, as described in the section on creating an area menu. You cannot delete any entries from the SAP menu.

[+] To avoid performance problems, you should activate the buffering function for the area menu. Click on the **Area Menu Settings** button to check the settings in the initial screen of the area menu maintenance. Usually, the buffering function is activated automatically for new menus.

User assignment

The area menu is assigned to users or user groups by means of an authorization role. This type of assignment requires the authorization to maintain roles and users. You can make the assignment as follows:

1. Start role maintenance via the following SAP Easy Access menu: **Tools • Administration • User Maintenance • Role Administration • Roles** (Transaction PFCG) and insert the desired area menu in the **Menu** tab via the **from Area Menu** button (see Figure 17.4).

2. Maintain the authorization data in the **Authorizations** tab and generate the profile.

3. You can assign the role to a user group or individual users (**User** tab).

In addition, you can store an area menu as the start menu in the user master record of a user. You can access the user maintenance section via the following path in the SAP Easy Access menu: **Tools • Administration • User Maintenance • Users** (Transaction SU01). Go to the **Defaults** tab and enter the name of the area menu in the **Start menu**

field. The area menu you enter there will then be displayed instead
of the SAP menu.

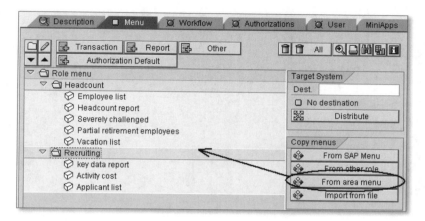

Figure 17.4 Copying the Area Menu into a Role

In summary, we can say that the area menu is used relatively rarely.
Usually the user menu is directly created and maintained with
reports and transactions in the authorization role. The task of creating the menu should not be regarded as a redundant step because the
area menu can be integrated into the role with a click of the mouse.
However, once you implement a change to the area menu, you must
not forget to adjust the role as well. Otherwise the changes will not
be made available to the user.

Perhaps you have identified other advantages of the area menu and use
this tool to a greater extent. As we would like to learn more about your
experiences, you should send us an email to the following address: kon-
takt@iprocon.de.

Your feedback

The Human Resources Information System (HIS) enables you to analyze personnel management data on the basis of hierarchical structures. Doing so does not require you to switch between the different modules. This chapter describes how you can quickly and easily run analyses using the HIS.

18 Human Resources Information System

The Human Resources Information System (HIS) provides a simplified access to reports for different submodules of the HR system. This avoids having to navigate through the SAP Easy Access menu to find a specific report.

To be able to use this tool, you must implement the Organizational Management module. The structures contained in Organizational Management must correspond to the business requirements of reporting, that is, a selected subtree should contain all objects that are supposed to be aggregated (see Section 2.5.1).

Organizational Management as the basis

18.1 Using the HIS

You can call the HIS via the SAP Easy Access menu path **Human Resources • Information Systems • Reporting Tools • HIS** or run Transaction PPIS.

SAP Easy Access path

In the initial screen (see Figure 18.1), you must select a view first. The standard SAP system contains the **Standard** view for reports on the Organizational Management structure as well as the **Training** view for reports on the business event catalog. The view you select defines which objects will be displayed in the structure graphic, and it determines which functions are available in the graphical display. Section 18.2 provides information about available Customizing options.

Once you have selected the view, the system provides several options in the **Graphical Display** area, which affect the objects made available in the structure graphic. For instance, in the example shown in the figures below, you can only select organizational units, organizational units with positions, organizational units with persons, or organizational units with positions and persons to be displayed in the structure graphic. This affects only the display in the structure graphic, but not the objects that are processed in the report.

[+] There are separate evaluation paths for the display and the object selection of the report.

Once you have selected a view and the objects it contains, you must select a root object to enable the graphical display. In addition, you can define the number of levels and the period you want to display.

You can define these parameters in the **Defaults** section for future calls of the HIS (see Figure 18.1).

Once you have started the HIS, the system displays a window that contains the structure graphic as well as a split window containing subcomponents including the associated reports (see Figure 18.2).

Press and hold the Shift key and select one or several objects that are supposed to be used for the report. Then select an area of application and double-click on a task function to start the report.

Usually, the report is started directly by means of a standard setting without the system displaying another selection screen, provided you have not disabled this function in Customizing.

You can customize the display in the structure graphic via the **Options** menu item.

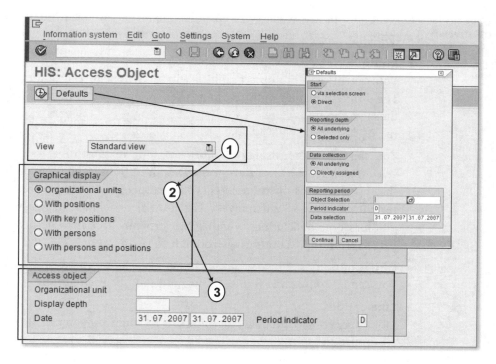

Figure 18.1 Initial Screen of the HIS

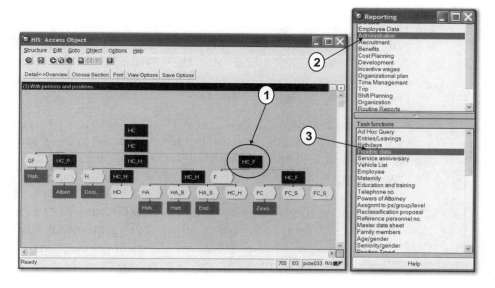

Figure 18.2 Starting Reports with the HIS

Several options are available to optimize the display in the structure graphic:

- **Multiple views**
  You can display multiple graphics windows next to each other. The different display options can be used independently in each of these windows.

- **View options**
  You can select the display of short and long texts of objects by selecting either the **Overview** or the **Details** option. Depending on the type or status of the objects, you can specify different colors for the objects to be displayed. The normal or feather structure graphics type determines whether the structure tree is to be displayed from top to bottom or from left to right.

- **Object options**
  You can customize the frame, filling, and font for each object.

- **Line options**
  Lines may contain arrowheads and text. In addition, you can also customize the font.

18.2 Customizing the HIS

You can access the Customizing section for the HIS via the following path from the IMG menu: **Personnel Management · Human Resource Information System · HIS**. The following items allow you to flexibly customize the structure graphic and the provided task functions:

- **Define data views**
  The data view defines the structures to be displayed in the graphics window. It defines the initial object, evaluation path, and the status vector that contains the list of available object statuses (e.g., planned or active). Moreover, you can create multiple variants of the graphical display. For example, the **Standard** data view provided by SAP for reports carried out via the Organizational Management module contains definitions of variants of the graphical display that include positions and persons. You can select these variants via checkboxes in the initial screen of the HIS.

The structures displayed in the HIS may originate from different areas of the SAP HCM system, such as Organizational Management or Training and Event Management. As it does not make sense to combine each report with each of the displayed structures, you should define the appropriate reporting subareas in Customizing.

[+]

▶ **Define Areas**
You can create groups of subareas. This can involve a separation by HR modules or the combination of subareas according to the requirements of a specific group of users.

▶ **Specify Data Retrieval**
The data retrieval process controls the import of the object set to be analyzed from the structure graphic. For example, all employees who have been assigned in Organizational Management can be included in a report even if the structure graphic displays merely the organizational structure and organizational units. The data retrieval settings are composed of selection report, the type of the start object, and two evaluation paths — one for direct child objects and the other for all lower-level objects.

▶ **Assign Users**
Users can be grouped into user groups that are provided with different task functions.

▶ **Define Task Functions**
A task function defines the call of an SAP or customer report. Here you can specify the report name and variant that is to be started upon the call. Furthermore, you can define the data retrieval for the objects to be analyzed.

Queries that are automatically generated as ABAP/4 programs can be integrated as well. You can retrieve the report name via **System • Status** in the selection screen.

[+]

18.3 Using the HIS in Practice

The HIS is intended for users who run strictly defined reports through varying sections in Organizational Management. These users may be managers who analyze different areas of their respon-

Target group

sibility or HR analysts who need to create reports for different areas of an enterprise.

The HIS is often neglected, partly because the SAP structure graphic has its limits since it does not provide any convincing and appealing display options despite the various configuration options it contains. Especially with regard to complex structures, you can easily lose your overview. Unfortunately, the printing options are not very good either.

In general, the attempt to simplify the reporting process and keep it as intuitive as possible is an approach that should be continued in the future. However, better technologies are available in the market that pursue this goal. The Manager's Desktop (MDT), which will be described in the following chapter provides a range of optimized options to achieve this purpose.

The Manager's Desktop (MDT) is specifically tailored to the needs of managers with personnel responsibility who need to have quick and easy access to relevant personnel information. This chapter describes how you can use the MDT to retrieve reports.

19 Manager's Desktop (MDT)

The Manager's Desktop (MDT) combines functions from several SAP ERP HCM components and from financial accounting. The tool was developed to provide management staff with an easy-to-use tool that supports them in handling administrative and strategic tasks. The MDT can be customized according to specific requirements. With regard to reporting, this means that reports, queries, and even SAP NetWeaver BI queries and workbooks can be provided in Excel format as well as on the Web.

Functions from various SAP ERP HCM components

To be able to use the MDT, you must implement the Organizational Management module from which the MDT retrieves the data of the employees who are assigned to the respective manager.

The following sections focus on the MDT functions in the area of HR reporting.

19.1 Functions of the MDT

The functions provided by the MDT may come from the areas shown in Figure 19.1:

▶ **Personal data**
Reports from the areas of Personnel Administration, Personnel Development, and Training and Event Management

▶ **Organization**
Reports from Organizational Management

▶ **Compensation Management**
Reports from the areas of Compensation Management and Personnel Cost Planning

▶ **Recruitment**
Reports on job advertisement campaigns and applicants

Figure 19.1 Initial Screen of the MDT

[+]   You can customize the MDT according to your own specific requirements. For instance, you can hide categories you do not need, rename categories, and add new ones. Furthermore, you can configure the functions within the individual categories (see Section 19.3). Thus, even though the MDT looks different, its basic functionality described in the following sections will remain the same.

19.2   Using the MDT

SAP Easy Access path   You can start the MDT from the SAP Easy Access Menu via the following path: **Personnel • Manager's Desktop**. Alternatively, you can call Transaction PPMDT. The initial screen (see Figure 19.1) can be deactivated for future use if you have not deactivated it previously in

Customizing. To start the MDT, you can click on one of the categories in the initial screen. The theme categories provided here can also be accessed via the buttons in the upper part of the screen (see Figure 19.2).

Figure 19.2 shows the two areas of the MDT: The available functions are displayed on the left, whereas the right-hand section displays the employees assigned to the manager in accordance with the structure defined in Organizational Management. Many of the functions represent different reports. If you drag-and-drop an object from the structure to a function, the system executes this function, that is, the report is executed for the area you selected. In this case, the system skips the selection screen and directly displays the list, as shown in the example in Figure 19.3. You can use the period set in the MDT for the report.

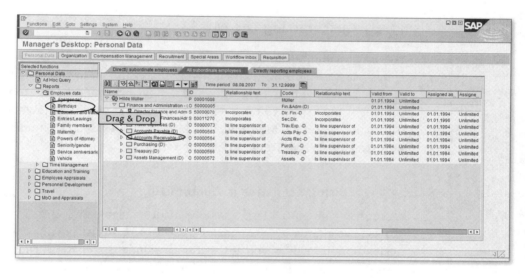

Figure 19.2 Starting a Report

Whereas the **Directly subordinate employees** tab displays only employees of a manager's own department, the **All subordinate employees** tab includes subordinate organizational units as well (see Figure 19.2).

Birthday list													
Personnel No.	Last name	First name	Entry	Leaving date	Date of Birth	Day	DoB	Year	Month	Gend.	Cost ctr	Org. Unit	Age of employee
00001007	Ulrich	Hanna	01.01.1994	31.12.9999	07.12.1955	07	0712	1955	12	2	2100	50000564	51
00001011	Förster	Claudia	01.01.1996	31.12.9999	01.01.1970	01	0101	1970	01	2	2100	50000564	37
00001014	Hintze	Gudrun	01.01.1995	31.12.9999	01.01.1960	01	0101	1960	01	2	2100	50000564	47
00900030	Tiemann	Christian	01.01.1994	30.12.1999	07.01.1957	07	0701	1957	01	1	2100	50000564	50
00900180	Knapp	Markus	01.06.1999	31.12.9999	20.09.1944	20	2009	1944	09	1	2100	50000564	62

Figure 19.3 Calling the Birthday List Report

When you start an Ad Hoc Query, the reporting set already contains the selected employees.

This function of the MDT enables you to use reports intuitively and to easily provide them to senior managers who do not use the SAP system on a regular basis.

19.3 Customizing the MDT

You can customize the MDT according to your individual requirements via Customizing. Particularly with regard to the functions made available, you have the option to remove existing ones and add your own functions. You can access Customizing via the following IMG path: **Personnel Management • Manager's Desktop • Customer Adjustment •** Define **Scenario-Specific Settings**.

19.3.1 Editing Scenarios in Customizing

A scenario contains all task functions made available to a user. You can use two alternative customizing options. The **Adjust existing scenarios** option enables you to customize standard scenarios. These customizations are even preserved during the installation of patches or upgrades. Alternatively, you can define your own scenarios. However, you should never change the standard scenarios. In any case, we recommend that you create a copy of the scenario you want to modify (see Figure 19.4) and then customize this copy according to your requirements, particularly if you plan to use the MDT extensively.

The evaluation path determines the identification of the root object. This is usually the chief position of the user who's logged in. The standard version considers the **directly subordinate** employees to be the ones that belong to a manager's own organizational unit, whereas the **all employees** option includes the employees of subordinate organizational units as well. The root object depends on the chief position of the current user.

Evaluation path

At this point (see Figure 19.4) you can skip the initial screen by activating the **Skip initial screen** option. In addition, you can display a virtual root so that the manager sees himself as the starting point of the structure, as shown in Figure 19.2. Furthermore, you can use the **Reorganization not permitted** setting to deactivate the execution of organizational changes via drag and drop, that is, if you check this option, the **Organization** theme category will be hidden.

Initial screen

If you maintain a **Referenced scenario**, the scenario will inherit all properties, that is, all settings, views, and views per category.

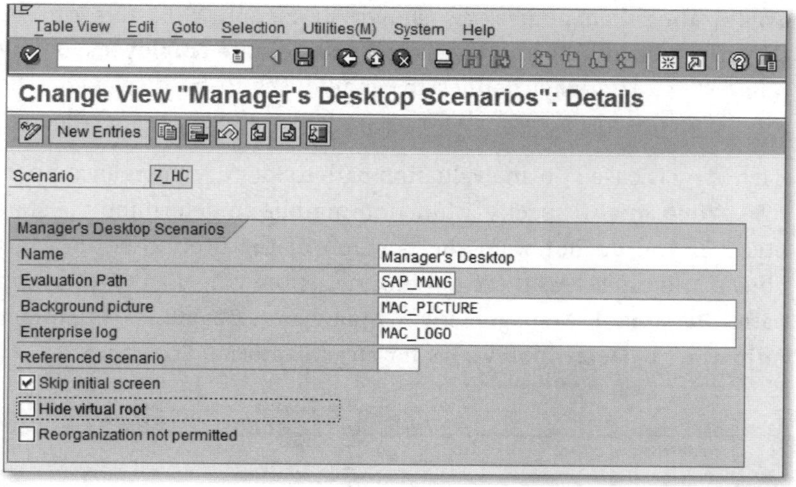

Figure 19.4 Defining an MDT Scenario

You can assign the scenario to a user via the user parameters. The MWB_SCEN parameter (see Figure 19.5) allows you to define which scenario you want to use after starting the MDT.

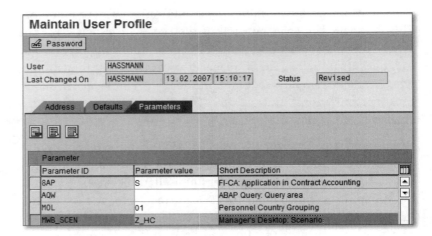

Figure 19.5 User Parameter MWB_SCEN

19.3.2 Views

Once you have created the scenario, you can define **Views of the organizational structure**. As shown in Figure 19.6, this can be **Directly subordinate employees**, **All subordinate employees**, or any other view. The view defines the employees to be displayed. The MDT contains a separate tab for each view in the order specified.

Each view is based on an evaluation path to identify the relevant persons. You can also specify a function module to determine the start object if you do not want the position of the user to be the start object. You can access these options in Customizing via the following path: **Personnel Management · Manager's Desktop · Customer Adjustment · Determine Views for Organizational Structure**.

Scenario	Eval.path	Numb	Evaluation path text	Sequence	Icon name	Column group
MWB1	B900	0	Directly reporting chiefs			ORGS
MWB1	MDTDIREC	0	Directly reporting employees	3	ICON_EMPLOYEE	MDT_ORGS
MWB1	MDTKOST	0	Cost centers	4	ICON_COST_CENTER	MDT_ORGS
MWB1	MDTREC	0	Applicants	5	ICON_EMPLOYEE	MDT_RECRUITMENT
MWB1	MDTSBES	0	Directly subordinate employees	1	ICON_EMPLOYEE	MDT_ORGS
MWB1	MDTSBESX	0	All subordinate employees	2	ICON_EMPLOYEE	MDT_ORGS
MWB1	MDTSBPJ	0	Project assignments	6	ICON_EMPLOYEE	MDT_ORGS
MWB1	MDTWB	0	Requisition	7	ICON_EMPLOYEE	MDT_WB_RQ
MWB1	SBES	0	Directly subordinate employees		ICON_EMPLOYEE	ORGS
MWB1	SBESX	0	All subordinate employees	98	ICON_EMPLOYEE	ORGS

Figure 19.6 Views of the Organizational Structure

Furthermore, you can assign these views to theme categories by selecting the following menu in the IMG: **Personnel Management** • **Manager's Desktop** • **Customer Adjustment** • **Determine Views per Category**. Here, you should redefine the views to avoid overwriting the entries with patches (Figure 19.7).

Scenario	Function Code	Eval.path	Numb
MWB1	STANDARDFUNCTION	MDTDIREC	0
MWB1	STANDARDFUNCTION	MDTSBES	0
MWB1	STANDARDFUNCTION	MDTSBESX	0

Figure 19.7 Views per Category

19.3.3 Function Codes

The menu on the left-hand side of the MDT consists of function codes (Figures 19.8 and 19.9). A function code can be a folder or an executable task function. The HOME type function code defines the top-level node. The NODE type function codes represent the subordinate folders, which contain the task functions.

Function Code	Type	Org.	Obje	Text	Function Module
RHPMSTKA	REPO	☑	☑	Job Chart	
RHPMSTUE	REPO	☑	☑	Budget in FTE	
RHPMSTUE_EXT	REPO	☑	☑	Enhanced Position Overvw	
RHPMVHHJ	REPO	☑	☑	Budget Year Comparison	
RHPMVMFS	REPO	☑	☑	Available Budget	
RHPMZWBI	REPO	☑	☑	Violations of Earmarking	
RHPMZWSH	REPO	☑	☑	Violations of Earmarking	
RPLMIT00	REPO	☑	☐	Employee Overview	

Figure 19.8 Function Codes – Overview

REPO (report) type function codes enable you to integrate reports in **Reports** the MDT. In the MDT, reports are always started without a selection screen, which is why the only way to manipulate the report execution consists of entering a variant.

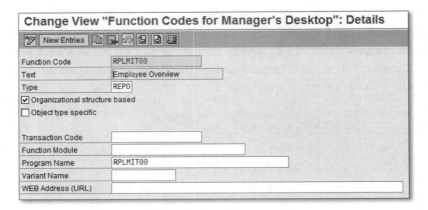

Figure 19.9 Function Codes – Details View

BI reports The BWR3 (BW reports, Web reporting) and BWEX (BW reports, Excel) types allow you to integrate BI reports in the MDT as well. To do that, you must merely maintain the function code, text, and type, and check the **Organizational structure based**. The link to the BI system is then established in Table T77MWBBWS (see Figure 19.10). The basic characteristic contains a characteristic that in turn contains the organizational structure in the BI system.

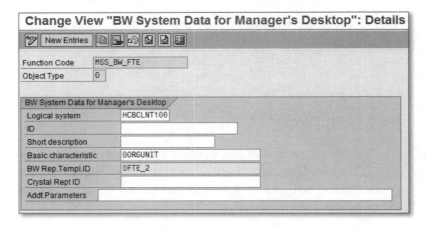

Figure 19.10 Function Code Settings for BI Reports

You should set the **Organizational structure based** flag for all function codes that are used with organizational objects. If you do not set this flag for any of the functions within the theme category, the system automatically executes the first function at each startup and displays this function in the left-hand pane. You can then select other functions.

The last setting you have to make must be carried out via the following IMG menu: **Personnel Management • Manager's Desktop • Customer Adjustment • Enhancement of Function Codes • Define Function Codes**. Here, the defined function codes are finally grouped into a hierarchical structure (see Figure 19.11).

Defining the structure of function codes

Scenario	Higher-level Fcode	No	Function Code	Function Module
Z_HC	HIS	1	ZHR_BW_HC1	
Z_HC	HIS	2		HR_HIS_READ
Z_HC	HRHAP_PA_NODE	10	HRHAP_PA_DOC_CREATE	
Z_HC	HRHAP_PA_NODE	20	HRHAP_PA_DOC_CHANGE	
Z_HC	HRHAP_PA_NODE	30	HRHAP_PA_DOC_LIST	
Z_HC	PA_PD_AP	10	APPRAISAL_DISPLAY	
Z_HC	PA_PD_AP	20	APPRAISAL_CREATE	
Z_HC	PA_PD_QR	10	ORG_QUALI_OVERVIEW	
Z_HC	PA_PD_QR	15	ORG_QUALI_MAINTAINED	
Z_HC	PA_PD_QR	20	PERS_PROFILE	
Z_HC	PA_PD_QR	30	POS_PROFILE	
Z_HC	PA_PD_QR	40	PERS_PROFILE_MATCHUP	
Z_HC	PA_PD_QR	81	ZQUALSRCH	
Z_HC	PA_PD_QR	82	Z_NACHFOLGE	
Z_HC	STANDARDFUNCTION	1	ADHOC	
Z_HC	STANDARDFUNCTION	2	HIS	
Z_HC	STANDARDFUNCTION	3	TRAIN	
Z_HC	STANDARDFUNCTION	4	PA_PD_AP	
Z_HC	STANDARDFUNCTION	5	PA_PD_QR	
Z_HC	STANDARDFUNCTION	6	TRIP_NODE	
Z_HC	STANDARDFUNCTION	7	HRHAP_PA_NODE	
Z_HC	TRAIN	1	TRAIN_HIST	
Z_HC	TRAIN	2	TRAIN_BOOK	
Z_HC	TRAIN	3	TRAIN_PREBO	
Z_HC	TRAIN	4	TRAIN_RESO_RESERV	
Z_HC	TRAIN	5	TRAIN_STOR	
Z_HC	TRAIN	6	TRAIN_BUDGET	
Z_HC	TRIP_NODE	1	TRIP_APPROVAL	
Z_HC	TRIP_NODE	2	TRIP_E_NODE	
Z_HC	TRIP_NODE	3	TRIP_P_NODE	

Figure 19.11 Hierarchy of Function Codes – Customizing

Function codes that have the **STANDARDFUNCTION** entry in the **Higher-Level FCode** column represent the first level under the root object. The function code with the Number 1 entry in the **No** column represents the function code of the Ad Hoc Query, whereas Numbers 2 through 7 represent additional folders. For each folder you can find function codes including reports and transactions. Figure 19.12 shows the effects of the Customizing settings.

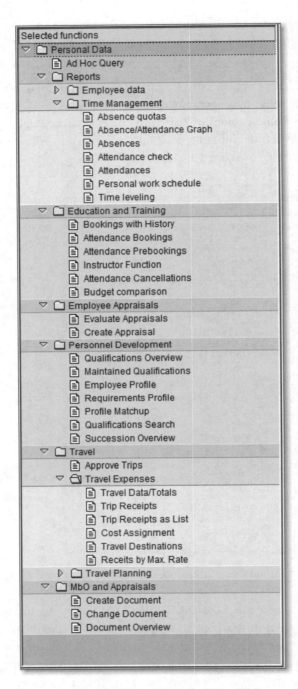

Figure 19.12 Function Codes Hierarchy in the MDT

19.4   Using the MDT in Practice

The MDT is a good tool for senior management staff to retrieve reports. The organizational structure it presents reflects the area of responsibility to which a user can apply the available functions. Subareas can be dragged onto function codes to create reports for these specific subareas.

The MDT can be used easily and intuitively, which represents a great advantage for users who do not regularly use the system.

Little customizing work is needed to provide the MDT to any user and to configure it individually with different scenarios for different groups of users. One of its major advantages is that it allows you to integrate reports from financial accounting as well.

However, the fact that the selection screens are generally hidden represents a disadvantage. It means you cannot influence the reporting process. In practice, this may require you to define multiple functions with the same report but in different variants. In general, you should use the MDT if you want to avoid using a portal (see Chapter 20). If you already use a portal, it does not make much sense to use the MDT because the portal avoids having to roll out the SAP GUI for all managers.

The SAP NetWeaver Portal is gaining an increasingly important role as a user interface in newer releases. This chapter provides information on how you can use the Portal for HR reporting purposes.

20   SAP NetWeaver Portal

This chapter provides an overview of how you can present reports using the SAP NetWeaver Portal. This includes using the Manager Self-Service (MSS), which replaces the Manager's Desktop (MDT) from the SAP R/3 system as a portal application. The following sections contain a detailed description of the Manager Self-Service including the Report Launchpad. Furthermore, you will learn how to use SAP NetWeaver BI in the Portal in conjunction with the BEx Web Application Designer and the Visual Composer.

As of Release SAP NetWeaver 2004s, SAP NetWeaver BI requires the use   [+]
of the SAP NetWeaver Portal for Web reporting purposes.

20.1   Manager Self-Service

The MSS is no HCM application. It contains functions from several modules and is part of the general business packages. One component of the MSS is the configurable Launchpad, which can be used to provide reports from different systems in a structured manner.

The Report Launchpad is a menu structure that enables you to launch   [+]
reports in the Portal. It can be compared to the report tree or the MDT
structure.

The Launchpad has been available with all its functions as of SAP ERP 6.0 and must be configured in the Customizing module of the back-end system.

20.1.1 Customizing the Report Launchpad

You can access the Customizing section for the Launchpad via the following IMG path: **Integration with Other SAP Components • Business Packages/Functional Packages • Manager Self-Service • Reporting • Set Up LaunchPad** (see Figure 20.1).

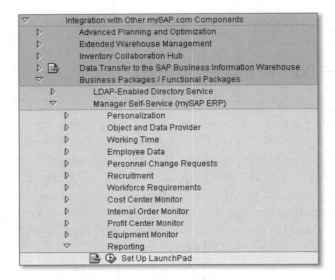

Figure 20.1 Report Launchpad in the IMG

The following functions are available to set up the Launchpad, which represents a menu structure that provides users with reports in a structured manner (see Figure 20.2):

- ► SAP NetWeaver BI Reports (Queries)
- ► SAP NetWeaver BI Reports (Web Templates)
- ► MDT functions
- ► Report Writer
- ► Transactions
- ► URLs

You can either define the functions as unchangeable in the Launchpad or deactivate them.

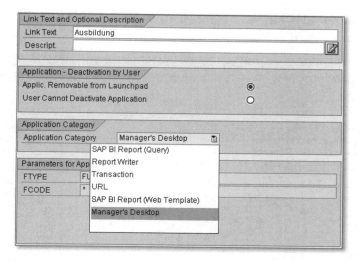

Figure 20.2 Functions of the Report Launchpad

Figure 20.3 shows how you can integrate a Web template, for example: The connection to the BI system is defined via the **RFC Destination** field in the **System** section.

> The system alias is defined in the Portal and is not checked in the back-   **[+]**
> end system. The input help provides only the values that have been used
> previously for setting up the MSS.

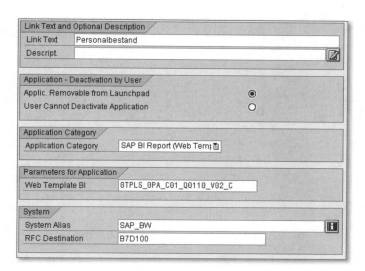

Figure 20.3 Integrating a Web Template in the Launchpad

20.1.2 Implementing MDT Data in an MSS Reporting Launchpad

A transfer function that is available in Customizing enables you to integrate previous MDT scenarios in an MSS Launchpad (see Figures 20.4 and 20.5).

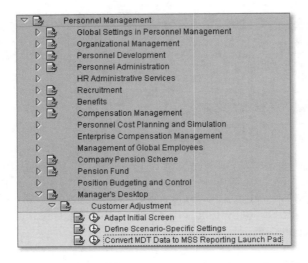

Figure 20.4 IMG Path for Integrating an MDT Scenario in the MSS Launchpad

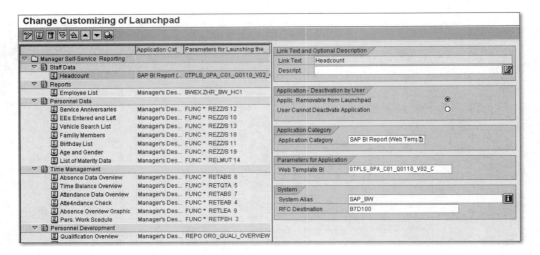

Figure 20.5 MDT Scenario after Integration into the Report Launchpad

The implementation tool creates nodes that reference functions of the MDT. However, this is not very useful with regard to the future maintenance and replacement of the MDT. For this reason, it makes sense to carry out the implementation manually or to reconfigure the system from scratch to facilitate future maintenance work.

Implementation tool

20.1.3 Key Figure Monitor

The Key Figure Monitor allows you to define key figures that you want to monitor and display in the Portal. This way you have the most important information available at one glance. The key figures may originate from both the BI and the ERP system.

The following information is available for each key figure in the Portal:

Key figure information in the Portal

▶ Key figure status represented by a traffic light (green, yellow, red)

▶ Current value of the key figure

▶ A trend indicator representing the historical development of the key figure

▶ A defined target value

▶ The absolute and percentage deviation

Figure 20.6 shows the IMG path to the Customizing section for the Key Figure Monitor.

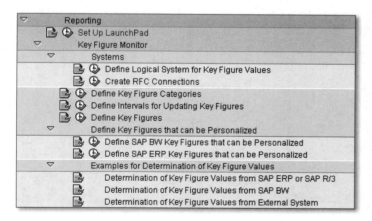

Figure 20.6 IMG Path to the Key Figure Monitor

[Ex]   In the example shown in Figure 20.7, we define a **Sick Rate** key figure that is made available in the ERP system by means of a report and
can be displayed in the Portal. The report and variant are stored with
the source data. The sick rate represents a negative key figure, that is,
the higher the value, the more unfavorable are the effects. You can
define threshold values that cause the traffic light color to change
from green to yellow and from yellow to red when reached.

Technical Name	ZHR_SICK_RATE
Name	Sick Rate
Description	Sick Rate
Source Data	
Source system type	SAP R/3 or mySAP ERP
Source System	
Report	ZHR_HC_PT01
Variant	PORTAL
User	
BW Web Template	
URL External System	
Format	
Key Figure Unit	HR
Key Figure Curr.	
No. Decimal Places	0.00
Value Range	
Key Figure Direction	Negative
Min. Value: Key Fig.	
Red->Yellow Thresh.	0.00000
Yellow->Grn Thresh.	0.00000
Targ. Value:Key Fig.	5.00000
Grn->Yellow Thresh.	7.00000
Yellow->Red Thresh.	10.00000
Max. Value: Key Fig.	100.00000
Periods	
Period Type	Month
Number of Periods	1
Interval	
Other Settings	
Personalization Type	Cannot be Personalized (Determine Value for Each Key Figure)
Comments	No Comments
Key Figure Category	STRA Strategic KPI category

Figure 20.7 Defining a Key Figure – Sick Rate Example

20.1.4 Web Templates for the MSS

The SAP Standard Content provides several templates for Web Cockpits that contain important queries with central key figures. You can complement these templates with your own applications containing BI content by using the BEx Web Application Designer and the Visual Composer.

The SAP Standard Content in SAP NetWeaver BI contains the following Web templates that can be used as patterns for the MSS:

Web templates in the Standard Content

- ▶ Headcount
- ▶ Headcount (Charts)
- ▶ Average age of Employee
- ▶ Average length of Service
- ▶ Number of Part-Time staff
- ▶ Number of Full-Time staff
- ▶ Percentage of Women
- ▶ Illness rate
- ▶ Illness rate (Charts)
- ▶ Overtime rate
- ▶ Overtime rate (Charts)
- ▶ Illness costs
- ▶ Illness costs (Charts)
- ▶ Overtime costs
- ▶ Overtime costs (Charts)

20.2 BEx Web Application Designer

The BEx Web Application Designer is a desktop application that enables you to create Web applications with business intelligence content. The HTML pages created using this tool provide a basis for interactive Web applications, such as Web Cockpits and iViews.

iView

An iView represents a content area within the Portal, which displays formatted data.

Figure 20.8 shows the four screen areas of the Web Application Designer:

► **Web Items**
The Web item describes the way in which the data are displayed, for instance, as a table or graphic.

► **Properties**
The **Properties** window allows you to define the properties of a Web item.

► **Web Template**
This is the area in which you create the Web application. Here you must position the Web items and determine the design. You can view this area in three different modes: in layout mode, as HTML code, and as an overview of items in a list.

► **Errors and Warnings**
This area displays errors and warnings that occur during the modeling of the Web application.

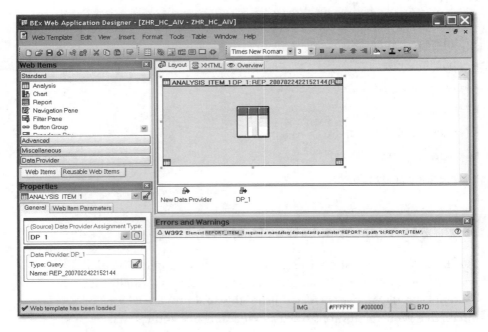

Figure 20.8 Web Application Designer

[Ex] In the following example, you will learn how to create a simple Web template.

1. After starting the BEx Web Application Designer via the Windows Start menu, you must log on to the SAP NetWeaver BI system. Then you can generate a blank template by clicking on the **Create new Web Template** button in BEx Web Application Designer.

2. Save the template by selecting **Web Template • Save as …** from the menu and specify a technical in the dialog that displays next, for example, ZHR_EXM_HEADCOUNT. Then enter a descriptive text, such as **Headcount**. You can save the template among your favorites or in a role.

3. To verify the result, you can view the template directly in the Portal by clicking on the **Execute** button.

4. Double-click on the **New Data Provider** button beneath the Layout area to add a query to the **Number of Employees per Personnel Area** (see Figure 20.9). To do that, select **Query** as the DataProvider type and choose an appropriate query via the input help. The query will appear as **DP_1** under the Layout window.

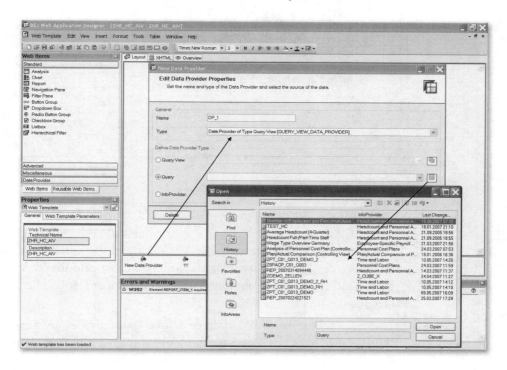

Figure 20.9 Inserting a New DataProvider into the Web Template

5. To be able to position different elements on a Web page, you must create a table by clicking on the **Insert table** button in the toolbar. In the window that displays next (see Figure 10.10), you should select two columns and two rows for the HTML table in our example. In addition, you can define other design features such as frames or the color of cells. The table allows you to firmly position web items in the table cells.

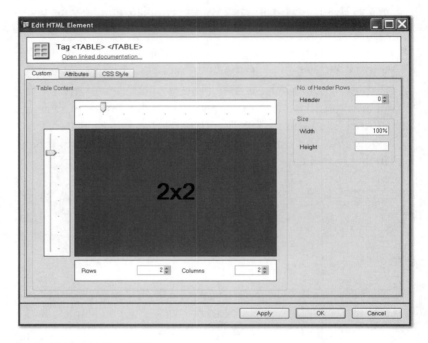

Figure 20.10 Inserting a Table

6. After that you can position the Web items in the table by dragging it (hold the left mouse button) into the relevant cell. The Web items are now placed in the table. For example, you can drag an analysis into the lower left-hand table cell, a chart into the lower right-hand cell, and a drop-down box into the upper left-hand cell (see Figure 20.11).

7. The data is automatically bound to the DataProvider because there is only one DataProvider in this example. If you use more than one DataProvider, you can select the relevant one via the **Properties** area in the lower left-hand pane.

Note, however, that you must configure the data binding for the drop-down box. To do that, go to the variable selection and enter the personnel area as a variable name (see Figure 20.12).

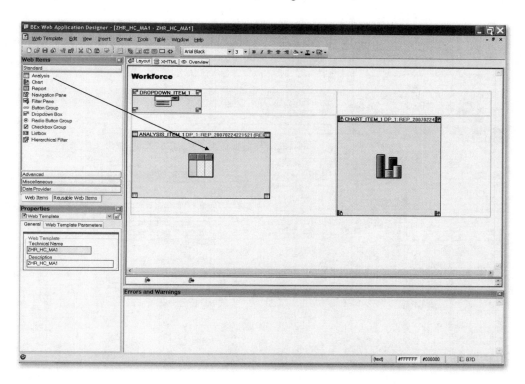

Figure 20.11 Positioning Web Items

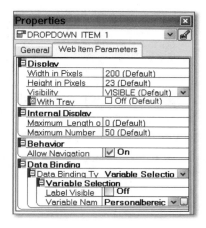

Figure 20.12 Configuring Properties for the Drop-Down Box

8. Format the background of the Web template by right-clicking on an empty space below the table and selecting the **Properties** option from the context menu. You can define the background color or font color, for example (see Figure 20.13). In practice, HTML pages are usually formatted using CSS templates (Cascading Style Sheets), which enable you to apply a defined design to multiple pages.

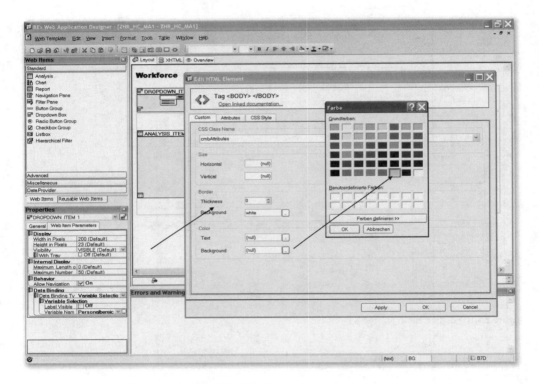

Figure 20.13 Formatting the Background

9. Now you can run the template and should obtain a result like the one shown in Figure 20.14. The drop-down box was used in the Web template to filter the personnel area, Chicago. Moreover, we used the navigation via the right mouse button to add a drill-down by employee subgroup.

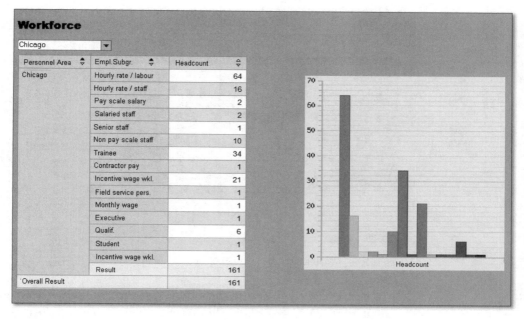

Figure 20.14 Example of a Completed Web Template

20.3 Visual Composer

As of Release SAP NetWeaver 2004s, SAP provides the Visual Composer as a new powerful tool that allows you to make BI data and data from other systems available in integrated applications within the Portal. SAP NetWeaver Visual Composer is not a desktop application, but an integrated application within the Portal. It represents a model-based development tool for both IT experts and users in the area of business analytics. It allows you to create applications by building models without any programming knowledge.

As an example, the following sections describe how you can create an iView with a table and graphic that provides information on the number of employees per age interval:

1. Click on the **New Model** button and specify a name for the model (see Figure 20.15).

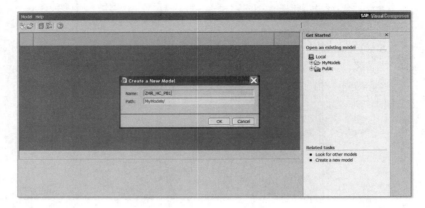

Figure 20.15 Visual Composer – Creating a New Model

2. To create an iView, double-click on **iView** and enter a name (see Figure 20.16). Then double-click on the iView to develop the contents.

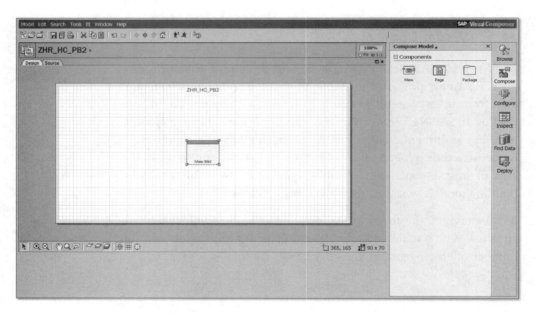

Figure 20.16 Creating an iView

3. Select **Find Data** from the list on the right and choose your BI System from the **Find Data Services** area. Select **Look for Query** in the **Look for** field and enter a search term in the **Query** field. Click on **Search**. The lower part of the window now displays a list of queries from which you can select one and drag it into the work area (see Figure 20.17).

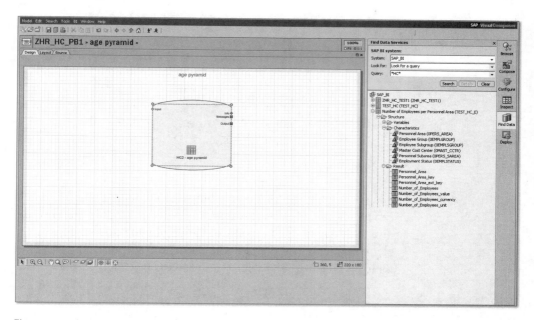

Figure 20.17 Inserting a Data Service

4. The system displays input and output points of the query to which you can link a data flow. We now want the output to flow as input into a table that in turn supplies a graphic with data. To do that, select these elements in the **Compose** area by double-clicking on them, and position them in the work area. You can drag the output of the query to the input of the table and vice versa to establish a link between the two.

5. The properties are displayed in the right-hand pane when you double-click on the elements. You can then configure table properties, for example, such as the visibility of columns or whether or not a table can be edited (see Figure 20.18). Regarding the graphic you can, for instance, select different graphics types or animations.

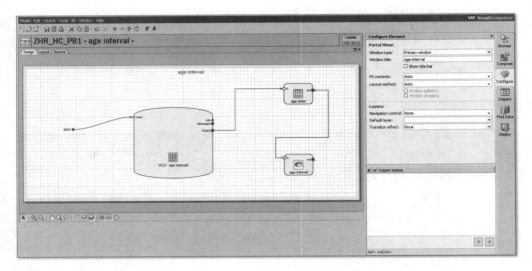

Figure 20.18 Modeling the Data Flow

6. The work area of SAP Visual Composer contains three views that can be selected via tabs at the upper border of the area: **Design**, **Layout**, and **Source**. The **Layout** area allows you to position the selected elements. Drag the elements to the required position and adjust their size according to your requirements (see Figure 20.19).

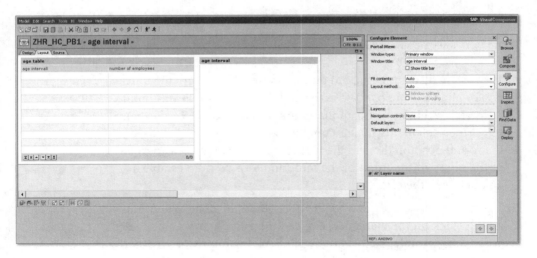

Figure 20.19 Defining the Layout

7. To be able to view the result, you must first click on the **Deploy** button, which enables you to generate a model in accordance

with the source code. After that you can launch the model in the Portal by clicking on **Execute** (see Figure 20.20).

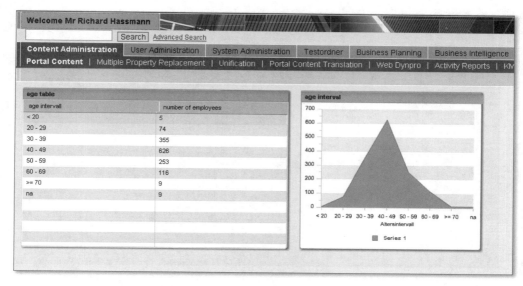

Figure 20.20 Display of the Age Interval in the Portal

This simple example demonstrates how intuitively you can operate the SAP NetWeaver Visual Composer as it allows you to develop complex models for the Portal without any programming knowledge.

20.4 Using the SAP NetWeaver Portal in Practice

The Portal will certainly establish itself as the standard user interface for the retrieval of reports for managers and other users who do not use the system regularly. At present, many enterprises have not yet upgraded to Releases SAP ERP 6.0 and SAP NetWeaver 2004s BI, both of which are a prerequisite for using the SAP NetWeaver Portal; however, we notice a growing interest in the Portal functions among companies that have nots used any Employee Self-Services up until now. Consequently, MSS will definitely replace the MDT as the standard user interface for managers.

This tendency is further intensified by the integration of Web reporting into SAP NetWeaver BI as well as by the powerful tools for the development of Web applications in the Portal.

APPENDIX

A   Further Reading

In order to become more familiar with some special topics, here are some reading recommendations:

- Krämer, Christian; Ringling, Sven; Yang, Song: *Mastering HR Management with SAP*. SAP PRESS, 2006.

- Krämer, Christian; Lübke, Christian; Ringling, Sven: *HR Personnel Planning and Development Using SAP*. SAP PRESS, 2004.

- Brochhausen, Ewald; Kielisch, Jürgen; Schnerring, Jürgen; Staeck Jens: *mySAP HR—Technical Principles and Programming*. 2nd edition. SAP PRESS, 2005.

- Egger, Norbert; Fiechter, Jean Marie R.; Kramer, Sebastian; Sawicki, Ralf Patrick; Straub, Peter; Weber, Stephan: *SAP Business Intelligence*. SAP PRESS, 2007.

- Egger, Norbert; Fiechter, Jean-Marie R.; Rohlf, Jens: *SAP BW Data Modeling*. SAP PRESS, 2005.

- Nolan, Gary: *Efficient SAP NetWeaver BI Implementation and Project Management*. SAP PRESS, 2007.

- Larocca Signorile, Danielle: *SAP Query Reporting*. Indianapolis, IN: Sams, 2007.

This Appendix contains an overview of all standard reports for the SAP HCM modules including their names, ABAP program names, and the corresponding transaction code. The sequence of the reports corresponds to the sequence in which they are presented in the chapters of Part III in this book. You can download an electronic copy of this Appendix from the publisher's Web site at www.sap-press.com.

B   Standard Reports in the SAP HCM Modules: Overview

B.1   Administration

Report	ABAP Program Name	Transaction Code
Flexible Employee Data	RPLICO10	S_AHR_61016362
HR Master Data Sheet	RPPSTM00	S_AHR_61016360
Date Monitoring	AQZZ/SAPQUERY/ H2DATE_MONITOR==	S_PH0_48000450
Education and Training	AQZZ/SAPQUERY/ H2EDUCATION=====	S_PH9_46000224
Time Spent in Each Pay Scale Area/Type/Group/Level	RPLTRF00	S_AHR_61016356
List of Maternity Data	RPLMUT00	S_AHR_61016370
EEs Entered and Left	AQZZ/SAPQUERY/ H2FLUCTUATIONS==	S_PH9_46000223
Service Anniversaries	AQZZ/SAPQUERY/ H2JUBILEE_LIST==	S_PH9_46000216
Powers of Attorney	AQZZ/SAPQUERY/ H2AUTHORIZATIONS	S_PH9_46000225
Family Members	AQZZ/SAPQUERY/ H2FAMILY_MEMBERS	S_PH9_46000222

Report	ABAP Program Name	Transaction Code
Birthday List	AQZZ/SAPQUERY/H2BIRTHDAYLIST==	S_PH9_46000221
Vehicle Search List	AQZZ/SAPQUERY/H2CAR_SEARCH====	S_PH9_46000220
Telephone Directory	RPLTEL00	S_AHR_61016354
Headcount Changes	AQZZ/SAPQUERY/H2STAFF_CHANGES2	S_L9C_94000095
Headcount Development	RPSDEV00	S_AHR_61016373
Assignment to Wage Level	RPSTRF00	S_AHR_61016378
Salary According to Seniority	RPSSAL00	S_AHR_61016376
Nationalities	RPSNAT00	S_AHR_61016374
Statistics: Gender Sorted by Age	AQZZ/SAPQUERY/H2GENDER_PER_AGE	S_PH9_46000218
Statistics: Gender Sorted by Seniority	AQZZ/SAPQUERY/H2GEND_P_SENIOR=	S_PH9_46000217
Logged Changes in Infotype Data	RPUAUD00	S_AHR_61016380
Log of Report Starts	RPUPROTD	S_AHR_61016381

B.2 Organizational Management

Report	ABAPProgram Name	Transaction Code
Existing Organizational Units	RHXEXI00	S_AHR_61016491
Staff Functions for Organizational Units	RHXSTAB0	S_AHR_61016492
Existing Jobs	RHXEXI02	S_AHR_61016497
Job Index	RHXSTEL0	S_AHR_61016498
Job Description	RHXDESC0	S_AHR_61016499
Complete Job Description	RHXSCRP0	S_AHR_61016501
Existing Positions	RHXEXI03	S_AHR_61016502
Staff Functions for Positions	RHXSTAB1	S_AHR_61016506

Report	ABAPProgram Name	Transaction Code
Periods When Positions Are Unoccupied per Organizational Unit	RHXFILLPOS	S_AHR_61018869
Staff Assignments	RHXSBES0	S_AHR_61016503
Position Description	RHXDESC1	S_AHR_61016504
Vacant Positions	RHVOPOS0	S_AHR_61016509
Obsolete Positions	RHVOPOS1	S_AHR_61018831
Complete Position Description	RHXSCRP1	S_AHR_61016511
Authorities and Resources	RHXHFMT0	S_AHR_61016507
Planned Labor Costs	RHXSOLO0	S_AHR_61016508
Existing Work Centers	RHXEXI01	S_AHR_61016514
Authorities and Resources	RHXHFMT0	S_AHR_61016516
Existing Objects	RHEXIST0	S_AHR_61016527
Structure Display/Maintenance	RHSTRU00	S_AHR_61016528
Display and Maintain Infotypes	RHDESC00	S_AHR_61016531
Start HR Reporting via Personnel Planning Structures	RHPNPSUB	S_AHR_61016533

B.3   Recruitment

Report	ABAP Program Name	Transaction Code
Variable Applicant List	RPAPL012	S_AHR_61015508
Applicants by Name	RPAPL001	S_AHR_61015509
Applicants by Action	RPAPL004	S_AHR_61015510
Applicants' Education and Training	RPAPL011	S_AHR_61015511
Applications	RPAPL002	S_AHR_61015512
Applicant Statistics	RPAPL005	S_AHR_61015513
Planned Activities	RPAPRT08	S_AHR_61015514

Report	ABAP Program Name	Transaction Code
Vacancy Assignments	RPAPL003	S_AHR_61015515
Vacancies	RPAPL010	S_AHR_61015516
Job Advertisements	RPAPL006	S_AHR_61015517
Recruitment Instruments	RPAPL008	S_AHR_61015518

B.4　Payroll

Report	ABAP Program Name	Transaction Code
Remuneration statement	RPCEDTD0	PC00_M01_CEDT
Remuneration statement with HR-Forms	H99_HRFORMS_CALL	PC00_M01_HRF
Payroll Journal	RPCLJNU0	S_ALR_87014259
Wage Type Reporter	H99CWTR0	S_PH9_46000172
Display Results	H99_DISPLAY_PAYRESULT	PC_PAYRESULT
Workers' Compensation Report	RPLWCOU0	S_AHR_61016148
Garnishment Details	RPCGRNU0	S_AHR_61016146

B.5　Time Management

Report	ABAP Program Name	Transaction code
Display Work Schedule	SAPMP51S	PT03
Daily Work Schedule	RPTDSH20	PT_DSH20
Absence/Attendance Data Overview	RPTABS20	PT64
Absence/Attendance Data: Calendar View	RPTABS50	PT90; PT90_ATT
Absence/ Attendance Data: Multiple Employee View	RPTABS60	PT91; PT91_ATT
Attendance Check	RPTEAB00	PT62

Report	ABAP Program Name	Transaction code
Absence/Attendance Overview Graphic	RPTLEA40	PT65
Time Statement	RPTEDT00	PT_EDT_TEDT
Cumulated Time Evaluation Results: Time Balances/Wage Types	RPTBAL00	PT_BAL00
Time Accounts	RPTDOW00	PT_DOW00
Display Absence Quota Information	RPTQTA10	PT_QTA10
Time Evaluation Messages	RPTERL00	PT_ERL00
Display Time Evaluation Results (Cluster B2)	RPCLSTB2	PT_CLSTB2

B.6   Personnel Development

Report	ABAP Program Name	Transaction Code
Profile Matchup	SAPLRHPP	PEPM
Profiles	SAPLRHP6	PEPP
Search for Qualifications	SAPLRHPD_SEARCH	PPPE_SEARCH_FOR_Q
Appraisals	SAPLRHPA_REPORTING	APPSEARCH
Profile Matchup: Positions/Holders	RHXPEP01	S_AHR_61015532
Profiles (Organizational Units)	RHXPEP02	S_AHR_61015533
Expired Qualifications	RHXPE_EXPIRED_QUALI	S_AHR_61015536

B.7　Training and Event Management

Report	ABAP Program Name	Transaction Code
Attendee List	RHXTEILN	S_PH9_46000434
Attendance List	RHXTEILA	S_PH9_46000433
Employee List	RHXFIRMA	S_PH9_46000432
Bookings per Attendee	RHXBUCH0	S_AHR_61016215
Attendee's Training History	RHXTHIST	S_PH9_46000431
Attendance Prerequisites	RHXKVOR0	S_PH9_46000430
Attendee's Qualifications	RHXQALIF	S_PH9_46000429
Attendance Statistics	RHXKURS2	S_ALR_87014085
Cancellations per Business Event/Attendee	RHXSTOR0 RHXSTOR1	S_PH9_46000424 S_AHR_61016216
Business Event Demand	RHXKBED0	S_AHR_61016220
Business Event Information	RHSEMI60	S_PH0_48000476
Business Event Dates	RHXKBRO1	S_AHR_61016219
Resources Not Yet Assigned per Business Event	RHXORES1	S_PH9_46000436
Resource Equipment	RHXRESA0	S_AHR_61016224
Instructor Information	RHSSREF0	S_PH0_48000096
Resource Reservation	RHRBEL00	S_ALR_87014087

B.8　Personnel Cost Planning

Report	ABAP Program Name	TransactionCode
Display an Existing Scenario Group	RHPP25LI	S_AHR_61015559

B.9 Benefits

Report	ABAP Program Name	Transaction Code
Eligible Employees	RPLBEN01	HRBEN0071
Participation	RPLBEN02	HRBEN0072
Changes in Benefits Elections	RPLBEN07	HRBEN0077
Change of Elibility Status	RPLBEN09	HRBEN0079
Changes in General Benefits Information	RPLBEN13	HRBEN0083
Health Plan Costs	RPLBEN03	HRBEN0073
Insurance Plan Costs	RPLBEN04	HRBEN0074
Savings Plan Contributions	RPLBEN05	HRBEN0075
Flexible Spending Account Contributions	RPLBEN08	HRBEN0078
Stock Purchase Plan Contributions	RPLBEN16	HRBEN0086
Costs/Contributions for Miscellaneous Plans	RPLBEN15	HRBEN0085
Vesting Percentages	RPLBEN06	HRBEN0076
Contribution Limit Check	RPLBEN18	HRBEN0088
Employee Demographics	RPLBEN11	HRBEN0081
Benefit Election Analysis	RPLBEN17	HRBEN0087
Enrollment Statistics	RPLBEN19	HRBEN0089

The following sample codings refer to Chapter 4, Queries, and demonstrate how you can extend InfoSets with your own additional fields.

C   Sample Codings for Chapter 4, Queries

Most infotypes allow you to assign user-defined text to them. This text can be included as an additional field in the InfoSet and be analyzed in queries. Let us first take a look at the DATA declaration for the additional field:

```
*** Data definition for reading the cluster
TABLES: pcl1, pcl2.
CONSTANTS: k_buffer VALUE 'BUFFER'.

INCLUDE rpcltx00.
INCLUDE rpc2cd00.
INCLUDE rpc2rdd0.
INCLUDE rpppxd00.

DATA: BEGIN OF COMMON PART k_buffer.
INCLUDE rpppxd10.
DATA: END OF COMMON PART k_buffer.
```

... and now the additional field (here, user-defined text from Infotype 0015):

```
CLEAR textit15.

MOVE-CORRESPONDING p0015 TO tx-key.
tx-key-infty = '0015'.
rp-imp-c1-tx.
IF sy-subrc = 0.
  LOOP AT ptext.
    CASE sy-tabix.
      WHEN 1.
```

```
          MOVE ptext-line TO textit15.
        WHEN 2.
        WHEN 3.
        WHEN OTHERS.
          EXIT.
      ENDCASE.
    ENDLOOP.
ENDIF.
```

To be able to analyze time balances, we must include an additional field for each time type in the InfoSet. Function module Z_HR_TIMETYPE_FOR_QUERY reads data from the clusters:

```
*** Declarations and includes that must be positioned
*** in front of the function are used to read the clusters.
tables: pcl2, pcl1.
include rpc2rdd0.
include rpc2cd00.
include rpclst00.
include rpc2b201.
include rpc2b202.
include rpppxd00.
include rpppxd10.

FUNCTION Z_HR_TIMETYPE_FOR_QUERY.
*"-------------------------------------------------------------
------------
*"*"Local interface:
*"  IMPORTING
*"     REFERENCE(PERNO) TYPE  PERNO-PERNO
*"     REFERENCE(YEAR)  TYPE  CHAR4
*"     REFERENCE(MONTH) TYPE  CHAR2
*"     REFERENCE(ZTYPE) LIKE  PC2B5-ZTYPE
*"  EXPORTING
*"     REFERENCE(NUMBR) LIKE  PC2B5-NUMBR
*"-------------------------------------------------------------
------------
clear: balance.
refresh: balance.

b2-key-pernr = perno.
b2-key-pabrj = year.
b2-key-pabrp = month.
b2-key-cltyp = '1'.
```

```
rp-imp-c2-b2.

loop at balance where zttype = zttype.
  numbr = balance-numbr.
endloop.

ENDFUNCTION.

*** Declarations and includes that must be positioned after
*** the function are used to read the clusters.
include rpppxm00.
include rpcmgr00.
```

The additional field **Time Balance XY** is created in the InfoSet (for example, Infotype 0007 [Planned working time]) with reference to PC2B5-NUMBR. In the **DATA** coding section, you must make the following declaration: YEAR(4) and month (2). The code for each additional field differs only in terms of the time type and the name of the additional field.

```
year = pn-begda(4).
month = pn-begda+4(2).
clear Z_ABW.
call function 'Z_HR_TIMETYPE_FOR_QUERY'
  exporting
    perno = p0007-perno
    year  = year
    month = month
    zttype = '0020'
  importing
    numbr = Z_ABW.
```

These examples show that complementing the InfoSets with additional fields is no big deal. Once you have defined the additional fields, they will be available for all future query analyses. You can use these sample codings as templates as well as a source of inspiration. Thus, a small extension to an InfoSet can quickly avoid the programming of a separate report.

D   Authors

Hans-Jürgen Figaj is the director of Projekt-kultur GmbH (*www.projektkultur.biz*), a consulting firm that's part of the AdManus Consulting Network and specializes in personnel management and SAP ERP HCM. As a certified SAP ERP HCM consultant, Hans-Jürgen has more than 10 years of experience during which he managed and supported projects that involved the modules of SAP ERP HCM.

Richard Hassmann is the director of Hassmann-Consulting GmbH (*www.hassmann-consulting.de*), a consulting firm that specializes in SAP ERP HCM within the AdManus Consulting Network. Richard Hassmann has more than 16 years of project experience with all modules of SAP ERP HCM. He implemented numerous requirements in the area of reporting in both national and international projects. In doing so, he used the standard tools of the SAP ERP system as well as those of SAP NetWeaver BI to implement numerous customer-specific reports and interfaces to many different external reporting tools.

Anja Junold has been working as an SAP ERP HCM consultant at iProCon GmbH (*www.iprocon.com*) since 2002. She has accumulated a lot of experience in HR departments of national and international enterprises. Anja Junold is a coauthor of the book, *SAP-Personalwirtschaft für Anwender*, also published by SAP PRESS. As the responsible body of the AdManus Consulting Network (*www.admanus.co.uk*), iProCon GmbH provides services related to SAP ERP HCM. The HR service tree reference model is an iProCon product, which can be ordered at *www.iprocon.de/referencemodel*.

AdManus is a network of small HR consulting firms (*www.*admanus.co.uk). Cross-company teams that are created within this network enable HR experts to continually extend their knowledge about SAP ERP HCM. AdManus consultants regularly present their experiences in collaboration with their customers at annual "SAP HR in Practice" events. Approximately six times a year, the AdManus Consulting Network publishes a free-of-charge newsletter for HR and IT experts who want to constantly extend their knowledge of SAP ERP HCM. You can order the newsletter at *http://www.admanus.de/english-news-letter*.

Index

Increase company productivity by learning to use HCM Performance Management efficiently

Prepare for, design, implement, and configure your HCM implementation

302 pp., 2007, 69,95 Euro / US$ 69.95
ISBN 978-1-59229-124-3

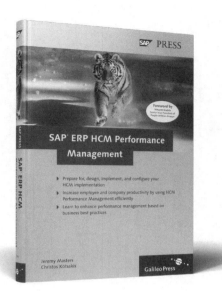

SAP ERP HCM
Performance Management

www.sap-press.com

Jeremy Masters, Christos Kotsakis

SAP ERP HCM Performance Management

From Design to Implementation

This comprehensive book is an indispensable reference for HR professionals, analysts, and consultants learning how to implement SAP ERP HCM Performance Management. The book teaches you everything you need to know about the Objective Setting and Appraisal (OSA) module within SAP so that you can identify and retain key talent within your organization. You'll take a step-by-step journey through the design and implementation of your own performance management application that will help you improve your companies' performance and talent management processes. The book covers all the latest releases, including the R/3 Enterprise Release (4.7), SAP ERP 2004 (ECC 5.0) and SAP ERP 2005 (ECC 6.0).

**Best Practices for Payroll,
Time Management, Personnel
Administration, and much more**

**Expert advice for integrating
Personnel Planning and
SAP Enterprise Portal**

**Based on R/3 Enterprise and
mySAP ERP HCM 2004**

629 pp., 2006, 69,95 Euro / US$
ISBN 1-59229-050-7

Mastering HR Management
with SAP

www.sap-press.com

C. Krämer, S. Ringling, Song Yang

Mastering HR Management with SAP

Get a step-by-step guide to the entire personnel
management process, from recruiting, to personnel
controlling, and beyond. This book comes complete
with practical examples regarding user roles, and
covers all of the new enhancements, improved
features and tools that have been introduced with
R/3 Enterprise. Uncover the ins and outs of
e-recruiting, organizational management, personnel
administration, payroll, benefits, quality assurance,
rolebased portals, and many others too numerous to
list. The book is based on Release 4.7 (R/3
Enterprise), and mySAP ERP 2004 (HCM)

**Solves difficult
US Payroll-related problems**

**Create custom wage types and
learn about the schemas and rules
specific to US Payroll**

**Discover advanced topics, such as
overpayments, accruals, payroll
interfaces, garnishments, and more**

332 pp., 2007, 69,95 Euro / US$ 69.95
ISBN 978-1-59229-132-8

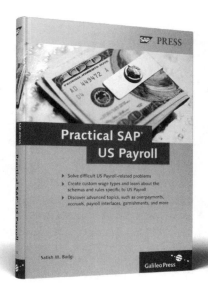

Practical SAP US Payroll

www.sap-press.com

Satish Badgi

Practical SAP US Payroll

„Practical US Payroll" has everything you need to
implement a successful payroll system. Readers will
learn how to create custom wage types, process
deductions for benefits and garnishments, handle
accruals, report and process taxes, and process
retroactive payrolls. From the hands-on, step-by-step
examples to the detailed wage type tables in the
appendix, this book is your complete guide to the
US Payroll system.

Learn how to implement and configure the SAP US Benefits Module

Work through the entire employee life cycle from enrollment to COBRA

Explore practical scenarios and examples to guide your own benefits processes

approx. 85 pp., 68,– Euro / US$ 85.00
ISBN 978-1-59229-164-9, Nov 2007

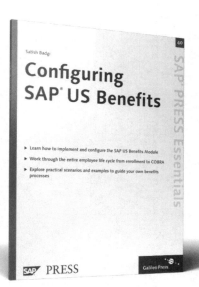

Configuring SAP US Benefits

www.sap-hefte.de

Satish Badgi

Configuring SAP US Benefits

SAP PRESS Essentials 40

Configuring SAP US Benefits is a comprehensive, hands-on approach to configuring SAP's US Benefits module. The book is written for payroll and benefits departments using SAP (power users), project teams, aspiring consultants, off-shore and outsourced benefit administrators, and benefit providers using or interacting with SAP customers. It provides the foundation for the entire benefits process of the employee lifecycle from enrollment, benefits changes, and FSA and Claims processing to termination and COBRA. In addition, the book details the US-specific benefits plans and teaches benefits managers how to configure them for their companies. Practical scenarios and examples are used throughout, including differentiating benefits by geography, unions, and employee groups; driving costs based on coverage and options; driving costs by groupings such as age and salary; enrollment changes and their impact within 30/60 days of life events; default plans vs. automatic plans; driving Infotype 0171 (defaults for groupings); and life events and benefit changes.

Integrate the Cross-Application Time Sheet with SAP HR, FI, PS, PM, CS and MM

Master employee time management from various decentralized locations

96 pp., 2006, 68,– Euro / US$ 85.00
ISBN 978-1-59229-063-5

Integrating CATS

Martin Gillet

Integrating CATS

SAP PRESS Essentials 7

One of the most important aspects of the Cross Application Time Sheet (CATS) is its integration with other SAP modules. This unique new guide provides readers with exclusive advice and best practices for integrating CATS with other key SAP modules. First, learn the fundamentals of CATS. Then, discover the concepts, practical applications and possible enhancements for CATS. You will quickly advance your mastery of CATS as you uncover little known tips, practical examples, and concise answers to your most frequently asked questions. Full of practical guidance and real-world scenarios, this book is for anyone interested in CATS.

Gain a holistic understanding of SAP

Make SAP-related decisions with ease

Learn about the SAP landscape, products, solutions, strategies, and more

approx. 426 pp., 34,95 Euro / US$ 34.95
ISBN 978-1-59229-117-5, Oct 2007

Discover SAP

www.sap-press.com

Nancy Muir, Ian Kimbell

Discover SAP

If you're new to SAP and want to learn more about it, or a decision-maker pressed for time, who needs to gain a holistic understanding of SAP, then this book is for you. A practical, reader-friendly guide for busy professionals, this comprehensive book helps you make quick sense of SAP solutions such as CRM, as well as application integration, SAP NetWeaver and enterprise SOA, embedded analytics, and many other core topics. Plus, learn about SAP as a company, its history, vision, strategies, and much more.

Discover what SAP Financials (FI) is all about and whether its right for your organization

Lean how this powerful, time-tested tool can improve your financial processes and save you money

approx. 350 pp., 39,95 Euro / US$ 39.95
ISBN 978-1-59229-184-7, Feb 2008

Discover SAP Financials

www.sap-hefte.de

Manish Patel

Discover SAP Financials

Business financials are an essential part of every business, large or small. Whether you just need basic accounting or you perform complex financial audits and reporting, your business needs a software tool that meets your needs. Discover SAP Financials explains how SAP can provide this solution. Using an easy-to-follow style filled with real-world examples, case studies, and practical tips and pointers, the book teaches the fundamental capabilities and uses of the core modules of SAP Financials. As part of the Discover SAP series, the book is written to help new users, decision makers considering SAP, and power users moving to the latest version learn everything they need to determine if SAP Financials is the right solution for your organization. This is the one comprehensive resource you need to get started with SAP Financials.

Learn how to integrate SAP SRM with other core SAP components

Uncover key insights on strategies, functionalities, and methodologies

695 pp., 2007, 69,95 Euro / US$ 69,95
ISBN 978-1-59229-068-0

Enhancing
Supplier Relationship Management
Using SAP SRM

▶ Learn how to integrate SAP SRM with other core SAP components
▶ Uncover key insights on strategies, functionalities, and methodologies
▶ Gain a detailed and practical understanding of SAP SRM to help you guide standardization and lower costs throughout your company

Sachin Sethi

Galileo Press

Enhancing Supplier Relationship Management Using SAP SRM

www.sap-press.com

Sachin Sethi

Enhancing Supplier Relationship Management Using SAP SRM

This book will help readers leverage valuable insights into strategies and methodologies for implementing SAP SRM to enhance procurement in their companies.
Tips and tricks, changes brought about by 5.0 and customization will be woven in throughout the book. It will provide detailed information on integration and dependencies of mySAP SRM with core SAP components like MM, IM, FI and HR.

Your guide to individual service-oriented architectures

Industry-specific solutions for implementing enterprise SOA

Volumes of lessons learned and best practices for redesigning your system architecture

approx. 350 pp., 69,95 Euro / US$ 69,95
ISBN 978-1-59229-162-5, Dec 2007

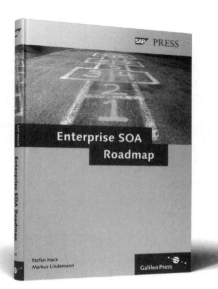

Enterprise SOA Roadmap

www.sap-press.com

Stefan Hack, Markus A. Lindemann

Enterprise SOA Roadmap

This book, intended for business leaders, IT managers and consultants, guides you step-by-step along the path to enterprise service-oriented architecture. Using a detailed analysis of more than 500 SAP Consulting projects in different industries as a basis, the authors deliver concrete recommendations on how best to roll out enterprise SOA in your own organization. You'll learn how SAP supports enterprises along their individual adoption paths, and benefit from the many lessons learned that are described in the book. In addition, you'll discover how to apply specific implementation options, arguments and best practices in your enterprise and how to sidestep potential implementation risks.

Learn about SAP Financials implementations from a real-world, business-oriented perspective

Discover the workings of the various Financials sub-modules

Explore practical case studies and real-world examples

approx. 550 pp., 79,95 Euro / US$ 79.95
ISBN 978-1-59229-160-1, Dec 2007

Optimize Your
SAP Financials Implementation

www.sap-press.com

Shivesh Sharma

Optimize Your
SAP Financials Implementation

The real work in SAP Financials begins after the implementation is complete. This is when it's time to optimize and use SAP Financials in the most efficient way for your organization. Optimization entails understanding unique client scenarios and then developing solutions to meet those requirements, while staying within the project's budgetary and timeline constraints. This book teaches consultants and project managers to think about and work through best practice tools and methodologies, before choosing the ones to use in their own implementations. The variety of real-life case studies and examples used to illustrate the business processes and highlight how SAP Financials can support these processes, make this a practical and valuable book for anyone looking to optimize their SAP Financials implementation.

Interested in reading more?

Please visit our Web site for all
new book releases from SAP PRESS.

www.sap-press.com